EIGHTEENTH-CENTURY SATIRE

EIGHTEENTH-CENTURY SATIRE

ESSAYS ON TEXT AND CONTEXT FROM DRYDEN TO PETER PINDAR

HOWARD D. WEINBROT

Vilas Profesor and Ricardo Quintana Professor of English,
University of Wisconsin–Madison

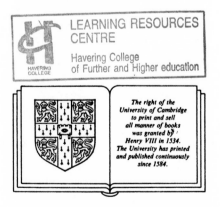

The right of the
University of Cambridge
to print and sell
all manner of books
was granted by
Henry VIII in 1534.
The University has printed
and published continuously
since 1584.

CAMBRIDGE UNIVERSITY PRESS
Cambridge
New York   New Rochelle   Melbourne   Sydney

CAMBRIDGE UNIVERSITY PRESS
Cambridge, New York, Melbourne, Madrid, Cape Town, Singapore, São Paulo

Cambridge University Press
The Edinburgh Building, Cambridge CB2 2RU, UK

Published in the United States of America by Cambridge University Press, New York

www.cambridge.org
Information on this title: www.cambridge.org/9780521325134

First published 1988
This digitally printed first paperback version 2006

A catalogue record for this publication is available from the British Library

Library of Congress Cataloguing in Publication data
Weinbrot, Howard D.
Eighteenth-century satire.
Bibliography.
Includes index.
1. Satire, English – History and criticism.
2. English literature – 18th century – History and criticism.
I. Title.
PR935.W39   1988   827′.5′09   87-26836

ISBN-13 978-0-521-32513-4 hardback
ISBN-10 0-521-32513-7 hardback

ISBN-13 978-0-521-03409-8 paperback
ISBN-10 0-521-03409-4 paperback

FOR GWIN AND RUTH KOLB

CONTENTS

Preface   *page* ix
Acknowledgments   xi
List of abbreviations   xii

Introduction: The Achievement of Dryden's "Discourse on
Satyr"   1

CONTEXTS

1   The Pattern of Formal Verse Satire in the Restoration and the
    Eighteenth Century   11

2   History, Horace, and Augustus Caesar: Some Implications for
    Eighteenth-Century Satire   21

3   Masked Men and Satire and Pope: Towards an Historical Basis
    for the Eighteenth-Century Persona   34

TEXTS

4   The Swelling Volume: The Apocalyptic Satire of Rochester's
    Letter from Artemisia in the Town to Chloe in the Country   53

5   The "Allusion to Horace": Rochester's Imitative Mode   68

6   "Natures Holy Bands" in *Absalom and Achitophel*: Fathers and
    Sons, Satire and Change   80

7   *The Rape of the Lock* and the Contexts of Warfare   100

8   "Such as Sir Robert Would Approve"? Answers to Pope's
    Answer from Horace   120

9   The Conventions of Classical Satire and the Practice of Pope   128

10 Persius, the Opposition to Walpole, and Pope   144

11 Johnson's *London* and Juvenal's Third Satire: The Country as
    "Ironic" Norm   164

12 No "Mock Debate": Questions and Answers in *The Vanity of Human Wishes*   172

13 Pope, his Successors, and the Dissociation of Satiric Sensibility: An Hypothesis   186

    Notes   204
    Index   254

PREFACE

I do not know whether contemporary readers will find this collection sublimely au courant or ridiculously archaic. Here are the splendors of reader response, reception criticism, intertextuality, awareness of covert political statement, "new historical" breadth of non-literary knowledge, family history, impatience with authoritarian received opinion, significant recovery of the underworld of letters, and, in the final essay, innovation that spurns the shackles of footnotes, manfully leaps the barriers of proof, and embraces the ample body of Dame Speculation. Here too, though, is a stubborn insistence on relevant historical grounding, testing of hypotheses with evidence rather than self-affirming preconceptions, the primacy of a shaping author who at his best knows reasonably well what he is doing, and who with unspoken eloquence convinces me not to impose my values upon him, but to let him and his culture speak for themselves if I am clever enough to awake the dormant past.

Given such hopeless, or perhaps hopeful, indeterminacy and binary opposition, I thought it best to correct only obvious errors in the following essays, while no doubt overlooking many of which I was not aware. I have accordingly resisted the temptation of making substantive changes and of quarreling with myself. It would have been rude to usurp a position for which so many will feel qualified. I also have left some overlapping of materials since, whatever the blow to authorial vanity, not everyone will want to read the book from cover to cover; those who prefer to read individual essays will not be deprived of knowledge. The essays themselves originally appeared between 1965 and 1988. The Introduction is new, and the essays on *Absalom and Achitopel* and *The Rape of the Lock* are so recent that they are virtually new. Two others appeared in journals with small circulation: "The Swelling Volume . . . Rochester's *Letter from Artemisia*," and "Such as Sir Robert Would Approve"? will seem unfamiliar to most students of eighteenth-century satire. I especially wish to see the Rochester essay enter the discussion of his best poem.

I am pleased and grateful to recall the several libraries, universities, colleagues, and research grants that helped to make lonely work both social and possible.

I am even more pleased to thank Gwin and Ruth Kolb, to whom this volume is warmly dedicated. It is offered to an admired couple I met thirty years ago. For a generation they have helped others to approach the high professional, pedagogical, and personal standards they exemplify. Their retirement from the University of Chicago reminds me that the achievement of human wishes may counter the vanity of human wishes.

ACKNOWLEDGMENTS

The author would like to thank the following editors, journals, and presses for permission to reprint material previously published:

"The Pattern of Formal Verse Satire in the Restoration and the Eighteenth Century," *Publications of the Modern Language Association of America* 80 (1965): 394–401.

"History, Horace, and Augustus Caesar: Some Implications for Eighteenth-Century Satire," *Eighteenth-Century Studies* 7 (1974): 391–414.

"Masked Men, and Satire, and Pope: Towards an Historical Basis for the Eighteenth-Century Persona," *Eighteenth-Century Studies* 16 (1983): 265–89.

"The Swelling Volume: The Apocalyptic Satire of Rochester's *Letter from Artemisia in the Town to Chloe in the Country*," *Studies in the Literary Imagination* 5 (1972): 19–37.

"The 'Allusion to Horace': Rochester's Imitative Mode," *Studies in Philology* 69 (1972): 348–68, University of North Carolina Press.

" 'Natures Holy Bands' in *Absalom and Achitophel*: Fathers and Sons, Satire and Change," *Modern Philology* 85 (1988), University of Chicago Press.

"*The Rape of the Lock* and the Contexts of Warfare," in *The Enduring Legacy: Alexander Pope Tercentenary Essays*, ed. J.P.W. Rogers and G.S. Rousseau (Cambridge: Cambridge University Press, 1988).

" 'Such as Sir Robert Would Approve'?: Answers to Pope's Answer from Horace," *Modern Language Studies* 9, no. 3 (Fall 1979): 5–14.

"The Conventions of Classical Satire and the Practice of Pope," *Philological Quarterly* 59 (1980): 317–37.

"Persius, the Opposition to Walpole, and Pope," in *Greene and Centennial Studies: Essays Presented to Donald Greene*, ed. Paul J. Korshin and Robert R. Allen (Charlottesville: University Press of Virginia, 1984), pp. 93–124.

"Johnson's *London* and Juvenal's Third Satire: The Country as 'Ironic' Norm," *Modern Philology* 73 (1976): S 56–65, University of Chicago Press.

"No 'Mock Debate': Questions and Answers in *The Vanity of Human Wishes*," *Modern Language Quarterly* 41 (1980): 248–67.

"Pope, his Successors, and the Dissociation of Satiric Sensibility: An Hypothesis," in Howard D. Weinbrot, *Alexander Pope and the Traditions of Formal Verse Satire* (Princeton: Princeton University Press, 1982), pp. 331–64, extracts from which are reprinted with permission of Princeton University Press.

ABBREVIATIONS

CE	The Works of John Dryden, University of California Press, Berkeley
CL	*Comparative Literature*
ECS	*Eighteenth-Century Studies*
EIC	*Essays in Criticism*
ELH	*English Literary History*
HLQ	*Huntington Library Quarterly*
MLQ	*Modern Language Quarterly*
MP	*Modern Philology*
PMLA	*Publications of the Modern Language Association of America*
PQ	*Philological Quarterly*
RES	*Review of English Studies*
SEL	*Studies in English Literature*
SP	*Studies in Philology*
SR	*Sewanee Review*
TE	The Twickenham Edition of the Poems of Alexander Pope
TLS	*Times Literary Supplement*
YE	The Yale Edition of the Works of Samuel Johnson
YR	*Yale Review*

INTRODUCTION
THE ACHIEVEMENT OF DRYDEN'S "DISCOURSE ON SATYR"

LATER SEVENTEENTH-CENTURY SATIRE was an incoherent setting of diamonds and coal. Poets of genius, or less, often lacked design, full awareness of the limits of their art, and modulation of tone. Butler's endless Hudibrastics stretch a joke until it breaks; Rochester's "Allusion to Horace" (1680) is written by a brilliant self-destructive solipsist often too intent on savaging his apparent inferiors than convincing us that they are inferiors worth savaging; Robert Gould, and even the more promising John Oldham, are best when shouting with graveled voices. The significant exception to this expandable list of course is John Dryden.

Whether through native gift, experience with dramatic dialogue, breadth of classical and modern reading, or all of the above, Dryden could give satire shape, variety, and appealing public urgency for private concerns. Both in the largely punitive *Mac Flecknoe* (1682, 1684) and the corrective heroic satire *Absalom and Achitophel* (1681), Dryden offers unity of plot, diversity of voice, and community of response between satirist and audience, and at times even between the satirist and the satirized: he teaches the once-profligate David-Charles II to adopt the values of the narrator-Dryden. In Dryden's hands, satire is purged of some of its energetic vulgarity – as evident in peer as in plebeian – and acquires good manners that can easily be rejected when "please" fails. As Dryden says in the preface to *Absalom and Achitophel*, those who wrongly "imagine I have done my Worst, may be Convinc'd, at their own Cost, that I can write Severely, with more ease, than I can Gently."[1] This is a truth seen by any reader of the consequent "Epistle to the Whigs" and *The Medall. A Satyre against Sedition* (1682) in which *"English* Ideots" run to see "The *Polish Medall"* of "A Monster" (ll. 2–4). Union of refinement and fatal power is also demonstrated in Dryden's familiar preference in the "Discourse" for "the fineness of a stroak that separates the Head from the Body, and leaves it standing in its place," to "the slovenly Butchering of a Man."[2] However fine the stroke, the bodyless head will hatch no more plots against its king. Dryden, after all, illustrates his point with the character of the traitor Zimri, the Buckingham in *Absalom and Achitophel*.

Notwithstanding Dryden's, and even Boileau's, practice, by 1692 later seventeenth-century English satire lacked a self-conscious, synthetic, and both authoritative and comprehensible history and assessment of the modern satirist's art. The ingredients had long been in place – an ongoing controversy regarding the derivation and corollary nature of formal verse satire; debate regarding the character and merits of Horace, Persius, and Juvenal; translations or imitations of all or significant parts of their respective canons; many satirists practicing varied species of the genre; and the modern example of Boileau, widely seen as the heir of Roman satire under an Augustan Louis XIV. Dryden's role would be to launder the soiled prose of Renaissance Latin by men like Casaubon, Heinsius, Rigaltius, and Scaliger; with apparent impartiality and admission of weakness to state the arguments on each side of each debate; and after his own judgment had played upon the wisdom of the distant past and near present, to transmit a benevolently despotic document that influenced satiric taste, theory, and practice until the decline of formal verse satire in the next century. Dryden dates his "Discourse" on 18 August 1692. He might as well have dated this preface to his English Juvenal and Persius the Year One, for like the Whig revolution to which Dryden objected, it consolidated trends, made a new contribution, and changed the future and the view of the past.

describe

✳

One of his chief tasks would be to make qualitative and personal and political distinctions regarding the three great Roman satirists. The easiest part was the discussion of Persius, for though Casaubon had championed the small body of Persius' crabbed satire, he gained few converts. Dryden nonetheless accepts and seconds both the moral and, we shall see, structural bases of Persius' art, and regards him as "the last of the first Three Worthies" but superior both to the Greek and to modern satirists, "excepting *Boileau* and your Lordship" Dorset, to whom the book is dedicated (p. 76).

Dryden's elegant compliment to Persius the diminished triumvir had at least two functions: one was to reinforce satiric clarity and the pleasure gained from an un-Persian immediacy of apprehension; the other was to offer sufficiently high praise so that his genuine literary virtues remained norms against which his brother-satirists could be judged.

Perhaps the chief of these was Horace, whose satire was becoming progressively more popular and threatened to replace the long-standing affection for Juvenalian and Persian roughness. The Francophile, superficially polite court of Charles II had fostered such "Augustan" taste, and any strong king, whether Tory James or Whig William, preferred to be addressed in the respectful Horatian tones of "a Court Satirist" who "comply'd with the Interest of his Master" (pp. 69, 68). For Dryden, Horace was the satirist in the court of a "Conquered People." Here is Dryden the supporter of a banished dynasty, ill at ease with the foreign king and, I suspect, thinking of himself in this description of disgruntled Romans under Augustus: "They cou'd not possibly have forgotten the Usurpation of that Prince upon their Freedom, nor the violent Methods which he had us'd, in the compassing of that vast Design" (p. 66). For all Horace's eminence as an instructor, rallier, and splendid poet of varied talents, as a satirist he is second to Juvenal and second in political morality.

Dryden's political and personal logic in the "Discourse" thus virtually dictate his preference for Juvenalian satire and for a modified form of the nation's earlier satiric taste. In Dryden's hands, the harsh cadence of Juvenal's rugged line would be polished while retaining its identity as elevated satire by a moral, perceptive outsider. That outsider, like Dryden himself, preferred an earlier dispensation, and is more serious than his main competitor. He attacks vice not Horatian folly; he is tragic not comic; he is rhetorically sublime and refuses the Horatian garbage of puns. Horace "was dipt in the same [illicit] Actions" of his monarch (p. 69), but Juvenal speaks truth to the corrupt power from which he is dissociated. Hence,

we cannot deny that *Juvenal* was the greater Poet, I mean in Satire. His Thoughts are sharper, his Indignation against Vice is more vehement; his Spirit has more of the Commonwealth Genius; he treats Tyranny, and all the Vices attending it, as they deserve, with the utmost rigour: And consequently, a Noble Soul is better pleas'd with a Zealous Vindicator of *Roman* Liberty; than with a Temporizing Poet, a well Manner'd Court Slave, and a Man who is often afraid of Laughing in the right place: Who is ever decent, because he is naturally servile.

For Juvenal, "*Roman* Liberty was to be asserted"; for Horace, the avaricious and flycatchers were to be scolded in easier times. "This Reflection at the same time excuses *Horace*, but exalts *Juvenal*" (pp. 65–66) and, it would seem, a "noble soul" like Dryden able to appreciate such qualities.

This exaltation takes two other forms – one is the relative manliness Dryden attributes to each satirist. He is not much moved by Horace, whose offered "Delight . . . is but languishing." Though "He may Ravish other Men," Dryden is "too stupid and insensible to be tickl'd" by Horatian "faint" wit and "Salt . . . almost insipid." The sexual imagery is less subdued upon Juvenal's appearance. He is "of a more vigorous and Masculine Wit," gives "as much Pleasure as I can bear" and "fully satisfies my Expectation . . .: His Spleen is rais'd, and he raises mine" (p. 63). No wonder that when Dryden apportions the prizes to these satirists he borrows from *Aeneid* v. 407–11 and awards Juvenal the majestic war horse, and Horace, for all his strength, the arrows of an Amazon probably conquered by a stronger male:

> The first of these obtains a stately Steed
> Adorn'd with trappings; and the next in Fame,
> The Quiver of an *Amazonian* Dame;
> With feather'd *Thracian* arrows well supply'd.[3]   (406–9)

The other exaltation of Juvenal is generic. Casaubon's *Prolegomena* (1605) to Persius had changed the derivation of satire and thereafter its conception and practice. Hitherto, the ambiguous tortured genealogy of the form rested largely upon either the Greek tragic satyr, or the woodland satyr, half man half goat, who whipped away one's vices. Casaubon, however, argued that satire actually was an adjective, not a noun, and that it was a variant of *satura*, full or abundant, with *lanx*, a plate or charger, understood. Satire would give one a full plate of wickedness to be attacked; it was nevertheless loosely held together by the boundaries of the charger itself, and descended from comedy not tragedy. To be truly satiric one therefore needed to lower one's voice and subject and avoid the heroic path. This view was especially popular in France, and was well promulgated in the several editions of André Dacier's influential translation and commentary on Horace (1681–89).

Dryden offered dual responses to this trend. On the one hand he declared a truce and discriminated between satiric modes and their respective best models: "what disreputation is it to *Horace*, that *Juvenal* Excels in the Tragical Satyre, as *Horace* does in the Comical?" (pp. 73–74). On the other, he preferred to praise Juvenal as the best satirist because associated with the best species of the genre. This goes far towards explaining Dryden's apparent digression on epic poetry, which he thinks superior even to tragedy, and which still can be written in a Christian nation. By establishing the transcendence of the heroic genre, he also establishes the transcendence of Juvenal's heroic (or sometimes "tragic") satire. The vices he lashes are among "the most enormous that can be imagin'd"; they also are "Tragical Vices" (p. 62) that evoke "Elevated . . . Sonorous . . . Noble . . . sublime and lofty" thoughts (p. 63). In contrast, Horace wrote on subjects "of a lower" and, we have seen, of a more compromising, "nature than those of which *Juvenal* has written" (p. 69). Heinsius thus wrongly confuses the part with the whole and claims that satire proceeds "in a low familiar way, chiefly in a sharp and pungent manner of speech." This confused description, Dryden observes, "is wholly accommodated to the *Horatian* way," and excludes "the Works of *Juvenal* and *Persius*, as foreign from that kind of Poem" (p. 77). Dryden's metaphors, again drawn from the sexual and equestrian, demonstrate his impatience with Horace and his apologists:

But how come Lowness of Style, and the Familarity of Words is to be so much the Propriety of Satire, that without them, a Poet can be no more a Satirist, than without Risibility he can be a Man? Is the fault of *Horace* to be made the Virtue, and Standing Rule of this Poem? Is the *Grande Sophos* of Persius, and the Sublimity of *Juvenal*, to be circumscrib'd, with the meanness of words and vulgarity of expresion? If *Horace* refus'd the pains of Numbers, and the loftiness of Figures, are they bound to follow so ill a Precedent? Let him walk a Foot with his Pad in his Hand, for his own pleasure; but let them not be accounted no Poets who choose to mount, and shew their Horsemanship. (p. 78)

That elevation so appealed to Dryden that he extended it to the serious genre of the mock-heroic. Though Virgil's fourth Georgic speaks about bees, for example, he "raises the Lowness of his Subject by the Loftiness of his Words; and ennobles it by Comparisons drawn from Empires, and from Monarchs" (p. 83). The *Lutrin* successfully learned from Virgil, to whom Boileau "scarcely" yields. Such a form is in fact "the most Beautiful and most Noble kind of Satire. Here is the Majesty of the Heroique, finely mix'd with the Venom of the other; and raising the Delight which otherwise wou'd be flat and vulgar, by the Sublimity of the Expression." Satire is "undoubtedly a Species" of "Heroique Poetry" (p. 84) with which it shares several traits of style and subject – as the author of *Mac Flecknoe* and *Absalom and Achitophel* well knew.

Dryden's penultimate contribution to the craft of formal verse satire also elevates Juvenal at the expense of Horace. Now, though, Dryden allies his genre with the dramatic, and returns to the tactfully treated Casaubon and Persius as norms. That great scholar preferred Persius because of his coherence and unity of design, which Dryden also accepts as the way in which "a Modern Satire shou'd be made" (p. 78). Horace often engaged in two or more arguments, "and the second without dependence on the first." Persius knew that "a perfect Satire . . . ought only to treat of one Subject" or theme. "As in a Play of the *English* Fashion, which we call a *Tragecomedy*, there is to be but one main Design: And tho' there be an Under-plot, or Second Walk of Comical Characters and Adventures, yet they are subservient to the Chief Fable, carry'd along under it, and helping to it; so that the Drama may not seem a Monster with two Heads" (p. 79). This coherence requires the poet to attack one vice that is the opposite of the virtue praised. Horace chose to ignore this precept of his art, whereas Juvenal "has chosen to follow the same Method of *Persius*, and not of *Horace*. And *Boileau*, whose Example alone is sufficient Authority, has wholly confin'd himself, in all his Satires, to this Unity of Design" (p. 80).

In stressing Juvenal's freedom of choice within a growing literary tradition, Dryden suggests perhaps his final, and overlooked, achievement. For all his essay's deserved respect for ancient masters, it is a "modern" cannonade in the battle between the ancients and moderns. The full title offers a revealing code word: "A Discourse concerning the Original and Progress of Satyr." The term "progress" was anathema to advocates of the ancients, for whom the world was in decline from approximately its Homeric past, when heroes, nature, and poets were at their untarnished golden apex. On this scheme, even civilized silver Virgil could but adapt his more glorious ancestor. Dryden inverts such assumptions. He chronicles the early, crude, Graeco-Roman satiric modes, sees them begin to mature in the Roman Lucilius, advance to Horace, add unity of design in Persius, meet full potential in Juvenal, and, though this never is quite clear, perhaps even fuller potential in the "living *Horace* and a *Juvenal*" of Boileau: "What he borrows from the Ancients, he repays with Usury of his own: in Coin as good, and almost as Universally valuable" (p. 12).

Boileau's presence helps to justify Dorset's, with whom he is coupled as a model of satiric greatness (p. 76). Dorset surely is overpraised because he was a generous patron; but he also had claims to be a modern satirist and the heir of a great tradition enriched by its latest practitioners as the genre improved. Dorset, for instance, can excel Horace by adding "that pointedness of Thought, which is visibly wanting in" him. Dorset also has more numbers, versification, and dignity than Donne (p. 6). Dorset thus exemplifies Donne's Renaissance Juvenalianism polished with Horatian elegance, and Horatian lowness raised by Juvenalian dignity and point. In the *Essay of Dramatick Poesy* (1668) Dorset was Eugenius, an advocate of the superiority of the modern English dramatist; here he is an example of the superiority of the modern English satirist.

Horace, on the other hand, had only the meager inheritance of Lucilius whom he "resolv'd to surpass . . . in his own Manner," a humble, low way that is a "dead Weight." Horace indeed won that race, but "limiting his desires only to the Conquest of *Lucilius*, he had his Ends of his Rival, who liv'd before him; but made way for a new Conquest over himself, by *Juvenal*, his Successor." Horace "cou'd not give an equal pleasure to his Reader, because he us'd not equal Instruments" (p. 64), one of which was Horace's own model of the limits of low satire. Dryden offers a central statement of Juvenalian progress and a modernism that, however offensive to Swift, combined the ancient and modern worlds in an improving tradition.

Anyone offended by Horace's second-place finish, Dryden says, should consider that Juvenal was talented, diligent, and studious. Moreover,

coming after him, and Building upon his Foundations might [he] not probably, with all these helps, surpass him? And whether it be any dishonour to *Horace*, to be thus surpass'd; since no Art, or Science, is at once begun and perfected, but that it must pass first through many hands, and even through several Ages? If *Lucilius* cou'd add to *Ennius*, and *Horace* to *Lucilius*, why, without any diminution to the Fame of *Horace*, might not *Juvenal* give the last perfection to that Work? (p. 73)

As Dryden also says, following Barten Holyday, Persius and Juvenal "chang'd Satire, . . . but they chang'd it for the better" (p. 70); and, Dryden adds in his own voice, "Why shou'd we offer to confine free Spirits to one Form, when we cannot so much as confine our Bodies to one Fashion of Apparel?" (p. 78). Any such offer would not be accepted by John Dryden who believed that cultures and the genres that express them improve through competition and available examples.

Dryden's manifold achievements in the "Discourse," then, include propagation and assessment of Continental Latin and French learning adapted to contemporary English needs; he places Horace, Persius, and Juvenal in their proper ranks in a satiric hierarchy, thereby slowing, but not stopping, the popularity of low comic Horatian satire adapted to the court, in favor of Juvenalian, political, opposition satire of the elevated tragic or epic kind. He also establishes the choice of satiric models as a form of political expression; at the best, he restores Juvenal's splendor, and at the least he establishes separate but equal comic and tragic satiric modes; he urges the pattern of coherent praise and blame as necessary in formal verse satire; and he insists on a modern progress through a limited but great past that grows greater as its satiric options increase.

＊

In preparing this collection of essays, I realized that these extraordinary achievements inform much eighteenth-century satiric practice and theory and significant aspects of the essays reprinted within. Though this is not a book with a unified thesis, it nonetheless offers a movement through time and satiric accomplishments from Dryden to Peter Pindar, from the solidification to the collapse of the greatest years of English verse satire that is not subsumed within another form – as it is in Byron's *Don Juan*.

These essays are divided into two sometimes overlapping classes. In "Contexts" the "Pattern of Formal Verse Satire" examines the knowledge of Dryden's design of a "perfect satire" throughout much of the eighteenth century. "History, Horace, and Augustus Caesar" amplifies Dryden's anti-Augustanism and examines the implications for so-called "Augustan" satire. "Masked Men and Satire and Pope" considers the persona in eighteenth-century satire and, implicitly, some of Dryden's view of how satirists "have prosecuted their intention" (p. 55) and communicated a sense of personal presence, whether positive or negative.

The essays in "Texts" examine specific poems by most of the major eighteenth-century verse satirists. "The Swelling Volume" analyzes Rochester's *Letter from Artemisia* (1679) and considers what the world of satire is like when Dryden's insistence on norms, or a praised and active virtue, is lacking. The study of Rochester's "Allusion to Horace" considers a satire and imitation before Dryden's best practice and "Discourse"; his valid assumption that poets learn from poets is one reason that Pope's imitations are so good, for he saw the imitation insufficiently exploited in Rochester. "'Natures Holy Bands' in *Absalom and Achitophel*" and "*The Rape of the Lock* and the Contexts of Warfare" study different modes of heroic satire and may suggest why Dryden thought so highly of that serious form, still so weighted with distorting modern clichés. The three following essays show how Dryden's view of the political statement inherent in the satiric model, and of the liberating nature of satiric choices, is fully exemplified in Pope. Someone for whom "Horace" is a synonym for "court sycophant" is not likely to use Horace as the impeccable literary, moral, and social norm he is so often mislabeled. The essays on Johnson's *London* (1738) and *The Vanity of Human Wishes* (1749) make plain, in the first case, the need to understand the history of interpretation in order to understand Johnson's modern Juvenal; in the second case it makes plain the strength of a better modern Juvenal handsomely elevated but nonetheless – again consistent with Dryden's view – surpassed by a modern competitor. The final essay, in effect, suggests the collapse of Dryden's tradition and the inward turning that renders satire irrelevant as a public act and art; in this new world harsh satirists like Churchill and Wolcot are most concerned with self-expression and regard earlier practitioners, to whom they may be in debt, as statues in a museum rather than part of a living tradition. By then, indeed, many of Wolcot's satires are called odes.

To be sure, these essays do, I very much hope, raise many other problems and aspects of scholarly and critical method. Throughout, for example, I insist on the need to examine eighteenth-century texts with eighteenth-century evidence, the better to see individual achievement within its tradition. Modern literary criticism has much to be said in its favor; that excludes critical imperialism in which vastly different works are colonized and made microcosmic clones of some larger theory more important than the literature itself.[4] I have assembled these essays on behalf of some eighteenth-century satiric literature, its contexts, and their modern students.

CONTEXTS

1 · THE PATTERN OF FORMAL VERSE SATIRE IN THE RESTORATION AND THE EIGHTEENTH CENTURY

THOUGH FORMAL verse satire was a major genre in the Augustan age, students of satire have generally been reluctant to define its essential traits. Perhaps the most illuminating study is Mary Claire Randolph's "The Structural Design of the Formal Verse Satire." She remarks that the satire of Lucilius, Horace, Persius, and Juvenal was "bi-partite in structure," that a particular vice or folly was attacked in "Part A," and its opposite virtue praised in "Part B." There is always more attack than praise in satire "since, paradoxically, in the very act of presenting the negative or destructive side of human behavior the satirist is establishing a positive foundation on which he can base his specific recommendation to virtue."[1] Whether introduced by direct exhortation, implication, or quotable proverb, the "admonition to virtue" is inevitably present in formal verse satire: "it must be there, spoken or unspoken, if the piece is to be more than mere virulence and fleeting invective . . . In any case, whatever the plan, the positive rational mode of procedure advocated or unmistakenly implied in a satire will be the precise opposite of the vice or folly ridiculed."[2]

Though accurate, Miss Randolph's remarks are based on classical Roman precedent, and she offers virtually no evidence about the influence of the structure on Restoration and eighteenth-century theory and practice. Nor does she indicate that any satirist or commentator other than Dryden and possibly Young, discussed the structure of formal verse satire. Dryden, she says, was "the only critic in English literature who has come reasonably close to an apprehension of the basic structure of the genre."[3] But Miss Randolph does not believe that Dryden's remarks, which are based on the classical pattern, influenced later satirists, for, she says, his "Discourse concerning the Original and Progress of Satyr" (1693) was overlooked and unappreciated. We must therefore infer that the pattern of satire that she describes was unknown to most English satirists.

Other scholars, applying Miss Randolph's insight regarding the structure of the genre, have found that Pope's satires exhibit the pattern of praise and blame;[4] but none of them has shown that in using this pattern Pope adheres to the concept of formal verse satire described by Dryden. That is, contrary to Miss Randolph's view, Dryden's concept of the form was well known during

the Restoration and eighteenth century; it influenced the theory of commentators, the expectation of readers, and the practice of satirists. Moreover, the
same concept was discussed by André Dacier in his important edition of
Horace (1681–89).

Dacier's essay on Roman satire supplied both a title and much information
for Dryden's "Discourse."[5] Furthermore, John Dennis often referred to him;[6]
there were at least three printed English translations of his essay "Sur les
satires d'Horace, où l'on explique l'origine & le progrès de la Satire des
Romains" (1687);[7] Jeremy Collier, Tom Brown, and Charles Gildon knew his
work well; Joseph Trapp, in his *Praelectiones Poeticae* (1711), frequently drew
upon him for his own discussion of satire,[8] and David Watson, in 1750, before
translating several of his "Remarques" on the satires and epistles of Horace,
calls them "a better Account . . . than I have any where met with."[9] Dacier's
La Poétique d'Aristote traduite en français avec des remarques (1692) further enhanced
his reputation, and he was considered, Gildon said in 1718, along with
Aristotle, Horace, and René le Bossu, among those who had made known and
fixed "the rules of criticism."[10] This broad influence justifies examination of
Dacier's remarks which, we will see, support the concept of satire described by
Miss Randolph.

In his prefatory essay on satire Dacier discusses Horace's attack upon vice
and praise of virtue. At first view, he says, we discover nothing in Horace's
satire which merits our affection. He seems more likely to amuse children than
occupy men. But, Dacier continues, "quand nous lui ôtons ce qui le cache à
nos yeux, & que nous le voyons jusques au fond, nous y trouvons toutes les
Divinitez ensemble, c'est-à-dire, toutes les Vertus qui doivent faire l'exercise
continuel de ceux qui cherchent sérieusement à se corriger de leurs vices."
Among the virtues which Horace hopes to teach in the two books of the satires
are those that are able "à regler nos passions, à suivre la Nature . . . [et] à
revenir de nos préjugez."[11] The most important job of the commentator on
Horace is to "montrer l'usage, la raison, & la preuve de des Preceptes; & de
fair voir, que ceux qui ne tâchent pas de se corriger sur un si beau modèle, sont
justement comme des Malades qui auroient un Livre tout plein de remedes
pour leurs maux, & qui se contenteroient de les lire, sans les comprendre, &
sans en connôitre l'utilité."[12] The commentator, therefore, aids the effect of
the satire's praise of virtue by making clear the utility, reason, and proof of
Horace's precepts.[13]

Dacier makes other important remarks when he discusses the *Epistles* of
Horace and asks whether they are not satires. Those who deny the name of
satire to the *Epistles* do not properly understand the nature of satire, he
declares, for they have founded their opinion on the praise of Maecenas and
Horace's other friends in the *Epistles*. Praise, they argue, does not belong in
satire. But the critics are mistaken about this point; satire may include praise
as well as raillery, as one can see in the little treatise preceding Dacier's

edition. Indeed, "Lucilius, qui passoit pour l'inventeur de cette sort de Poëme, ne faisoit pas toûjours la guerre au vice, dans ses Satires, il y loüoit aussi très-souvent la vertu. Horace lui-même n'at-t-il pas loüé Auguste & Mecenas dans les siennes? Et Perse n'a-t-il pas loüé Cornutus?"[14] Dacier concludes that it is not the mere presence of praise which differentiates the *Satires* from the *Epistles*, for some praise is essential to the satiric structure. What does differentiate them is the distinct way in which each functions in the satiric balance of praise and blame. Horace, Dacier explains, perceived that lack of order and method was the fault of the satirists preceding him. He therefore decided that his two books of *Satires* would, in general, attack vice, and that his two books of *Epistles* would praise virtue. Thus the four books fall under the rubric of satire; considered as a unit they carefully preserve the balance of praise and blame. Since the long passage from Dacier's "Remarques sur le titre des épîtres," so far as I know, does not appear in any other modern discussion of satire, it must be quoted in full:

Il a mis d'abord ses deux premiers Livres de Satires, parce que dans le premier il travaille à déraciner les vices; & que dans le second il s'efforce d'arracher les erreurs & les fausses opinions. Après ces deux Livres, viennent les Epîtres, qui peuvent fort bien être appellés la suite de ses Satires; & il les a mises après les Satires, parce qu'il s'attach à y donner des preceptes pour la vertu, & à allumer dans nos cœurs l'amour qu'elle merite. Ainsi ces quatre Livres sont un cours de Morale entier & [par]fait. Les deux premiers sont proprement . . . *destinez à redarguer* [to reprimand] *& à refuter.* Et les deux derniers sont . . . *destinez à insinuer & à enseigner.* Dans cette division Horace suivoit les maximes de Socrate, qui n'en seignoit jamais rien, qu'il n'eût auparavant déraciné du cœur de ses disciples tout ce qui pouvoit être contraire aux sentimens qu'il leur vouloit inspirer; & cette methode est très-conforme à la nature & à la raison. Il faut arracher d'un champ toutes les épines & les méchantes herbes & le bien preparer, avant que d'y semer le bon grain. Un bon Medecin tâche de dissiper & de chasser les mauvaises humeurs de son malade, avant que de lui donner les alimens solides pour lui fair revenir la santé avec l'embonpoint. C'est, sans doute, de cette pratique des Medecins que Socrate & Platon ont pris ces purifications, ou plûtôt ces purgations dont il est tant parlé dans leurs Livres . . . Socrate ne suit pas seulement cette methode dans chaque Dialogue, où il refute toûjours avant que d'enseigner: il lie aussi par-là plusieurs Dialogues ensemble, comme Horace a lié ces quatre livres . . . Cela explique admirablement le dessein d'Horace. Ses deux premiers Livres de Satires sont les purgations, . . . dont il se sert pour combattre nos passions, & pour nous délivrer des erreurs dont nous sommes remplis: & les deux derniers sont les enseignemens, . . . la doctrine pure & saine, qu'il fait succeder à ces maladies de l'ame dont il nous a gueris. C'est pourquoi ces deux derniers Livres plairont toûjours davantage à ceux qui se trouveront libres de toutes sortes de faux préjugez.[15]

This passage may have been known to Charles Gildon who, in 1692, edited *Miscellany Poems Upon Several Occasions: . . . With an Essay upon Satyr by the Famous M. Dacier.* Whether he knew it or not, he made clear the requirement that satire praise the virtue opposed to the vice attacked. For Gildon, however, satire is too personal and hence ineffectual. It does not do part of its proper job – making the virtue sufficiently explicit. Panegyric and epic poetry are more useful, for they deal extensively with "a Noble, and taking prospect of *Virtue.*"

Thus the *Aeneid* has contributed more to the progress of virtue than Horace's *Satires*, since it forms noble images in the mind, whereas the *Satires* merely expose vice and define virtue by the uncertain path of negatives. The reader is left rambling in the dark, and so may take the opposite road. Both epic and panegyric, however, affirm positively, and paint so exact a portrait of virtue that no one can mistake it or not know it immediately. "But that which is most of all," he adds, "*Panegyric* has the effectual force *Satyr* pretends to, in chacing away *Vice* and *Folly*, by discovering the *Properties*, and *Beauties* of their contraries."[16]

One year later Dryden issued his "Discourse concerning the Original and Progress of Satyr," prefixed to his translation of Juvenal and Persius. It is the most important contemporary English discussion of formal verse satire, and contains the clearest pronouncement on the structure of form. Dryden rejects Heinsius' definition of satire which, he says, is "wholly accommodated to the Horatian way [of low familiar speech]." He will therefore discuss his "own trivial thoughts" on the making of a modern satire, thoughts, he insists, which "will not deviate in the least from the precepts and examples of the Ancients."[17] Satire must attack only one vice and praise only one virtue. Dryden believes that Horace did not adequately follow this rule of the genre, since Persius – writing some seventy years later – was the first to point out the design of a perfect satire:

it ought only to treat of one subject; to be confined to one particular theme; or at least, to one principally. If other vices occur in the management of the chief, they should only be transiently lashed, and not be insisted on, so as to make the design double. As in a play of the English fashion, which we call a tragi-comedy, there is to be but one main design; and though there be an underplot, or second walk of comical characters and adventures, yet they are subservient to the chief fable, carried along under it, and helping to it; so that the drama may not seem a monster with two heads. (*Essays*, 2: 102–3)

To better preserve variety, he urges, the vice attacked may be illustrated with several examples in "the subdivisions of it, and with as many precepts as there are members of it." Dryden then adds a rule for perfecting this unity of theme in "the design of true satire":

The poet is bound, and that *ex officio*, to give his reader some one precept of moral virtue, and to caution him against some one particular vice or folly. Other virtues, subordinate to the first, may be recommended under that chief head; and other vices or follies may be scourged, besides that which he principally intends. But he is chiefly to inculcate one virtue, and insist on that. Thus Juvenal, in every satire excepting the first, ties himself to one principal instructive point, or to the shunning of moral evil. (*Essays*, 2: 104)

However, he emphasizes that the admonition to virtue may not be explicit; it may be implicit in the attack on the vice. Even in his sixth satire – a harsh attack upon women – Juvenal includes "a latent admonition to avoid ill women, by showing how very few, who are virtuous and good, are to be found amongst them" (*Essays*, 2: 104).

Persius, the originator of this method of satire, was also the most consistent practitioner of it, since he always inculcates a profitable Stoic doctrine and exposes "the opposite vices to it": "every satire is a comment on one particular dogma of that sect [the Stoic] ... In general, all virtues are everywhere to be praised and recommended to practice; and all vices to be reprehended, and made either odious or ridiculous; or else there is a fundamental error in the whole design" (*Essays*, 2: 104–5).

Miss Randolph has observed that Dryden emphasizes this "design" in the headnotes to each satire as well as in the essay. In the "Argument *of the first Satyr*" of Juvenal, for example, Dryden clearly notes the form of the genre when he remarks that though Juvenal here "strikes indifferently at all Men in his way: In every following Satyr he has chosen some particular Moral which he wou'd inculcate; and lashes some particular Vice or Folly."[18] Similarly, in the "Argument of the Sixth Satyr" of Juvenal, he again insists on the unity of the satiric structure. He reminds the reader that the real subject of Juvenal's attack is the lust of women, while the rest of their vices are but digressions to be skimmed over: " 'Tis one Branch of it in *Hippia*, another in *Messalina*, but Lust is the main Body of the Tree. He begins with this Text in the first line, and takes it up with Intermissions to the end of the Chapter."[19] And in the "Argument of the Eighth Satyr" (translated by Stepney), Dryden makes clear Juvenal's praise of honorable and good actions – as opposed to statues and pedigrees – as the defining traits of nobility. He thus advises his friend Ponticus to lead a virtuous life and praises the worth of noble and meanly born persons like Cicero, Marius, and Servius Tullius, and attacks the debauchery, luxury, cruelty, and other vices of the high-born Nero and Catiline.[20]

Dryden's view of the satiric pattern of praise and blame is expounded in his "Discourse" and illustrated in the Arguments prefixed to Juvenal's poems. He bases his theory on the practice of the ancients and of Boileau, on discussions of Renaissance commentators on Horace, Persius, and Juvenal,[21] and on Dacier's essay on satire. Dryden made this earlier view popular, gave it an English dress, and immense new authority. In all likelihood, his conception of satire influenced subsequent writers. Through much of the eighteenth century his reputation as a poet remained high, and his merits as a translator, though not always appreciated, were often discussed. In 1785, for example, Edward Owen attacked both Dryden's Juvenal and Persius, and his essay on satire;[22] in 1791 Boswell referred to the "excellent Dedication of his Juvenal,"[23] and as late as 1802, William Gifford discussed both Dryden's translation and his remarks in the "Discourse."[24] Moreover, one finds frequent allusions to Dryden's work throughout the Restoration and eighteenth century. In *De re poetica* (London, 1694), a collection of representative ideas on poetry, Sir Thomas Pope Blount quoted Dryden's remarks in his "Dedic. *before* Juvenal" on the origin of invective satire (p. 42). In John Ozell's translation of Boileau's *Works* (London, 1712), a bookseller's note referred to and quoted approvingly Dryden's discussion of the mock-heroic; the discussion quoted follows Dryden's description of the "design of a proper satire" (Boileau 1: 138). Sir Richard Blackmore, in his "Essay on Wit" (1716), alluded to the "Dedication of *Juvenal*, made *English*, to the late famous Earl of *Dorset*."[25] In his letter "To Matthew Prior, Esq.; Upon the Roman Satirists" (1721), John Dennis observed that "the Generality of Readers are more delighted with *Juvenal* than they are with *Horace*, because *Dryden* is more delighted with him [in the 'Discourse']."[26] Edward Young, perhaps following Dryden's precedent, briefly compared the beauties and faults of Horace and Juvenal in the Preface to his *Love of Fame* (1725–28). Dryden also had said that Boileau was "a living Horace and a Juvenal," a remark which was later echoed in Young's "*Boileau* has joyn'd both the *Roman* Satirists."[27] In 1728 John Oldmixon paraphrased Dryden's first note to Persius' First Satire thus: "DRYDEN says, the Commentators confess, that this *Labeo* is no where mention'd, but in this Satyr of *Persius*; yet *Casaubon* has found out that his Name was *Atticus Labeo*, and that he made a *foolish* Translation of *Homer*."[28] And in 1750 David Watson admitted that he was "greatly obliged" to "Mr. *Dryden*, in his admirable Preface before the *English* Translation of Juvenal."[29]

Samuel Johnson knew the translation of Juvenal and Persius at least as early as 1728, when he took with him to Oxford "Dryden's Juvenal."[30] His admiration for Dryden was so great that in the first volume of the *Dictionary* (1755) there are about 5,600 illustrations from his works. Only Shakespeare is cited more often (8,694 times), whereas Pope provides illustrations for only 2,108 words.[31] These quotations include more than 470 citations from the "Dedication to Juvenal" and prove that Johnson knew well the exact passages in which Dryden discusses the design of formal verse satire. For example, Johnson illustrates the word *underplot* with a sentence which occurs immediately after Dryden's initial statement about the unity of the satiric structure. Similarly, his illustration of the second meaning of *declamatory*, "appealing to the passions," is taken from the passage in which Dryden notes Juvenal's adherence to satire's *ex officio* rule to give the reader "some one precept of moral virtue, and to caution him against some one particular vice or folly." His illustration of *arraignment* is also taken from the same paragraph and immediately precedes the sentence which includes *declamatory*. In the paragraph following this passage, Dryden said that Persius' "kind of philosophy is one which is the Stoic, and every satire is a comment on one particular dogma of that sect." Johnson may also have had these words in mind when he used part of the "Argument of the First Satyr" of Persius for his illustration of *dogma*. At any rate, this illustration shows that Johnson knew the headnotes in which Dryden provides historical justification for his theory of satire: "Our poet was a stoick philosopher, and all his moral sentences are drawn from the *dogmas* of that sect."[32]

Moreover, Johnson not only had "Dryden's Juvenal" with him in 1735, three years before he wrote *London*,[33] but also referred to it frequently while preparing the *Dictionary* and writing *The Vanity of Human Wishes* in 1748. Thomas Birch records that by August 1748 Johnson's amanuenses had almost finished transcribing his authorities; that by September of 1749 a small part of the *Dictionary* was "almost ready for the Press"; and that, on 20 October 1750, 120 sheets – the first three letters of the alphabet – had already been printed.[34] It is impossible to say on exactly which letter Johnson was working in the autumn of 1748, but it is likely that much or all of letter *A* had been completed. Examination of the illustrative quotations under this letter shows that Johnson cited the translations of Juvenal twenty-six times, including two citations from "*Dryd. iun.*," Persius ten times, and the "Dedication to Juvenal" eight times. We also know that he gathered these and other quotations from "all such English writers as were most correct in their language";[35] his immediate selection of "correct" Dryden again indicates that Johnson knew the "Discourse" well before 1748.

Although less explicit than Johnson's, the remarks of several other writers also suggest indebtedness to Dryden's essay; in any case, these authors clearly show awareness of the form of a "true" satire. In the "Letter Concerning Enthusiasm" (1708), for instance, Shaftesbury sarcastically echoed this notion of the satiric form:

> If the knowing well how to expose any Infirmity or Vice were but a sufficient Security for the Vertue which is contrary, how excellent an Age might we be presum'd to live in! Never was there in our Nation a time known, when Folly and Extravagance of every kind was more sharply inspected, or more wittily ridicul'd. And one might hope at least from this good Symptom, that our Age was in no declining State; since whatever our Distempers are, we stand so well affected to our Remedys.[36]

Even minor writers and translators in the century were aware of the demands of the satiric pattern. Thomas Sheridan briefly summarized the individual satires in his translation of Persius (1728), and made clear the balance of praise and blame in each. *Satire* II, for example, attacks hypocrisy and superstition, and "points out a properer Way of publick *Worship*," while *Satire* III shows the "Folly of *Procrastination*; and the great Necessity there is of employing our Time to the best Purposes."[37] Shortly thereafter, Walter Harte, in his *Essay on Satire* (1730), stressed that though the moral of the satire "must be clear and understood," it is "finer still, if negatively good." Hence Capeneus "obliquely shows / T'adore those Gods *Aeneas* fears and knows."[38] Pope was also aware of the satiric pattern, since on 31 July 1738 Aaron Hill wrote to him about the second part of "One Thousand Seven Hundred, Thirty Eight." The poem, he says, combines Juvenalian acrimony with Horatian ease, and "it opposes just *praise* to just *censure*, and thereby doubles the *power* of either."[39] John Brown, writing his *Essay on Satire* (London, 1745), described satire's role in a similar way:

> To paint the heart, and catch internal grace;
> By turns bid vice and virtue strike our eyes,
> Now bid a WOLSEY or SEJANUS rise;
> Now with a touch more sacred and refin'd,
> Call forth a BRUTUS' or a SCIPIO's mind.   (p. 23)

Perhaps the most eloquent of the minor poets' discussions of the double-nature of satire may be found in the prefatory matter to *The Tears of the Muses* (1738). Aaron Hill there remarks that satire is "a poetical *Janus*; of whose Opposite two Faces, the fairest and best drawn you will find to be *Panegyric*." Hence he is justified in dedicating his poem to the distinguished "President, Officers, *and* Committie, of the Society for Encouragement *of* Learning."[40] This concept of satire seems to him "to be *New*: or not *practis'd*," for most satire is "either too *rough*, or too *gentle*," and therefore either "*corrodes*" or is merely "sportive and wanton, with what It shou'd *correct*, and discountenance." He thus proposes that the satirists copy the art of the painters, "who, by opposing their *Shades* against *Lights*, call out Darkness into open Distinction."

So, Enormities, which *Satirists* wou'd censure, are but dimly and imperfectly mark'd, till the *Defect* admits Disgrace, from the Neighbourhood of *Perfection*. – Then Contempt stings more sharply, in *One*, by the compar'd Admiration of the *Other*: Besides, that the Censur'd are driven, at the same Time, from their last little Refuge of Vanity, and can no longer recriminate upon the Censurer his *Ill-nature*, and Malevolence of Purpose.[41]

This author to the contrary, the form – as we have seen – was long known to satirists and expected by readers. Hill, we recall, was aware of it in one of Pope's poems, and Shaftesbury, Addison, Bishop Warburton, Edward Burnaby Greene, and Edward Owen,[42] all expressed awareness of the "bi-partite" structure of satire. Warburton, for example, in his edition of Pope's *Works* (1751), clearly pointed to Pope's ability to teach the virtue opposed to the vice attacked. In the *Epistle to Bathurst* (*Moral Essay III, of the Use of Riches* [1733]) the poet teaches the use of riches to others, "by the *abuse* that stands opposed to it." Thus "the *true use* of Riches [is shown] in a description of the *abuse*, and how that use is perpetually defeated by *Profusion* and *Avarice*." Warburton noticed a similar technique in Pope's *Epistle to . . . Burlington, of Taste* (*Moral Essay IV, of the Use of Riches* [1731]). He glosses "*What brought Sir Visto's* ill-got wealth *to waste?*" thus: "He then illustrates the above observation by divers examples in every branch of *wrong Taste;* and to set their absurdities in the strongest light, he, in conclusion, contrasts them with several instances of the *true*, in the Nobleman to whom the Epistle is addressed."[43]

But Pope was not always praised for his use of the form. Owen Ruffhead, in his *Life of Pope* (1769), severely criticized Pope's inattention to the proper balance of praise and blame in *The Characters of Women, to a Lady* (*Moral Essay II* [1735]). Here the satirist defeated his purpose, since he too harshly attacked the foibles of the sex, and scarcely ever interspersed moral precepts, "which may teach them to avoid or amend what is reprehensible. There is but one single line in the whole essay, in which he has offered any thing like *advice* to the fair." Young, according to Ruffhead, was not guilty of this mistake, for in the conclusion of the fifth satire in his *Love of Fame* he directed the sex not only to the "*whom*" they should charm but also "*how*, they should study to charm."[44] The *Epistle to Burlington*, however, deserves great praise because of its properly made satiric structure. In this epistle Pope not only pleasantly ridiculed false taste, but also showed the premises of true taste, first observing, for example, that "*good sense* is the foundation of *true taste*, whose office it is to embellish nature with suitable ornaments."[45] Ruffhead later says that it is also "observable . . . with what happy dexterity the poet, in exposing the absurdities of false taste, has negatively prescribed the rules of true taste." Furthermore, he continues, we should note the "admirable beauty in the conclusion of this poem . . . where the poet . . . gives a short summary of his precepts for true taste."[46] Indeed, Pope carried the principle of praise and blame into the *Dunciad* as well as the *Epistles*. Though his main intention was to attack bad writers and bad men, he nevertheless sincerely praised such men as Dryden, Congreve, and Addison, and even praised Cibber himself on the strength of his *Careless Husband*.[47]

Finally, Thomas Warton, in his *History of English Poetry* (1774–81), found the same pattern in Elizabethan satire. Though Hall turned the readers' eyes towards the obscene and immodest object, the effect of this "is to be counteracted by the force and propriety of [Hall's] reproof, by shewing the pernicious consequences of voluptuous excesses, by suggesting motives to an opposite conduct, and by making the picture disgustful by dashes of deformity."[48]

To this list of critical remarks we might add the practice of several satirists, including Dryden. We know that in the headnotes to his translation of Juvenal and Persius Dryden made clear each poem's attack on vice and praise of the opposite virtue. The pattern is similar in *Absalom and Achitophel* (1681), where he "taxes" the apparently extreme political innovations of the Whigs and praises the moderation of the Tories.[49] The satiric structure is also present in Young's *Love of Fame*. In his Preface Young remarks that his seven "character-istical" satires are really subsumed under one object of attack: "what men aim at by [vice and folly], is, generally, public opinion, and esteem. Which truth is the subject of the following Satires; and joins them together, as several branches from the same root. An unity of design, which has not (I think) in a set of Satires been attempted before" (sig. A3ᵛ). We soon see that each branch of the love of fame attacked has its own opposite virtue praised. For example, Young attacks nobles who spend and build unwisely, and then says:

> By your Revenue measure your expence,
> And to your *funds* and *acres* join your *sense:*
> No man is blest by *accident*, or *guess*,
> True *wisdom* is the price of *happiness*.[50]

He then censures the foppery, false gaiety, ostentation, and guilty intrigues of nobles at court, and offers the virtues of the happy country as an antidote to their refined misery.[51] Indeed, the pattern of praise and blame is present with such a vengeance in the seven satires that, it seems to me, its repetition ultimately helps to lessen the merit of the poem.

Moreover, the same satiric pattern explains the extended panegyric on George I in the seventh satire. Having surveyed its effect, Young turns to the cause of the universal passion. Though Ambition was sent "by heaven's indulgence . . . To warm, to raise, to deify mankind,"[52] it has different effects upon different minds: "Ambition in the *truly-noble mind*" is always joined with virtue to perform noble deeds. "In *meaner minds* Ambition works alone," but puts on the aspect of virtue in order to deceive and conquer. In the "*basest minds*" Ambition wears no mask: "All I have sung are instances of *this* [base Ambition]," he says, and then adds generalized counsel imploring his victims to "desist from your erroneous strife."[53] Virtuous Ambition can be found only where reside the several traits of wisdom, inward dignity, outward state, good purpose, great achievement, public blessings, and desire for deserved glory. All of these are exemplified in the long portrait of George I, the most eminent example of true Ambition, and the most likely model for emulation.

Our understanding of Johnson's *Vanity of Human Wishes* is also enhanced once we see that it exhibits the pattern of praise and blame. In this satire even the most innocent wishes directed to earthly powers, wishes for satisfaction of some worldly aspect of life, lead to misery, death, or disgrace, whereas wishes addressed to God, wishes for a healthy mind, obedient passions, a resigned will, love, and faith, all result in man's security, gain, calm, and happiness.

We have seen, then, that the concept of formal verse satire as incorporating attack upon a particular vice and praise of its opposite virtue was well known at least from the publication of Dacier's essay on satire (1687) to the final volume of Warton's *History of English Poetry* (1781). In England, this concept was made popular through Dryden's "Discourse concerning the Original and Progress of Satyr"; several major and minor authors either referred to it or implied knowledge of it. But the discussion of the form had more than theoretical interest. The judgments of Dennis, Hill, Warburton, and Ruffhead suggest that the pattern influenced the reader's expectations of satire, while the satires of Dryden, Young, Pope, and Johnson, and the prefatory matter to *The Tears of the Muses*, suggest that it influenced the practice of satire as well. Adherence to the pattern of praise and blame is probably a necessary and not sufficient cause of success in formal verse satire; but it should be clear that knowledge of the pattern was an important literary force during the Restoration and the eighteenth century.

2 · HISTORY, HORACE, AND AUGUSTUS CAESAR

SOME IMPLICATIONS FOR EIGHTEENTH-CENTURY SATIRE

CONTEMPORARY LITERARY SCHOLARSHIP has made impressive gains in reclaiming the classical background of eighteenth-century literature. We no longer think of Pope's *Dunciad* as a plotless ramble, or of his *Imitations of Horace* as unfortunately derivative; instead, they are carefully wrought poems that include and evaluate the classical past as transmitted by Continental and English commentators. Modern writers who hold this view regard the classics as normative, as one of the eighteenth century's main sources of inspiration, emulation, and imitation. Augustus Caesar, the apparently central Roman model, often lends his name to our period, and we hear the term "Augustan" applied sometimes to all the authors between 1660 and 1800, sometimes to the "orthodox" and "conservative" during those years, and sometimes to those who flourished during a prescribed segment, during, say, the "age" of Swift and Pope. Then as now Augustan implies a variety of excellences, but may be reduced to the omnibus belief that during the reign of Augustus Caesar the throne was a center of value. The exalted character of the monarch induced stable government, the arts of peace, protection by heaven, refinement of style, and patronage of great authors. These characteristics combined to create civilizing forces of permanent achievement for all mankind, and standards against which further achievements should be measured. As Laurence Echard put it in his *Roman History* of 1695, "never were more glorious, or at least, more pleasant Times . . . all Wars and Contests ceasing, all Arts and Sciences flourishing, and all Riches and Pleasures increasing."[1]

There is little doubt that such a concept of the Augustan age was attractive, functioned as a mythic force, and offered a basis of analogy for eighteenth-century history. Dryden, we know, praises Charles II as Augustus in *Astraea Redux* (1660); Pope celebrates Anne's present and wished-for accomplishments in the Augustan England of *Windsor Forest* (1713); Smart's georgic *Hop Garden* (1752) sings of Augustus as "Sovereign of Science! Master of the Muse"; and in *The Bee* (1759) Goldsmith assumes that during the Roman Augustan age "language and learning arrived at its highest perfection," and considers the period in England that might be so labeled.[2]

These remarks, and others like them, have lent eloquent support to those who read eighteenth-century literature in light of genial Augustan backgrounds. As one student recently observed, "'Augustanism' is gradually replacing 'neo-classicism' as a term for what we admire in the literature of the eighteenth century."[3] Accordingly, we hear that the unnamed English "Augustans saw in Horace's poetry, a concentrated image of a life and a civilization to which they more or less consciously aspired";[4] and that *Mac Flecknoe* embodies "the anti-world of the true Augustan ideal which Horace and Virgil tried to establish in their relationship with the throne."[5]

It will not, I hope, seem ungenerous to complain that we have now been overpaid in such antique coin, and than an inflationary spiral must bring on devaluation. There probably was consent, by most writers who bothered to think about it, that Augustanism as peace based on strength, stable government, and patronage of the arts was good. But beneath this pleasant overview there was a variety of changing and changeable attitudes towards Augustus during the 140 years in question. Augustanism, for example, seems to reach its positive peaks shortly after the accession of Charles II and again, for Tories at least, with the Peace of Utrecht. It reaches its low point when Bolingbroke's *Craftsman* attacks a tyrannical Augustus Caesar and likens him to George I and to George Augustus, King of England. Thereafter, classical and modern texts offered an attractive and open armory from which anti-Augustan weapons were frequently drawn.

In fact, throughout the Restoration and eighteenth century there existed a substantial and articulate voice that denied the poetic myth of the virtues of Augustus. He was, among other things, the butcher of Romans during the Triumvirate's proscription; accused of being too warm in the fields of love, sometimes with men, sometimes with his own daughter, and too cold in the fields of war; the trivial pagan ruler during the birth and childhood of Jesus; the foolish, perhaps malicious, selector of the brutal Tiberius; the paradigm for the absolute Louis XIV and thus suspect by English partisans of a limited constitutional monarchy.[6] Though this anti-Augustanism was often associated with political opposition and the fashion of exalting the Roman republic, it induced belief on both sides of the political spectrum. I suggest, in short, that the eighteenth century's friendly attitude towards Augustus Caesar has been overstated. Numerous historians, commentators upon history, men of letters, politicians, and ordinary citizens were, at the very least, ambivalent regarding the glories of Augustus, and often regarded him as politically dangerous and, ultimately, a destroyer not protector of literature. I further suggest that such a background has implications for the literary historian: T.W. Harrison has convincingly shown how Virgil and his *Aeneid*, a political poem written to help secure Augustus on the imperial throne, lost esteem during the eighteenth century precisely because of association with Augustus.[7] I will offer a complementary hypothesis: Horace was also blemished by his association with the Augustan court and was diminished as a moral, political, and satiric norm. This disillusion contributed to the decline of favor for Horatian satire, and helped to buttress Juvenalian satire which was popular during the seventeenth century, and though *perhaps* less so during the first third of the eighteenth century, nevertheless still eminently alive and influential.

There is, of course, no doubt that Horace had enormous appeal and was often looked to as a guide and authority. Pope tells the readers of *The First Satire of the Second Book of Horace Imitated* (1733) that *"An Answer from Horace was both more full, and of more Dignity, than any I cou'd have made in my own person."*[8] Eighteenth-century writers, however, not only were able to change their minds, but also able to compartmentalize their reactions, to use one poem as an authority and to criticize another, to find style exemplary and some aspects of content offensive. In the Preface to his widely read edition of Horace, André Dacier berates Horace's frequently sinful personal life, but generally praises the morality of his poems.[9]

Such compartmentalization is also found in attitudes towards Augustus, who is admired for his ability to make peace, encourage the court poets, and provide stable government, but blamed for waking the nascent despotism that finally ruined the republic and its values. The brief moment of splendor under Augustus was, many felt, both exaggerated in quality and purchased at too high a price. Hence St. Evremond, who largely admires Horace and Virgil and once believed in the wisdom of Augustus as a governor, also embodies one of the main attacks upon him: namely, that in his reign the arts actually declined. He argues that the later commonwealth, not the Augustan age, is the flowering of Roman genius,[10] and he tells the Maréchal De Créqui that under Augustus Roman

Parts as well as Courage began ... to decay. Grandeur of Soul was converted to Circumspect Conduct, and sound Discourse to Polite Conversation. . . . *Augustus* himself leaves us no great Idea of his Latinity. What we see of *Terence*, what was reported at *Rome* of the politeness of *Scipio* and *Laelius*, the Reliques of *Caesar*, and what we have of *Cicero*, with the complaint of this last for the loss of what he calls, *Sales*, . . . *Urbanitas, Amaenitas*, . . . all together make me believe, . . . That we must search some other time than that of *Augustus*, to find the sound and agreeable Wit of the *Romans*, as well as the pure and natural Graces of their Tongue.[11]

In some authors compartmentalization was second to condemnation. Echard's pro-Augustan royalism, for instance, quickly fell into disfavor, and by 1743 was attacked in Fielding's *Voyage from this World to the Next*. There the shade of Livy commends "the judicious collection made by Mr. Hooke [his "patriotic" *Roman History*], which, he said, was infinitely preferable to all others; and at my mentioning of Echard's," the narrator observes, "he gave a bounce, not unlike the going off of a squib."[12] And by 1771 Echard's book was labeled a tasteless, hurriedly composed work that, even among bad modern histories of Rome was "in particular, . . . lame and defective."[13]

Fielding was hardly alone in drawing upon Roman authors to degrade the genius of Augustus. Such attacks, based upon a variety of historical sources, were often accompanied by the belief that the usurper destroyed letters. Nat Lee's unintentionally comic masterpiece, *Gloriana or the Court of Augustus Caesar* (1676), uses accepted historical fact and myth, and his own fertile wit. He portrays Augustus as an elderly, half-crazed, sexually famished tyrant who banishes Ovid and is still remembered for his share in Cicero's murder.[14] Dryden's "Discourse concerning . . . Satyr" (1693) borrows from Tacitus, Suetonius, and a commentary upon Sextus Aurelius Victor, to show that Augustus was responsible for the diminution of the vigor, honesty, and quality of satire. The Emperor "thought in the first place to provide for his own reputation by making an edict against lampoons and satires, and the authors of those defamatory writings which . . . Tacitus . . . calls *famosos libellos*." Horace lost the freedom to reprehend "the worst of villanies"; the subjects of his satire "are of a lower" and, Dryden implies, an inferior "nature than those of which Juvenal has written."[15]

Since everyone opposed tyranny, both Whig and Tory, court and Opposition during the eighteenth century lament Augustus' depradations upon liberty. In 1728 Thomas Gordon dedicates his translation of Tacitus to his patron Robert Walpole, and argues that under Augustus "Truth was treason." No one "would venture to speak it . . . and when Flattery bore a vogue and a price there were enough found to court it, and take it. Hence the partiality or silence of Poets and Historians."[16] Nathan Hooke, who in 1738 dedicated the first volume of his *Roman History* to Alexander Pope, reminds us that "the odium of Cicero's death fell chiefly on *Antony*, yet it left a stain of perfidy and ingratitude also on Augustus which explains the reason of that silence which was observed about him, by the writers of that age; and why his name is not so much as mentioned either by *Horace* or *Virgil*."[17] Conyers Middleton, whose *Life of . . . Cicero* (1741) was subscribed to by the Royal Family, numerous peers, and men of letters,[18] agrees concerning the reason for the Augustan poets' neglect of Cicero,[19] adds that the birth of Octavius nurtured the seeds of the death of Roman liberty (1:230–31), and makes clear that "after CICERO's death and the ruin of the Republic, the *Roman* oratory sunk of course with its liberty, and a false species universally prevailed," so that oratory was fit only for "the making panegyrics, and servile compliments to . . . Tyrants" (2:534–35). And in 1760 the aging Boy-Patriot George Lyttelton added his pen to the attack upon the honesty and value of Augustan letters. In the ninth dialogue of his *Dialogues of the Dead*, Lyttelton's Cato berates Augustus as the murderer of the commonwealth, Cicero, and the noblest Romans. Messala, on the other hand, urges that under Augustus' "judicious patronage, the Muses made Rome their capital seat. It would have pleased you," he tells Cato, "to have known Virgil, Horace, Tibullus, Ovid, Livy, and many more, whose names will be illustrious to all generations." But Cato would not be so pleased and brusquely tells Messala: "Your Augustus and you, after the ruin of our liberty, made Rome a Greek city, an academy of fine wits, another Athens under the government of Demetrius Phalareus. I would much rather have seen her under Fabricius and Curius, and her other honest old consuls, who could not read." For Lyttelton's Cato, Augustus has perverted Roman letters, and Messala slinks off, finally drawing the only possible conclusion: "I see," he says, "you consider me as a deserter from the republick, and an apologist for a tyrant."[20] By 1793 Arthur Murphy – who dedicated his book to Edmund Burke – had translated Tacitus and in the process made clear that Augustus also diminished the quality of historical writing. Though in his time, Tacitus says, "there flourished a race of authors from whose abilities that period might have received ample justice . . . the spirit of adulation growing epidemic, the dignity of the historic character was lost."[21] Murphy and Tacitus again repeat this charge in Book I of the *History* (3:5–6, 461n), and amplify it to include biography when they discuss the *Life of Agricola* (4:52–53, 347n). Shortly thereafter, in a note to Tacitus, Murphy paraphrases Seneca's attack upon Augustus' initiation of bookburning, even though nothing in these "writings affected the public . . . The policy" under Augustus, Seneca and Murphy say, ". . . of punishing men for their literary merit was altogether new. Happily for the good of mankind, this species of tyranny was not devised before the days of Cicero . . . The gods, in their just dispensations, took care that this method of crushing the powers of the mind, by illegal oppression, should begin at the point of time when all genius ceased to exist" (4:348).[22]

Moreover, by mid century the outcry against Augustus had gained support from France, already well into the throes of repudiating the absolutism of her own Augustus, but well away from the Jacobin ravages that brought some moderation of anti-Augustan passion. In 1674 Louis Moréri's *Le Grand Dictionnaire historique* praised every aspect of Augustus' reign;[23] by 1734 Montesquieu's *Considérations sur les causes de la grandeur des Romains et de leur décadence* still respected Augustan stability, but called Augustus himself "a smooth and subtile Tyrant, [who] led [the Romans] gently into slavery."[24] In 1751, with the publication of the *Encyclopédie* this ruler is the destroyer of the republic, the enchainer of his people, and the murderer of accurate historical writing.[25] During the same year, Bonnot de Mably told the readers of his *Observations sur les Romains* that Augustus killed satire because it disturbed his vices.[26] It is no wonder that in his *Questions sur l'encyclopédie* (1770–72), Voltaire observes: "il est donc permis aujourd'hui de regarder *Auguste* comme un monstre adroit & heureux," and later adds that Virgil and Horace, in praising Augustus – "un fort méchant homme" – show "des âmes serviles."[27] And in 1782 the republican but anti-Jacobin Jean Dusaulx makes politically inspired anti-Horatian remarks that gain wide currency in England. He finds that France's learned neighbors were right in calling Juvenal "Prince des satiriques," and severely blames Horace's role in seconding Augustus' efforts "à métamorphoser les citoyens en courtisans."[28] By 1791 those neighbors had repaid Dusaulx's compliment by translating part of his "Discours" as "A Parallel Between Horace and Juvenal." Dusaulx and the *Literary Magazine* admire Horace's ability to write elegant verse while accommodating himself to the tyrant and his court, saying what he wished to hear, and not saying what he did not wish to hear – praise of the proscribed Cicero, for example. But Juvenal was a different sort of poet: "Horace had learned to support the yoke of a master, and to lead the way for the deifying of tyrants; Juvenal, on the other hand, did not cease to exclaim against usurped power, and to recall to the Romans the glorious ages of their independence." Juvenal "could speak of nothing but vice and virtue, slavery and liberty, folly and wisdom. It may be said of him . . . that he staked his life on what is true," whereas the writer with "exquisite politeness, is less to speak the truth, than what shall be grateful to those in power."[29] In short, in France as well as England several major authors and commentators believed that by encouraging flattery, servility, and tyranny, and discouraging free and just evaluation of all aspects of the state and its leader, Augustus lowered the quality of letters.

I will soon examine some implications of this view for literary studies, but first I should address myself to a troubling question: if Augustus is in fact the enemy of literature, how do we account for the works of Virgil and Horace that appeared during his reign? Perhaps what I call compartmentalization offers one answer: they are transcendent poets who can teach us much about art and some aspects of ethics, but must be viewed suspiciously regarding political morality. St. Evremond and Lyttelton suggest a second answer – Horace and Virgil are major poets but are overrated and not worth the price paid. Another is exemplified by Robert Andrews, who argues that the court poets knew that Rome was fallen, and that the only way for them to save their country from utter destruction was beautifully to sing "the oracles of political Wisdom, charming the Savage [Augustus] into Clemency."[30] But the most interesting argument comes in the three-volume work by Thomas Blackwell, Principal of Marischal College in the University of Aberdeen: *Memoirs of the Court of Augustus*, an autographed and inscribed set of which was presented to George III, was praised by Robert Jephson in 1794, and appeared on Shelley's reading list in 1814 and 1816.[31] Published between 1753 and 1763, Blackwell's work is a compendium of the eighteenth century's ambivalent, often hostile, attitude towards Augustus and his poets. He grants the genius of the Augustan wits, but adds that "it is matter of Lamentation that such Men should have been under a Necessity of stooping to flatter a flagitious Youth. – Miserable was the Plight of their Country, when it was *requisite* and *proper* to make such Compliments."[32] Augustus actually debased poetry by demands for flattery, and debased the theatre by using it merely to feed "the Curiosity of a restless People," engross "their Thoughts," and make "them forget all Affairs of State, in which they had formerly had so great a Share" (3:379). We are, then, faced with the paradox of a prince who diminished letters yet lived in an age famous for them. Blackwell's answer includes hostility to Augustus and an attempt to put as good a face as possible on the court poets, who were, he believes, really republicans manqués:

What we loosely term the *Stile of the Augustan Age*, was not *formed* under *Augustus*. It was formed under the Common-Wealth, during the high struggles for Liberty against *Julius Cesar*, and his Successors the Triumvirs, which lasted upwards of fifteen Years. The Men who had been *formed* under *Augustus shone* under *Tiberius*, and strictly, spoke the Language of his Age. *Cinna*, therefore, and *Varus, Gallus*, and *Pollio, Junius Calidius, Virgil*, and *Horace*, with all their contemporary Poets, learned the Language of *Liberty*, and took the masterly Tincture, which that Goddess inspires both in phrase and Sentiment. This gave them that Freedom of Thought and Strength of Stile, which is only to be acquired under *Her* Influence; which, when joined to the Politeness that accompanies the slippery Transition from Freedom to blind Obedience, produced the *finished Beauty* we admire in their Works. Those who wrote before them, were rough, and sometimes harsh – though exalted and manly. Those who came after them, were enervated, flimsy, and full of Conceits which *mimic* true Wit: – or, if they aimed at *sublime*, they were turgid and unnatural; if at *Turns of Thought*, they fell into meer Witticism. This is the first Step towards Degeneracy. The liveliest Instance I know of it is *Manilius*, who was quite modelled under *Augustus*, and whose truly great Genius, wide Learning, and exalted Subject, have not been able to guard him from the Infection of Slavery, I mean the *Concetti* or *Sheer-Wit* that then began to be in vogue. Let not therefore *Virgil* or *Horace*, or *Valgius* or *Varus*, be looked upon as *courtbred* Poets under *Augustus*: No more than *Milton, Waller*, or *Cowley* were under Charles II. They were free-born Romans, some of them early venturing Life and Fortune in the Cause of Liberty, who were called to Court, and protected and encouraged by the Prince's Ministers; in return for which they did him and them the greatest of all services. The *Roman* Model copied by *Virgil* was *Ennius*, as Lucilius did by *Horace*.

The *Roman* Composition began to degenerate even under *Augustus*.   (3:467–68)

It is worth noting that in 1756 Samuel Johnson reviewed the second volume of Blackwell's *Memoirs* and objected not only to his "furious and unnecessary zeal for liberty," but also to his vain tones of discovery when his audience had long known what he had to say.[33] Apparently, by about mid century attacks on Augustus as a tyrant and threat to the preservation of letters were commonplace.

Some of the remarks I have quoted earlier – Dryden's, for one – suggest that these commonplaces may have influenced eighteenth-century literature and the beliefs of contemporary and later writers in England and France, Whig and Tory, historian, poet, novelist, or concerned citizen. The anonymous author of *Plain Truth, or Downright Dunstable* (1740), for example, labels Horace and Virgil *"flattering, soothing Tools"* who were "Fit to *praise* Tyrants, and *gull Fools*."[34] The court poets do not live in a golden age, but "monstrous times"; they are *"Weeds"* who "ornament a Tyrant's nest"; they sing "hateful Lays / Still trumpeting the *Tyrant's praise*."[35] In his ode to Huntingdon (1748) Mark Akenside calls Augustus an "imperial Ruffian" unworthy of praise by even one "polluted Bard."[36] Several years thereafter, in John Cleland's novel *The Woman of Honour* (1768), Launcelot Grevelle tells the Marquess of Soberton that he is sorry Antony has been so well treated by dramatists, but consoles himself with the knowledge that his suicide was brought about "by one of his own gang, that cowardly and cruel in cold blood, Augustus, whose successes, as they are called, were the ruin not only of his own family, . . . but of the greatest republic." As a result of "sinking into slavery" under Augustus, Rome's "annals, after that period, became . . . the reproach of humanity, the disgrace of history, and the scorn of curiosity."[37] In 1773 Johnson insists that "no modern flattery . . . is so gross as that of the Augustan age, where the Emperour was deified," and he cites Horace (*Odes*, III.v.2) as a crass example.[38]

In order to suggest a more explicit influence and ramification of this anti-Augustan view, I would like briefly to focus upon Horace's reputation and Horatian satire during the eighteenth century, though much could also be done with Virgil's *Aeneid*, a "party piece" on the side of usurpation, Pope told Spence, in which there was not one honest line.[39] Reuben Brower argues that "for the small yet influential class that created what we call eighteenth-century civilization, Horace was a kind of 'cultural hero,'" and that "Pope and his friends – writers, statesmen, artists, country gentlemen of many degrees of grandeur – often saw their own world through Horace's eyes and to a surprising degree tried to shape the actuality to fit the dream."[40] But this view seems to me both overstated and at best partially applicable to Horatian satire. After all, Horace was in the court party, whereas during the peak of Pope's career he was opposed to the court, and not likely to find a cultural hero associated with the minions of Walpole. Furthermore, though it is obviously true that Horace was widely read, widely translated, and had continuing appeal, his odes, epodes, and literary criticism were responsible for much of his fame, whereas the battle for preeminence as a *satirist* was never clearly resolved on his side. In 1692 and again in 1718 even the genteel Joseph Addison contents himself with stating the respective merits of Horace and Juvenal and proclaiming the familiar notion that they "are perfect Masters in their several ways."[41] Boileau and Pope were often regarded as combining both Horatian ease and Juvenalian ferocity,[42] while in England alone one would be hard put to find many significant, polite so-called Horatian satires to place against the larger number of more "Juvenalian" works by Oldham, Gould, Rochester, Dryden, Swift, the best of Young, much of the later Pope, Johnson, and Churchill. Indeed, that the triumph of eighteenth-century Horatianism is but a myth is indicated by Joseph Warton's feeble attempt to refute Montesquieu's judgments on British satire in Book 19, chapter 27, of the *Esprit des lois* (1748). For Montesquieu "the character of a nation is . . . particularly discovered" in its literary performances. In England "satirical writings are sharp and severe, and we find amongst them many Juvenals without discovering one Horace."[43] In rebuttal Warton merely cites a few of Dorset's poems and urges that he "possessed the rare secret of uniting energy

28

with ease"[44] and thus is properly Horatian. Perhaps Warton is correct about Dorset, but if so it is the exception that proves the rule, or at least the generalization.

Moreover, as bawdy burlesques of the classics suggest, if Horace could serve as an elegant norm he could also be turned to amusing or miserable use. Pope's *Sober Advice from Horace* (1734) includes ample references to pimps, casual adultery, exposed buttocks, plump thighs, and the proper sort of wench with whom one should debauch. Chesterfield is concerned both with making use of one's spare time and with a certain natural function. He pleasantly advises his son to purchase a cheap edition of Horace, tear off a couple of pages for each visit to the "necessary-house," read them, and then use them as a sacrifice to Cloacina.[45] And in 1748 Smollett allows a learned innkeeper piously to mouth Horace while cheating the gullible Roderick Random (ch. 10).[46]

But the main blemish upon Horace's reputation as a satirist (indeed as a court poet) was his lamentable willingness to serve Augustus, the usurper who insists upon flattery and upon satire of mild folly not extreme vice. For the self-consciously patriotic Englishman such a pose must have been objectionable, and was at the heart of Dryden's preference for Juvenalian satire. Juvenal's spirit, Dryden argues,

has more of the commonwealth genius; he treats tyranny, and all the vices attending it, as they deserve, with the utmost rigour: and consequently, a noble soul is better pleased with a zealous vindicator of Roman liberty than with a temporizing poet, a well-mannered Court slave, and a man who is often afraid of laughing in the right place; who is ever decent, because he is naturally servile. (2:132).

Dryden's censures were well known throughout the eighteenth century, and in 1721 John Dennis tells Matthew Prior that the generality of readers prefer Juvenal to Horace because Dryden does.[47] Lewis Crusius was among that generality, and in his *Lives of the Roman Poets* (1726) he embodies accepted wisdom regarding Horace and Juvenal's lashing of vice,[48] and is confident that he "will appear a true generous spirited *Roman*, and a friend to liberty and virtue" (2:84). It is thus not surprising that though Crusius gives full credit to Horace, and some to Persius, he argues that "JUVENAL has undoubtedly improved on both" (2:80). Corbyn Morris prefers Juvenal to Horace because the severe attack of true satire shows "a generous free Indignation, without any sneaking Fear or Tenderness; It being a sort of partaking in the Guilt to keep any Terms with Vices."[49] Such partaking in vice, we may infer from previous evidence, though Morris does not so state, is well exemplified in Horace's relationship with his emperor. In 1745 we again hear a traditional evaluation of the two satirists based to some degree, I suggest, on political purity. Horace, John Brown says in celebration of Pope's death, "Politely sly, cajol'd the foes of sense"; but Juvenal's "mighty numbers aw'd corrupted *Rome*, / And swept audacious greatness to its doom."[50] And in 1763 Gibbon insists that republican "love of liberty, and loftiness of mind distinguishes Juvenal from all the poets who lived after the establishment of the monarchy." Horace, Virgil, and Ovid, among others, "sing the ruin of their country, and the triumph of its oppressors . . . Juvenal alone never prostitutes his muse."[51]

One of the most telling examples of the rejection of Horace is in Alexander Pope, a putative bastion of eighteenth-century Horatianism. His growing disillusion may have been encouraged by Joseph Spence who, in *Polymetis* (1747) and other places, wrote eloquently regarding Virgil's political poem.[52] But Pope's disillusion was not limited to Virgil, as the epitaph he penned about himself indicates:

> HEROES, and KINGS! your distance keep:
> In peace let one poor Poet sleep,
> Who never flatter'd Folks like you:
> Let Horace blush, and Virgil too.[53]

At other times Pope proudly told Spence and his readers that he had never flattered, especially in what he thought the cause of tyranny.[54] Hence the very conception of the *Epistle to Augustus* (1737) includes satire upon Horace as well as George II; but the first Dialogue of the *Epilogue to the Satires* (1738) is of even greater importance for establishing Pope's ultimate anti-Augustan and anti-Horatian stance. The poem begins with the remarks of a court devotee ironically labelled "Friend."

> Not twice a twelvemonth you appear in Print,
> And when it comes, the Court see nothing in't.

In a note to this couplet Pope says: "These two lines are from Horace [*Sat.* II.iii.1–4]; and the only lines that are so in the whole Poem; being meant to give a handle to that which follows in the character of an impertinent Censurer" (*Imitations*, p. 297n). Pope both dissociates himself from Horace's authority and uses him to offer a clue to the characterization of his own adversarius. Junius Damasippus, the vaguely parallel Horatian character, has a dual history: in Cicero's *Letters* he is an agent in the purchase of works of art, and in Horace's satire he is a former art dealer who is a convert to stoicism and thinks the whole world mad.[55] Renaissance and contemporary commentators blended the two and helped Pope to his now unused "handle."[56] The Friend, obviously an enemy, is trying to buy Pope's art and induce his own stoicism regarding court activities. Though Horace satirizes the stoic, he gives him a serious hearing and admits his basic point. Pope rejects stoicism and the easy view of universal madness, and disdains everything his interlocutor has said. In the process he uses the conventional critical language that described Horatian satire, shows how easily it can be adapted to modern political corruption, and actually portrays the Friend unconsciously adhering to the anti-Augustan tradition I have been describing. Moreover, he has the Friend employ only the most ambiguous part of Persius' description of Horace – his "sly insinuating Grace"[57] – and ignore the affirmative lines immediately thereafter (as they appear in Dryden's translation of *Satires*, I, 231–38). In the process, Pope's Friend places Horace in the court, with the tyrannical Augustus, and against the exposure that the free satirist must make while, by implication, Pope associates himself with a "Juvenalian" Lucilius who "never fear'd the times; / But lash'd the City, and dissected Crimes" (2:748). Horace, as now interpreted by a contemporary "Augustan," opposes the essential values of Alexander Pope:

> But *Horace*, Sir, was delicate, was nice;
> *Bubo* observes, he lash'd no sort of *Vice*:
> *Horace* would say, *Sir Billy serv'd the Crown,*
> Blunt *could do Bus'ness*, H–ggins *knew the Town,*
> In *Sappho* touch the *Failing of the Sex,*
> In rev'rend Bishops note some *small Neglects,*
> And own, the *Spaniard* did a *waggish thing,*
> Who cropt our Ears, and sent them to the King.
> His sly, polite, insinuating stile
> Could please at Court, and make AUGUSTUS smile:
> An artful Manager, that crept between
> His Friend and Shame, and was a kind of *Screen.*   (lines 11–22)

One must, I think, disagree with John Butt's judgment that the *Epilogue* "is the most Horatian of Pope's original work," especially since, in the last two lines quoted, Horace is clearly equated with Walpole.[58] Though this poem is labeled "Something like Horace," aside from the dialogue form it is designed to be very little like Horace and very much like Juvenal. The satirist is the enemy of the corrupt court not its friend; he cannot laugh at folly but must attack vice whatever the consequences; his indignation makes verse for which he may be banished or belittled by the court, and so must make his own court in the country; he is a satirist for whom receipt of the court's praise would mean defeat. Thus the last allusion in the second Dialogue dramatically inverts Dryden's translation of lines 170–71 of Juvenal's first satire, a sort of prologue to the other fifteen. Juvenal says:

> Since none the Living-Villains dare implead,
> Arraign them in the Persons of the Dead.   (2: 677)

And Pope says in his own line 251: "Are none, none living? let me praise the Dead." Juvenal's beginning is Pope's end, the "last poem of the kind printed by our author, with a resolution to publish no more" (p. 327n), we hear in the concluding note to the second part of the *Epilogue*. With the exception of the final book and version of the *Dunciad*, Pope obeyed his resolution, but in the meanwhile he had contributed to the discrediting of Augustus and Horace as exemplary political and satiric models for some of the best writers of his age and the next. Samuel Johnson twice turned to Juvenal for his own imitations, and it seems reasonable to say that no major or significant minor work of directly Horatian inspiration appeared after 1738.

31

I hope that this review will induce reconsideration of two accepted but mistaken modern notions of Restoration and eighteenth-century literary history: the first sees Horace as "a moral instructor illuminated by the best of classical knowledge, and to be further brightened by the light of Christian revelation."[59] And the second accepts the English "Augustans' pervasive esteem for Horace" and the "nearly related if not synonymous" positive use of "Augustanism and Horatianism."[60] In the former Horace is, largely, normative and an authority for eighteenth-century writers; in the latter all good Augustans imitate Horace and eschew Juvenal, and any one with the opposite view is, by definition, not Augustan and an aberrant creature one can easily ignore. According to this theory, Juvenal is revived in the later half of the century because of its failure in taste, misreading, and movement away from good irony and towards bad sentimental quasi-Christian declamation.

The errors of method and judgment in these views should be pointed out: confusion of the part for the whole, of, for example, Horace's odes and literary criticism with his satires;[61] ignorance of entire areas of discussion of the classical past; rejection of solid contrary evidence in contemporary texts; and acceptance of clichés in place of the difficult and complex amalgam of historical thought during the period. My counterhypothesis is that though Horace was fashionable, frequently imitated and translated, a guide in some secular matters, rightly admired for his art, and even used by some theologians for purposes of instruction,[62] much of his audience also associated him with a dubiously benevolent despot they had been taught to mistrust. Such historians, their editors, commentators, translators, and the numerous men of letters on either side of the Channel who agreed with them, helped to clarify both (apparent) parallels between Rome and England and the value of such parallels as a guide to "their judgments in current political controversies."[63] Thus, depending upon one's bias and historical moment, James II, William III,[64] George I, George II, or any other head of state, need not be contrasted with a virtuous but compared to a vicious Augustus Caesar. As a corollary, Juvenal, though less imitated, did embody what Dryden called "the commonwealth genius," and was often more admired than Horace for his independence from the court: Pope's last great triumphs in formal verse satire are anti-Augustan and anti-Horatian.

There are generally several causes for one literary effect, and the diminution of Augustus and Horace as political norms is but one part of an explanation for the renewed attention to Juvenalian satire during the later eighteenth century. Nevertheless, with Horace thus tainted, contemporary authors even more openly turned to Juvenal as a guide, and found major figures in preceding and present generations to buttress their beliefs. Perhaps this is one reason for the pro-Juvenalian remarks I have already cited, and perhaps why, in 1755, Johnson selects an evaluative illustration from Henry Peacham's *Compleat Gentleman* (3rd ed., 1661) for his fourth *Dictionary* definition of the adjective *round*: "In his satyrs Horace is quick, *round*, and pleasant, and as nothing so bitter, so not so good as Juvenal";[65] why in 1787 Sir John Hawkins believes that "in two instances [Johnson] nearly equalled the greatest of the Roman satyrists";[66] and why in 1800 the respected Alexander Adam tells readers of his *Classical Biography* that "many" prefer Juvenal's satires to those of Horace.[67]

When we remind ourselves that as students early in the eighteenth century both Johnson and Hawkins were subject to Dryden's pro-Juvenalian judgments, and that Adam's remark is representative not aberrant, it should be clear that Juvenal's works did not need to be revived – they were never dead, and were as well understood then as now. And they attracted enthusiastic readers as different as the devout Samuel Johnson, who memorized all of Juvenal, and the "enlightened" Edward Gibbon who was, one suspects, unblemished by Christian sentimentality. At any rate, the popularity of Juvenal is as likely to be a function of the growth of anti-Augustan attitudes as the growth of Christian declamation and bad taste. Consequently, if we continue to use the term "Augustan" to characterize any or all of the years between 1660 and 1800, we should be aware of that period's anti-Augustan stance, its reservations regarding the political morality of the court poet Horace, and the possible influence of such reservations upon the mutations of literary history.[68]

3 · MASKED MEN AND
SATIRE AND POPE

TOWARDS AN HISTORICAL BASIS FOR
THE EIGHTEENTH-CENTURY PERSONA

IN RECENT YEARS criticism that uses a theory of the persona to analyze eighteenth-century texts has been attacked, defended, and chronicled, and refuses to enter geriatric decline. Briefly, the theory holds that literature, particularly eighteenth-century satire, should not be read as an expression of the real author's real values. The work's main speaker, like its other actors, is assigned a mask or persona in a dramatic fiction whose players may believe something other than the words uttered through their masks. Indeed, the author's own beliefs are irrelevant in any case, since, for example, "Pope" as rhetorician and poet not Pope as man speaks to us. Other critics have challenged this view. They argue that masking is not peculiar to literature, that the author expects us to see through any disguise he might assume, that he appeals to verifiable historical data in his attack upon known enemies in public life, and that the work indicates, even if indirectly, what the author actually believes. Practically speaking, there is no intermediary or mask between us and the real author.[1]

Two dominant schools have developed in response to this debate: discussion of a work from one point of view, and combining of each.[2] So far, however, the argument remains at the level of competing modern hypotheses without an historical anchor. We need to ask whether the concept of the persona actually was known and used during the eighteenth century. The complex answers to this simple question may be as helpful, or distressing, for the partisan as the synthesist. These answers may also illumine aspects of authorial practice and audience response in the eighteenth century, and evoke reconsideration of a familiar assumption in the study of Alexander Pope.

※

Modern critics are not alone in fretting about the existence or efficacy of a persona in literature. Several classical writers thought that some authors expressed themselves all too much in their work. Chamaeleon claimed that Aeschylus brought drunken characters into his satyr plays because he himself was drunk when he wrote them; Satyrus insists that Euripides is an unpleasant man because "the man resembles his characters"; Quintilian

34

argues that Afranius "spoiled his plots by introducing nasty pederastic love-affairs, thus revealing his own character." Cicero and Quintilian both agree that the lawyer must feel the emotions he wishes to rouse on behalf of his client. "We must believe," Quintilian says, "that the sufferings which we are deploring have happened to *us* ... We must *be* those people about whose grievous ... sufferings we are protesting," and "take that sorrow tempo-rarily on ourselves." This occasional equation of speaker and writer also appears in theories of literary psychology. Horace claims that if a poet "would have me shed Tears [he] must first shed them" himself. Far later, Longinus argues that the poet who wishes to evoke sublimity in his reader must possess sublimity in his own soul. When Euripides describes the passage of Phaethon through the sky "the Poet's soul mounts the chariot with him; the poet then partakes in all his dangers, and accompanies the horses in their airy flight."[3]

Several ancients also made the opposite case – not that a pederast portrays pederasts, or that a sublime poet evokes sublimity but, as Cicero puts it in his *Tusculan Disputations*, one feigns the pose appropriate for the situation:

Do you think I am angry when I make a somewhat bitter and passionate speech in court? Or again, when the case is over and done, and I am writing the speech down, am I angry as I write: 'Will someone pay attention to this? Clap him in irons!' Do you think Aesopus was ever angry when he acted this or Accius when he wrote it?[4]

Ovid, Martial, Apuleius, Ausonius, and others asked their readers not to confuse their works with their lives. Catullus observes that "it befits a devoted poet to be pure himself; there's no need for his verses to be the same."[5]

These examples suggest that ancient theories of composition and reponse included both the assumption of a literal speaker revealing himself, and of a figurative speaker revealing his role in a fiction and in his creator's art. We should not be surprised to find both reactions in the eighteenth century.

Richard Steele's *Tatler*, No. 242 (1710), insists that "good-nature [is] an essential quality in a satirist, and that all the sentiments which are beautiful in this way of writing must proceed from that quality in the author." Mere railing coxcombs fail in their art because they cannot adequately communi-cate the good nature which they lack.[6] The causal relationship between per-sonal spirit and public act is made more forthright yet in the second of Edward Young's *Two Epistles to Mr. Pope* (1730):

> No mortal can write well, but who's *sincere:*
> In all that charms or strongly moves, the Heart
> Must aid the Head, and bear the greater part.
> Can they, tho' tongu'd as Angels sweet, perswade
> The Soul to day, who Yesterday *betray'd?*
> Wit in a *Knave,* my Brethren! is no more
> Than Beauty, in a rank, abandon'd *Whore.*[7]

35

Commentators upon the relevant remarks of classical writers were equally forthright. Richard Hurd's note to line 102 of the *Ars Poetica* thus mentions Euripides, Aristotle, Cicero, and Quintilian, and exhorts writers of tragedy "to examine their own hearts" for tenderness "before they presume to practise upon those of others."[8]

Numerous eighteenth-century examples, however, support versions of a theory of the persona: these make clear that it was perceived in ancients and moderns and was used and discussed by pedagogue and politician, critic and author. Lord Shaftesbury, for example, shifts masks to advantage in the *Miscellaneous Reflections*, which normally portray him as a serious philosopher considering his *Characteristics* (1711). Near the end of the first chapter he quotes part of an old ballad and a light ode to Horace. "I forget," he says, pretending to scold himself, ". . . that I am now speaking in the person of our grave inquirer. I should consider I have no right to vary from the pattern he has set, and that whilst I accompany him in this particular treatise, I ought not to make the least escape out of the high road of demonstration into the diverting paths of poverty or humour," – which he nonetheless does in order to please the fatigued reader he might otherwise lose to Morpheus. Two years later, Richard Steele showed himself as capable of endorsing an impersonal as a personal theory of art. His *Englishman*, No. 7 (1713), insists upon discrete genres and the voices "which distinguish those various kinds from one another," whether pastoral, elegy, or ode. "The same Man," he continues, "under these various Denominations, is, in Effect, so many different Persons." If he foolishly confuses these characters, blame "not the Muse, the Lover, the Swain, or the God, but *Bavius* at hard Labour in his Studies."[9] The writer of the *London Journal* on 4 December 1725 was also committed to the coherence of the speaker's persona. Though Christian poets have banished pagan superstition, that outmoded theology still inspires noble poetry. Even "the most serious Christian" should be able "to write, as a Poet, upon the *Pagan* Model. Are not poets allowed to personate all *Characters* fit to be presented; and ought they not always to write in that character which they personate for the Time being?"

The writers of periodical essays also used a mask – whether that of Mr. Tatler, Mr. Spectator, Mr. Rambler, or any of numerous others. Samuel Johnson's final *Rambler*, No. 208 (1725), announces his familiarity with this convention:

The seeming vanity with which I have sometimes spoken of myself, would perhaps require an apology, were it not extenuated by the example of those who have published essays before me, and by the privilege which every nameless writer has been hitherto allowed. "A Mask," says Castiglione, "confers a right of acting and speaking with less restraint, even when the wearer happens to be known." He that is discovered without his own consent, may claim some indulgence, and cannot be rigorously called to justify those sallies or frolicks which his disguise must prove him desirous to conceal.[10]

Later in the century, Boswell records this conversation between Johnson and Dr. Shipley, the Bishop of St. Asaph:

> The Bishop said, it appeared from Horace's writings that he was a cheerful contented man. JOHNSON. 'We have no reason to believe that, my Lord. Are we to think Pope was happy, because he says so in his writings? We see in his writings what he wished the state of his mind to appear. Dr. Young, who pined for preferment, talks with contempt of it in his writings, and affects to despise every thing that he did not despise.'

Boswell himself also observes that the apparently "surly ... severe and arbitrary" Milton was able to evoke the "sweetest sensations of which our nature is capable." He offers his own explanation for this phenomenon, and then adds a note by Edmond Malone, who thinks it "a proof that [Milton] felt nothing of those cheerful sensations which he has described: that on these topicks it is the *poet*, and not the *man* that writes."[11]

Johnson himself inspired persona criticism, some of it at his own expense. In 1785, John Scott borrows much of the tone and method of Johnson's *Lives of the Poets* (1779–81), examines some of the same works, and reaches different conclusions. "Lycidas," he argues, is a pastoral elegy, and so requires a distinction between the speaker's real and assumed voice. "Milton is *pro tempore* a rustick poet," and therefore while a "supposed shepherd" draws his images "from the business of the field." As the poem progresses, Milton's speaker enriches his voice by "combining the characters of shepherd and poet."[12]

Awareness of masking as a satiric technique was enhanced through the engravings that often guided contemporary readers of formal verse satire. Dryden's Juvenal of 1693, for instance, shows the muse placing a satyr's mask on the solemn Juvenal, while a putto flying above and between them presents the laurel wreath to the poet at his right. Richard Bentley's edition of Horace also includes a putto holding a satyr's mask, as a sign of one of the several genres in which Horace wrote. The mask was not always that of the familiar satyr, or even a single mask. The Henninius Juvenal of 1685 thus includes a satyr holding a long rope, on which are placed eleven different masks – including the old, the young, the grave, the gay, the arch, the innocent – appropriate for the exuberant genre. Several years thereafter, the engraving on the title page of John Brown's *Essay on Satire* (1745), dedicated to Pope, shows the triumphant Muse of Satire flying through the clouds with thunderbolts in her right hand and a somber mask in her left. By 1751 the engraving designed to face Pope's *Epilogue to the Satires* (1738) in Warburton's edition illustrates these lines printed beneath it:

> O Sacred Weapon, left for Truth's Defence,
> Sole Dread of Folly, Vice and Insolence!
> To all but Heaven-directed Hands denied,
> The Muse may give thee, but the Gods must guide.

The muse is giving Pope his pen with her right hand, while holding the mask of a concerned man in her left. In the center, a goddess on an elongated cloud holds a spear which points to the muse's pen she guides on Pope's behalf, while behind him blindfolded Justice holds a sword whose hilt she presents to Pope.[13]

Another visual tradition showed satire not putting on but stripping off a mask, commonly one of hypocrisy, and makes clear that masking could be a satiric subject as well as satiric technique. The frontispiece to Schrevelius' 1671 Juvenal and Persius thus includes a bare-breasted two-faced woman whose skirt raised to her calf reveals a large clawed foot and a tail. She holds two burning hearts in her left hand and a mask, presumably removed by the satires within the book, in her right hand.[14] The engraving in John Brown's *Essay on Satire* may also allude to this tradition, for it is hard to determine whether the mask held by the angry muse is one to be worn, or one stripped from the monsters falling beneath her and thus denied access to the temple of virtue in the right rear of the engraving. In any case, satire clearly was thought to use an appropriate mask for the good poet and, as one of its tasks, to remove an inappropriate mask from the bad person. Indeed, in some cases that bad person was the satirist himself who, his enemies argued, wrongly assumed the mask of virtue.

Since, in fact, modern discussion of the persona tends to concentrate on satire, I shall do so as well, and hope to suggest some of the ways in which its wearers were subject. Verse satire, whose conventions often were adapted by prose satirists, spawned most of the abundant response.

Many commentators still believed that the roots of satire lay in earlier comic drama, or at the least included dramatic conventions; they thus regarded satire as especially subject to the playing of roles. As Isaac Casaubon said in his influential *Prolegomena* to Persius (1605), all satire is related to dramatic plot and "is complicated by the shifts of personae."[15] In 1680 the Père de la Valterie added that "la Satyre est une espece de Comédie, où il y a différents Acteurs, qui parlent sans que leur personnage soit marqué. La première [satire de Perse] est toute de cette sorte." In the next century, the Abbé le Monnier would say that with the exception of the second and sixth satires Persius gives us little dramas in which two interlocutors engage one another. "L'un d'eux, dans le cours de la pièce, fait intervenir des personnages fictifs avec lesquels il commence un nouvel entretien. Ces acteurs fictifs en appellent d'autres à leur tour." And as William Boscawen said of Horace's conversational satire, he there discusses topics "sometimes in his own person (introducing occasional questions or arguments from a supposed objector), sometimes in the person of another, sometimes in a Dialogue between himself and some other speaker, and sometimes in a Dialogue, in which the speakers are two different persons."[16]

These dramatic persons take several roles. A satirist might cast himself as reasonably close to his public personality, and thereby use the echo of his real voice to amplify his speaker's voice. André Dacier remarks that in *Satires* i.i.25, "ut pueris olim," Horace imitates the beginning of Lucretius' fourth book, but with a significant difference, for he is not playing the epicurean, but "le personnage d'un Philosophe qui enseigne & qui corrige." Horace invents a congenial role and plays it well. This is also true for the angry moralist Juvenal, who punishes rather than wittily instructs. Hence, Barten Holyday observes, in the third satire Juvenal speaks "in the person of *Umbritius*" who darkly arraigns Rome's many sins and sinners. At the end of the next century, Edward Owen notes the relationship between the structure of the third satire and the character of its speaker. That poem, he says, "seems not to be strictly methodical, and that too with propriety; being supposed to be the extemporary effusions of honest indignation."[17]

This mask is inappropriate for a good man portraying a comparably good man. Another option included portraying a character who in some way is superior to the satirist, and whose words would be discredited if uttered by him. Horace, for example, was rather a glutton, and so could not recommend culinary moderation. In *Satires* ii.ii he therefore puts much of the poem's wisdom in the mouth of the simple, temperate Ofellus, and hides his own inadequacies. As David Watson renders Dacier in 1743, "The Poet knew very well, that such Rules from his own Mouth, would appear ridiculous, who was known to be so much a Lover of good Company and good chear." Some years thereafter, Thomas Blackwell described Horace's practice and placed it in a larger context of the relationship between the poet and his audience: "By introducing various Characters, and making them talk each in their own style, you put a PERSON *between* you and the PUBLIC, and out of *his* mouth can say many things which you could not have said so well, or possibly not said at all from your own."[18]

One variation of this kind of mask is the young man playing the elder and lecturing his own contemporaries. Persius puts on either the mask of the stoic teacher or the student. In *Satire* ii, Dryden argues, Persius "himself sustains the Person of the Master, or *Praeceptor*, in this admirable Satyr, where he upbraids the Youth of Sloth, and Negligence in learning. Yet he begins with one Scholar reproaching his Fellow Students with late rising to their Books: After which he takes upon him the other part, of the Teacher." Similar remarks are commonplace in later discussions of Persius. In 1719 Henry Eelbeck observes that in the third satire Persius "desires the young Men, under the Person of a *Stoic* Philosopher, that they should" study philosophy and avoid vice. William Gifford inherits and uses this tradition for his 1817 version of Persius, when he berates the literal-minded who see inconsistencies in Persius' satires:

the real inconsistency rests with those who persist in bringing the author on all occasions in *propria persona* . . . It is one of years and gravity who opens the third Satire; it is a preceptor who alternately seeks to shame, to alarm, and to encourage his pupil, and who concludes his admonition in a strain of indignant reproof which a youth could not with decency assume towards his fellows.[19]

Of course the satirist might also portray someone who is beneath his own character in different ways, so that he can undermine a common belief, threaten from a safe distance, or suggest that a speaker is untrustworthy. Barten Holyday says that in the thirteenth satire Juvenal mocks the notion of sacrificial altars to the gods, "Which the Poet speaks not as his own belief, but by way of Satyre, to express the common Atheisme of those Times." Some years later, Dryden adds that Juvenal employs a figurative speaker for his exalted, morally deficient, victims. In *Satire* I he "not only gives a fair warning to Great Men, that their Memory lies at the mercy of future Poets and Historians, but also with a finer stroke of the Pen, brands ev'n the living and personates them under dead mens Names." According to the *Craftsman* of 27 December 1729, No. 182, Horace uses a comparable technique in *Satires* II.iii, where he "put . . . into *another Person*'s Mouth [Damasippus] what He could not speak so freely *Himself*," and used him "to vent his *own Reflections* on the Vices and Follies of those Times," especially the "*Male-administration*" in the Augustan government. Edward Owen later says that at line 92 of *Satire* I, Persius "speaks . . . in the person of foolish admirers" whom we are not to believe. Saint-Marc describes Boileau's variation on this device of employing a lesser speaker for his own purposes. He reminds us that in Satire Ten Boileau's unfaithful rendering of a line from Juvenal is intentional, for "Ce n'est pas lui qui parle, mais *Alcippe*, un homme du monde, qui doit avoir perdu de vuë depuis long temps les *Satires* de *Juvenal*." Alcippe's antiquated notion of an "outré" Juvenal is not Boileau's.[20]

Boileau embodies a fourth typical device of the masking satirist – hiding his true emotions, the better to reveal them. According to Pierre le Verrier and Boileau himself, Satire Nine, "A Mon Esprit," was the product of Boileau's anger at being libeled by his enemies. At first he decided to reply in a serious apologia; but he quickly saw that he played the part of an angry man and that he fell into the same error as the poets who had attacked him. Since showing his anger would not do, Boileau changed his plan. As le Verrier reports,

Dès qu'il eut trouvé le moyen de parler à son esprit, il ne fut plus embarrassé de dire tout ce qu'il vouloit dire. Aussy personne ne s'est offensé de ce qu'il a mis dans cet ouvrage, quoiqu'il soit presqu'entièrement composé des mêmes termes et des mêmes invectives que la colère arrachoit à tant de Poëtes malcontens. Tant il est vray que souvent le tour qu'on donne aux choses sert infiniment à les faire passer.[21]

One might say, that by assuming an extrinsic Horatian mask, Boileau communicates his intrinsic Juvenalian anger.

We recall that Juvenal was forced to brand the living only by personating them "under dead mens Names." Such a strategy suggests another reason for assuming a mask – self-protection, as the example of Persius shows. In *Satires* I Persius uses overtly what Horace and Juvenal had used covertly. "Quisquis es, o modo quem ex adverso dicere feci" (line 44), Persius says in words translated by Dryden in 1693 as, "Thou, whom I make the adverse part to bear," and by Swift's sometime friend Thomas Sheridan in 1728 as, "My Friend, whoever you are, whom I have engaged in this Dispute." In Latin or in English, readers could see a self-conscious poet giving his hostile *adversarius* the character of a mindless partisan of ugly modern literature, including that of the Emperor Nero. The Prologue also included a masker, but this man was neither a nonce-adversarius nor an interlocutor, but Persius himself playing a role. Edward Owen observes that in these ironic lines

> The poet assumes . . . a fictitious character, that of a necessitous scribbler, with two views: 1. To ridicule the silly pretensions of vain-glorious poets; and 2. To show, that with all their pretensions to inspiration, they only wrote, as Pope expresses it, 'obliged by hunger and request of friends.' But all this is banter. He was himself a Roman Knight of birth and fortune, and had his own well-improved genius to depend upon for success . . . Even without this knowledge of the author's real character, any attentive reader may clearly see that he is not in earnest from the exaggerated cast of phrase or buskined stile which he affects.[22]

Persius needed to protect himself because of the corrupt and corrupting state in which he lived. The normal complexity of dramatic satire is heightened in Persius, Isaac Casaubon argues, because of his intentional obscurity as a satirist in Nero's age. Hence, "I easily forgive the poet when I reflect that he poured in some ink of cuttlefish on purpose, out of fear of that most cruel and bloodthirsty of tyrants against whom [his satires] were [written]; nor do I doubt that the very wise preceptor Cornutus supported such writings, who as an old man repeatedly whispered to him the words, 'be obscure'."[23] This reasoning would echo through several generations of commentators and remained one support for the theory of the persona. Dryden is indebted to Casaubon when he says that in the Prologue the author concealed his name and quality because "He liv'd in the dangerous Times of the Tyrant *Nero*; and aims particularly at him, in most of his Satyrs. For which Reason, though he was a *Roman* Knight, and of a plentiful Fortune, he wou'd appear in this Prologue, but a Beggarly Poet, who Writes for Bread." The fourth satire uses a similar technique for a similar reason: "here, in the Person of Young *Alcibiades*, he arraigns [Nero's] Ambition of meddling with State Affairs, without Judgment or Experience. 'Tis probable that he makes *Seneca* in this Satyr, sustain the part of *Socrates*, under a borrow'd Name: And, withal, discovers some secret Vices of *Nero* . . . which had not yet arriv'd to publick Notice."[24] Virtually all commentators on Persius from Casaubon to Gifford, from 1605 to 1817, schooled their readers in the relevance of a mask for the verse satirist, and especially for the self-protective, if courageous, political satirist. Here is Thomas Brewster's gloss on part of the fourth satire.

Nero it seems was a kind of Mohock in his Diversions; and committed numberless Indecencies, nay even Robberies and Cruelties, disguised under the Habit of a Slave. Sometimes he met with a vigorous Opposition, and at last was soundly beaten: for which Reason, he went afterwards attended with a parcel of Gladiators. *Casaubon* observes that it is to this *Persius* here alludes, *Si Putea multa* & c. but the Poet (says he) designedly left the Words capable of another Construction; to the End that if he should be accused of glancing at the Emperor, by Means of this Ambiguity he might elude the Charge.[25]

The satirist had yet another reason to assume a mask that obscured his true self and allowed him to play a part. For centuries he had been required to defend his role as scourger of the wicked. He attempted to do so by anointing himself as the agent of God, history, law, the best part of the state, or his own temperament forced to resist evil. He might also argue that he hurt no one in any case, and that he was only responding to and not initiating attacks. Whichever path he chose, he must seem to be a good man untainted by the vices he attacks in others.

Pierre des Maizeaux puts the case in its most extreme form when he discusses one reason for Boileau's success. "A Satiric Poet," he says, "shou'd, to a great share of Equity and Uprightness, joyn an ardent Love for Virtue and a perfect Exemption from the Vices which he lashes in his Writings: By this he gains the Favour of good Men, and secures himself against the Malice of his enemies."[26] The English were less absolute in demanding adherence to the letter of this stern law. Only a saint can be perfectly free of vice, and eighteenth-century saints were not frequent perpetrators of formal or other satire. Aaron Hill meets des Maizeaux's arguments by invoking what he calls a figurative speaker.

Satire, Hill argues in the Preface to his unsigned *Tears of the Muses* (1738), can only be reconciled to humanity "by the general Benevolence of its *Purpose*: attacking Particulars, for the Public Advantage." It cannot meet its end of reformation if it is either too rough or too gentle, and so should seek a middle ground, in which it blames faults, praises virtues, and heightens our contempt for vice by showing achievable norms. As a result, those satirized cannot "recriminate upon the Censurer his *Ill-Nature*, and Malevolence of Purpose." Hill then introduces his solution to the problem of how an imperfect man earns the right to censure other imperfect men, especially "where the Subject is so invidious, as *Satire*." Indeed, he claims, "Decency" makes it "a *Duty*" for the satirist

to abandon his personal Self, and insinuate Opinions, with *Modesty*. I mean from the Mouth of Some *figurative Speaker*, whom He ought to *suppose* of more Consequence; and whose Sentiments the Reader will *be sure* to receive with less Scruple . . .

Who is there, to say truth, so unguilty of the Follies of Life, that he dares, in his own proper person, stand out and *justify* the Right he assumes, of reproaching the Conduct of Others?

Reproof is too bitter a Potion, to be welcome from our Sense of its Use. And the administering hand should be *dear*, not *disgustful*, if it would incline us to taste it, with Pleasure. (pp. vii–viii)

Though no one can be a satirist in "his own proper person," the good man seems to come close, for he is guilty of folly not of vice, is good-natured, and wishes to help his fellows. The figurative speaker has "more Consequence" and is an idealized version of the good man; the mask thus is appropriate and shows some of the better traits of the writer behind it. As Samuel Johnson says while quoting Castiglione, one may speak more freely behind a mask, but, as Johnson goes on to say, "I always have thought it the duty of an anonymous author to write, as if he expected to be hereafter known."[27] Alexander Pope either was known upon publication or shortly thereafter, and his personal and political enemies were quick to recognize what they thought too great a disparity between the figurative and the real speaker. Indeed, the mask as satiric subject was perhaps as lively an issue as the mask as satiric technique – as the response of both opposition and Walpole administration writers makes clear.

✳

Visual evidence suggests that one function of the satirist is to remove the mask of hypocrisy and reveal the truth beneath it. This convention is especially familar during the satirically hyperactive late 1720s and 1730s, when Thomas Gilbert's *The World Unmask'd* (1738) stabs, tortures, and lashes its way through hordes of scoundrels. Gilbert anticipates himself in *A View of the Town: In an Epistle to A Friend in the Country* (1735), where he claims that

> Satire, like a true mirrour to the fair
> Shews not what we affect, but what we are;
> Plucks from the splendid courtier all disguise,
> And sets the real man before our eyes. (p. 7)

Gilbert was a foot soldier in the opposition's army and trained himself under its most illustrious man of letters: "O *Pope*, though scourge to a licentious age, / Inspire these lines with thy severest rage" (p. 18), he orates. The opposition may also have inspired his metaphor of unmasking, which appears often in its political journalism, and normally refers to Walpole or his minions. In the *Craftsman*, No. 441 (1734), for example, one of Caleb D'Anvers's correspondents bemoans the fate of Rome and warns that the people of Britain will be comparably betrayed "by electing Those to represent Them, who are hired to betray Them; or by submitting tamely, when the *Mask* is taken off, or falls off, and the attempt to bring *Beggary* and *Slavery* is avow'd, or can be no longer conceal'd." Walpole was often labeled one Roman tyrant or another, as he was in *The Fate of Favourites* (1739), where he is

Appius who wished to alter the constitution of Rome and establish the Decemviri in its stead. At first the nobility and the people like the new government, "but no sooner was he stept into the Tyrant's Seat, than, as Livy tells us, he threw off the *Mask* of Hypocrisy, . . . shew'd the Native Pride of his Heart, and infected all his Companions with his own Vices. He despis'd the Senate, and us'd the People ill" (p. 37). This author is both describing Appius–Walpole's removal of his mask, and removing it himself, as many of his colleagues tried to do.

The administration was not remiss in using these conventions for its own ends and in claiming that the opposition was in fact the hypocritical masker. Thus, according to Thomas Cooke, by assuming names like Socrates, Cato, and Sir Walter Raleigh, the wicked and inept writers of the *Craftsman* hope "to deceive the credulous into a Belief of . . . having the same virtuous Principles" as their namesakes and thereby "to gain Favour in their [readers'] Eyes, and to impose their various Falsehoods on them for so many Truths."[28] Walpole's *Daily Gazetteer* was especially adept at pointing out the inappropriate mask of its detractors. On 2 December 1735, No. 137, it claims that there are "modern Traytors, under PATRIOT MASK"; and on 9 July 1737, No. 638, it implicitly likens Bolingbroke to Pompey in his conflict with Caesar, the enemy of liberty: "History . . . that takes off the Mask, has shewn *Pompey* with all his fine Pretensions, to have shared the same Views as *Caesar.*" By 21 April 1738, No. 883, the *Gazetteer* offers a sustained critique of the opposition's inappropriate persona. If the author of the Preface of the reprinted *Common Sense* had dropped the mask of virtue, and said that he was an unprincipled writer merely seeking to profit from political turmoil, his readers would angrily have rejected the wretched book and its author. Since the truth would not suit his malign purposes, it was "highly necessary for him to assume another Character, and to talk in a different Style . . . He makes his Appearance on the Stage like an ancient Legislator, that is come to reform the World, and to point out to us the Paths that Lead to Truth and Virtue." The *Gazetteer* urges us not to confuse the appearance of political virtue with the reality of the vicious false oracle.

The *Gazetteer* also used hostile persona criticism as part of its attempt to discredit Alexander Pope. On 27 March 1738, No. 861, it responds to Pope's imitation of Horace's *Epistles* i.i, to Maecenas, whom Pope transforms into Bolingbroke, Walpole's great tormentor. The *Gazetteer* was not amused, and argued that the poem's ethical posture was impossible to justify in light of its compliments to such a man: no one who wished to encourage virtue and discountenance vice would choose "such a Patron" if he really wished "to recommend Virtue and Goodness." In fact, Bolingbroke "was endeavouring to subvert the Laws and Constitution of his Country, and to introduce in the stead of it, Tyranny and absolute Power." Pope himself is tarred with this brush, for his own hypocrisy, bad judgment, or both, subvert his poem's speaker. One cannot believe in a man who praises a traitor. Pope is more to be blamed, we hear on 6 July 1739, No. 1261, for pronouncing his several kinds of nonsense behind the inappropriate mask of Horace. In *To Augustus* (1738), Horace's *Epistles* II.ii, Pope had criticized much contemporary poetry, associated himself with "the *most celebrated* Bards of Antiquity, [and] rashly, I wish none had thought *ridiculously*, assum'd the Style and Authority of Horace; and in that superior Light" condemned everyone but himself and his few friends, like Bolingbroke. Consequently, "you found Mankind generally set against you," and are put "*up to Sale at less than Half-Price*, in the Face of the whole World." Whether or not the *Gazetteer*'s own pose is convincing, it has again made clear its sensitivity to the theory of the persona and its ham-fisted exploitation of perceived weakness in its practice by Pope. The *Gazetteer* recognizes Pope's satiric technique, declares it inept, and makes his inappropriate mask of benevolence its own satiric subject.

In so attacking Pope and his mask, the administration both reflected and encouraged a trend that grew after 1733 and the appearance of Pope's first imitation of Horace, *Satires* II.i. Though Pope claimed that "*An Answer from Horace*" would help his cause, it actually provided yet another charge against him. *Fortescue*'s conclusion, in which Pope pretends that Sir Robert approves of him and his opposition cause, immediately was subject to contempt and reversal. Pope, respondents urged, actually would be jailed, fined, garrotted, hanged, or otherwise harshly treated as an enemy to the state, to his Horatian original, and to the truth of his own miserable character.[29] As the author of *An Epistle to the Little Satirist of Twickenham* (1733) puts it, after using Pope's own words from *Fortescue*, and testing them in recalcitrant "reality,"

> Leaf by Leaf your Writings I have turn'd
> To find the Page wherein your Faults are mourn'd;
> Still self-blown Praise presents itself to View,
> As if Vice *heard ye, Trembled*, and withdrew. (p. 9)

Two years later Thomas Bentley joined the increasingly shrill chorus singing the difference between Pope the real and Pope the figurative speaker. His *Letter to Mr. Pope, Occasion'd by Sober Advice from Horace* (1735) attacks that poem, *Fortescue*, *Arbuthnot*, and Pope's religious, political, and moral wisdom as embodied in its praise of the erring and heretical Bolingbroke. Indeed, Bentley continues, questioning the validity of Pope's mask, "You make a great ado with your *Virtue only* and your *Uni aequus virtuti atque ejus amicis*. VIRTUE ONLY in Capitals is one of the Marks to know you by. Is BOLINGBROKE," he asks in outrage, "one of your *Virtutis Amici?*" Unvirtuous Pope's true motto should not be "TO VIRTUE ONLY and HER FRIENDS, A FRIEND," as he claims in *Fortescue* (line 121), but "*To my self only and my Friends a Friend.*" Far from being the patriotic satirist he pretends to be, Pope utters "Shocking Words, and almost treasonable!" (p. 12). In light of these and other crimes Bentley asks: "How dare you impose upon the Public at this

45

rate? 'Tis *sly*, if not dishonest" (p. 16). He concludes with an insult again based upon the conflict of man and mask. For all Pope's proud "strutting and swelling" because of his "fine verses" he is really a "little Creature, scarce four Foot high, whose very Sight makes one laugh" (pp. 17–18). As the author of "Modern Characters" (1739) puts it after lambasting Pope's hypocrisy, excesses as presumed defender of freedom, and attempted close imitation of Horace, "Is this to imitate the glorious *Roman*, who would scorn to be the Dupe of the Seditious, or . . . *Faction*?" Not at all. Pope's "Prostitution of the celestial poetic Art, is owing to the persuasive *Poison* of the *Grand Incendiary*" Bolingbroke.[30]

Bentley, the *Gazetteer*, Lady Mary, and others all believed that Pope's Horatian mask was ill-fitting, and his satire without foundation. Thomas Newcomb, whose Horace returned from the underworld to publish a bill of divorcement from Pope, knew one reason for all this playing of roles – the fear of prosecution.[31] His *Supplement to One Thousand Seven Hundred Thirty-Eight. Not written by Mr. Pope* (1738) is a parody and inversion of Pope's dialogues. A and B chatter away, with A the adversarius who now gets the better of most arguments, and B the figure of "Pope" often made to sound silly, corrupt, or self-seeking and self-protective. A recognizes B's method: "if a falsehood in a rhime they spy, / It is not you, but *A.* and *B.* that lie." Quite right, Newcomb's B responds; he intends to avoid legal responsibility for his words:

> B. Tho' one my satire dreads, and t'other blames,
> *Bufo* and *Bavius* are unmeaning names!
> Folks call it libel, when there's nothing in't;
> I but translate – 'tis *Don* and *Horace* print.
> The town quite wicked, and quite guiltless I,
> Those only make the libel, who apply. (p. 23)

Much of the severity of such attacks is exemplified in John, Lord Hervey's *Letter to Mr. C–b–r, On his Letter to Mr. P–* (1742). Lord Hervey argues that Pope "is constantly labouring to obtain, and keep up by *Art*" a self-designed but inappropriate public character (p. 19). Consequently, "whenever he has endeavoured to personate . . . *Benevolence, Disinterestedness, Humanity*, or *Virtue*, he has play'd them so ill, they have sat so awkwardly upon him, and the Mimickry has been so coarse, that all his Attempts have been constantly exploded, the Cheat seen through, and the wretched Actor despised" (p. 18). After further attack upon Pope, and his praise of Bolingbroke, Hervey concludes that Pope is the reverse of his mask – he is "a *bad Companion*, a *dangerous Acquaintance*, an *inveterate, implacable Enemy, no body's Friend*, a *noxious Member of Society*, and a *thorough bad Man*" (p. 25). Clearly, in attacking Pope's poems, his enemies often used a theory of "reality" as a weapon against him and his theory of the persona, and concluded that the satirist was a counterfeit hero. For them, an intended *vir bonus* becomes an actual *vir malignus* so that, as Lord Hervey puts it, perhaps without objectivity,

46

when Mr. *Pope* professes a Love to Mankind in general, whilst he is treating *every Individual in detail* in the manner he does, I give his Professions just the same Credit that I give to the Professions of any old, sowre, tyrannical Fellow, who calls himself a Patriot, pretends to love his *Country*, and wish the Welfare of his Fellow-Citizens, at the same time that he beats his Wife, Scolds his Children, starves his Servants, cheats his Tradesmen, abuses his Acquaintance, and screws up his Tenants till they break.   (p. 25)

We may indeed ask, "Who was that masked man?" We may also be ready to draw some tentative conclusions regarding the eighteenth-century's theory and practice of the persona and their relevance for students of Pope.

✳

One point is obvious: persona criticism is not anachronistic when applied to eighteenth-century texts. Commentators assumed that authorial role-playing was common to many literary forms, and frequently used terms like *masks, person, personate, character, part* and *figurative speaker*.[32] No one who has experienced the mixed blessing of reading Pope's manuscripts can doubt that, where appropriate, he shaped and reshaped the idealized character of his speaker.

Much of the contemporary criticism of that speaker, however, suggests a view of Pope different from the benevolent Horatian in his anglicized Sabine farm at Twickenham. Modern readers who accept the face value of Pope's persona forget that his successes often were more substantial in his poems than in the reality they failed to change.[33] Some eighteenth-century readers rejected Pope's presumed Horatian mask, which they saw as shaped by anti-Augustan hands. As Lady Mary and Lord Hervey said of *Fortescue*, with its English and Latin on facing pages, "on one side we see how *Horace* thought; / And on the other, how he never wrote." Thomas Newcomb's Horace says to Pope: "If you quote more – I must protest, / And swear your Sense is none of mine." The angry author of *Characters* makes an appropriate inference in 1739: "you from *Juvenal* would snatch the Rod, / And scour along the Path in which he trod."[34]

Pope also snatched the rod from the severe Persius, whose conventions often were relevant for opposition satirists of the 1730s. Like Pope, Persius lived in a world of political and literary decline induced by a presumably tyrannical, tasteless monarch and his imitative court. Pope satirizes his own monarch in a variety of ways: he invents an incorrigible adversarius who represents some of the court's unattractive values; he uses a mask for himself and disguises for his royal or administration victims in order to avoid their punishment; he becomes "obscure" when attacking his tyrants; and he finally retreats to the inner lives of poetry and philosophy to help compensate for the loss of outward pleasures, one of which is a flourishing state. If this does not sound like Pope's case, look again at Thomas Brewster's version of Casaubon on Persius' fourth satire, and substitute only "King" or "Minister" for "Emperor": Persius "designedly left the Words capable of another Construction; to the End that if he should be accused of glancing at the Emperor, by Means of this Ambiguity he might elude the Charge." Pope's mask, the evidence suggests, often was perceived as being more Juvenalian and Persian than Horatian, and thus easily "exploded." The reductive and still fashionable notion that Pope and other imitators show "a conscious and thoughtful act of identification . . . with a poet of Augustan Rome" is better mythology than literary history.[35]

Perhaps paradoxically, recognition of masking suggests that the voice of the speaker was thought to be the author's. As we have seen, belief in a separable persona was not universal, and some of those who did accept it had reservations. Samuel Johnson endorsed the persona both in his private conversations and his public art; but he also denigrated "Lycidas" because Milton did not feel the grief his speaker appears to feel, and he mocked Pope's world-weary pose in his letters to Swift because its "pretended discontent" was a "fictitious part which he began to play before it became him."[36] The term *before it became him* is a variation of a major theme in the eighteenth-century's attitude toward the persona. Lord Hervey and the *Gazetteer* were predisposed to savage the works of Pope and his allies, and used the presumed conflict between man and mask as a handy excuse; but their general, if not specific, point was well taken. Satire relies upon the authenticity of its central details and arguments, and those arguments often are made convincing by the voice of the speaker. If he appears to lie or to support persons of dubious worth, he will not convince us of his own virtue or that of his cause; but the author of *An Epistle to the Little Satirist of Twickenham* asserts that he turned over all of Pope's writings without finding "the Page wherein your Faults are mourn'd," as Pope's speaker had maintained in *Fortescue*. Good men, we are to infer, do not say the thing that is not. As late as 1781 Johnson found Pope's praise of his noble friends counterproductive: "he can derive little honour from the notice of Cobham, Burlington, or Bolingbroke."[37] Remarks like these also were applied to the opposition, to the administration, and to writers from other periods. Different readers had different views of what reality might be, but they normally assumed that when the speaker claimed to be a good man, the mask and the man should be closely related. The author, especially if a controversialist, tried to make his assumed role a reflection of his best, public self so that appearance could be verified within the acceptable limits of poetic license. However liberating the mask might be, one should write, Johnson said, as if "he expected to be hereafter known."

In some cases hostile readers refused to accept the intended similarity between man and mask; in others the author emphasized, or was thought to emphasize, the difference, and again assumed that knowledge of the real author would be a guide to his intention, as Edward Owen observes when he claims that in Persius' Prologue "any attentive reader may clearly see that he is not in earnest from the exaggerated cast of phrase . . . which he affects." (Where the author genuinely was unknown, his opponent in political disputes would invent an appropriately ugly reality for him.) Persius employs a similar revelatory mask in the first satire when he falls into elaborate praise of the dreadful verse beloved by his adversarius (lines 110–11). This technique and, probably, Persius' example are behind Pope's temporary pose in the *Epilogue to the Satires*. In the first *Dialogue* he proclaims: "*Virtue*, I grant you, is an empty boast; / But shall the Dignity of *Vice* be lost?" (lines 113–114). Certainly not! "This, this, my friend, I cannot, must not bear" (line 127). In the second *Dialogue* he cries out – "Spirit of Arnall! aid me while I lye. / COBHAM's a Coward, POLWARTH is a Slave" (lines 129–30). In each case our knowledge of Pope's real beliefs clarifies any potential ambiguity; if we are ignorant of such belief, "any attentive reader" can determine that the "exaggerated cast of phrase" signals Pope's denial of his own words. Each dialogue invites us to recognize the intentionally jerrybuilt mask; we do so more easily because we are aware, or are made aware, of what the author believes.

I suggest, then, that at least four, sometimes overlapping, points have emerged from this discussion: (1) the eighteenth century inherited and used a complex, though not universally accepted, theory of the persona which was especially appropriate in formal verse satire, and became a familiar satiric technique; (2) when Pope's political enemies responded to that technique, they demanded that the mask reflect the good man as they defined it; therefore they condemned Pope either as inept or as a liar, for his presumed Horatianism actually showed Persian and Juvenalian opposition to the government, and his own malign, Bolingbrokean, vision; (3) when Pope's personal and literary enemies responded to that technique, they asked for external verification of the acts of kindness and self-abnegation Pope boasted of in his own poems and, in their judgment, failed to perform in reality; in each case – political and personal – satiric technique becomes satiric subject; (4) this and related evidence suggest that a theory of the persona as a mask portraying an idealized or other figurative speaker should be based not merely upon rhetoric or disembodied art, but, where possible, also upon the "known" character of the speaker, though that word was and is subject to biased interpretation. In principle, the persona was acceptable to many eighteenth-century readers; in practice, it bore the emblem *caveat scriptor*, and was subject to rigorous examination and demands for verisimilitude. Perhaps such historical evidence can provide a firmer basis for the ongoing debate regarding the existence and uses of literary personae in the eighteenth century and beyond.

TEXTS

4 · THE SWELLING VOLUME

THE APOCALYPTIC SATIRE OF ROCHESTER'S *LETTER FROM ARTEMISIA IN THE TOWN TO CHLOE IN THE COUNTRY*

Mᴏᴅᴇʀɴ ʀᴇᴠᴀʟᴜᴀᴛɪᴏɴ of Restoration and eighteenth-century literature has helped Rochester's reputation as both man and poet: many of the nastier myths of his life have been exploded, his poetry has been reliably edited, and critical and scholarly studies have illuminated aspects of his intellectual context and poetic achievement. The *Letter from Artemisia in the Town to Chloe in the Country* (1679), however, has received sparse critical comment and is excluded from the latest, weighty, anthology of contemporary literature.[1] This is unfortunate, not only because of our ignorance of the poem that is probably Rochester's masterpiece, but also because the *Letter* helps to show Rochester's broad exercise of satiric talent and, especially, his mastery of the most pessimistic form of serious contemporary satire.

Of course it is difficult to label and classify the varieties of so-called "Augustan" satires, but three broad and, sometimes, overlapping classes may be found. I call these punitive satire, formal verse satire, and apocalyptic or revelatory satire.[2] In the first the poet hopes to punish an adversary rather than correct him, as in Rochester's "On Poet Ninny" (1680), a lampoon upon Sir Carr Scroope. Though there are certain implicit and explicit norms – beauty is preferable to ugliness, pride is bad – the main thrust of the satire is towards abuse rather than instruction:

> Thou art a thing so wretched and so base
> Thou canst not ev'n offend, but with thy face. (lines 6–7)[3]

In formal verse satire, normally in heroic couplets and based in part upon the examples of Horace, Persius, and Juvenal, the poet attacks one central vice and praises its opposite virtue. Such a form requires the presence, however faint, of a workable and working norm for this world. Two of Rochester's major poems fall roughly at opposite ends of a spectrum of formal verse satires. The "Allusion to Horace" (1680) affirms related norms – the critical perception of the sheltered aristocratic poet, and poetry which eschews mere popular acclaim. Both the speaker and the friends he mentions fulfill these positive values:

> I loathe the rabble; 'tis enough for me
> If Sedley, Shadwell, Shepherd, Wycherley,

Godolphin, Butler, Buckhurst, Buckingham,
And some few more, whom I omit to name,
Approve my sense: I count their censure fame. (lines 120–24)

But the "Allusion" is also punitive in its attack upon Dryden, who is the central target of Rochester's anger, and whose rhymes are "stol'n, unequal, nay dull many times" (line 2). He wonders whether

those gross faults his choice pen does commit
Proceed from want of judgment, or of wit;
Or if his lumpish fancy does refuse
Spirit and grace to his loose, slattern muse? (lines 89–92)[4]

Though Rochester is anchored in Horace's relatively mild *Satires* I.x, his poem hovers near the borders of punitive satire, just as the *Satyr against Mankind* hovers near those of revelatory satire.

That poem is often regarded as the embodiment of Rochester's "furious contempt for mankind" and his gloomy view that man is a beast.[5] The fury of Rochester's satire cannot be denied; but the force of his argument suggests that he still cares enough to want us to reform, and has hope enough to offer a clear alternative through which correction is possible. Speculative reason is "an *ignis fatuus* in the mind" (line 12) and is the false reasoning he attacks. On the other hand,

I own right reason, which I would obey:
That reason which distinguishes by sense
And gives us rules of good and ill from thence,
That bounds desires with a reforming will
To keep 'em more in vigor, not to kill.
. . .
My reason is my friend, yours is a cheat. (lines 99–103, 106)

The final paragraph of the poem's "epilogue" describes "a meek, humble man, of honest sense" (line 212), an ideal clergyman who at least *may* exist.

If upon earth there dwell such God-like men,
I'll here recant my paradox to them. (lines 216–17)

Even at the end of this harsh formal verse satire the speaker is willing to keep the corrective norm alive. Rochester's slight expectation of change – rather than a demonstrated probability – is surely more extreme in this work than in more moderate satires like Pope's epistles to Arbuthnot or Bathurst, in which the adversarius finally embraces Pope's own values. The *Satyr* thus moves towards the revelatory or apocalyptic mode, which primarily intends to depict the terrible situation within or without us and, often, to suggest massively destructive results. This sort of satire is partially at work in *A Tale of a Tub* (1704), sometimes bursts from the genteel surface of Edward Young's *Love of Fame* (1725–28), and is particularly clear in *The Dunciad in Four Books* (1743). I believe that this is also the most illuminating way to view the *Letter from*

Artemisia in the Town to Chloe in the Country. It has been discussed in terms of the conventions of the novel and of Restoration comedy,[6] but, as I hope to show, in ways the poem is grimmer than Swift's *Tale* and perhaps even the final *Dunciad*. In the *Letter* Rochester presents us with a world of interlocking sins and sinners with a collective ability to seduce the weak and reach out beyond the confines of the poem's 264 lines. Artemisia's words frame the poem and indicate its direction; as her reluctant beginning evolves into the eager promise of a volume to come, her better values collapse and a whore's triumph. Instead of the country going to the city to seek news of debauchery, the city actively communicates debauchery; Artemisia sows infamous tales which Chloe will reap; the town and the country begin to blend; and the poem takes on a quality of rapidly spreading evil. In the process the poem pictures venal and murderous women, stupid or foolishly clever men, the mere memory of what heavenly love could be, and the hellish actuality earthly love has become.

The Reluctant Correspondent

The poem begins with the first part of Artemisia's frame, her protest against the essentially unfeminine act of writing poetry, something she does only, "Chloe, ... by your command" (line 1). She supports her reluctance to engage in "lofty flights of dangerous poetry" (line 4) with the perils to both wit and woman in so writing. If "the men of wit" (line 13), she argues, are so often "dashed back, and wrecked on the dull shore, / Broke of that little stock they had before!" how would a less talented woman's "tottering bark be tossed" (lines 10–12)? Hence she "gravely" advises herself that "poetry's a snare" (lines 15–16), that the poet will sadden the reader and be thought mad, and that as a jester or tool of pleasure for the town one is "Cursed if you fail, and scorned though you succeed!" (line 23). Although Artemisia had responded only to a command, and had concluded "That whore is scarce a more reproachful name / Than poetess" (lines 26–27), she quickly becomes "Pleased with the contradiction and the sin," and stands "on thorns till I begin" (lines 30–31). She is "well convinced writing's a shame" (line 25), but abandons her conviction in the face of her urge to do "the very worst thing" (line 29) she can.

Such a movement is a microcosm of what happens to Artemisia and her world in the *Letter*, and is consistent with the important similarities between wit and woman. Like the putative wit, Artemisia will explore a "stormy, pathless world" (line 9), and will be dashed back upon the shore. He reveals his creative deficiencies; she reveals her moral deficiencies and is broke of the little stock of virtue with which she starts the poem. He becomes the fiddle of the town – the jester, as Professor Vieth glosses it; she is also potentially a fiddle – an instrument to amuse and please whoever chooses to pick her up.

55

The wit, we will see upon the Fine Lady's appearance, must know the truth about woman at his own cost; Artemisia also pursues the truth about woman and the world she inhabits at her own, but somewhat different, cost, as she already is pleased with sin and becomes worse than a whore in being a poetess. The two opening paragraphs, then, establish the contradictory nature of woman, the tentative virtue of Artemisia herself, and the similarities between wit and woman.

But Artemisia cannot be condemned from the start. For all her obvious blemishes, hers is still the voice that presents the best values of the poem, values which, if preserved, could have preserved her society as well. We know little about Chloe, except that she orders her friend to write in unfeminine rhyme and expects "at least to hear what loves have passed / In this lewd town" (lines 32–33) and who is currently sleeping with whom. Such matters, Artemisia tells Chloe, are "what I would fain forget" (line 37). Poor Artemisia cannot "name that lost thing, love, without a tear, / Since so debauched by ill-bred customs here" (lines 38–39). She is not so misguided that she cannot see the right path, and though apparently incapable of achieving love herself, she can describe its source, what it was and should be. The following affirmation serves as an ideal against which the current status of love is measured, and from which Artemisia – the only character with even a hope for change – so badly strays. Love, she says, is "This only joy for which poor we were made" (line 50):

> Love, the most generous passion of the mind,
> The softest refuge innocence can find,
> The safe director of unguided youth,
> Fraught with kind wishes, and secured by truth;
> That cordial drop heaven in our cup has thrown
> To make the nauseous draught of life go down;
> On which one only blessing, God might raise
> In lands of atheists, subsidies of praise,
> For none did e'er so dull and stupid prove
> But felt a god, and blessed his power in love. (lines 40–49)[7]

The piling on of positive words for the portrait of blessed, innocent, heavenly love is as clear as the pejoratives in the portrait of contemporary, earthly love that follows. What should be a joy is "an arrant trade" (line 51); a refuge for innocence and a director of youth becomes a refuge for rooks, cheats, and tricks (lines 52–53); direction by Heaven is taken over by fallen women (lines 54–58); those same women, created free by God, "Turn gypsies for a meaner liberty" (line 57) and become slaves to distorted senses and fashion. The perfection of God's blessing and His generous passion of the mind is twisted:

> To an exact perfection they have wrought
> The action, love; the passion is forgot. (lines 62–63)

Spiritual love surrenders to secular love, God's design to woman's. As a result of this collapse of values the senses are also out of order. Such women are "deaf to nature's rule, or love's advice" (line 60), and so desire undesirable men, covet merely fashionable lovers, and do not even enjoy the amiably gross weaknesses of the flesh, since they "Forsake the pleasure to pursue the vice" (line 61):

> 'Tis below wit, they tell you, to admire,
> And ev'n without approving, they desire.
> Their private wish obeys the public voice;
> 'Twixt good and bad, whimsey decides, not choice.
> Fashions grow up for taste; at forms they strike;
> They know what they would have, not what they like.
> Bovey's a beauty, if some few agree
> To call him so; the rest to that degree
> Affected are, that with their ears they see. (lines 64–72)

Artemisia wins our approval as she is offended by these betrayals of Heaven's wishes, love's aims and end, nature's carnal desires and the senses. Indeed, she has been fulfilling one part of the similarity between wit and versifying woman – that of self-revelation. Having shown her own weakness, she re-engages at least some of our sympathy through her awareness of what love should be, and her disapproval of what it is. Hence, though she is a willing participant at the Fine Lady's place of assignation, she nevertheless disappears and allows the Lady her own words and actions.

This change of voice allows Rochester to enlarge the poem's point of view and to lend "objective" support for a scene intended to illustrate several of Artemisia's remarks regarding the action love. We had seen Artemisia's equation of herself with the exploited woman (and wit), the fiddle of the town; she is abused and hardened but nevertheless capable of preserving a vision of redeeming love. If there is any hope for the Restoration world, the opening part of her frame suggests, it is in that lingering memory. Artemisia is thus an improper vehicle for the ensuing section, in which a town-woman recently arrived from the country depicts, defends, and unconsciously debases the destructive battle of the sexes that Artemisia temporarily deplores. Like Artemisia, the Fine Lady also reveals herself, but what she reveals is so ugly that for the time being, at least, Artemisia is preserved as a tainted norm who disapproves of what she sees, whereas the Lady is an active participant and, as we will find, the "creator" of an even uglier character.

The Fine Lady

The Fine Lady presents three categories of the action love: wife and husband, wife and gallant, wife and beast. The first demonstrates the sharp contrast between heavenly love's generous passion of the mind and earthly love's debasement of mind. The Lady's linguistic pyrotechnics, for example, are made clear at once. The husband had prevailed with his wife "through her own skill, / At his request, though much against his will / To come to London" (lines 75–77). The earlier image of love as a "cordial drop" that Heaven has put in "the nauseous draught of life" (lines 44, 45), contrasts with the Fine Lady's wish that her husband drink a brew that offers ill effects for him and ill opportunities for her.

> "Dispatch," says she, "that business you pretend,
> Your beastly visit to your drunken friend!
> A bottle ever makes you look so fine;
> Methinks I long to smell you stink of wine!
> Your country drinking breath's enough to kill:
> Sour ale corrected with a lemon peel.
> Prithee, farewell! We'll meet again anon."
> The necessary thing bows, and is gone. (lines 85–92)

The process of dehumanizing and bestializing will become even more overt, though it is obvious enough in this passage. The relationship between husband and wife is a matter of social and economic necessity, devoid of any human emotion but disdain and, perhaps, shame on her part for needing such a booby (line 82).

Nor is the relationship with the gallant any better. His presence may force the husband to leave, but it is without clear benefit to himself: "The gallant had been, / Though a diseased, ill-favored fool, brought in" (lines 83–84). And that is all. Once the husband is gone she does not run into the arms of a lusty paramour, but flies upstairs to gossip with the mistress of the house and to insist upon the wisdom of having only a fool as husband or lover. The Fine Lady, then, has her country-fool husband and town-fool gallant, one a necessary the other a fashionable thing.

The only physical or quasi-sexual contact we see (the later episode between Corinna and the fool is narrated) occurs with the Lady and a pet monkey. She courts him, smiles at him, is generally seductive, and provides an obscene parody of love:

> She to the window runs, where she had spied
> Her much esteemed dear friend, the monkey, tied.
> With forty smiles, as many antic bows,
> As if 't had been the lady of the house,
> The dirty, chattering monster she embraced,
> And made it this fine, tender speech at last:
> "Kiss me, thou curious miniature of man!
> How odd thou art! how pretty! how japan!
> Oh, I could live and die with thee!" Then on
> For half an hour in compliment she run. (lines 137–46)

Throughout much of the *Letter* both man and woman are reduced to subhuman levels; she is "an arrant bird of night" (line 121) or "a fly, / In

58

some dark hole" (lines 205–6). The Fool is "Ever most joyful when most made an ass" (line 130), or is an "unbred puppy" (line 240), or "an owl" (line 250). But this unpleasant scene – and its probable pun on die – carries the poem's dehumanization of love to its fullest degree, especially since the monkey in its own right and as a near relation to the ape was commonly regarded as the embodiment of base sexuality and man's and woman's lowest drives.[8]

Rochester, I suggest, is using the embrace of the Fine Lady and the monkey as an emblem of what human sexuality and love have become – lust channeled into fashionable bestiality. All other liaisons in the poem are based upon passionless modes, misplaced revenge, a self-destructive desire for forbidden knowledge, or prostitution. Rochester is not attacking mere lust, since such a desire would almost be healthy – nature's voice – in comparison with the unfeeling world we actually see. He is attacking the absolute withdrawal of positive human emotion from human sexual embraces, so that the woman can be warm, friendly, and sexual only with the fashionable pet, a creature close to man – indecently so, Edward Topsell says (p. 4) – yet infinitely below him. In so doing she becomes more bestial than the beast she courts, both because normally the ape or monkey "courted" the Lady, and because the monkey is merely acting its prescribed role, whereas she is a product of willingly demeaned reason. The fool, the Fine Lady says, is "Ever most joyful when most made an ass" (line 130), and the Lady, Artemisia insists, becomes "an ass through choice, not want of wit" (line 151). The woman who reduces man to an ass becomes one in the process, and she makes herself a fit mate for a monkey (transformed from miniature of the mistress to miniature of man) when she embraces and becomes a "dirty, chattering monster" (line 141) as well.

In short, the scene with the monkey is a logical extension of three themes in the poem. First, we recall that "Fashions grow up for taste; at forms they strike; / They know what they would have, not what they like" (lines 68–69). Under such circumstances even the ugly Sir Ralph Bovey may be judged more than handsome and other women will agree. The Fine Lady's gallant is "a diseased, ill-favored fool" (line 84), and must owe his fortunate position to just such sense-defying fashion as also leads her to court the monkey.

The Lady and her values, moreover, continue the substitution of the secular for the spiritually ordered world. She knows "everything," apparently with God's blessing, yet chooses to be an ass (lines 150–51). This is fitting, since God's vision is clearly different from woman's as here portrayed. Nature is inadequate "in making a true fop" (line 154), and God Himself "never made a coxcomb worth a groat. / We owe that name to industry and arts" (lines 159–60). This product of civilization who insists upon her wisdom in marrying a fool has also made herself "An eminent fool" (line 161). Along the way she alters God's design for her, and is ignorant of her true character:

she . . . had turned o'er
As many books as men; loved much, read more;
Had a discerning wit; to her was known
Everyone's fault and merit, but her own.
All the good qualities that ever blessed
A woman so distinguished from the rest,
Except discretion only, she possessed. (lines 162–68)

The play upon turning over "as many books as men" suggests the loss of love as a generous passion of the mind, and the blindness that comes when one rejects the truth and kind wishes of God and seeks faults with the aid of human wisdom. The final step in the replacement of God's design by woman's emerges at the end of the Lady's tale, in which the whore Corinna seduces and financially rapes a country fool after she herself had been abandoned by a wit. In this parody of divine purpose God, who ordains all things including the cordial drop of love, is replaced by "Nature," who provides vengeance, victims, and continued vice for whores.

"Nature, who never made a thing in vain,
But does each insect to some end ordain,
Wisely contrived kind keeping fools, no doubt,
To patch up vices men of wit wear out." (lines 252–55)

In spite of this inversion of order, however, the reader is carried along by the remnant of moral sanity in Artemisia. From the moment of the Fine Lady's introduction she voices her partial disapproval of this gross-voiced creature (lines 78–79) with malfunctioning taste in her husband, lovers, animals, language, manners, books, and personal perception. But Rochester does not leave us secure – as he might have in a formal verse satire – with the knowledge that as long as there is one good person who preserves the ideal of love there is yet hope. No more, indeed, than he lets us wholly disapprove of the Fine Lady or approve of the poor victimized man. Though Artemisia sees much to deplore in her, she also sees that she is a "mixed thing . . . / So very wise, yet so impertinent" (lines 148–49), and that she has "All the good qualities that ever blessed / A Woman" (lines 166–67). Indeed it is attraction to the Fine Lady's world that ultimately breaks Artemisia's little store of virtue; and it is also Rochester's ability to communicate the "mixed thing" that prevents this poem from being merely another anti-feminist tract or a black-and-white moral allegory.[9] Specifically, let us examine the role of the man in creating the debauched world that also debauches him.

The Lady and Corinna: the Wit and Fool

Like Artemisia, the Fine Lady sees that there is a dangerous relationship between wit and woman. The Wit is a threat to the Lady because he knows or seeks to know woman's true nature, and in the process of knowing may destroy his comfort and her worldly success. The Fine Lady, for instance, relates that when she was married "men of wit were then held *incommode*" (line 104), primarily because they insisted upon clearly perceiving the difference between appearance and reality. Wits are:

> Slow of belief, and fickle in desire,
> . . . ere they'll be persuaded, must inquire
> As if they came to spy, not to admire.
> With searching wisdom, fatal to their ease,
> They still find out why what may, should not please;
> Nay, take themselves for injured when we dare
> Make 'em think better of us than we are,
> And if we hide our frailties from their sights,
> Call us deceitful jilts and hypocrites.
> They little guess, who at our arts are grieved,
> The perfect joy of being well deceived;
> Inquisitive as jealous cuckolds grow:
> Rather than not be knowing, they will know
> What, being known, creates their certain woe.
> Women should these, of all mankind, avoid,
> For wonder by clear knowledge is destroyed.
> Woman, who is an arrant bird of night,
> Bold in the dusk before a fool's dull sight,
> Should fly when reason brings the glaring light.   (lines 105–23)

The portrait here is hardly flattering to women, and again illustrates the difference between the truth of Heaven's love – "This only joy for which poor we were made" (line 50) – and "The perfect joy of being well deceived" (line 115) which has replaced it. Woman represents deception of husband, lover, and reason itself where possible. But the Wit is not much better (nor is the urban or rural fool): his knowledge does not bring him pleasure, destroys the illusions he might otherwise live by, and serves no broadly effective purpose of exposure, since even "though all mankind / Perceive us false, the fop concerned is blind" (lines 131–32), and thus courts the woman nonetheless.

A brief contrast with section 9 of Swift's *A Tale of a Tub* will make clear the Wit's complicity in the unhappy world of the *Letter*. In the *Tale* happiness as "a perpetual possession of being well-deceived" is pronounced by a modern madman. Yet behind him, indeed through him, we are aware of Swift's own insistence that knowledge of man's ugliness is necessary before we can move towards his potential beauty, that self-deception is bad because it inhibits self-improvement, that you shall know the truth, however unpleasant, because it shall make you free to seek something better, the ultimate truth in God. The savage satire of that work would not be possible if Swift did not strongly feel and need to communicate the dangers to a Church, state, and culture worth saving. The anger of the "real" speaker in the *Tale* grows with the aberration his persona communicates.

In the *Letter*, however, the Wit is divorced from any theological or moral basis for his action. He does not urge us to see the earthly truth in order to correct it and work towards a corollary higher truth. He sees only the deception, depravity, and despair at the heart of life, and actually contributes to others' and his own unhappiness by offering an inadequate cerebral counter-vision, inadequate moral life (he debauches whomever he pleases and whoever pleases him), and inadequate emotional response. He is neither angry, nor spiritual, nor an effective source or model for change. He is merely destructive of his own and others' ease and offers a barren secular vision that is not even a distant shadow of the sort of divine love and truth Artemisia describes early in the poem. Under such circumstances the Wit – unlike Swift in the *Tale* – helps to make the world he deplores. He already shares many of its values, offers no viable alternative, and worsens the situation by causing those he has jilted to seek revenge upon fools who, though sublimely sub-human and delighted when made asses, surely are punished out of proportion to their crime.

This disproportion is made clear in the Fine Lady's own story of Corinna – a tale within a tale that exemplifies the Lady's point regarding fools and wits just as the Lady herself exemplifies Artemisia's regarding the action love. Moreover, Corinna's story not only continues to show ruptured human relationships and the perversion of God's plan for His love on earth; it also moves the poem from black comedy to overt tragedy, from figurative to literal destruction of the family, and provides the final impetus to draw the tottering Artemisia into the Lady's world.

At first Corinna's adventure is sad, and well illustrates one consequence of the unstable Wit's social life. She was a prosperous young whore – "Youth in her looks, and pleasure in her bed" (line 196) – until she doted upon a man of wit,

> Who found 'twas dull to love above a day;
> Made his ill-natured jest, and went away.
> Now scorned by all, forsaken, and oppressed,
> She's a *memento mori* to the rest;
> Diseased, decayed, to take up half a crown
> Must mortgage her long scarf and manteau gown.
> Poor creature! who, unheard of as a fly,
> In some dark hole must all the winter lie,
> And want and dirt endure a whole half year
> That for one month she tawdry may appear. (lines 199–208)

The Wit has rendered Corinna outcast and sub-human, probably because he has exposed her, forced her to run from his searching reason that seeks to satisfy his own need to know and then move on. However, her state is not irreparable, since "A woman's ne'er so ruined but she can / Be still revenged on her undoer, man" (lines 185–86). Yet in this case the poor Fool and his family must pay for the Wit's crime. The newly arrived country-Fool "Turns spark, learns to be lewd, and is undone" (line 223) as he courts Corinna. The

Wits have "searching wisdom, fatal to their ease" (line 108), and "Fools are still wicked at their own expense" (line 225). Both are self-destructive, but the Fool is more victimized – in part because he is paying the Wit's penalty, but largely because his entire family is destroyed in the process. The Wit makes Corinna a *memento mori*; Corinna makes the Fool die. He

> falls in love, and then in debt;
> Mortgages all, ev'n to the ancient seat,
> To buy this mistress a new house for life;
> To give her plate and jewels, robs his wife.
> And when t' th' height of fondness he is grown,
> 'Tis time to poison him, and all's her own.
> Thus meeting in her common arms his fate,
> He leaves her bastard heir to his estate,
> And, as the race of such an owl deserves,
> His own dull lawful progeny he starves.   (lines 242–51)

The poem adopts the abandonment of conventional cause and effect that characterizes tragedy; that is, ordinary events have results vastly out of proportion to their usual expectations. A Wit "seduces" and abandons a whore; several months later she revenges herself upon the Wit by seducing a young country-fool, bankrupts his family, kills him, acquires his estate, neglects his children, and, in the process, becomes a paradigm of the good life of those women who deal with fools. It is now that the parodic perversion of divine order emerges (lines 252–55), as all things do seem to be connected – each part has its reason for being, "Nature" ordains that "kind keeping fools" be provided "To patch up vices men of wit wear out." By synecdoche, woman is vice and man her tailor.

Let us sum up the world of this letter; with the exception of Artemisia early in the poem, women reveal themselves as destitute of divinely inspired love; they are contradictory, enjoyers of sin, foulers of their own nest, tasteless, passionless creatures motivated by fashion and desire for revenge, and reduce others and themselves to the sub-human. Man is either a blind, easily duped fool or a restless wit disturbed by the vision of harsh female reality he seeks, yet incapable of correcting it; he is also a prime cause of the revenge by women upon fools and their families. The poem portrays pleasureless adultery, a diseased and unattractive gallant, a murderous town wench, a murdered lover, a bastard child, and distortion of divine love and order. The true emblem of this world of bestial humans with a passion for the mode is the embrace of the Fine Lady and the monkey.

But this vision is not dark enough for Rochester. I suggested earlier that Artemisia's disapproval of the society she portrays is mixed and that the progress of her first two paragraphs – from reluctance to desire to write in verse – embodies her change in the poem at large. I do not wish to overstate the "dialectical" qualities of the poem since, after all, Artemisia's initial coyness may merely be a gossip's conventional desire to excuse her urge to chatter. Nevertheless, the view of Artemisia's decline is supported through her muted reaction to the tale of Corinna. After that tale Artemisia has a splendid opportunity to reject the world the Fine Lady has been describing. She might, for example, elaborate upon the dangers of the morality portrayed, as Rochester does in the *Satyr against Mankind*. Or she might briefly condemn it and dissociate herself from it, as Pope was to do at the end of his first *Dialogue* of the *Epilogue to the Satires* (1738): "Yet may this Verse (if such a Verse remain) / Show there was one who held it in disdain" (lines 171–72). Artemisia's latent attraction to the Lady was implicit in her earlier dissection of this "distinguished" woman and her "good qualities" (lines 167, 166); but now the several lines of reservation – her foppery, sexual license, folly, blindness, lack of discretion – are condensed into one tepid remark that comments on the Lady's rambling discourse – her inability to be pertinent – at least as much as on her wisdom: during the Lady's long talk there were "some grains of sense / Still mixed with volleys of impertinence" (lines 256–57). Perhaps Artemisia has been worn down by and drawn into the vigorous world she describes, as so many ordinary writers are in *The Dunciad*. Perhaps the Fine Lady's judgments concerning the need to avoid wits and cultivate fools have convinced her that as long as love inspired by Heaven is forgotten, she had better make her own market, forget the background of chastity and female heroism and fidelity associated with her name, and live as best she can.[10] In any case, unlike the formal verse satirist, at a strategic point in the poem Rochester has her ignore an opportunity to reject the Lady's values and, instead, diminishes her earlier criticisms. We are more impressed with what Anne Righter calls Artemisia's amusement, delight, and exasperation than with any desire to expose or punish. And we are, I think, equally impressed with how much that world should be punished.

The final paragraph is even more important in characterizing Artemisia's inverted growth, as she concludes with a promise of awful tales swelling to a volume. Hitherto the letter's partially decent voice, she now becomes an agent for the propagation of infamy. Like the wits who reveal their meager talents for writing, she reveals her meager moral fiber and perseverance. She is "dashed back, and wrecked on the dull shore, / Broke of that little stock [she] had before" (lines 10–11). She does not merely abdicate her own judgments; she accepts the Lady's. Instead of attempting to substitute the ideal of spiritual love, she warms to a new task of spreading – indeed planting – infamy:

> But now 'tis time I should some pity show
> To Chloe, since I cannot choose but know
> Readers must reap the dullness writers sow.
> By the next post such stories I will tell
> As, joined with these, shall to a volume swell,
> As true as heaven, more infamous than hell.
> But you are tired, and so am I.
>   Farewell.   (lines 258–64)

Rochester is probably alluding to the biblical warning that as one sows so shall he reap. Here, however, the sowing comes from Artemisia in the city, the reaping will be from Chloe in the country – the locations are connected in a widening web of depravity (witness the Fine Lady's arrival from the country, and Corinna in town ruining the Fool's family in the country). Chloe's request initially induces a reluctant reply that comes to 264 lines; Artemisia's promised letter is offered without invitation, and includes an ominous biblical allusion that denotes planting, growth, and harvest of a volume. Heaven, which had been a touchstone for divine love, becomes a touchstone for the truth of diabolical victory. Artemisia, to repeat, is neither exposing nor condemning when she claims that the tales will be "more infamous than hell' (line 263). By refusing to do so, or by doing so in mild terms in the ambiguous "volleys of impertinence" (line 257), she is encouraging such hellish values to take root. Rochester as satirist is severely critical; Artemisia no longer is. He may be motivated by the Juvenalian need to satirize vice triumphant; she is merely exhilarated, and by tolerating the morally intolerable fosters the decline of God's "one only blessing" (line 46).

The structure of the poem not only shows Artemisia's increasing acceptance of the world she describes. Perhaps even more significantly it also shows a series of characters, one virtually "creating" the other, who fall more deeply into a self-regarding world. At the start Rochester offers us Artemisia, who responds to Chloe's command that she write, but laments the contents of her letter – "what I would fain forget" (line 37) – and still remembers the proper sort of love. Artemisia then turns the poem over to the Fine Lady, who enjoys the contents of her tale and recalls Chloe's role for Artemisia. Just up from the country, she seeks news of how love is governed and "who are the men most worn of late" (lines 101–2) – exactly the sort of question that Artemisia assumed rural Chloe would want answered. But where Artemisia also offers a picture of "that lost thing, love" (line 38), the communicative Lady offers her own picture of a flourishing love that is mere modish and unsatisfying lust. As Artemisia created the Lady, a "mixed thing" (line 148), so the Lady creates the abandoned Corinna; the lost, selfless love of Artemisia is turned on its end and becomes the propagated, selfish love of Corinna. Innocence surrenders to criminality, and the safe director of unguided youth becomes the wicked director of a prostitute who ruins the country-boy. The cordial drop is discarded from our cup, and life will no longer go down. What is thrown up quickens in the land of atheists, there is no praise of God's power in love, and woman helps her true joy to disappear in the face of plate, jewels, and land purchased by revenge, prostitution, and murder. The movement from the modest involvement of Artemisia, who knows and gives us the Lady, to the deeper involvement of the Lady, who knows and gives us Corinna, heightens the apocalyptic quality of the satire and mirrors the movement from dead spiritual to living diabolical love. At the start of the poem Artemisia at least has values she can set against the Lady's; in the middle the clever Lady has misguided values; at the end Corinna has no values at all – or only self-serving ones. Artemisia sees that such a society's works are "more infamous than hell' (line 263), but instead of purging them she spreads them. One must at least suspect that Chloe will end like the Fine Lady – or worse – if she is to reap similar food. Artemisia's norm of defeated love is a mere ten lines; the Lady's norm of prostituted, triumphant love is sixty-six lines.

Moreover, the rhyme scheme of the final two couplets is different from the rest of the poem's and thus catches our attention. Rochester has used end-stopped couplets, run-on couplets, half-lines, half rhymes, masculine and feminine rhymes, and several triplets, in a virtuoso display of poetic technique and colloquial dialogue. Now, however, he invites us to focus on the conclusion, as he presents the poem's only rhymed quatrain and supplies an important relation of rhyme and reason. The rhyme words are *tell, swell, hell,* and *farewell,* and offer one related comment: the poem will swell to tell of hellish stories which signify a farewell of any hope for the cordial drop of Heaven's love. City and country, man and woman, wit and fool, narrator and character are part of a world gathering momentum as it parodies and replaces "This only joy for which poor we were made" (line 50). The beautiful twelve-line passage describing "Love, the most generous passion of the mind" (line 40) will be obscured even more than it now is in the true stories willingly sent and received.

Conclusion: A Note on this Satiric Mode

Next to such perceptions the so-called pessimism of the *Satyr against Mankind* is not very frightening, especially since the speaker of that poem preserves his anger against the vices he exposes. To polarize, in the *Satyr* the interlocutor succumbs to his opponent, the normative speaker in the poem; in the *Letter* the opponent (Artemisia) succumbs to the values of the interlocutor (the Fine Lady). In the *Satyr* the main voice is triumphant in affirming its values; in the *Letter* it is defeated, there is no working norm, the ideal of love is proclaimed lost even before we hear it, and the narrator is too flimsy an anchor to hold on to the remnants of virtue. Her loss of control of that virtue is implied in her loss of control of the other characters in the poem. Samuel Johnson's formal verse satire *The Vanity of Human Wishes* (1749) works towards a climax that affirms the existence and acquisition of religious, spiritual wishes that are neither vain nor human. Rochester's *Letter* reverses that process; it quickly announces the death of the spiritual ideal and works towards a climax that affirms the existence and acquisition of devilish, selfish, and earthly love.

That is why the apocalyptic or revelatory satire of, say, Swift's *Tale* and the final version of *The Dunciad* are proper analogues for Rochester's poem, though they are obviously not congruent in many ways. The speaker in *The*

Dunciad must finally beg the goddess Dullness for a few moments more to finish his poem before he, his civilization, and its values are put to sleep. Yet he will not capitulate, he must be conquered. Swift's narrator, on the side of dullness as soon as the *Tale* begins, and confident of writing more by its end, is sometimes undercut by a recognized sane person behind him. But Rochester's poem takes the path between dead hero and partially triumphant madman, and shows us, instead, the morally downward movement of a once decent woman and a once decent world. *The Letter from Artemisia in the Town to Chloe in the Country* is an apocalyptic satire that proclaims the triumph of Hell.[11] It is one of the best of its kind and, as Artemisia predicted, one of the saddest.

5 · THE "ALLUSION TO HORACE"
ROCHESTER'S IMITATIVE MODE

IN RECENT YEARS students of Restoration and eighteenth-century satire have learned a new respect for the variety and sophistication of the Augustan imitation.[1] No longer do we praise the modern poet for imitating, say, Horace, closely, or blame him for imitating freely.[2] Nor are we surprised to find him both free *and* close at different moments in the same poem, or to find that he has imitated only a portion of the parent-poem or that he has, in Dryden's words, written in a manner "not to translate his [the author's] words, or to be confined to his sense, but only to set him as a pattern, and to write, as he supposes that author would have done, had he lived in our age, and in our country."[3] For Dryden, however, this is a pernicious form, since it violates the translator's demand to show his "author's thoughts" and thus is "the greatest wrong which can be done to the memory and reputation of the dead."[4] Another of Dryden's objections, however, may be taken as a central aspect of the creative power of the imitation – a form that is not a malign species of translation, but a separate, if related, genre which, depending upon the author's intention, uses the parent-poem as an integral part or as a central backdrop for its own purposes. Dryden observes that in imitation " 'tis no longer to be called [the initial poet's] work, when neither the thoughts nor words are drawn from the original; but instead of them there is something new produced, which is almost the creation of another hand. By this way, 'tis true, somewhat that is excellent may be invented, perhaps more excellent than the first design."[5]

It is ironic that Rochester, so great a literary enemy of Dryden, should adapt this loose form of imitation – though, of course, like Boileau, from whom he also learned a great deal, he never pretends to offer his reader a translation.[6] Rochester knew of the more literal or close form of imitation as translation, and must have found it an inadequate vehicle for his purposes and temperament. In July of 1673 Dryden wrote to Rochester informing him of Etherege's alteration of Boileau's first satire: Etherege, "changing the French names for English, read it so often that it came to their ears who were concern'd, and forced him to leave off the design, ere it were half finish'd."[7] During the following year, Rochester wrote his poem "Timon," a free version of Boileau's third satire which, in turn, freely adapts Horace, *Satires* II.viii.

Sometime between 1674 and early 1676, he wrote *A Satyr Against Mankind*, and late in 1675 or early in 1676 he wrote his "Allusion to Horace."[8] The "Allusion" is closer to the original's structure and intention than the *Satyr*; but both fall under that class of imitation which radically alters the original's meaning and offers something new from another hand.

The term "allusion" is discussed by Thomas Dilke, in the Preface to his own work, *XXV Select Allusions to Several Places of Horace, Martial, Anacreon, and Petron. Arbiter* (1698). Dilke has "familiarly adapted" his authors to the "present Circumstances of Time and Custom," so that they might easily be understood. " 'Tis true," he continues, "I have taken a great deal of liberty both as to the manner of Composure, and as to the Matter itself, and may sometimes seem to be very foreign from the subject propos'd." But such freedom is inherent in this sort of imitation: "Indeed 'tis my Opinion that Allusions properly admit of this scope, as soon as the hint is receiv'd, I think the Alluder may be allow'd to follow the Thread of his own Fancy."[9] The term has also been defined in Johnson's *Dictionary* (1755): "That which is spoken with reference to something supposed to be already known, and therefore not expressed; a hint; an implication."

Other contemporary lexicons and encyclopedias also offer helpful definitions or illustrations. Although Edward Bysshe does not define the word in his *Art of English Poetry* (1702), he does use it to mean the pointing to, or abstracting of, parts of a poem for one's own purposes.[10] John Kersey states that allusion is "speaking a Thing in reference to another."[11] Edward Phillips borrows this definition and adds that "an Allusion is made to an History, Custom, Wise-saying, &c. when we Speak or Write any thing that has relation to it."[12] Nathan Bailey, in his turn, borrows the Kersey–Phillips definition and Phillips' amplification, but adds another meaning: "A Dalliance or Playing with Words alike in Sound, but unlike in Sense, by changing, adding or taking away a Letter or two."[13] Bailey's source for the latter definition may be Ephraim Chambers' *Cyclopaedia* (1728). "ALLUSION*," Chambers reports, is

ALLUSIO, in rhetoric, a figure whereby something is applied to or understood of, another, by reason of some similitude of name, or sound.

*The word is formed of the Latin *ad*, and *ludere* to play. Camden defines *allusion* as dalliance, or playing with words like in sound, but unlike in sense; by changing, adding, or subtracting a letter or two; whence words resembling one another become applicable to different subjects.

Thus the almighty, if we may use sacred authority, changed Abram, *i.e.* high father, into Abraham, *i.e.* father of many. Thus the Romans played on their tippling emperor Tiberius Nero, by calling him Biberius Mero: and thus in Quintillian the sour fellow Placidus is called Acidus.

Allusions come very near to what we popularly call puns.[14]

Johnson's definition and illustrative quotation for the noun *parody* also cast light upon the nature of allusion. *Parody* is a "kind of writing in which words of an author or his thoughts are taken, and by a slight change adapted to some new purpose." Johnson then quotes a passage from the 1729 edition of the *Dunciad* in quarto, with notes, and in the process suggests the relationship between serious parody and allusion: "The imitations of the ancients are added together with some of the *parodies* and allusions to the most excellent of the moderns."[15]

The conflated meanings of "allusion" current during – and after – the writing of Rochester's poem, then, include "speaking a thing in reference to another," "changing, adding, or taking away a Letter or two," and adapting the thought of the work to the "present circumstances of Time and Custom" according to the alluder's "own Fancy." Even allusion as brief as partial reference or quasi-pun includes awareness of the original and the author's right to change it as he sees fit. Rochester extends this notion to a complete poem and practices allusion as an extremely free form of imitation: he supposes that we already know Boileau's eighth satire and Horace's tenth satire of the first book. Indeed, in most contemporary printed and manuscript versions of the latter poem, he (or the copyist or bookseller) offers part of Horace's first line as a reminder;[16] in others it is called an "Imitation,"[17] and in 1714 it was printed together with Horace's poem.[18]

John L. Moore has ably shown how independent from Boileau Rochester is, though one suspects that examination of the complete *Satyr*, including its "new" conclusion, would strengthen his case even more. But criticism of the "Allusion to Horace" has not advanced significantly beyond Johnson's remarks in his "Life of Rochester":

His Imitation of Horace on Lucilius is not inelegant or unhappy. In the reign of Charles the second began that adaptation, which since has been very frequent, of ancient poetry to present times; and, perhaps, few will be found where the parallelism is better preserved than in this. The versification is, indeed, sometimes careless, but it is sometimes vigorous and weighty.[19]

For our immediate purposes, the question of parallelism is essential, for upon reading the two poems it becomes clear that, though they often proceed in the same direction, they often diverge as well, and that Rochester has designed that they never meet. Moreover, comparison and contrast of these satires, and a brief analysis of the varieties of "Augustan" poetic imitation, may suggest reasons for the modest success of Rochester's poem.

✳

Horace's *Satires* i.x, actually begins with i.iv, in which Horace had praised Lucilius' wit and satiric sharpness, but criticized his speed of writing, harsh metrics, and refusal or inability to write correctly (lines 6–13). The contemporary partisans of Lucilius attacked Horace and rushed to the defence of their apparently maligned idol.[20] Horace thus begins the latter poem with direct reference to the former: he is defensive, troubled, forced to insist that he praised Lucilius and is not a mere scoffer attempting to lower the past in order to elevate the present and his role in it. Accordingly – in about the first half of the poem – he carefully creates the image of a modest and judicious critic, one who offers praise and blame to poets of the past or present without prejudice or self-interest. He is instructive, aware of distinctions between poetic modes and styles, offers advice regarding the tone of satire as presently conceived, and makes clear that he is aware of the limitations of his own genius. Hence he insists – as he did in i.iv – that the satiric sharpness of Lucilius is admirable, but adds that this virtue hardly implies all others, just as Laberius' low scenes of mime may be splendid as *mime*, but utterly different from distinguished poetic discourse. The satiric poet should add terseness, variety of styles – whether of orator, poet, or wit – and jesting humor in addition to his harsher laughter. On the other hand, he should exclude a mixture of Greek and Latin verse. It is not only tiresome old stuff indeed, but also a disservice to the development of native Latin poetry. At this point, Horace finds two ways to bolster his character in the reader's eyes: he admits that he too was tempted to write in such a mingled form, and adds that Romulus himself appeared in a dream and warned him away from this error.

> When I, a *Latin*, once design'd to write
> *Greek* Verse, *Romulus* appear'd at night;
> 'Twas after Twelve, the time when dreams are true,
> And said: *Why* Horace, *what do'st mean to do?*
> *'Tis full as mad the* Greeks *vast heaps t' encrease,*
> As *'tis to carry Water to the Seas.*[21]

Horace, then, is aware of the temptation of such a hybrid mode, and could resist only through quasi-divine and patriotic intervention; he thus lessens the degree to which Lucilius, presumably innocent of such help, is culpable, and also reinforces his commitment to Rome, a commitment that an attacker of the Roman literary heritage would not be likely to share.

Horace also makes clear his awareness of others' strengths within different genres. He knows that among the moderns Fundanius excels in comedy, Pollio in tragedy, Varius in epic, and Virgil in pastoral, and that there is still room for a contemporary's success in satire. Others who have attempted the form (like Varro of the Atax) are below his own achievement; yet he himself admittedly remains *inventore minor* (i.x.48):

> Yet than *Lucillius* less I freely own,
> I would not strive to blast his just renown,
> He wears and best deserves to wear the Crown.   (p. 417)

Only after Horace employs effective precept and example of good and bad poets, shows awareness of his own strengths and shortcomings, and has established both the sanity of his evaluation of his peers and of himself, does he directly reintroduce what had been obliquely discussed after the first verse paragraph of the poem – his "attack" upon Lucilius' blemishes and his own stature.

> Doth not *Lucillius Accius* Rhimes accuse?
> And blame our *Ennius*'s correcter Muse?
> For too much lightness oft his Rhimes deride,
> And when he talks of his own Verse, for Pride?　　　　　(p. 417)

Having thus added Lucilius' authority to his own, Horace addresses himself to an audacious question. At this point the unbiased reader is aware that Horace has not malevolently attacked Lucilius and that he is correct regarding Lucilius' faults. The question then raised is *why* was Lucilius so deficient? Was it lack of genius or the rough nature of the satiric themes he employed? The answer is – neither. Instead, Horace argues that Lucilius' deficiencies stem from a desire to please an unpolished audience. In so doing, Horace continues to shift away from defence of himself for unjustly attacking Lucilius and towards a demonstration that he is Lucilian. Moreover, he also suggests that those to whom he is responding, the implied adversarii of the poem, are actually the enemies of Lucilius; they would propagate what Lucilius himself would abandon if he were living in the Augustan age of more correct literary values which insist that one improve his work:

> did He now again new life Commence,
> He would correct, he would retrench his Sense,
> And pare off all that was not Excellence;
> Take pains, and often when he Verses made,
> Would bite his Nails to th' quick, and scratch his Head.　　　　　(p. 418)

Significantly, Horace follows these lines with others in his own voice, reiterating the value of painful revision. As a result, such a Lucilian–Horatian author would reject the popularity of the schoolroom and its teachers, and the professional authors' guild: that is, precisely those critics who berated Horace at the beginning of the poem.[22] Since Horace and Lucilius are allied, the pedagogues' quarrel with Horace is also a mistaken quarrel with the author they presume is a model for emulation; such a bad, non-Augustan audience willing to accept Lucilius' flaws is responsible for them. Horace concludes by exemplifying those for whom he and, if it were chronologically possible, Lucilius, prefer to write – not Demetrius, a trainer for the mimes, or the bad poets Fannius and Hermogines Tigellius, but those who are clearly Augustan:

> Let *Plotius, Varius*, and *Mecaenas* love,
> Let *Caesar, Virgil, Valgius* all approve
> What I compose; to these would I could joyn
> The *Visci*, and *Messala*'s Learned Line,
> And *Pollio*, and some other Friends of mine.　　　　　(p. 418)

The relevant Latin of I.x.82 (the second line above) is *Octavius*, not *Caesar*: it is now thought to refer to Octavius Musa, a poet and historian, and not to Augustus Caesar. But Creech's error – that of many of his contemporaries – is understandable and reiterates the exalted nature of Horace's audience, which would make Lucilius even greater by insisting that he blot and amend.[23] Demetrius and Tigellius, in contrast, urge the transcendence of Lucilius in his uncorrected form and thereby reproduce the sort of audience that endangers the poet it praises. Horace has moved from apparent attack upon Lucilius to real alliance with him, and from apparent defense of himself against foolish critics to real attack upon them.

Thus for Horace, Lucilius is blemished but great; Horace is on Lucilius' side; the attackers are wrong, and the refined court of Augustus is responsible for much of the success of Horace and would be responsible for improving the quality of Lucilius' efforts. Horace shows his kinship with Lucilius by borrowing an important device from him. Eduard Fraenkel observes:

In a section of his earliest published book (the twenty-sixth in the collection of his works), presumably a kind of proem to what was to follow, Lucilius had spoken, both in general terms and naming some individual persons, of the readers whom he did not wish to have and of those he would like to have. To that section belonged the line (593) *Persium non curo legere, Laelium Decumen volo*; the gist of a pronouncement made in the same context is preserved in Cicero's well-known paraphrase [*De orat.* II.xxv] *neque se ab indoctissimis neque a doctissimis legi velle, quod alteri nihil intelligerent, alteri plus fortasse quam ipse.* Horace borrows from Lucilius the idea of listing desirable and undesirable readers, but he uses it not in a proem but in the epilogue of his book. Lest such an outspoken pronouncement might seem vain or ponderous, Horace makes it arise easily and naturally from a discussion on the risks of hankering after the wrong kind of popularity.[24]

Though I have only touched upon a few of the major historical issues behind the poem, I believe that this analysis is a reasonably accurate gloss upon Horace's intention as understood in the later seventeenth century. It will immediately be clear that Rochester's position is different from Horace's in numerous respects, but especially so in his attitude towards the main satiric target – John Dryden.

✳

Significant differences between the two poems begin in Rochester's second line. Horace sincerely praises Lucilius as an inventor of satire; but Rochester regards Dryden's dramatic verses as "stol'n." Similarly, Horace's genuine regard for Lucilius as a sharp satirist is replaced by Rochester's dubious praise of Dryden's "plays, embroidered up and down / With wit and learning [which] justly pleased the town" (lines 5–6). Rochester thus dissociates himself from Dryden: we do not see a satirist defending himself for having attacked the inventor of the form and his admitted superior; instead, we see a satirist attacking a dramatist who is neither his superior nor an inventor.

Moreover, the term *embroidered* suggests that what intelligence there is in Dryden's plays is ornamental and decorative rather than an intrinsic part of the drama.[25] Lines 12 and 13 confirm our suspicion regarding the praise of Dryden and his "just" pleasing of the town, since we now hear that "your false sense / Hits the false judgment of an audience." The illicitly pleased audience is not in Horace's corresponding lines (though it is assumed later in the poem): Lucilius-induced laughter is a lesser but genuine pleasure. Though Lucilius' audience is not of the best, it is surely a notch above the "clapping fools" and "the rabble" who praise Dryden. Furthermore, "the Court" (lines 14–19) must be added to the list of those who improperly praise, and so Rochester again diverges from the parent-poem, since there Horace's friends were not only from the court but seemed to include Caesar himself. Rochester baits his monarch; Horace flatters his. Rochester gives grudging and damning praise to Dryden, and concludes that pleasing "the rabble and the Court" – the vulgar of low or high social rank – is something, at least,

> Which blundering Settle never could attain,
> And puzling Otway labours at in vain.　　　　　　　　(lines 18–19)

In the following section (lines 21–40) Rochester evalutes Elizabethan and contemporary dramatists. The parallel passage in Horace contains praise for the mingled jesting and serious mode of the old comedy, advises the moderns to adapt this, and criticizes Hermogenes and his school for never reading, and thus not profiting from, these plays. But Rochester is talking about Dryden as a modern dramatist; and so when he praises other modern dramatic wits he is obliquely condemning Dryden. Horace associates himself with Lucilius and discredits those who claimed he had attacked him; Rochester dissociates himself from Dryden, amplifies his original attack, and covertly, as well as overtly, criticizes him:

> Of all our modern wits, none seems to me
> Once to have touched upon true comedy
> But hasty Shadwell and slow Wycherley.　　　　　　　(lines 41–43)

Both the subsequent praise of Shadwell as a poet of nature, and of Wycherley as a poet of art, exclude Dryden from the higher ranks of comedy. Shadwell "scorns to varnish his good touches o'er / To make the fools and women praise 'em more" (lines 48–49), Dryden had his "false sense" please "the false judgment of an audience / Of clapping fools" (lines 12–14). Similarly, Wycherley "earns hard whate'er he gains: / He wants no judgment, nor he spares no pains" (lines 50–51), whereas Dryden's rhymes were not earned but "stol'n, unequal, nay dull many times" (line 2), and he is a poet of primarily quantitative output (lines 8–9, 93–97).

Rochester again departs from the original in the rest of his discussion of the genres and the poet who excels in each. At this point in his poem Horace shows that he must succeed in "correct" satire, which Lucilius had ignored. The poet remains personal and positive: Horace is not competing with Lucilius but fulfilling the form which he had so brilliantly invented. But the notion of Horace as a refined extension of Lucilius is foreign to Rochester's purpose, since – in terms of the poem, at least – Rochester has no desire to follow Dryden as a dramatist; he thus chooses Buckhurst "For pointed satyrs" (line 59), and Sedley for amorous love-poetry (a genre not discussed by Horace) as a way of returning to qualitative evaluation of Dryden. Where Sedley is seductive and successful – "the poor vanquished maid dissolves away / In dreams all night, in sighs and tears all day" (lines 69–70) – the amatory songs in Dryden's plays are merely gross, and may also reveal something about Dryden's limp sexuality:[26]

> Dryden in vain tried this nice way of wit,
> For he to be a tearing blade thought fit.
> But when he would be sharp, he still was blunt:
> To frisk his frolic fancy, he'd cry, "Cunt!"   (lines 71–74)

Rochester, then, ironically praises and really attacks Dryden, excludes him from the ranks of good dramatists, and shows him to be ineffectual in his dramatic "love" poems. With all this in mind, the reader again doubts the sincerity of Rochester's praise of Dryden.

> But, to be just, 'twill to his praise be found
> His excellencies more than faults abound;
> Nor dare I from his sacred temples tear
> That laurel which he best deserves to wear.[27]   (lines 77–80)

Rochester then introduces lines with an important reservation, and proceeds to tear away Dryden's laurels. The same lines also further distinguish him from Rochester at precisely the point at which Horace was cementing his relationship with Lucilius:

> But does not Dryden find ev'n Jonson dull;
> Fletcher and Beaumont uncorrect, and full
> Of lewd lines, as he calls 'em; Shakespeare's style
> Stiff and affected; to his own the while
> Allowing all the justness that his pride
> So arrogantly had to these denied?   (lines 81–86)

Dullness, pompous fullness, and lewdness are the traits which, according to Rochester, belong to Dryden himself. Of course Horace carefully avoids any such presumption in describing Lucilius' quarrels with his predecessors, and assumes that Lucilius' accurate strictures serve as proper precedent for his own. Dryden's pride and arrogance thus contrast with the normative behavior of both Lucilius and Horace. The latter honestly praises his great master; Rochester shows a despicable contemporary berating his betters, and places

Dryden in the distasteful situation that Horace's detractors attempted to place him in.

Unlike Horace, Rochester thus "impartially" (line 87) attacks his author's pride and arrogance. Horace gains our sympathy through association with a good man of letters; Rochester through dissociation from a bad man of letters. Horace throws the burden of Lucilius' deficiencies on to the inadequate demands of his rough age, but this alternative is impossible for Rochester, since Dryden is of the present age. Hence he raises three questions regarding Dryden's lack of literary merit, and each depends solely upon Dryden's internal literary state. He wonders whether

> those gross faults his choice pen does commit
> Proceed from want of judgment, or of wit;
> Or if his lumpish fancy does refuse
> Spirit and grace to his loose, slattern muse? (lines 89–92)

The questions are not overtly answered because, unlike Horace's answer, by implication all three charges are accurate. It is, presumably, Dryden's lack of wit, among other things, that makes him so poor an amatory poet ("Dryden in vain tried this nice way of wit" [line 71]; his lack of judgment leads him to substitute quantity for quality (lines 93–101); and as "a vain, mistaken thing" (line 104) he wishes to please a poor theatrical audience. It thus follows that Dryden does not refuse spirit and grace to his muse: as a man of neither wit nor judgment he has none to give.

Rochester's strategy continues to be radically different from Horace's. The latter argues that were Lucilius now alive "he would correct, he would retrench his sense." Rochester's same advice (lines 98–101) is given to one who is alive, chooses not to follow it, and seeks to please the rabble. Rochester himself has "no ambition on that idle score" (line 110) and prefers, instead, to be censured by a few critics and poets he respects.

> I loathe the rabble; 'tis enough for me
> If Sedley, Shadwell, Shepherd, Wycherley,
> Godolphin, Butler, Buckhurst, Buckingham,
> And some few more, whom I omit to name,
> Approve my sense: I count their censure fame.[28] (lines 120–24)

Horace is truly pro-Lucilian; Rochester truly anti-Drydenian. The former's main intentions are to defend himself and to define the best satiric mode for a correct age; the latter's to attack Dryden and bad drama that seeks the favor of the mob, whether high or low. Horace discusses his own satiric role in the literary culture of the court; Rochester functions as a gadfly in literary culture and attacks the court. The throne is at the center of value in the former; the throne is associated with the playhouse and rabble in the latter. In short, when compared to Horace *Satires* I.x, Rochester has in fact produced something new which is the creation of another hand; but that new creation can be seen only when set against the old, since as an allusion it is "spoken with reference to something supposed to be already known, and therefore not expressed."[29] Such an imitation, in which some parallelism is preserved and some altered, could not have been ignored by poets who either translated or carried the imitation as a form to its highest level of achievement. It is not only the source of much phrasing for Creech's translation of the same poem in 1684,[30] but may also have been one of Pope's main models of imitative freedom from the original.[31] And it is surely an example of what Thomas Rymer meant when he said of Rochester's method:

> Whatsoever he imitated or Translated, was Loss to him. He had a Treasure of his own, a Mine not to be exhausted. His own Oar and Thoughts were rich and fine: his own Stamp and Expression more neat and beautiful than any he cou'd borrow or fetch from abroad.[32]

Rochester's poem tells us much about his allusive mode of satiric imitation; but it also provides a paradigm of that sub-species of imitation which both hopes for the reader's awareness of the parent-poem and is largely neutral in its attitude towards it. With the exception of implied differences between the quality of Horace's emperor and Rochester's king, there is little thematic interplay between the two poems; and even this contrast is blunted by means of Rochester's praise of noble figures – like Buckhurst – whom he hopes to please. There is no real sign that we are to judge Horace's age as better or worse than Rochester's. Though Lucilius is superior to Dryden, the intentions of Horace and Rochester are so different that, though the former clarifies the latter, we cannot draw any further inference.

"Augustan" imitation is remarkably complex; we do not fully understand the modern poem unless we understand its attitude towards the poem imitated. In the *First Satire of the Second Book of Horace* (to Fortescue, 1733), Pope is aware that "*an Answer from* Horace *was both more full, and of more Dignity, than any I cou'd have made in my own person.*"[33] There is an implicit metaphor in Pope's attitude and posture: like his illustrious forebear he too must defend his satiric role from those who would silence him in order to harm virtue. Horace was the victor and convinced Trebatius, a guardian of the law in the legal sphere, that he should continue to write; Pope's defense of himself and use of Fortescue are similar. The poem is thus essentially optimistic; it assumes an historic community of thought, problems, and rational men who exist and have some power, however grim the world might in fact appear. In *Fortescue* Pope regards his parent-poem as normative and full of dignity.

This was not the only alternative for an imitator. One thinks of Prior's *English Ballad, On the Taking of Namur* (1695), a comic parody of Boileau's *Ode sur la prise de Namur* (1692), in which Boileau's flattery of his king and glorification of a minor victory are ridiculed. Or, on a more serious level, one turns to Johnson's imitation of Juvenal's tenth satire, *The Vanity of Human Wishes* (1749), in which Juvenal's pagan harshness, the philosophic laughter of Democritus, and the unpredictable quality of the goddess Fortune, are replaced by Johnson's Christian piety, the speaker's rejection of laughter at the human situation, and the safe, stable, world that "celestial wisdom" can make for mankind. In these poems – and many more like them – the original is used not as a subdued argument from authority, but as a clear argument for the superiority of the imitator and his culture – whether English as opposed to French, or Christian as opposed to pagan.

Yet another imitative mode is the mingling of acceptance and rejection of the parent-poem, as in Pope's *Epistle to Augustus* (1737). Here the literary values of Augustus and his age contrast with those of George Augustus in England, but the Roman political values are regarded as negative models all too extant in contemporary England.[34] One suspects, as well, that a poem like Johnson's *London* (1738), from Juvenal's third satire, also falls into this broad class. Only the worst attributes of Domitian's bad Rome can be evoked to characterize Walpole's London; yet Johnson, nevertheless, uses Juvenal's conclusion – in which Umbritius promises to listen to Juvenal's satires when he too quits Rome – as a sign that, today as yesterday, the virtuous retreat but continue to fight the vicious. Like Umbritius before him, Thales must write satire and define the good life.

Rochester's characteristic mode of imitation provides still a fourth way – the way which I have called relatively neutral in attitude towards the parent-poem. Though there are occasional lapses, he generally follows his own path, with minimal use of the original. He may invite challenge on qualitative grounds, and comparison and contrast on thematic grounds; and he may – or may not – show his own genius thereby. But he also shows the limitations of such neutrality. Boileau and Horace, their values and culture, are not actors in Rochester's poems; they are known but static figures who provide the backdrop but not much more. Johnson's change of the pagan "Fortuna" to the Christian "celestial wisdom" functions as the culmination of two movements in *The Vanity of Human Wishes*: the acceptance of Christian values in the modern poem, and the rejection of pagan values in the Roman. Similarly, Pope's substitution of Bolingbroke for Maecenas in his imitation of Horace, *Epistles* i.i, immediately warns his audience that the poet is in political opposition to the English court, whereas Horace is in sympathy with his. The contrast of English discord with Roman concord structures our understanding of the relationship between the two poems and the cultures they represent.

It is clear that Rochester's poem lacks such resonance, such sustained qualitative assessment of the past and comparison with the present. The "Allusion to Horace" has neither the striking independence of the *Satyr Against Mankind*, nor the eloquent "dependence" of Pope's *Epistle to Augustus*. I would thus suggest that collateral analyses of the imitation and the parent-poem, together with discussion of the role the latter poem plays in the former, can be a tool of both understanding and evaluation. Of course it is evident that Rochester is not as great a poet as Horace, and simply pales in comparison. Moreover, in the poem before us his attack on Dryden is not only personal and unjustified, but unconvincing, since the poetic "world" within which Dryden exists is not fully realized, as the world of Shadwell or Cibber in other unjustified attacks surely is. As both Pope and Johnson observed, the versification sometimes is harsh and inelegant. And, as I have implied, the character of Rochester's speaker lacks Horace's convincing tones of an essentially disinterested, patriotic, personally involved yet ethical and fair poet.

One should grant these as convincing reasons for Rochester's diminished achievement; but at least as convincing a reason is that he chose a form whose finest conventions were just evolving and just beginning to be defined. Perhaps it is unfair to judge Rochester's "Allusion" on the standards of the *Epistle to Augustus*, written some sixty years later, for each man is attempting a different sort of poem. Yet, I believe, one reason that Pope's poem is so complex in its attitude towards the original is that Rochester's is so simple. Though Rochester's imagination is fertilized by the poem imitated, he nevertheless, as Rymer claims, disdains help "from abroad." In so doing, however, he limits himself to his own mine or its immediate environs, and thereby limits the expanse of his poem. He normally parallels or diverges from Horace and only rarely touches him. The reader innocent of Horace can read Rochester's "Allusion" with relatively little loss of understanding;[35] nor is his understanding substantially enriched after reading Horace. The hint or implication that allusion implies remains precisely that; the reader is teased by a promise that is never fulfilled, whereas in the *Satyr against Mankind* – which, unlike the "Allusion," was never printed next to its original – the reader is not directly referred to another text through the very title of the poem,[36] and in the *Letter from Artemisia* (1679) there is neither a specifically announced nor implied literary parent. In the "Allusion," on the other hand, the reader is frustrated by a static backdrop, by suggestions of historical similitude and dissimilitude which remain inchoate. One of the central reasons why Rochester's poem is not fully satisfying is that the creative strengths of imitation as a genre were not yet clear; these could not be fully realized until the limitations of Rochester's mode in the "Allusion to Horace" were absorbed. Paradoxically, Rochester's refusal to be substantially in debt has limited his wealth, and Pope grew rich by inverting his example.

6 · "NATURES HOLY BANDS" IN
ABSALOM AND ACHITOPHEL
FATHERS AND SONS, SATIRE AND CHANGE

THE OPENING LINES of *Absalom and Achitophel* have long been considered an *apologia pro regis libidine*. Here is a sophisticated exchange between men of the world, one of whom happened to be the divinely appointed gentleman king whose actions were applauded by the poet, his well-connected readers, and God.[1] Attacks on Charles' private life, the argument runs, were both irrelevant and a stalking horse for attacks on his kingship. During the last several years, however, a few students of the poem have objected to this interpretation. In criticism as in politics vocal minorities may be heard without being listened to. In 1971 A.E. Dyson and Julian Lovelock expressed surprise that "some critics have sought to excuse the censure of the King" either as a rhetorical device "or even worse, as a celebration of the King's humanity."[2] Nonetheless, in 1976 K.E. Robinson rightly complained of the continuing "critical orthodoxy" that absolved Charles of responsibility for his sexual actions.[3] As recently as 1981 Jerome Donnelly lamented that "The most widely accepted readings of *Absalom and Achitophel*" view Dryden's attitude towards Charles "as one of almost unreserved admiration."[4] Each of the two latter revisionists also shares a corollary of his skepticism – King Charles as King David must evolve into a better person if he is to become the better monarch capable of speaking lines God sanctions.[5]

These studies have been strengthened by another salutary trend, one perhaps related to the new interest in family history during the Restoration and the eighteenth century. Donnelly has amplified scattered remarks of others and made plain that as a culpable father Charles must acknowledge a superior model before he can improve. This movement, in turn, has served to relocate the poem's decidedly mixed genre, which had long been confidently placed within the heroic kind;[6] its hero, after all, was king by divine right, a type of Christ, emblem of grace, and natural enemy of the forces of Satan and Chaos ranked against him. The hypothesis, or assumption, of genre was a function of the hypothesis of royal character – or vice versa as the case may be. With an assumption of a dominant satiric mode, however, different questions suggest themselves. These include the nature of characterization and the placement of characters, and ask how the endangered king becomes the enlightened secure king. They include the role of satiric norms and ask what model or models would allow that king to change, so that both political sides can agree on civic standards and avoid civil war. They also include questions concerning rhetoric, which ask how the narrator can be an admitted royalist while claiming to be a moderate and hoping to persuade Whigs, and how he can criticize the king whose favor he must gain. Finally, such questions ask what external, contemporary evidence from history, politics, theology, or paper wars might substantiate whatever answers one finds.

I propose, then, to enlarge upon and synthesize happy trends in Dryden criticism, and to suggest ways to rethink some assumptions and conclusions regarding his greatest poem.

✳

The patriarchal basis of Charles' power was of course central to royalist theories of divine right. Dryden, however, largely avoids Filmer's dogmatic insistence on Adam's paternal kingship, either to preserve his own appearance of moderation or to avoid a suspect argument. Locke observes that Filmer's putative biblical theory ignores the mother's authority, though the Bible gave equal weight to her in establishing parental power over children.[7]

Dryden nonetheless knew that both Whigs and Tories believed in "Natures Holy Bands" (line 339). Shaftesbury seeks fortune for his son, and Locke argues that "Reverence, Acknowledgement, Respect and Honour ... is always due from Children to their Parents."[8] Though there are limits on each side's power, by "the Law of God and Nature" even the adult offspring must always seek his parents' welfare. Locke's remarks well support Gordon Schochet's view that there is an "underlying patriarchalism" in much Whig political thought:

God having made the Parents Instruments in his great design of continuing the Race of Mankind, and the occasions of Life to their Children, as he hath laid on them an obligation to nourish, preserve, and bring up their Off-spring; So he has laid on the Children a perpetual Obligation of *honouring their Parents*, which containing in it an inward esteem and reverence to be shewn by all outward Expressions, ties up the Child from any thing that may ever injure or affront, disturb, or endanger the Happiness or Life of those, from whom he received his; and engages him in all actions of defence, relief, assistance, and comfort of those, by whose means he entered into being, and has been made capable of any enjoyments of life. From this Obligation no State, no Freedom, can absolve Children.[9]

Dryden's family setting thus recalls the obligations of child to parent shared by each "party," even though circumstances made that setting more attractive to royalists. No one in the early 1680s could forget that Charles II was endangered in part because he was the son of the beheaded Charles I. Samuel Pordage's *Azaria and Hushai* (17 January 1682) laments "The Scandal of a curs'd Conspiracy, / Against our King and Father to rebell" (p. 14).[10] On 18 July 1683 the author of *A Congratulatory Pindaric Poem, For His Majesties Safe*

Deliverance from This Hellish and True Plot, says that the king was victimized "For that great Crime of his, of being his Father's Son" (p. 3). The author of *An Answer written on Sight, by a Loyal Hand* (14 September 1683) pleads to the Whigs: "Though *CHARLES* the Father you did Murther, / Forbear the Son, and Plot no further." Shortly thereafter the evoker of *Sylla's Ghost: A Satyr Against Ambition* (4 October 1683) makes a similar point. Lord Grey wishes to kill Charles II "For none other Crime than this alone, / For being his Glorious Martyr'd Father's Son" (p. 8; see also p. 12). On 7 January 1684 *The Recanting Whig* wonders how he can atone for all he has done "To a Martyr'd Fathers too much injur'd Son."

The perpetrators of such wickedness found analogues in Phaethon, Icarus, Satan, Catiline, Brutus, Cromwell, and vipers. Accordingly, Monmouth's opponents easily roused emotion against an illegitimate son suspected of seeking the death of his generous king and father. Dryden raises the problem while avoiding the charge:

> Some thought they God's Anointed meant to Slay
> By Guns, invented since full many a day:
> Our Author swears it not; but who can know
> How far the Devil and the *Jebusites* may go? (lines 130–33)

Others were less oblique. The writer of *A Lash to Disloyalty* (13 August 1683) berates "Insatiate *Monmouth*!" for seeking "thy Fathers Death" and "Royal Father murdered" (p. 1) to gain the crown beyond his birth. Long after the Exclusion Crisis, Charles Hopkins could explore the natural anger evoked by two simultaneous ugly crimes. A faithful subject in the *Female Warrior* (1700) warns: "On your own Head a double Guilt you bring, / Warring against a Father and a King" (p. 23). Such wars and the way to resolve them form one of the bases of *Absalom and Achitophel* and supply its narrator with his bond first to the king and then to any reader sensitive to domestic or national family structures.

The poem as rhetorical document thus begins with its address to the reader. Dryden affirms his moderation, his association with the reasonable "honest Party," and his dissociation from the violent fringes of either side. Moderation does not mean indecision, for the introduction plainly aligns the speaker with the king's party and personality. Dryden's own affection for Absalom ingratiates him with the king, whose forgiving temper the speaker here imitates. Like the king, he has "endeavour'd to commit" the faults of extenuation, palliation, and indulgence: "*David* himself, cou'd not be more tender of the Young-man's Life, than I would be of his Reputation" (pp. 3–4).

Such alignment signals Dryden's wish to make his art a model for life in at least two senses. He does not conclude the biblical story because he could not "shew *Absalom* Unfortunate." Indeed, he would prefer to rewrite history and reconcile Absalom and David: "And, who knows but this may come to pass" for "There seems, yet, to be room left for a Composure." But, he warns, the alternative is reality, pity, and the *Ense rescindendum*, the surgeon's work turned to the hangman's, "which I wish not to my very enemies." Far better, Dryden hopes, to allow his "good natur'd Errour" of forgiving Absalom as Charles forgives Monmouth. "God is infinitely merciful; and his Vicegerent is only not so because he is not Infinite" (pp. 4–5). The king's poet, Dryden might have added, is not as merciful as that vicegerent only because he is, as it were, even less infinite than the king, several of whose values as benevolent, forgiving, but potentially stern monarch he shares. The king soon must become the chastiser of vice he prefers not to be. Like his sovereign, Dryden can ameliorate the sting of his satire; like his sovereign, he can convince those who abuse his kindness that he can be severe as well as gentle (p. 3).

Alliance with the king's mercy and filial piety allows Dryden room respectfully to satirize the king himself. Dryden wished that the Absalom outside the poem would change upon seeing his conduct impartially portrayed; but he allows David the opportunity to change within the poem, and so makes his key statement regarding satire only after he has bonded himself to the king. "The true end of *Satyre*, is the amendment of Vices by correction. And he who writes Honestly, is no more an Enemy to the Offendour than the Physician to the Patient, when he prescribes harsh Remedies to an inveterate Disease" (p. 5). On the principle of *ad exemplum regis*, a sick king makes a sick nation; if the king's vices are amended Absalom's can be as well. Dryden's introduction thus lays out his overt and covert satiric design. The latter must be deftly implemented or the narrator will squander the good will presumably gained in his association with the king. Dryden meets this problem in the poem's deservedly famous opening lines, which are not an "apology" or "insinuated condonement of . . . promiscuity" in the king's private life, as they have been called.[11] Rather, they lay out a theory of causation: unacceptable conduct breeds unacceptable conduct.

✳

Dryden lacked the occasion to savage Charles for his royal lust, as Rochester did in "A Satyr on Charles II" (1674):

> Poor prince! thy prick, like thy buffoons at Court,
> Will govern thee because it makes thee sport.
>
> . . .
>
> Though safety, law, religion, life lay on 't,
> 'Twould break through all to make its way to cunt.[12]

Dryden nonetheless both granted the point of such attacks and their implicit compliment to the monarch's sexual exploits. One could do worse than the blame by praise of telling Charles II that he himself was infinitely virile, though attached to a barren wife, "A Soyl ungratefull to the Tiller's care" (line 12).

83

But Charles is to blame. He listens to nature's prompting, not to the restraints of law (line 5); he forsakes concubines and bride through indiscriminate sexual use (lines 6, 9); he forsakes the Judaeo-Christian God of design and imitates a deity who thoughtlessly "Scatter'd his Maker's Image through the Land" (line 10). One such "image" is Absalom himself, who shares his father's strengths and weaknesses. Absalom too is born for love, is naturally pleasing and graceful, and is given everything he wishes in spite of violating the law. Accordingly, "With secret Joy indulgent *David* view'd / His Youthfull Image in his Son renew'd" (lines 31–32).

Parallel and comparison and contrast are among Dryden's typical modes of proceeding in *Absalom and Achitophel*. He thus shows how Israel shares Absalom's image, but without the physical charm of the wayward youth. His movements are "all accompanied with grace" (line 29); Israel tries "th' extent and stretch of grace" (line 46). David "To all [Absalom's] wishes Nothing . . . deny'd" (line 33); Israel is "God's pamper'd people . . . debauch'd with ease" (line 47). Absalom is guilty of "Some warm excesses which the Law forbore" (line 37) including murder (line 39); Israel "No King could govern, nor no God could please" (line 48), and no nation is "by Laws less circumscrib'd and bound" (line 54). Israel regards David as "An Idoll Monarch which their hands had made" (line 64); Absalom later accepts Achitophel's view that "the People have a Right Supreme / To make their Kings; for Kings are made for them" (lines 409–10). The Israelites' murmurings and Absalom's sedition, illegitimate complaints and an illegitimate son, are unified by an illegitimate leader: "*Achitophel* still wants a Chief, and none / Was found so fit as Warlike *Absalon*" (lines 220–21) who, in turn, would be made a vassal to the crowd and accept "Kingly power . . . ebbing out" (line 226). David has literally created his own revolution, as his own worst traits, made attractive through an engaging presence, in turn encourage the nation's worst traits and lend coherence to chaos. If "The true end of *Satyre* is the amendment of Vices by correction," the poem must show David corrected or Israel ruined.

The image of a guilty king was readily available in the biblical story which, together with some of its commentaries, portrays the morally irregular David as hardly the type of Christ he too often has been called. Shortly before Dryden's poem appeared, for example, the author of *Absalom's Conspiracy: Or, the Tragedy of Treason* (1 July 1680) made plain that "The king was careless, drown'd in his Pleasures."[13] Bishop Simon Patrick's account of David's adultery with Bathsheba and virtual murder of Uriah, her husband and his loyal officer, includes words like crime, idleness, sloth, sin, guilt, foul, vile, and corrupt. Patrick shows that David's "very Nature was altered, and become base and degenerate; now he had given himself up to Sensuality." His consequent marriage to Bathsheba "*was evil in the eyes* of God."[14] By 1697 Pierre Bayle summarized much of the received awareness of David's uncertain virtue. He caused his own grief, for "his Indulgence to his Children was excessive, and he himself was the first that suffered for it." Had he punished, "as he ought," Absalom's murder of Amnon, "he would not have run the Hazard of being entirely dethroned." Alas, Bayle laments of the varied miseries in David's private and public life, "What Scandal is here given to pious Souls, to see so much Infamy in the Family of this King!"[15]

Hostile readers clearly saw that Dryden invoked the tradition of David as the fallible paragon, and attacked this strategy to discredit a popular poem. On 10 December 1681 Henry Care's *Towser the Second. A Bull-Dog*, replied to *Absalom and Achitophel* and labeled Dryden a mad dog menacing or biting everyone, including "our Royal *CHARLES*, / And his two Mistresses." Four days later "A Person of Honour" published his *Poetical Reflections on a Late Poem Entituled Absalom and Achitophel*. He complained that Dryden's poem was "a Capital or National Libel." The king as portrayed is "a broad figure of scandalous inclinations" whose "irregularities" render him more "the property of Parasites and Vice, than suitable to the accomplishments of so excellent a Prince." Worse yet, Dryden darkens David's "sanctity in spite of illuminations from Holy Writ" (sigs. B1^{r-v}). The author of *A Key (with the Whip) To open the Mystery and Iniquity of . . . Absalom and Achitophel* (13 January 1682) bitterly charged Dryden with committing "scandalum magnatum *yea of Majesty itself*" (verso of dedication) and with sparing "Nor *Queen, nor King*, in thy pernicious Book" (p. 25). On 6 April 1682 Elkanah Settle made a similar point in his *Absalom Senior: Or Achitophel Transpros'd*. Dryden's poem has "*this one unpardonable Fault, That the Lash is more against a* David, *than an* Achitophel." This "unmannerly Boldness" both attacks "the publick Justice of the Nation" and affronts "even the Throne itself" (sig. A2^r). By 24 July of the same year another hostile poet issued *A Satyr to His Muse. By the Author of Absalom and Achitophel* and has that satirist record the "Whoring life" of David, "By whom Uriah was so basely Slain" (p. 4).[16]

These respondents hoped further to taint Charles by their assumed outrage, and to taint Dryden's poem by confusing the part with the whole. They enhance the scandal by denying it, and imply that a loyal poet is unconscionable to write such stuff, and that the unlawful David is not countered by the new David under God's law. Such remarks show that David's virtue was perceived as very fragile indeed. In the earlier phase of *Absalom and Achitophel*, then, David makes his own rebellion by propagating his own lawlessness in his lawless son and lawless nation. How he remedies that situation is in part a function of other fathers and sons who join the narrator in two essential activities: in general, by establishing increasingly assured and numerous public voices of reason, restraint, and law to which the king as father of his nation listens and from which he grows; and in particular, by establishing through Ormond and Ossory the normative relationship between father and son that also serves as an instructive paradigm for the king. Along the way Dryden allows Absalom and Achitophel to discredit themselves through their words, political theory, and Miltonic context, and suggests equally unpleasant biblical contexts for Achitophel's other colleagues. Phillip Harth has demonstrated that Dryden could not have hoped to influence Shaftesbury's trial;[17] but he could have hoped to influence consequent attitudes towards the incorrigible Shaftesbury and the corrigible king, and he certainly hoped that Monmouth would draw the appropriate inference and take the appropriate side.

Dryden's hope was shared by the admiring author of *Absalom's IX Worthies: Or, A Key to a late Book or Poem* (10 March 1682): "Thy Lines will make young *Absalon* relent, / And though 'tis hard *Achitophel* repent." With the general reconciliation, tearful, protective, "Godlike *David*" fully recognizes that he "owes his Son and Subjects to thy Verse" (sig. A1ᵛ). The author of *Good News in Bad Times; Or, Absalom's Return to David's Bosome* (30 November 1683) also sees the demise of the Whigs, the reform of Monmouth, the intercession of York on his behalf, and the consequent reunion of father and son and subject and monarch. Though these reunions were fanciful, in the enclosed world of Dryden's poem the king can reform after he watches a salutary filial relationship and its links to the divine, and listening to salutary prophetic advice.

✳

Achitophel produces a son after his own image, "a shapeless Lump, like Anarchy" (line 172); he also wishes to produce his twin by becoming Absalom's surrogate father and supplying values and the royal birth that David denies him. Achitophel has refused "his Age the needful hours of Rest," punished "a Body which he could not please" and now is "Bankrupt of Life" (lines 166–68). He thus steals from David's nest while implicitly admitting to the defects of age he attributes to David. Achitophel's first speech shows his own apparent power: he elevates Absalom to prince, to Christ in his nativity, and to a second Moses leading his people to freedom in the promised land. He is, finally, a "*Saviour*" and "Royal Youth" (lines 240, 250) who must accept Heaven's invitation to be king. To do so he must also accept Achitophel's breaking of international alliances, shaking of public pillars of support, usurping of titles, inverting of order that makes treason safe and the profane sacred, and substituting the people for the crown as a source of power. Achitophel debases David in the proportion that he elevates Absalom, turning David into Lucifer. The monarch "like the Prince of Angels from his height, / Comes tumbling downward with diminish'd light" (lines 273–74). Achitophel also replaces divine order with fortune and chance as he strips David of all his friends – including the son whose duty and gratitude obliged him to defend, relieve, assist, and comfort his father.

Substitution of fathers is another way in which Dryden taps Tory and Whig paternal feelings. Algernon Sidney was one of the many Whig theorists who argued that "No man can be my father but he that did beget me; and it is absurd to say I owe that duty to one who is not my father, which I owe to my father, as to say, he did beget me, who did not beget me; for the obligation that arises from benefits can only be to him that conferred them" – as Achitophel did not so confer to Absalom.[18]

In spite of this misalliance, Dryden's narrator again joins his royal master in attenuating, excusing, and praising Absalom. Some of that credit is due to a young man of such sound familial and political perception that he ably refutes Achitophel and, in the process, condemns himself from his own mouth. Absalom also shows why, in the best sense, he is not his father's son, for he finally refuses to extend the benefit of the doubt to his father that his father extended to him. Dryden reminds us of this difference of behavior through repetition of the same phrase. The father calls the son's murderous act "a Just Revenge for injur'd Fame" (line 40); the son tells Achitophel, "What Millions has he Pardon'd of his Foes, / Whom Just Revenge did to his Wrath expose" (lines 323–24). This son, though, later blames his father who "Exalts his Enemies, his Freinds destroys" (line 711). Absalom's surrender to Achitophel's values is signaled by repeated personal pronouns and by abuse of family ties:

> Why should I then Repine at Heavens Decree;
> Which gives me no Pretence to Royalty?
> Yet oh that Fate Propitiously Enclind,
> Had rais'd my Birth, or had debas'd my Mind;
> To my large Soul, not all her Treasure lent,
> And then Betray'd it to a mean Descent.
> I find, I find my mounting Spirits Bold,
> And *David*'s part disdains my Mothers Mold.
> Why am I Scanted by a Niggard Birth?
> My Soul Disclaims the Kindred of her Earth:
> And, made for Empire, Whispers me within;
> Desire of Greatness is a Godlike Sin.   (lines 361–72)

The emphasis on *I*, *me*, and *my* removes the mask of community interest; the insult to his mother is both humanly offensive and a violation of Whig family dogma; and the last line signals his change of divine analogy. Before falling, Absalom said of his father's mercy also extended to his son: "His Crime is God's beloved Attribute" (line 328). Now the crime has become Absalom's, and is the devil's not God's, in the self praise and unwitting self-condemnation in "Desire of Greatness is a Godlike Sin." The excessive mercy of David becomes the excessive ambition of Absalom, a change Achitophel notices; his increase in satanic rhetoric is signaled by the Miltonic inversion of "Him Staggering so when Hells dire Agent found" (line 373).

Achitophel's fresh forces of argument include an extreme statement of the contract theory of government, which he turns into family theory. "The

People have a Right Supreme / To make their Kings; for Kings are made for them" (lines 409–10). The people have become the patriarchs, and the king is the son who must obey. Filmer's *Patriarcha* has become Achitophel's, but with a change in the cast of characters.

Achitophel also discredits the filial bond between father and son and, again in violation of Whig theory, labels it mere paternal self-love:

> Nor let his Love Enchant your generous Mind;
> 'Tis Natures trick to Propagate her Kind.
> Our fond Begetters, who would never dye,
> Love but themselves in their Posterity.   (lines 423–26)

Even that love is questionable. If David loves his "Darling Son" (line 433) why cheat him of his birthright? James will be given a crown he does not deserve, will reverse his brother's vice, and will meditate revenge. Under such conditions nature herself must continue to be redefined. "Natures Holy Bands" that restrain the son from harming his father now become "Natures Eldest law" (line 458) of self-defence and Achitophel's defence of violent revolution. Achitophel also uses another metaphor of retreat from civilized repression, one perhaps drawn from the biblical Absalom's humiliating and incestuous seduction of his father's concubines. To "Commit a pleasing Rape upon the Crown" is at once to possess prince and law (lines 474–76). The virile scatterer of his image has become like one of his own slaves or concubines; he is a passive woman "Secure" (line 475) under the weight of the new values of Achitophel's new royal son.

✳

Achitophel unites several other factions behind that son. Zimri, Shimei, and Corah are the leading players, and share several overlapping functions. Each serves internal poetic and structural needs. As the Duke of Buckingham, Zimri parallels Barzillai, the Duke of Ormond, who begins the loyalist catalogue. Zimri is "all Mankinds Epitome" (line 546) in contrast to Amiel, Edward Seymour, who elicits the wise words of Commons, "*Israel*'s Tribes in small" (line 906). As one of the "Princes of the Land" (line 543) he has at least a metaphoric title that Achitophel bestows on Absalom as "Auspicious Prince" (line 230). Discrediting such a leader thus discredits much of the movement he represents. He is demonstrably incoherent, unreliable, unpredictable, dubiously sane, and "always in the wrong" (line 547). So is Shimei. Bethel's reputation for republican cruelty during the civil wars and his self-involved acquisition of money contrast with David's mercy and varied generosity;[19] and his biblical support of Absalom and cursing of David and his servants contrast with David's temperance and refusal to allow usurpation. Corah, in turn, is ugly in body and spirit, at once recalling Achitophel's ugly son and contrasting with David's beautiful son. His body is an emblem of the cause of which Absalom should be wary.

These characters also amplify the theme of improper paternity associated with an evil plot. Like the Whigs, Zimri embodies political and moral disorder, instability, and ultimate infertility. Within a month he

> Was Chymist, Fidler, States-Man, and Buffoon:
> Then all for Women, Painting, Rhiming, Drinking;
> Besides ten thousand freaks that dy'd in thinking.   (lines 550–52)

As Jerome Donnelly has suggested, the dead freaks may recall Buckingham's notorious liaison with the Countess of Shrewsbury, which generated an illegitimate "child who died shortly after birth."[20] Buckingham's insufficient procreation contrasts with Charles' amplitude, just as his desire to lead the opposition contrasts with Achitophel's ability to do so. Zimri is "wicked but in will, of means bereft" (line 567) and is associated with impotence of which Charles is free.

He also is free from a sexual weakness associated with Oates, who was discharged from the Royal Navy for sodomy, and parallels Buckingham's undisciplined heterosexual lust and incomplete paternity. Numerous works attacking Oates associated his sexual deviance with his political deviance. Such scandalous and abusive things, as Narcissus Luttrell called them,[21] included John Dean's *Oates's Bug[gering] Bug[gering] Boarding School, at Camber-well* (8 March 1684) which showed the schoolmaster using 300 boys and reviving a Turkish seraglio in his nominal place of youthful education. Thereafter, *The Sodomite, or the Venison Doctor, with his Brace of Aldermen-Stags* (13 September 1684), characterized Oates' more mature taste and its monstrous consequences. We hear

> how a *Doctor* had Defil'd
> Two *Aldermen*, and got 'em both with Child,
> Who Long'd for *Venison*, but were beguil'd.
> The *Pasty* lost, they could no longer tarry,
> With *two Abortive Births*, & *shapes* as vary,
> They fell in *Labour* and of both Miscarry.

Dryden's poem assumes an educable audience, one main part of which is David and Absalom. The portraits thus allow them to objectify their own state – Absalom's cause in Oates' ugly body, David's unbridled sexuality in ducal philandering and infant death. This device allows its own expansion and warning evoked by the biblical characters. One part of the Zimri tale, for instance, also is addressed to Absalom, and makes plain that in rebellion not even a pretender is safe. In 1 Kings 16.11 Zimri kills King Elah and so exterminates his line that "he left him not one that pisseth against a wall, neither of his kinsfolk, nor of his friends." When Zimri's short reign is threatened by Omri and his troops, Zimri incinerates himself in the king's palace. Bishop Patrick's concise comment on Zimri as a traitor and usurper "abandoned by God" places him in a relevant historical context: "So *Sardanapalus* ended his Life" (2:424). David also is warned through his biblical opposition. Shimei is an emblem of deserved punishment deservedly inflicted. David patiently suffers Shimei's insults, Bishop Patrick observes, not "out of meer Greatness of Spirit" that disdains baseness, "but acknowledges the Justice of them, and bears them with a singular Patience, out of Humility, and Reverence to God, who had so ordered it." Moreover, "what were the Revilings of a Stranger, to the murderous Intentions of a Son? And how could he withstand God, who inflicted this Punishment upon him for his Sins?" (2 Sam. 16. 10–11; 2:325). On this hypothesis, David again makes his own world, and must make another before he can improve. And here too Shimei is useful, for he represents himself as God's prophet and thus, Patrick says following Grotius, is free from "the Respect that is to be used to Kings, in not giving them publick Reproaches," for "this alone could make it lawful to speak evil of the King, if God, in a special manner enjoined it" (verse 10; 2:325). The false prophet Shimei, we shall see, contrasts with the true prophet Nathan just as the false corrector of the king, Bethel, contrasts with the true correctors, the loyal representatives of church, Lords, and Commons. But these men can appear in the poem only after Shimei has been inflicted on David, and he has seen what he has wrought.

Perhaps of greatest importance, however, is the three enemies' shared trait of defeat by David. They have shown David the fruits of his folly; they also show him the fruits of patience, fidelity to God, and the ultimate triumph of the state's justice when supported by God's power. Accordingly, Numbers 25 enlarges upon Zimri's own threat to himself. He wishes to be chief and thinks himself above the law, blatantly takes a woman in contempt of Moses' and of God's authority when Israel had begun its repentance, and induces his own and the woman's death by Phineas' javelin of God's justice: "So the Plague was stayed from the Children of Israel" (verse 8). As Bishop Patrick says, the story "argues *Zimri* to have been very impudently wicked, who thought himself so great a Man, that no Judge durst meddle with him" (1:676). Commentary on Shimei also is instructive. Dryden complains that "During his Office, Treason was no Crime" (line 597), and that he packed juries to liberate the like-minded from secular law: "For Laws are only made to Punish those, / Who serve the King, and to protect his Foes" (lines 610–11). 2 Samuel, however, demonstrates that such triumphs over law are brief and ineffectual, and that divine power and justice protect the anointed. Though Shimei curses David, and would have killed him if he could, "all the Mighty Men were on [David's] right hand, and on his left," and so, Patrick observes, "*Shimei*'s Rage was little less than Madness; for he could not hurt *David*, but might have been immediately killed himself" (2:324). He is not killed only because David does not allow the eager Abishai to act: "There was admirable

Discipline observed in this small Army, none of which durst stir without *David*'s Order, or Leave" (verse 9; 2:325). Shimei's illusory power is twice brought home – first in 2 Samuel 23, when the now triumphant David agrees to spare him, and finally in 1 Kings 2. 44–46, when David's son Solomon executes Shimei: "The Lord shall return thy wickedness upon thine own head" (verse 44). Temporal power fails before the restored state's power replete with divine justice.

Corah's death supplies the third such lesson. Dryden recalls Corah's biblical relevance by describing Oates' "*Moses*'s Face" (line 649) – that is, his challenge to the authority of Moses and his brother Aaron as God's chosen priests. Oates' "Zeal to heav'n, made him his Prince despise" (line 672); his analogue Corah defies Moses and accuses him of duplicity, arbitrary acts, and usurpation of authority. Like the other characters this one also tells us about the benevolent adversary. Moses is generous and forgiving towards his people, intervening on behalf of the wavering congregation, in fulfilled hopes that God will distinguish between the seducer and the seduced. The merciful God encourages merciful Moses, who in turn encourages a wavering people to make the right choice. Like Jotham in the poem, some Israelites choose the wrong side and are allowed to change, as David himself must. Furthermore, Corah's actions evoke a brief speech from Moses that is a relevant if distant analogue to David's at the end of *Absalom and Achitophel*. Bishop Patrick's paraphrase upon Numbers 16–28 sounds like a comment upon the restoration of Charles and the later Exclusion Crisis:

I have been commissioned by *God* to do all the things with which those Men find fault; particularly to take upon me the Government of them, and to put *Aaron* and his Family into the Priesthood, and make the *Levites* only their Ministers . . . It was none of my own device or contrivance: I did it not out of an ambitious desire to be great myself, or out of private affection to my Brother. (1:623)

The consequences are plain. Corah and his allies are swallowed up by the earth, though Corah may have been struck by God's lightning; the priesthood of Moses and Aaron is confirmed; and the destroyed false priests become "A Monument of *GOD*'s Displeasure against those that affront his Ministers; to give Warning unto all Posterity not to follow their pernicious Courses" (26.10; 1:680). God's law and power are again allied with those loyal to Him – however much they waver – and again smite the unbelieving. To receive such authority, the teacher must abjure "private affection" and act as if he actually accepted the governance of his people – as thus far in the poem David has not.

A king in name only can be replaced by a king in name only. The poem's internal logic drives towards a necessary inference: the nation requires a new king but he is the old David not the new Absalom. That young man was changed by listening to Achitophel's bad advice; David must change by listening to others' better advice. His ability to do so at once defines his prudent humanity and confirms his divine anointing. The process starts with the poem's own narrator.

✻

Dryden had been both indulgent and forgiving towards Absalom; but that tone and strategy change as Dryden juxtaposes the hated Corah as Absalom's friend, with the hitherto acted upon youth who now deludes the people, does Achitophel's work, and lies about David. Absalom "forsakes the Court" (line 683), but he tells the people that he was banished for them (line 700). He was forgiven for murder, but he claims to be "Expos'd a prey to Arbitrary laws" (line 701). He pretends to wish that, Christlike, he "alone cou'd be undone" (line 702) on their behalf, while he seeks the throne to which he is not entitled. He threatens his king and father with civil war, while he insists that such war would be his father's fault (lines 715, 720). As Achitophel's voice in Absalom's body, he also accepts the new genealogy that Achitophel had offered. Achitophel called him savior (line 240); the crowd "their young *Messiah* bless" (line 728) and make him the "Guardian God" of every new consecrated house he enters (lines 735–36). Accordingly, Absalom not Achitophel becomes associated with the devil or with others who soared too high against paternal advice. He runs from east to west showing his glories, "And, like the Sun, the promis'd land surveys. / Fame runs before him, as the morning Star" (lines 732–33). The morning star is Lucifer, and the young man trying to be like the sun as symbol of kingship, is Phaethon, who stole Apollo's chariot and would have set the world on fire if Zeus had not destroyed him with a thunderbolt. (Some versions of the myth include quarrels regarding Phaethon's legitimacy and Apollo's, or Helios', wrongful indulgence of his handsome son's wish.) Here indeed would be an *Ense rescindendum* if Absalom continued his adventure.

The narrator himself thus encourages us and his monarch to think less well of his potentially murderous son, and begins the poem's and the monarch's new direction. Irony, urbane banter, apparent flattery of phallic prowess, the give-and-take of debate and dialectic – all these disappear with the narrator's answer to his own question, whose key pronoun counters the egoism of Absalom's first person plural: "What shall we think!" (line 759). Dryden, the ally of the indulgent father, becomes the ally of the embattled king in need of political theory and of instruction regarding his son. He may join with the crowds and their representatives, madly rebellious, threatening "To Murther Monarchs for Imagin'd crimes" (line 790), threatening kingship and orderly government, and turning the apparent solidity of a Lockean contract into the actuality of the Hobbesian "Nature's state; where all have Right to all" (line 794). The nature of Charles' sexual lust and the nature of holy bands between father and son, and even nature as the self-serving law of self-defence, become the nature of life as nasty, brutish, and short. Dryden's political coda implies nearly as much about proper fatherhood as it tells about proper kingship. It also supplies the benevolent transition to the king's small party, as the Miltonic context changes from Satan to Abdiel.

Barzillai, the Duke of Ormond, as paragon of the family, begins the catalogue of worthies and immediately brings the "Relief" (line 811) that besieged David requires – namely, the satiric norm of proper relationship between father and son that denotes the proper relationship between king and subject, one explicit in Barzillai's role in 2 Samuel 17.27 and 19.31–39. The several elegies on Ossory include the unsigned *An Second Elegy on that Incomparable Heroe, Thomas Earl of Ossory* (1680) which suggests that link. Ormond is secure in his greatness, not because of his own worth and pure virtue, "No nor in *Charles* his great Affection; / But only, 'cause he had so great a Son." That son also supports and learns from the true royal line.

> Thanks mighty *Hector* of our second *Troy*,
> Thanks for *Astyanax* thy hopeful *Boy*,
> Young *James*, who influenc'd with *Charles* his Care,
> May shortly prove in *Valour* too thine *Heir*.

Dryden himself included the father in more tactful ways, for his Ormond as mighty Hector was valuable not only for his son, but as a model of the old virtues insufficiently practiced either by the court or country party. The aristocrats Absalom and Achitophel support rebellion to sink the nation and raise themselves; Barzillai opposed rebels, suffered for and with his king, and knew him when he was "Godlike" (line 823) in more than propagation. Barzillai's eight legitimate sons offer a silent rebuke of Charles' eight illegitimate sons. In seeking a crown, Absalom thus is merely "Made Drunk with Honour" (line 312) falsely bestowed by Achitophel; Barzillai is more genuinely "crown'd with Honour" (line 818). Achitophel's son was deformed; Absalom's "motions [were] all accompanied with grace"; and Barzillai's son is "with every Grace adorn'd" (line 831). One of these graces was protecting his father from the threats of Buckingham and Shaftesbury, in obvious contrast to Absalom as agent of those threats.[22] The narrator accordingly uses the word "honour" three times for that unAbsalom-like man who "All parts fulfill'd of Subject and of Son" (line 836). Absalom runs from east to west to promote himself; Barzillai's son runs in a "Narrow Circle, but of Pow'r Divine, / Scanted in Space, but perfect in thy Line!" (lines 838–39). In contrast, David's divinity was one of lust (line 19), and his line therefore imperfect and destructive. David's son Absalom won renown in war and threatens to use his skills against his father (lines 23–24; 456–60; 715–20) and against the uncle under whom he had once bravely fought; Barzillai's son also wins renown loyally fighting under James and for David ((lines 840–45). Israel is all too worthy of the rebellious Absalom it resembles; "But *Israel* was unworthy of [Ossory's] Name" (line 846), and God takes him to His own world. Even there he serves his king, for "From thence thy kindred legions mayst thou bring / To aid the guardian Angel of thy King" (lines 852–53). The warm tribute to Barzillai also is a loving corrective for David, who can see the ongoing value to him, to the state, and to heaven in the man whose "Fruitfull Issue" (line 829) benefitted the nation, the family, and the father. David has seen the consequences of his own actions in his son, has heard his poet and free subject offer correctives on his behalf, and now sees that the old values of Barzillai remain models for royal conduct.

Dryden encourages this return to order through other vignettes of faithful individuals from the church, Lords, and Commons. In so doing he furthers one other essential and one other hopeful movement. Again we see the example of proper sons nurturing proper goals in support of the state, as Absalom did not:

> The Prophets Sons by such example led,
> To Learning and to Loyalty were bred:
> For *Colleges* on bounteous Kings depend,
> And never Rebell was to Arts a friend.   (lines 870–73)

As the poem progresses, David seems to respond to this poetic re-education, and now becomes less indulgent towards Absalom. Adriel's loyal service is rewarded with honors "That from his disobedient Son were torn" (line 881). "Sharp judging Adriel" himself, in fact, reinforces the image of the poet and the other respectful critics of a king bound by law. Adriel is "True to his Prince; but not a Slave of State" (lines 877, 879). Immediately thereafter, perhaps like the poet who once praised Cromwell, both the father and the son see the possibility of change and its consequences for the state. Jotham

> onely try'd
> The worse awhile, then chose the better side;
> Nor chose alone, but turn'd the balance too;
> So much the weight of one brave man can doe.[23]   (lines 884–87)

This return to order is epitomized in two other ways – Amiel in the Sanhedrin ably and loyally represents "*Israel*'s Tribes" and can "speak a Loyal Nation's Sense" (lines 906, 905). Israel, once "a Headstrong, Moody, Murmuring race" (line 45), is becoming verbally and intellectually coherent. We see the return of the sober moderate men – and of their rhyme words (line 885) – who previously had "Inclin'd the Ballance to the better side" (line 76) before Absalom subjected himself to Achitophel and anarchy. David and Israel are being educated together, as loyalists unite and perform their own role in government and in correcting the king and nation.

Earlier, Dryden had been spokesman for that nation's best values. Now he prudently allows his superiors to speak directly to the king on behalf of the three estates they represent:

> These Ills they saw, and as their Duty bound,
> They shew'd the King the danger of the Wound:

That no Concessions from the Throne woud please,
But Lenitives fomented the Disease:
That *Absalom*, ambitious of the Crown,
Was made the Lure to draw the People down:
That false *Achitophel*'s pernitious Hate,
Had turn'd the Plot to Ruine Church and State:
The Councill violent, the Rabble worse:
That *Shimei* taught *Jerusalem* to Curse.   (lines 923–32)

Here too Dryden may be calling upon the less attractive parts of the biblical David, who must be reminded of his duties as God's anointed, and be made to suffer through his children. In 2 Samuel 12, God sends the prophet Nathan to instruct David through a parable of a rich man taking a poor man's lamb and slaying it for his own company. The tale angers David, who declares that such a man must make fourfold restitution and die: "And Nathan said unto David, Thou art the Man" (verse 7); David grieves, admits his guilt, and is spared by God, though he loses his infant child borne by Bathsheba and later loses his sons Amnon, Absalom, and Adonijah.

This cautionary tale of sin, punishment, loss of children, repentance, and a message brought from God's true prophet is clear enough, especially when set against the public railings of the false prophet Corah. In 1680 Nathan already had been pressed into poetic service as "God's dread Prophet" to warn the patricidal, rebellious Absalom that God shall destroy him, for "Rebells to Fathers doubly meritt Hell."[24] The apposite commentary, however, relates Dryden's narrator and David's dutiful advisors to Nathan the prophet, each of whom fulfilled his duty by telling the king unpleasant but necessary truths. Bishop Patrick said of Nathan's parable and its relevance for modern kings: "This was a prudent and respectful way of awakening *David*, . . . Which was so managed, that the Prophet did not condemn *David*, but made him condemn himself. And many have very pertinently observed from hence, that there is never more use of Wisdom and Discretion, than in the Contrivance of Reprehension; especially of Princes and great Persons." Moreover, Patrick says, glossing Nathan's statement "Thou art the Man," reproofs "of Men in Authority are to be managed very mannerly." The content should "be plain and downright; so that they may be made sensible of their Guilt," guilt aggravated because of "the Obligations he had to God; who had preferred him to the highest Dignity, when he was in a low, and sometimes desperate Condition" (2:307–8). David's deserved punishment, Patrick argues, comes from divine not secular law. Upon the death of his illegitimate son, David thus prays in the synogogue and thanks God "for the Pardon of his Sin . . . He acknowledged also the Justice of God and did not complain of his Severity. He submitted to his holy Will, and beseeched him, perhaps, that the remaining Afflictions might be moderated and made profitable to him" (2:309). The tangible sign of this repentance is the legitimate son of David and Bathsheba,

Solomon, whom God loved and made famous: "Such is the wonderful Goodness of God to truly penitent Sinners; who . . . thereby incline the divine Goodness to shew further Mercy to them" (2:310). As with much else in the poem's biblical and English history, this context is suggestive rather than congruent. Nonetheless, the figure of Nathan as a genuine prophet superior to Corah allows David to see himself and declare his own guilt. Nathan thereby reinforces Dryden's role as an instigating narrator who transfers authority to the ministers appropriately counseling the king.

In the "Life of Dryden" Johnson complains that David's speech is more the product of romance than of logical structure: "Who can forbear to think of an enchanted castle, with a wide moat and lofty battlements, walls of marble and gates of brass, which vanishes at once into air when the destined knight blows his horn before it?"[25] Had the vanishing been "at once" it indeed would have been romantic; but as I hope to have shown, David's speech is carefully prepared and culminates the varied lessons set before him, not the least of which is his own responsibility in making the world and the son that threaten to destroy him. If David is to survive, he must correct and restore himself – like Barzillai he must be a good father to a well-tutored loyal son; like Jotham he may try the worse awhile but then must choose the better side and bring others with him; like the poet he must understand and speak political sense so that his subjects can know what they should think. As a result of all this, he will again become like the David who had been enthusiastically restored. David demonstrates that he has learned the lessons of Dryden's Nathan-surrogates.[26]

✳

David's speech immediately signals his change and the consequent change of those who depend on him – the patient, indulgent, pagan parent of disruption abjures his earlier fault. The king who had been "inspir'd by some diviner Lust" (line 19) to beget Absalom now speaks "from his Royal Throne by Heav'n inspir'd" (line 936). The king who had been godlike (line 14) in procreating, now is godlike in speaking with God's voice to a subdued audience: "The God-like *David* spoke: with awfull fear / His Train their Maker in their Master hear" (lines 937–38). The speech's genealogy and function insure that it is the only one in the poem that allows neither reply nor exchange. Such a metamorphosis, we recall, is based firmly on royal acceptance and correction of errors – one of which is the improper perception of his son and his people. David thus recognizes that his mercy has been taken for weakness because "So much the Father did the King asswage" (line 942). With his return to kingship, he also returns to manhood, and shifts the image of sexual and political weakness to Absalom. Achitophel would use Absalom to shake "The Pillars of the publick Safety" (line 176); David insists that

"Kings are the publick Pillars of the State" and that if his "Young *Samson*" wants "To shake the Column, let him share the Fall" (lines 953, 955–57). Moreover, these words imply that as king, David himself may be forced to break nature's holy bands if his son threatens the state. Indeed, in the second edition David speaks four new lines in which he shares Dryden's wish that Absalom reject Achitophel and again be his own "Darling Son" (line 433). As father to his nation, David must eliminate rebels who threaten the public peace. Hence, godlike King David, with the power of justice, says of Absalom:

> But oh that yet he would repent and live!
> How easie 'tis for Parents to forgive!
> With how few Tears a Pardon might be won
> From Nature, pleading for a Darling Son!   (lines 957–60)

God, not Achitophel or the people, makes kings, and the agent of God knows the true heir to his throne: "*Esau*'s Hands suite ill with *Jacob*'s Voice" (line 982).

That allusion to Genesis 27.22 has wider implications than are usually seen, for the rejected son Esau at first angrily plans to find his brother and violently regain his birthright. Their mother Rebecca, who instigated the substitution, urges Jacob's flight to her brother until Esau is mollified. Over the years Jacob honors and loves God, is richly rewarded, and upon again meeting his equally well fortuned brother, sends him generous presents. After Jacob wrestles all night with the angel of God, he gains the confidence to face Esau: "And Esau ran to meet him, and embraced him, and fell on his neck, and kissed him, and they wept," and, Jacob adds, "I have seen thy face, as though I had seen the face of God, and thou wast pleased with me" (Genesis 33.4, 10). The tale of Esau and Jacob begins with usurpation, and ends with forgiveness and reconciliation between man and man and man and God. As Bishop Patrick says "For *Esau*'s Kind Reception of him he could not but look upon as a Token of the Divine Favour towards him" (1:117–18). Evocation of Esau thus comments upon David's plea to Absalom: "But oh that yet he would repent and live!"

If Absalom rejects such a model, he will be subject to the rigors of the law and not to David's native mercy. The poem begins with a world in which "no law deny'd" (line 5) David's lust; it then characterizes an unappreciative nation freer from law's limits than any other (line 54). Thereafter, it details several attempted violations of law. Achitophel urges Absalom "To pass your doubtfull Title into Law" (line 408) and usurp his father's role and throne; this would distort "Natures Eldest Law" (line 458) of self-defence into potential patricide and regicide; and it would threaten to turn the source of law into the source of lawlessness if the king is successfully seized by his enemies (line 476). These men can "make Treason Law" (line 582), and free their allies "from Humane Laws" (line 609). In David's final speech, however, divine law augments such corrected human law, as David subjects himself and his nation to hitherto deficient regulation and order. He reforms himself as well as his world: "The Law shall still direct my peacefull Sway, / And the same Law teach Rebels to Obey" (lines 991–92). But his questions suggest both a similarity to the narrator and a wrenching from his normal pattern. Severity is an act of will rather than unguided inclination:

> Oh that my Power to Saving were confin'd:
> Why am I forc'd, like Heav'n, against my mind,
> To make Examples of another Kind?
> Must I at length the Sword of Justice draw?
> O curst Effects of necessary Law!   (lines 999–1003)

These effects were drawn out by his enemies, of course including Absalom and Achitophel, who could neither accept nor understand mercy. Hence, "Law they require, let Law then show her Face" (line 1006) – that is, to tempt death with the sword that Dryden had hoped need not be used.

We have seen the examples of fathers and sons who serve as negative models and then, in examples of Barzillai, the satiric norm that begins the poem's final movement towards David's corrected vision. Dryden uses another image of parent and offspring to show the self-consuming nature of rebellion. The female viper was thought to have bitten off the male's head, which he put in her mouth in order to fertilize her eggs. To revenge their father's considerable discomfort, the adult offspring destroy their own mother (perhaps as this Absalom had also tried to do), an analogue well adapted to the future David predicts for his plotters:

> Against themselves their Witnesses will Swear,
> Till Viper-like their Mother Plot they tear:
> And suck for Nutriment that bloody gore
> Which was their principle of Life before.   (lines 1102–15)

The civil war his enemies wished on him redounds upon themselves, as "on my Foes, my Foes shall do me Right" (line 1,017).

The final couplet of David's speech is both an obvious and subtle sign of his victory, and of his response to the portrait Dryden has encouraged him to see in the poem. Earlier, Achitophel evoked Absalom's wavering answer to his temptation, and encouraged his vice: "Him Staggering so when Hell's dire Agent Found, / While fainting Vertue scarce maintain'd her Ground" (lines 373–74). David absorbs those rhyme words and transforms them in his victory on behalf of law, God's agent and Absalom's and Israel's father: "For Lawfull Pow'r is still Superiour found / When long driven back, at length it stands the ground" (lines 1,024–25) – as follow'd by the epic tag "He said."

Given such a dispensation Dryden needs, finally, to give "external" warrant for David's change from misplaced mercy and pagan licentiousness, to law and divine approbation. He does so by characterizing God's nod of "Consent" and voice of thunder – the consent presumably both to David's and the plotters' transformation. Paradoxically, that transformation is shown through a 21-year-old event, so that the poem's conclusion is simultaneously forward and backward looking. By reverting to his old self he reverts to the image Achitophel had tried to erase:

> He is not now, as when on *Jordan*'s Sand
> The Joyfull People throng'd to see him Land,
> Cov'ring the *Beach*, and blackning all the *Strand*.   (lines 270–72)

The king is indeed even greater, for he creates new time that peacefully extends far into the future by recreating the David and the obedient Israel of the past, as nation and monarch again are one:

> Once more the Godlike *David* was Restor'd,
> And willing Nations knew their Lawfull Lord.   (lines 1030–31)

They know their king because both he and Israel have restored themselves. David becomes a true father once he becomes an obedient son to the true God, whose will he carries out by helping to defeat the Belials and Beelzebubs of the world, a contest that far surpasses anything in the secular Virgilian associations of a distant Jove who merely aids Aeneas' imperial expansion.[27]

Absalom and Achitophel, then, exploits assumptions shared by Whigs and Tories – the honor and love due from the son to the father, and the violation of those duties by the title characters. The poem also makes plain that however much it sides with the king, part of its greatness as a satire is in its willingness respectfully to place blame where it belongs. By so doing, Dryden also shows that David is not an unswerving absolute monarch, but a great man and king able to change and again be known to his God and nation. David's vices are amended by Dryden's friendly, physician-like healing satire which, at a crucial point, yields to the experienced seconding ministers' voices and then to David's. In the poem, at least, David's wisdom affirms Dryden's view of satire. Absalom and Achitophel could neither read nor respond so well. Shaftesbury died in exile in Holland; Monmouth was executed after a foolish rebellion against James II in 1685. Contrary to Dryden's hopes, the devil was not saved, and the sick disciple was not spared a fatal *Ense rescindendum*. The real triumph of Dryden's poem, though, is the gradual education of the restored father and king, as nature's holy bands become bands between king and country and king and God, and a world is regained.

7 · *THE RAPE OF THE LOCK*
AND THE CONTEXTS OF WARFARE

Until recently, all of us knew the essential facts and interpretations regarding *The Rape of the Lock*. It was written as a jeu d'esprit to unify two neighboring Catholic families in hopes that Arabella Fermor and Robert, Lord Petre, would be reconciled. In 1712 it appeared in two cantos; in 1714 in five, with the full machinery of the sylphs and gnomes; and in 1717 in Pope's first collected *Works*, with Clarissa's speech added. The poem, we were told, sets Pope's fragile culture against the superior culture evoked in his parody of epic devices. Pope does not taint Homer's epic, but the modern pseudo-heroes whose moral diminution is well reflected in the sylphs and the trivial act of cutting off a woman's lock of hair. On this hypothesis, even Clarissa, Pope's own spokeswoman, provides good sense because that is all such a world can aspire to. As three shrewd and very different modern commentators have put it, "in mock-epic a dignified genre is turned to witty use without being cheapened in any way"; "the essence of Pope's wit in the *Rape of the Lock* lies in ... the appeal of a better world of noble manners and actions. Cutting the lock is ... more than absurd"; or in another severe judgment, Pope's lines "do violence to Homer's passages, adulterate them, because the weak and sordid modern culture adulterates the simple purity of the Homeric life."[1]

However inadequate, these familiar views served some useful purposes – they directed us to the poem's mock form, epic forebears, and moral norm of Clarissa's speech. All things are subject to decay. In an aberration to which I must in part contribute, the poem's elegant lightness now is darkened by learned allusions; the sylphs are demonic and satanic; Pope's mock epic itself is a capitalist tool and the product of an elitist male poet who ridicules women; and Clarissa's speech is either ironic, or a woeful constraint upon woman's role, or both. She has been called a "narrow, hypocritical" opportunist, and "ostrich-like" in preparing one for old age and death; she also is "an envious prude" who wants to harm Belinda to help herself with the baron; and she is so filled with "high-minded insincerity" and "falsity" that in comparison even Thalestris' angry, martial harangue is "honest, life-engaging."[2]

Though much of the direction of these inquiries seems to me both wrong and wrongheaded, the search for new light on *The Rape of the Lock* is welcome. We should indeed rethink the poem's epic contexts, the function of its mock-heroic, and Clarissa's and Thalestris' roles in the poem. Discussion of the epic begins with Homer's Anglo-French reputation during the later seventeenth and earlier eighteenth centuries.

A Schism among the Wits

From at least the early Renaissance, Homer was regarded as the father of the poets, the master of all knowledge, and classical antiquity's preeminent poet. He also was ideologically pure, since the moral of his *Iliad* was the need for a unified state under Jove's vicegerent. In 1660 John Ogilby thus dedicates his translation of Homer to Charles II and prudently says "that which may render [Homer] yet more proper for Royal Entertainment is, That he appears a most constant assertor of the Divine Right of Princes and Monarchical Government." In Hanoverian 1714 that argument was less compelling, but Homer apparently was not. Richard Fiddes speaks of Homer's "universal Esteem . . . in all Ages," the "universal Genius" he embodies, and the "Danger . . . either to revive, or raise Objections against" him. One year later Thomas Parnell concludes his "Essay on . . . Homer" prefatory to Pope's *Iliad* by reminding us that Homer was the comprehensive "Father of Learning," and left behind him "A Work which shall always stand at the top of the sublime Character, to be gaz'd at by Readers with an Admiration of its Perfection, and by Writers with a Despair that it should ever be emulated with Success."[3]

Nonetheless, all was not placid in the world of letters, and Fiddes and Parnell write as if cloistered from the preceding half century's bitter literary debates. Hostility to Homer had been growing throughout the seventeenth century, especially in France. Desmarets de Saint-Sorlin, for example, wrote several impassioned works urging the virtues of his modern Christian century, and the vices of ancient, pagan, Greece and Rome. By 1671 Gabriel Gueret had written his *Parnassus reformé* and reported that all was changed in the republic of letters. War has broken out among authors, the academy is divided, and there is a schism among the wits. The French academy itself became an anti-Homeric command post, first under the leadership of Charles Perrault in 1687, and then of Houtar de la Motte in 1714.[4] The polite label for this impolite confrontation was the *querelle des anciens et des modernes*, in which Homer figured prominently for two generations in England as in France. By 1707, for example, Samuel Cobb complained that Homer was "so much the Ridicule of our *Beaux Esprits*."[5]

This effort was helped by successful attacks on Aristotle's science, which gave aid and comfort to attacks on his literary criticism. As Saint-Evremond put it, natural philosophers observed errors in Aristotle's physics, and poets "spy'd out faults in his *Poeticks*, at least with respect to us." Consequently, Pierre Bayle observes, by the later seventeenth-century faith in Aristotle "has been violently shaken." The abbés Jean Terrasson and Jean-François de Pons recognized, respectively, the roles of Perrault and Houtar in what they regarded as the moderns' victory over the ancients. Accordingly, Terrasson said that "the Fall of *Aristotle* had already . . . prepared Men's Minds" to reject the ancients and this victory "carried its Light into Homer."[6] Homer and Aristotle thus were the chief dragons guarding the ancients' gates to Parnassus; slay them and all the other dragonettes – Bossu, the Daciers, Rymer, Dennis – would die as well. That is what the Anglo-French moderns, many of whom also admired classical, especially Latin, literature, set out to do. The many opponents of Homer found four basic areas of weakness: plot, language and decorum, the nastiness of the gods, and the brutality of the heroes.

"Absolutely sunk and Ruin'd": Anti-Homeric Paradigms

As René Rapin reported, the *Iliad* has two incoherent actions. That of the Trojan War is imperfect since within the poem it lacks both a beginning and an end; that of Achilles' anger against Agamemnon lacks an end and a middle, for rage against Hector soon replaces it. The defective plot has neither the regularity nor proportion "in which alone consists the Perfection of a Great Work."[7] Even after the death of Hector, which ought to have concluded the poem, we find two more books "which are Foreign to the Purpose, the Principal Action being perfect without them" (p. 178). Homer's plot also includes too many improbable miracles, requires that everything be "done by Machines" (p. 147), and that the most commonplace of wisdom can be ferried to the world by peripatetic gods. Digressions are equally troubling, for Homer rarely keeps to his subject, piles episode upon episode, and is hurried along by his uncontrolled imagination. Every encounter encourages him "to tell Stories, and derive Genealogies" (p. 153).

Homer's linguistic and moral decorums were no better than his fable. Rapin was outraged that "Kings and Princes in *Homer* talk to one another with all the Scurrility imaginable." Agamemnon treats the father and priest Chryses insolently, and that priest himself then behaves without dignity, charity, or patriotism by calling down Apollo's curse on the Greeks, when his office required that he pray for them "and for the Preservation of the Government." Homer violates several other social and literary conventions: "Fathers are harsh and cruel, the Heroes weak and passionate, the Gods expos'd to Miseries, uneasie and quarrelsome, and incens'd against one another" (pp. 152–55). Shortly thereafter, the Abbé D'Aubignac filled his own *Dissertation sur l'Iliade* with specific and general complaints concerning the gods' and heroes' language and conduct towards one another: "Mars appelle Minerve mouche de chien, Dianne appelle son frère Apollon un fou, et Junon appelle Dianne une chienne. Achille nom Apollon le plus méchant de tous les Dieux, et Hector l'appelle un chien et un fou." Indeed, when the gods and men were not fighting, they debased themselves by eating. D'Aubignac also laments that "ils sont toujours à table, ils ont toujours le verre à la main; et toute la félicité de leur vie céleste et glorieuse, n'est qu'une goinfrerie perpétuelle." Homer wrongly leaves before us "une image de gens attachés à la crapule."[8] As the appearance of Mars and Venus trapped in Vulcan's net shows, the unmajestic gods also lack the "Air of Gravity . . . Essential to an Heroick Poem." Nor are the human beings more reverent to the gods; the story of Venus being wounded by Diomedes borders on burlesque (p. 160).

Thus harried, Homer's gods found themselves fleeing for their celestial lives through much of Europe. Even René le Bossu, who convinced himself and others that the gods were allegorical, admitted that "some" think Homer gave those gods "such *Manners* as turn them into mere Swine." This judgment was shared by many, including Giambattista Vico, who regarded the gods as villainous, by Houtar who called them despicable, by Saint-Hyacinthe who labelled them vicious, powerless, and often worse than the fools who asked their help, and by Andrew-Michael Ramsay, who thought them debased.[9]

Homer's heroes, especially Achilles, are as unattractively criminal as the gods they resemble. According to Rapin, Homer blundered in making Achilles "not so much as Rational" but brutal, a vice Aristotle knew to be "directly opposite to Heroick Vertue" and one that disgraced Achilles by causing the needless death of so many men "whom he sacrific'd to his Grief and Discontent" (pp. 124–25). This barbarous and cruel hero, Rapin concludes, epitomizes "Imperfections and Vices" (p. 131). D'Aubignac both berates the princes who argue like thieves over their booty and seem to make war for gain not for honor (p. 84), and rejects the horror of their incessant bloody combat and vaunting insults to the dead and dying. In 1693 Samuel Wesley labels Achilles "a perfect Almanzor, with not one spark of Vertue, and only remarkable for his extraordinary Strength and little Brains." The widely read Pierre Bayle exemplifies such resentment. He wonders how any one can still admire the *Iliad*, or how Horace could boast of memorizing all of that poem in which Achilles behaves with such inexcusable venality. His acts "are so repugnant, not only to heroic virtue, but even to the most common generosity; that we must conclude, either that Homer had no idea of heroism, or that he designed to draw the character of a brutal wretch. He represents Achilles, wishing himself brute enough, to devour Hector's raw flesh."[10] No wonder that in 1715 Jean Terrasson says that as for battles, one should "imitate all the Poets in the World except Homer" (2:306).

His imperfections were enhanced by the many well-known burlesques which Pope knew and, as the *Dunciad* makes plain, provided congenial devices for him. In addition, the burlesques also put in rude form what more solemn commentators had put in polished form. For all the burlesques' vulgarity, they reflect and enlarge an important body of literary, social, and cultural criticism.

Homer à la Mode

The motives of these often obscene poems include exposing Homer for what he is to make plain that he is not a superior of the moderns. Charles Cornwall admits that the *Iliad* may be pleasing, but insists that it is no more "Than a Parcel of wild, imaginary undertakings" in which an absurd hero does absurd things beyond the reach of man in some never-never land – "and this, forsooth, must be call'd *An Hero*. And . . . must have the exalted Title of *An Heroick Poem*." Actually, it is uninformed and "very inferiour, and paultry" when contrasted with Christian dispensation.[11]

One reason for this slovenly inadequate mind and its poem was offered in a commonplace regarding Homer's genealogy. He was not an exalted man of letters, but a beggarly poet rambling about Aegean Smithfield fairs, singing for his supper, and patching together various incoherent rhapsodies concerning Troy or Ulysses. Alternatively, he never existed at all, and was simply the name given to a rag-tag assortment of ballads which, 500 years later, Pisistratus of Athens organized into loose medleys called the *Iliad* and the *Odyssey*.[12] Nothing could be expected from such a poet, who, Burnet and Duckett rationalize, may as well be translated into burlesque verse that a Yorkshire milk-maid could understand.[13] Such language also was appropriate, Abbé Terrasson probably would agree, because as "the Original, Source, and Principle of all Burlesque Morality" Homer "presents the most open Vice and Obscenities and formally recommends the most shameful Actions" (2:204). Consequently, the Homer of the parodists supplies a full menu of luscious sins. Many of these writers assumed that Homer's plot was absurd, and so they mingled burlesques of barbarous language and decorum, the heroes, and the gods. No one fared well.

Neither the crudity of rhetoric nor of table manners escaped the parodists' notice. A literal translation of Achilles' harangue to Agamemnon in Book 1, Burnet and Duckett claim, will seem more like a "a Dialogue between two *Watermen*" than "the Speech of one great King to another about a Parson's Daughter, whom they had made a whore of" (pp. 11–12). James Scudamore and the pseudonymous Nickydemus Ninnyhammer characterize the Greeks' disgusting culinary adventures in which, for example, a newly butchered heifer is so mangled, cut, torn, and hashed it was "enough to make / One spew; it would so turn one's Stomach."[14] *Deuteripideuteron* of 1681 is even more graphic as it reverses roles. In its epic feast the Cyclops is the hero who turns two of Ulysses' men into his own rough meal:

> He dasht their brains against the Bed-post;
> Brains (though but few) fell on the ground,
> Comixt with blood, and there this Hound
> Tearing them piece-meal with gub-teeth
> Sat down and eat them just like Beef.
> First he their thighs devour'd gladly,

> Then on their yellow Buttocks fed he,
> Nay guts and garbage, which look nastily;
> One would not eat a turd so hastily;
> As he their flesh and bones did swallow;
> Nay made the very Pr—s to follow:
> And Sav'd the Piss, that ran down heels,
> In a huge Bowl, to drink at meals.[15]

The heroes embodied another form of criticized epic barbarism, sexual vulgarity and indifference to everything but self-gratification. The putative Henry Fitzcotton's Achilles thus tells us how he and his men satisfy their tender longings:

> When convents happen in our way,
> Each takes his nun, that very day:
> We make an honest dividend;
> And when that's done – why there's an end.

Such amusements and deposits were meager in comparison with the many other references to pudenda, sexual functions, and ancillary acts. In *Homer A la Mode. The Second Part* (1681) Agamemnon promises to give Achilles anything, including all of his daughters, if he will return to the war. He swears

> By *Gargantua*'s monstrous ware,
> And by *Pantagruel*'s huge Tarse,
> And by the foistings of mine Ar—
> Nay, and I'le swear by that same Odpiece
> Of flesh hangs dangling in *Jove*'s Codpiece.[16]

Lest Homer's women should demand equal treatment, Nickydemus Ninnyhammer parodies Book III of the *Iliad*, in which a reluctant Paris and an eager Menelaus box in order to end the war and, as Hector puts it, determine who "May take fair *Nelly* and go f—k her" (p. 52). She watches the unequal battle, observes her husband's "swinging B—ks" (p. 57), and retires as her lover is saved by Venus' intervention. The pimping goddess insists that Helen go to bed with Paris, searches her out, and finds that so inventive and communal a spirit hardly needs a man:

> in a Garret
> She found her f—gg—g with a Carrot;
> With many a Finger F–k–g Neighbour,
> All groping, just as at a Labour. (p. 63)

In so iconoclastic a tradition the ancient warriors and wise men received no quarter. For many writers even the courage of those exemplary killing machines was suspect. At different times, both the frightened Greek and Trojan sides beshit themselves, cut their own throats, abandon their men, require the help of the gods to conquer a lone hero, and scarcely deserve that exalted name. As Nickydemus says, Achilles also is a cry-baby, for when he

105

surrenders Briseis he "cry'd and roar'd like any Noddy" and "for that Oyster-whore his Mother / He bawl'd, and made an heavy pother" (p.13). Similarly, the Nestor of *Homer A la Mode* in 1681 makes plain that most of the Greeks are witless, that Agamemnon has "few" brains (pp. 8, 12), and that the other Greek leaders are a filching knave, a fool, and a clown (p. 20).

The parodists also knew that the gods were as scurrilous as those who prayed to them. Their sexual vulgarity could take the form of a goddess seducing a god in order to get brutal wishes granted for a mortal. Achilles thus asks his mother Thetis for a small favor – convincing Jove to permit the Trojans to slaughter all the Greeks as their punishment for angering him. "Draw your stool nigher" to Jove, James Scudamore's Achilles urges "And stroke his knees, or something higher" (p. 48). Nickydemus' Vulcan gives the gods the giggles and Juno incontinence when he explains that after being thrown out of heaven and falling for three days, "I sprain'd Two Legs – but not my middle" (p. 18). Charles Cornwall is especially rich in divine dalliance of varied sorts. To hide the battered Paris, Venus "Piss't full in *Menelaus*' Eyes" (p. 49); she then becomes "The pimping *Cytharaean* Queen: With naked Breasts, and brazen Face" (p. 53) who coerces Helen into bed with Paris, and hears that matron lament – "aren't we cunning Prigs, / To dance to all your bawdy Jigs?" Thanks to Venus, any booby now can have "A Lick at *Helen*'s Gallipot" (p. 54). This crassness is present as well in Thomas Bridges' long, later-eighteenth-century culmination of the burlesque tradition. Diomedes' wounding of Venus after she protects the vulnerable Aeneas is a comic rendering of sex and violence. Diomedes

> with his tool the goddess enter'd;
> With such a force he drove it in,
> It made the light heel'd gipsy grin:
> Strait from the place where he did stick her
> There came a bright transparent liquor.

Apollo then explains the incident to Mars:

> The whelp at *Venus* push'd and hit her
> With such a tool, I thought he'd split her;
> But she in dangers ever calm,
> Receiv'd it in her sweaty palm,
> There held it fast, and made it stand,
> And *spend* its venom in her hand.[17]

Neither milk-maid nor maid-of-honor could misunderstand such sexual play in the burlesques of Homer: whether in the natural or supernatural, male or female worlds, sex was casual, illicit, violent, self-propelled, prostituted, any or all of the above, and provocation for bloody and lengthy warfare about an irresponsible adulterous woman and her cowardly lover.

Pope's *Rape of the Lock*, then, does not emerge from a perceived grand past that dwarfs an inadequate present. For many commentators, the opposite was true. They might agree that the *Rape* and its contrasting Homeric backgrounds do show the triumph of heroic grandeur, but with more than compensating modern manners and achievements. As Pope's contemporaries recognized, the eras of great epic ventures in Greece and Rome were disjointed and savage times that one would not wish to relive; a great poem is little recompense for great slaughter. In 1735 Thomas Blackwell thus observes that "tho' the Pleasure arising from a Taste of the sublimer kinds of Writings, may make" readers "regret the Silence of the [epic] Muses" today, nonetheless we must wish *"That we may never be a proper Subject of an* Heroic Poem."[18]

Indeed, the more characters in *The Rape of the Lock* embrace epic values and conventions, the less pleasant they are. The baron's prayer to the goddess of Love, for example, includes a mischievous combination of Achilles' and Ulysses' traits – he hopes "by Force to ravish, or by Fraud betray";[19] the gods themselves are characteristically unreliable and later grant only half his prayer so that he acquires but cannot keep the lock (2.45). Both Belinda's triumphant vaunting after her victory in the card-game (2.99–100) and the baron's refusal to return the raped object (3.161–70; 4.131–40) are adaptations of epic heroes' ungenerous self-absorption, like Achilles' refusal to return Hector's body until his suppliant father ransoms it.[20] Sir Plume's driveling speech (4.127–30) is consistent with several commentators' notions of heroic wisdom. The final scenes' collapse of social values and rise of universal violence that pleases the interested gods also is drawn from the Homeric epic.

On the other hand, when the poem is most modern and least disagreeable, it negates epic values. Unlike the apparently rambling *Iliad*, *The Rape of the Lock* is meticulously coherent.[21] It also begins with an allusion to the "dire Offence [that] from am'rous causes springs" (1.1) – as with the genocide of the Trojan War because of Helen, and the eternal enmity between Rome and Carthage, and its consequent sacking because of Aeneas' abandonment of Dido. In Pope's poem, sexual rapaciousness is sublimated into a courtship ritual. The card-game also is a mating dance and a ritualized expression of potentially violent sexual energy. That world's violence also is restrained through ceremony, so that "with Sword-knots, Sword-knots strive" (1.101); the sword is sheathed, ornamented with ribbons, and serves more like a male peacock's feathers than an instrument of death.[22] Unlike the characteristic exhortation to kill, Clarissa's speech is an exhortation to engage life. The epic feast is not the Homeric culinary debauch, but an elaborately civilized coffee and tea service that also is an emblem of the pacific interdependence of modern trading nations thought to be God's will.[23] Moreover, this poem also is presented by a protective, encouraging narrator, who begins and ends in his own benevolent voice, and, unlike Homer, refuses to allow the creatures he has made to come to bad ends. He has memorialized Belinda in art, and Belinda has ennobled him by the folly that evoked his poem: "It will be in vain to deny that I have some Regard for this Piece, since I Dedicated it to You," he says in his prefatory letter's first line (p. 142). "*This Lock*, the Muse shall consecrate to Fame, / And mid'st the Stars inscribe *Belinda*'s Name" (5.149–50), he says in the final couplet. For Homer, there is harmony within Achilles, among the Greek leaders, and between men and gods only after the venting of vast amounts of blood. For Pope, such harmony returns after affectionate scolding and a brief allusion to the difference between the permanence of art and the transience of the life we had best live while we can.

Such a view is not inconsistent with Pope's willingness to spend some twenty years translating the deservedly esteemed *poet* Homer. But he was as eclectic and often judicious in his affection for Homer as for Virgil and Horace, each of whom he and many others faulted on moral and political grounds. Pope says, for example, that Homer's plot is "a confused Heap of Beauties," his love of slaughter is offensive, and his use of some metaphors is indecent. Pope will not even translate the animal's name to which Ajax is likened in Book XI;[24] he assumes that Agamemnon's hold on Chryses' daugher is motivated by lust not by kingly prerogative; and he regards Thetis' advice that Achilles stop mourning Patroclus and take Briseis to bed as an outrage to decency and in its "Expression . . . almost obscene" (TE, 8:543n; *Iliad*, XXIV.168). In several places he thus makes plain that he has absorbed the ancients' and, especially, the moderns' objections to Homer. As he says at the end of a long attack on Homer's combats of the gods in *Iliad* XXI.566, "*Homer* never better deserv'd than in this place the Censure past upon him by the Ancients, that as he rais'd the Characters of his Men up to Gods, so he sunk those of Gods down to Men" (TE, 8:445n).

These deviations were heresies to a true Homerophile like Madame Dacier, whose second edition of her own translated *Iliad* (1719) includes a gratuitously insulting addendum on Pope's ignorance for even suggesting that Homer's divine robes had moth holes. Perhaps one reason for her rage was that she sensed Pope's mediating role among Homer's detractors. The serious commentators establish a large body of hostile critical discourse; the parodists employ that discourse to reduce Homer to absurdity; Pope then plays a variation on both themes. He accepts each group's criticism of Homer, but unlike his prose ancestors does so in a pleasing way; unlike the parodists he does so in a polite way. The reader drugged by an academic treatise or scandalized by a frigging Helen would find *The Rape of the Lock* a perfect mine for sapping Homeric walls. No wonder Madame Dacier groused that "The most inveterate Enemies to *Homer* never said any thing more injurious, or more unjust against that Poet" than Pope did in the preface to his *Iliad*.[25] As I hope to show, Pope's rejection of Homer's deification is as present in the body of his mock poem as in the preface and notes to his real translation.

In light of these reclaimed, indeed subversive, contexts and contrasts we may wish to reconsider some of the older critical dogmas with which I began – that Pope's poem shows how "weak and sordid modern culture adulterates the simple purity of the Homeric life" and that his mock epic does not cheapen the distant "dignified genre." We may also wish to reconsider two newer critical dogmas – for several commentators Thalestris is to be applauded, and for many others Clarissa is to be excoriated.

Belinda and Thalestris

The fragility of Belinda's world has long been recognized in images of broken china vessels;[26] but it also is a dangerous world which kills those who make improper moves on its battle field. Britain's statesmen at Hampton Court "doom" women there; even the ordinary heroes and nymphs so interpret behavior that "At ev'ry Word a Reputation dies" (3.5, 15–16). The famous couplet, "The hungry Judges soon the Sentence sign, / And Wretches hang that Jury-men may Dine" (3.21–22), suggests that Belinda is in danger of a parallel social death, degradation, and dishonor (4.107–12).[27] Like other martial or sexual warriors, however, she courts the death she hopes to avoid. The sylphs' advice in Canto 1 that she beware of man, for example, vanishes once she awakens and reads a love letter (1.114–20); she also soon uses traditional female war-paint for a sexual skirmish at Hampton Court.[28]

The game of ombre there tell us much about Belinda's values. She declares herself the challenger, the ombre or man who hopes to defeat her opponent the baron.[29] As the challenger, she has the right to declare the trumps, and does so in a radically biblical way: "*Let Spades be Trumps!* she said, and Trumps they were" (3.46). Pope gives her both God's creative mantle and a version of the words Longinus cited as the archetype of divine sublimity, in which thought and deed are simultaneous.[30] Since she seems as confidently in control of her world as any god, she "swells her Breast with Conquests yet to come" (3.28) and makes herself even more attractive to her hopeful lover.

The card-game takes the form of a miniature epic battle, in which each side advances, retreats, and takes prisoners on "the Velvet Plain" (3.44). The battle also cleanses human hostility and becomes a surrogate sexual confrontation, in which the "*Queens* . . . hands sustain a Flow'r, / Th' expressive Emblem of their softer Power" (3.39–40), knaves hold phallic "Halberds in their hand" (3.42), and the King of Spades puts forth a sexual "manly Leg" (3.57). When Belinda seems to be winning, the baron rallies, pours forth his diamonds, routs her cards, "And wins (oh shameful Chance!) the *Queen of Hearts*. / At this, the Blood the Virgin's Cheek forsook," and she sees herself "in the Jaws of Ruin" (3.88–89, 92). With the score tied at four tricks apiece, Belinda in turn rallies and uses her King of Hearts to win the game, which she celebrates with shouts of victory. Belinda, then, shows herself sexually enticing, socially aggressive, apparently dominant, and willing to confront the baron in a game whose rules announce and sublimate cruder passions. At the subsequent coffee-table-cum-epic feast, ceremony and rules begin to collapse.

The baron indecorously clips Belinda's lock, refuses to return it, and shows that he now is master of their world. Belinda must regain authority or suffer a predictable social death, one, Pope's additions and notes make plain, she herself encourages. In new lines added in 1714 Belinda ignores the sylphs' three warnings of the baron's approach, forces Ariel's withdrawal when he sees "An Earthly Lover lurking at her Heart" (3.144), and implicitly permits the lock to be taken by the man to whom she has just puffed her breasts, and by whom her heart had been put in "wild Disorder" (3.79). Belinda nonetheless can turn the "rape" into the purest chastity if she abandons childish games and fantasies of omnipotence and makes a prudent choice. Pope clarified the nature of that choice in his portrait of the fashionable upper-class malady, the spleen.

Ariel's surrender means Umbriel's assumption of power, which he improves by taking an epic journey to the underworld. Traditionally, this served at least two relevant purposes – to bring the tools of the gods to man, and to bring the future to the hero. Umbriel thus acquires a bag which holds "the Force of Female Lungs, / Sighs, Sobs, and Passions, and the War of Tongues," and a vial with "fainting Fears, / Soft Sorrows, melting Griefs, and flowing Tears" (4.83–86). Aeneas' subterranean adventure shows him Rome's imperial expansion and fulfillment; Umbriel's shows him Belinda's potential world of migraine headaches, ill-nature, painted, wrinkled, ancient maidens, religious hypocrites, lampoons, affectation, languishing pride, and horrible visions. Perhaps above all, we see the consequences for maids – a word repeated four times – who accept such sexual and other frustrations: with spleen, "Maids turn'd Bottels, call aloud for Corks" (4.54).

Upon returning to the world, Umbriel finds Belinda sunk in Thalestris' arms, releases spleen's bag of Furies over their heads, and evokes Thalestris' furious, consuming speech, as "*Belinda* burns with more than mortal Ire, / And fierce *Thalestris* fans the rising Fire" (4.93–94). After some heated jeremiad, she defines honor as appearance rather than virtue, and characterizes herself and the danger she believes Belinda is now in:

> Methinks already I your Tears survey,
> Already hear the horrid things they say,
> Already see you a degraded Toast,
> And all your Honour in a Whisper lost!
> How shall I, then, your helpless Fame defend?
> 'Twill then be Infamy to seem your Friend. (4.107–12)

When Sir Plume's foolish speech fails to regain the lock from the baron, Umbriel breaks the Vial of Sorrows over Belinda's head; she then worsens a bad situation, and remains trapped by her own self-pity. She curses the day and wishes that she had abjured the seductive court for "some lone Isle, or distant *Northern* Land" (4.154). Her beauty should have been hidden "from mortal eye, / Like Roses that in Desarts bloom and die" (4.157–58). If only, she moans in lines immediately thought indecent, the baron had "been content to seize / Hairs less in sight, or any Hairs but these!" (4.175–76).[31] Belinda thus accepts two sets of threatening values – sexual withdrawal that leads to the sexual anorexia in the Cave of Spleen, and moral withdrawal that leads to virtue as a public pose and beauty as an object of sterile adoration rather than productive attraction. On the poem's own terms, Thalestris as a guide leads Belinda down dangerous roads.

Thalestris and the Amazons

Pope colors our response to Thalestris in other contextual ways. As an Amazon she came trailing malevolent associations. If Amazons existed, commentators agreed, they either cut off, burned off, or stunted by binding the right breast in order to strengthen the right arm and clear an obstruction in pulling a bow string or throwing a spear. This form of body sculpture was joined by worse for the male children who were returned to their fathers by an occasional dovish mother, or if less fortunate were killed, castrated, crippled, to which Pope must have been especially sensitive, or enslaved as the case may be.[32] Since children of either sex emerge from traditional copulation, the Amazons insured that such acts were unblemished by affection. As Samuel Johnson translates the Abbé Guyon's commonplace *Histoire des Amazones* in 1741, "lest any Lady might give Reason for Suspicion that she had any tender Passion for the other Sex, no Virgin was allowed to pay this annual Visit [to men of the neighboring nation], 'til she had, by killing three Men, shewn how much she detested them, and how much her Race deserved to be propagated."[33]

Such a tale contributed to the image of Amazons in general and Thalestris in particular as types both of the aggressive and sexually hungry woman. In 1679 the amorous author of *The Enjoyment* praises his Silvia for rousing his phallic heroism: "She like some Amazon" delights in the sexual combat that can "gently raise his head" when he is briefly conquered and at rest (p. 2). As what John Biddle called "shameless lewd Viragoes," however, Amazons often were vilified rather than exalted for their sexual prowess. By 1693 Dryden's Juvenal refers to a "strutting Amazonian Whore."[34] Thereafter, Pierre Danet, Père Gautruche, and Claude Marie Guyon agree that, in Danet's words, the Amazons "prostituted their Bodies to Strangers" whom they took, according to Guyon, "without Distinction of Affection." By mid century Lord Chesterfield used Amazons to characterize Dutch ponderousness. Dutch women at home, he writes, "are mere *Amazons*, and their husbands are the wretched captives, destined to perpetuate the *gynarchy*. Accordingly, they people at a great rate, and with all the gravity imaginable."[35] Moreover, by choosing the name Thalestris, Pope evoked an Amazon whom Plutarch, Diodorus Siculus, and especially Quintus Curtius described as cupidinous in her meeting with Pope's partial namesake.[36]

The story of Thalestris' visit to Alexander the Great was often doubted and often told. When Alexander was camped in Hyrcania, Thalestris sent word that "there was a Queen come to visit him, and desiring to be something more intimate." She arrived with 300 women, saw Alexander, "alighted, bearing two Lances in her hand," and commenced to examine his frame, bearing, and excessively ornamented costume. Her disappointment in these baubles to the contrary, "she was not asham'd to tell him, she came to be got with Child, and that she was not unworthy to be gratified after that manner; that if it was a Son, she would restore it to the Father, if a Girl, she'd keep it her self." She then "desir'd him not to frustrate her expectation; her desire to be satisfied was more vehement than the King's, so that thirteen days being consum'd in those Enjoyments, she return'd to her Kingdom."[37]

She also returned to the Restoration stage. In 1667 John Weston made her tale a bedroom, or camp tent, farce in *The Amazon Queen. Or, The Amours of Thalestris to Alexander the Great*. Thalestris, like any sensible Restoration wit, rejects Alexander's offer of marriage, and wants only one year's sexual companionship to get herself a girl-child; a useless boy will be delivered to his father. When she also stipulates that they be faithful to one another for that year, Alexander rejects such harsh terms, and they part, much to Thalestris' shame. As she says to Hippolyta, "with my people great will be the stain, / That with this *Macedon* I have not lain" (p. 17). After she and sexually attracted Ptolemy later stab one another, they decide on more amiable combat, and she tells him – Alexander now out of sight out of mind – "you shall do what you to me propound" (p. 48).

Thereafter, the Reverend Edward Young was of course looking for ammunition when he wrote his satire against women in 1725, but he would have struck responsive chords when he presented a crude, blunt and heretical Thalestris who "justly gives the jealous husband pain" and proves that "A Shameless woman is the worst of *Men*."[38] Whatever the consequences for Restoration rakes or Dutch demographics, Amazonian relations between consenting adults were not thought likely steps to connubial bliss in the eighteenth century.

Nor is that bliss possible among the dead. In spite of formidable martial skills, in most representations of Amazon battles they lose. Visual evidence often shows women defeated by one source of their beauty. As Pope says of Belinda, "Fair Tresses Man's Imperial Race insnare, / And Beauty draws us with a single Hair" (2.27–28). Numerous classical pots and friezes show a naked well-muscled male warrior drawn to an Amazon's long hair which he pulls in order to unhorse her, drag her to the ground, and more easily cut her extended throat, spear her elongated torso, or club her taut body. This is the dreaded Amazonomachia, the literal war between the sexes that destroys the bodies designed to reproduce the beautiful men and women killing one another.[39]

There are, then, important implications in Pope's choice both of an Amazon and of this one among others. I hypothesize that she embodies and enlarges in one character both of Belinda's dangerous traits: her subdued aggression as seen in the card-game, where she is the challenging ombre who wishes to make a world in which she is superior; and her concomitant and conflicting sexual desires manifest in that game's suggestive skirmishes, her swelling breasts, the earthly lover lurking at her heart, and her ever-offered lock, about whose rape she is thrice warned. As a projection of much that is wrong but is attractive to Belinda, Thalestris is a powerful motivating voice which must have an equally powerful foil. That is one main reason why in 1717 Pope added Clarissa's speech, so that Belinda could have an authoritative, clear, and attractive guide away from the hostility of the epic and the ultimate defeat of the Amazon, and towards the sort of victory appropriate for her – if only she would listen. As we shall see, the problem becomes not one of sexual desire, but how to manage it in an acceptable way. Belinda is poised between virginity and marriage, and within this poem's values and Catholic context, she must choose adult marriage or choose wrongly.

Clarissa: "To Open more Clearly the Moral of the Poem"

So optimistic a view of Clarissa's speech, however, is foreign to what has been called the recent "open season against her."[40] If she is a norm, the argument goes, why does she become the baron's instrument and arm him for the fight as a lady does her knight in romance (3.125–30)? Either she is out of touch with Belinda's real needs, or wishes to have the baron for herself and is trying to hurt Belinda. I do not find these objections persuasive. For one thing, a woman arming a knight need not denote romantic exchange. As Spenser's "Letter of the Authors" makes plain, in *The Faerie Queene* Una arms the "clownish" Red Crosse when she still thinks him a country bumpkin unfit for the task, and at first accepts him "much gaine-saying." Moreover, whether Clarissa, the scissors, or both are the instruments of ill (3.126) does not mean that Clarissa's rather than the baron's motivation was bad; bad action can have a good end if properly controlled. In addition, since the ploy is called one of the "New Stratagems" (3.120) that rise in the baron's nominal mind as the steam rises from his coffee, he and Clarissa could hardly have had time to hatch a plot – though there is time to get caught up in an adolescent flirtation. Nor is it likely that Clarissa would help herself with the baron by urging Belinda to marry him. Such contradictions either are illogical or too complex for the simple characterization in *The Rape of the Lock*. Finally, Pope,

Warburton, or both forgot that Clarissa had given the baron a scissors, for in the 1751 edition she is called "*A new Character introduced in the subsequent Editions to open more clearly the MORAL of the Poem*" (TE, 2:199n). I thus suspect, on the one hand, that the earlier action need not bear too heavy a burden, and, on the other, that Clarissa's name was too apt not to be used for demonstrable wisdom.

If that earlier action is a magnet for interpretation, it probably should be seen not as a rival's mischief, but as a friend's kindness. Solid Clarissa knows what the airy sylphs must learn – that the baron and Belinda are appropriate suitors; as an ally she hopes to bring them together by joining an apparently harmless trick. As Ralph Cohen puts it, before Clarissa's eclipse, "her sophisticated approach to adaptation is apparent when she assists the Baron in the rape though she has clearly not anticipated the consequences that follow this action. She sought to satisfy the wish in Belinda's heart, but did not calculate upon the gulf between form and frankness."[41] Since the lock nonetheless must be regained, though, how better to do so than by such sane adaptation, by, say, inviting its wicked ravisher to return it at tea, then at supper, then at a ball, and then at the nuptials consequent upon so many visits to so good-humored a belle? Clarissa's error is not in providing the scissors, but in overestimating her rhetorical powers and Belinda's ability to accept her guidance. Instead, she too is carried away in Thalestris' call to arms and is trapped in the modern Amazonomachia, one nonetheless dramatically softened from the horrors of ancient warfare. Whatever Pope's achievement with Clarissa's speech, however, he made clear his often overlooked intention. John Dennis' severe *Remarks on Mr. Pope's Rape of the Lock* (1728) observe that in the *Lutrin* Boileau, unlike Pope, "seems to have given broad Hints at what was his real Meaning." Pope writes this refutation in the margin – "Clarissa's Speech."[42]

As the bearer of that meaning, she receives special praise, is graceful, given the honorific "Dame" (5.35), and has the presence immediately to silence the noisy reproaches around her with the simple wave of her fan (5.7–8). She also enjoys the narrator's implicit support. Like him, she wishes for a peaceful marriage contract between the combatants; her "trust me, Dear" (5.31) is echoed in the narrator's own "trust the Muse" (5.123) as he relates the apotheosis of the lock; her advice to accept the human situation and the transience of female beauty is reiterated in the narrator's knowledge that Belinda's own "fair Suns" must set, and that "all those Tresses shall be laid in Dust" (5.147–48); her consequent awareness that Belinda must check pride in her beauty (5.33–34) reinforces the narrator's hope that the beautiful woman will have "Sweetness void of Pride" (2.15); and her recommendation of the healing, enticing value of good humor (5.31–34) and the plea to have "good Sense preserve what Beauty gains" (5.16) draw on Pope's own introductory letter to Arabella Fermor. He tells her that this poem "was intended only to divert a few young Ladies, who have good Sense and good humour enough to laugh" both at their own and their sex's follies (p. 142).[43] Clarissa's muted retort also is the final address, is the same length as Thalestris', and is a counter to it. If Belinda is to become an adult, she must have demonstrable options on which to exercise her freedom of choice.

Belinda thus hears an alternative to Amazonian values, and we thus see Pope sharing his moral authority with the clarifying woman who enriches his poem and his narrator's judgment. That narrator regards Belinda as an adored object whose beautiful face makes him forget her flaws (2.16–18). Sisterly Clarissa speaks of mature prudence, subtly alerts Belinda to the consequences of attracting and rejecting men, and characterizes the enlarging world still available "whate'er we lose" (5.30). She also adds a hitherto absent didactic tone in her nine probing questions and their spoken or unspoken answers within twenty-six lines. By so doing, she briefly changes the poem's focus from potentially destructive male worship of beauty, to the more important potentially constructive female use of beauty. Thereafter, her verbal presence gives the narrator's post-battle peroration the united force of male and female human wisdom, so that both sylph and gnome are excluded from the poem's final paragraph infused with Clarissa's power. The narrator gains as much authority from Clarissa as she gains from the narrator.

That authority begins with Sarpedon's speech to Glaucus in the *Iliad*, XII.371–96. This speech was one of Pope's favorites, long was regarded as a paradigm of aristocratic responsibility, and was singled out by Madame Dacier and Pope as wisdom worthy of the gods.[44] Sarpedon is introduced with pomp, so that we will expect greatness from him (TE, 8:94n; *Iliad*, XII); by birth he is the superior of all combatants on either side, and thus unlike them has "the Manners of" a perfect hero and deserves "universal Esteem" because of his superior merit (TE, 8:263n; *Iliad*, XVI.512n. See also TE, 8:268n; *Iliad*, XVI.605n). Before going into battle against the Greeks, Sarpedon tells his cousin that they are honored as gods in Lycia, given land, privilege, "foaming Bowls" and feasts enhanced by music. They must deserve such dignities through princely conduct – here, by embracing an ethic in which they either give or take martial glory. Everyone must die, and princes should "give to Fame what we to Nature owe" (TE, 8:96; *Iliad*, XII.394) before age diminishes the nobility of their sacrifice. On this scheme, the leader repays the debt of national homage with his own or his enemy's life in battle. The advice indeed is godlike, for when this son of Zeus and Laodemia was finally slain by Patroclus, Zeus commanded Apollo to preserve his body from Greek desecration and cleanse, anoint, and transport it to an honored place in Lycia. Glaucus, on the other hand, though also noble, is not so well connected or clever as his relation. When opposed to his family's former guest Diomedes, they refuse to fight and instead exchange compliments and gifts of armor. Since Glaucus' armor was gold and Diomedes' bronze, the Greek outsmarted the Lycian who, as in *Iliad*, vi.288–95 (TE, 7:340–41), evoked the expression "gold for bronze" as an emblem of an uneven trade.[45] With these two names as announced backdrop, Pope can suggest that Clarissa's advice both has epic and divine roots, and is offered to someone of lesser wit.

Such divinity, however, was not untarnished, and as with several matters Homeric was subject to reconsideration. In Book 2 of *Paradise Lost* Milton uses Sarpedon's speech on Satan's behalf. Like Sarpedon, he must reciprocate the splendor and power which adorn and arm his throne (2.446–73) and repay "These Royalties" by accepting "Of hazard more" – that is, take upon himself the fight against humankind (2.445–46). This successful ploy, Milton's narrator tells us, is but a "god-like imitated State" and part of the vain wisdom and false philosophy endemic to Hell (2.511, 565). Shortly thereafter, the Père D'Aubignac deflates Sarpedon's speech by insisting that its emphasis on plentiful food and drink "n'est pas capable d'émouvoir des goinfres et des pauvres misérables" (p. 117). Sarpedon's speech, then, was noble but potentially flawed and irrelevant for non-Amazonian women. Clarissa meets the challenge of respecting and transcending her source, of avoiding duplicity and sensuality while insisting upon the obligations of those in power, and of turning noble death into useful life.

Unlike both Belinda and Thalestris, Clarissa rejects vanity and suffering presumed pain merely to be worshipped from without while being hollow within. Instead, since she alone of the three women speakers is not tainted by the Cave of Spleen, she can introduce two essential terms foreign to her colleagues – internal good sense and virtue to balance external appearance:

> How vain are all these Glories, all our Pains,
> Unless good Sense preserve what Beauty gains:
> That Men may say, when we the Front-box grace,
> Behold the first in Virtue, as in Face![46]
> (5.15–18)

She also introduces concepts that answer the social bankruptcy of Belinda and Thalestris. Woman is not to be degraded by Belinda's own image of herself as a vegetating flower dignified only by its beauty. Instead, she must learn and accept the extensive housewife's cares, for if mere dancing and dressing kept away defacing illness and the wrinkles of age, "who would learn one earthly thing of Use?" (5.22). *Use* is more than utilitarian; it is both related to the parable of the talents and to the medieval *usufructus* that Pope advocates in later satires on the use of riches, where land and wealth are God's temporary gifts to one in service to many. "'Tis Use alone that sanctifies expense" (line 179), Pope tells Burlington in 1731. As Swift also told his congregation, God made "all the Works of Nature to be useful, and in some Manner a Support to each other" in order to solidify "the whole Frame of the World." One's advantages thus are not personal property but "only a Trust ... lent him for the Service of others."[47] As such a steward, the girl whom both Belinda and Thalestris characterize as acted upon can become a vigorous woman who in winning her battle of the sexes improves herself and her presumed combatant. She cannot negotiate this enlarging pre-nuptial rite of passage if she becomes an Amazon literally or figuratively destructive of life or of heterosexual community. As Clarissa bluntly states, "she who scorns a Man, must die a Maid" (5.28). Therefore,

> What then remains, but well our Pow'r to use,
> And keep good Humour still whate'er we lose?
> And trust me, Dear! good Humour can prevail,
> When Airs, and Flights, and Screams, and Scolding fail.
> Beauties in vain their pretty Eyes may roll;
> Charms strike the Sight, but Merit wins the Soul.   (5.29–34)

With such an ethic, Belinda need not be a bottle calling for a cork, nor the baron a dim-witted peer whose chief attraction is his title; she becomes a woman of merit, and he a man of soul. If Belinda accepts this counsel of metamorphosis, she can regain her lock and earn an equal share in the consequent human family unavailable to unseen and untouched roses.

That floral image, in fact, suggests one further function of Clarissa's potential prothalamion. We recall that the card-queens in Belinda's hand held a "Flow'r, / Th' expressive Emblem of their Softer Pow'r" (3.39–40) – that is, the flower as traditional symbol of virginity. "If thou beest yet a fresh uncropped flower, / Choose thou thy husband, and I'll pay thy dower," the King of France says to Diane in *All's Well that Ends Well* (5.3.327–28). If Belinda is an unseen, unplucked rose, often thought the "Flower of Love,"[48] and dies in the desert, she abandons her ultimate weapon in the battle of the sexes, whose peace conference is the marriage bed. Pope's poem is profoundly "traditional" in its insistence on courtship and marriage; it is profoundly, perhaps cynically, "realistic" in its knowledge of the modern sexual barter that replaces ancient sexual rape.

Addison's *Spectator*, No. 128, 27 July 1711, offers an appropriate gloss for "good humour," and its meaning in *The Rape of the Lock*. He observes that "Men and Women were made as Counterparts to one another, that the Pains and Anxieties of the Husband might be relieved by the Sprightliness and good Humour of the Wife. When these are rightly tempered, Care and Chearful-ness go Hand in Hand; and the Family, like a Ship that is duly trimmed, wants neither Sail nor Ballast," each being equally important for smooth sailing. Accordingly, the sexes are fulfilled by one another, and "Their Virtues are blended in their Children, and diffuse through the whole Family a perpetual Spirit of Benevolence, Complacency, and Satisfaction." "A Man must be a Savage," John Hughes adds on 15 February 1712 (No. 302), not to be improved and humanized by the good humour of such a woman.[49]

Clarissa's speech, then, is indeed the moral center of *The Rape of the Lock*. It rejects spleen, girlhood, hostility, isolation, powerlessness, inutility, folly, and frustration in favor of good humor, womanliness, affection, community, power, use, and virtue. More's the pity that when Belinda now has her own choice of Hercules the sign on her cross-road points towards Thalestris and the Amazonomachia this poem was designed to avoid. Belinda rejects Clarissa as "To Arms, to Arms! the fierce Virago cries, / And swift as Lightning to the Combate flies" (5.37–38). The lightning of attraction in Belinda's eyes in Canto 1 has become the lightning of destruction in Canto 5. Hence once Clarissa's wisdom is rejected, the repressed sexual and physical combat of the card-table is acted out in appropriately diminished but serious form – as wounds, looks, snuff, and bodkins harm the combatant while the delighted gnomes, mimicking the Homeric gods, watch or join the battle. The unleashing of sexual tensions is as clear:

> See fierce *Belinda* on the *Baron* flies,
> With more than usual Lightning in her Eyes;
> Nor fear'd the Chief th' unequal Fight to try,
> Who sought no more than on his Foe to die.　　　　　(5.75–78)

From 1714 on several critics, and perhaps Arabella Fermor herself, complained of the poem's indecencies. In 1728 William Bond berated "this *Chaste Performance*" and angrily said – "Every Body knows what, *Dying upon a fair Lady* means."[50] Pope's narrator, though, was not angry, for unlike Belinda he shares and augments Clarissa's advice regarding the pacification of sexual death. Commentators on the narrator's role have wisely emphasized his direct but affectionate correction of Belinda, and shown how he urges her not to seek untouched permanence in life, but in mythology or art – namely, his own poem. They have not, however, fully appreciated the implications of his allusion to Catullus, known both as an erotic poet and as the celebrant of sexuality in marriage. When Belinda's lock is metamorphosed to a comet, "Not *Berenice*'s Locks first rose so bright, / The Heav'ns bespangling with dishevell'd Light" (5.129–30). In the "Coma Berenices" Berenice promises Aphrodite to sacrifice her abundant hair if her husband Ptolemy returns safely from the wars. When he does, she places her luxuriance upon an altar in Aphrodite's temple, and later is told that the vanished hair became a constellation as a sign of divine approval for such wifely behavior. Berenice is a helpful deus ex machina, a forerunner of Clarissa's wisdom, and another anti-Amazonian model of generosity for Belinda.[51]

That allusion is indeed a fit way to end a discussion of *The Rape of the Lock*, composed during the period when Pope in his young manhood was writing his own "marriage group" or courtship poems. Catullus reminds us of Pope's inheritance of retreat from pleasure in epic warfare and its butchering heroes and unreliable malevolent gods, and both the gods' and heroes' insufficiently controlled sexuality. It also recalls two other major points – Pope's fidelity to the essence of the poem's superceded occasion, his desire to join two neighboring aristocratic Catholic families in marriage, and his insistence that for all the comedy in their diminished world, their little events have serious implications, and can improve upon Homeric values. We find such improvement most notably in Clarissa and her friend the narrator – and not in the Amazon who maims infants, women, men, and the blending of virtues Addison saw as the consequence of the good-humored wife and the balanced marriage. Clarissa surpasses the ethics of Sarpedon who probably would have shown even less interest in Thalestris than the reluctant Alexander the Great. If Sarpedon so reacted, he again would have endeared himself to the other great Alexander whose comment upon Paris and Helen's reconciliation in Book III of the *Iliad* epitomizes his attitude in *The Rape of the Lock*: "since both the Sexes have their Frailties, it would be well for each to forgive the other" (TE, 7:218n; *Iliad*, III.551).

8 · "SUCH AS SIR ROBERT WOULD APPROVE"?

ANSWERS TO POPE'S ANSWER FROM HORACE

Eighteenth-century imitations can be troublesome poems to read and evaluate, for they demand at least three kinds of related historical and critical knowledge: the meaning of the parent-poem as the modern author might have understood it; the modern author's intention and achievement in light of that understanding and his own contemporary purposes; and the immediate response to the imitation, its reception by readers likely to have known what we must acquire.[1] I shall be concerned with the dangers of ignoring the third kind of knowledge, as exemplified in the controversy regarding the satirist's real or apparent triumph in Pope's *First Satire of the Second Book of Horace Imitated* (1733).

One side argues that the conclusion, in which the lawyer Fortescue agrees that Pope can continue to write satire if Sir Robert approves, is a "virtual confession of defeat," or is a "dangerous and unreliable alliance" that signals ominous things to come.[2] The other side argues that the victorious Pope is exonerated by the pro-administration lawyer, whose acceptance of Pope's case involves "his simultaneous acceptance of" Pope's "larger world order," that Pope's enemies "are vanquished, and [his] *adversarius* is metamorphosed into coadjutor"; and that the poem is a triumph in which Pope's "vision of the ideal community, epitomized by his grotto, is not a never-never-land, but rather a viable alternative."[3]

A full examination of the poem's manuscript and varied contexts is necessary to resolve these contradictory readings, and to determine which side is most nearly correct.[4] *The First Satire of the Second Book of Horace Imitated*, however, evoked several immediate responses; these are useful for determining whether Pope's enemies thought themselves vanquished or victorious, and whether they and Pope's other readers thought his adversarius an ultimate ally. If his apparent victims felt chastened or outflanked they were likely to have been silent or might risk publicizing their shame – as Shadwell does when he complains that *Mac Flecknoe* (1684) wrongly calls him an Irish poet, "when [Dryden] knows I never saw *Ireland* till I was three and twenty years old, and was there but four months."[5] Alternatively, if those enemies granted an occasional accurate point, but felt that point was improperly understood, they might have focussed on it and offered clarification. The administration does this in other cases, when its political press argues that so-called corruption actually is an effective way to keep government functioning smoothly.[6] If, finally, they were angry at what they thought improper and unfair claims and tactics, they were likely to have been vocal, indignant, and threatening, as Aaron Hill was (more subtly) when his letters encouraged Pope to withdraw an apparent insult to him in *The Dunciad* of 1729.[7] The evidence suggests that outrages and indignation, rather than a civilized mea culpa, were the responses to *Fortescue*,[8] and that reports of the demise of Pope's opponents have been greatly exaggerated. The putative corpses, at least, would have protested their premature burial and, as we will see, read the final exchange of the satire in a way quite different from some of Pope's later devotees.

The lines come after Fortescue's initial advice to "write no more" (line 11), Pope's affirmation of his satire as necessary in modern Britain, his noble defence of beleaguered Virtue, his characterization of his grotto as the secure place of rest and spiritual and intellectual nourishment, and his final question to a presumably re-educated fellow jurist, "What saith my Council learned in the Laws?" (line 142).[9] Fortescue's answer recognizes Pope's moral stance while making clear the irrelevance of morality in the face of law and power.

> *F.* Your Plea is good. But still I say, beware!
> Laws are explain'd by Men – so have a care.
> It stands on record, that in *Richard*'s Times
> A Man was hang'd for very honest Rhymes.
> Consult the Statute; *quart.* I think it is,
> *Edwardi Sext.* or *prim.* & *quint, Eliz:*
> See *Libels, Satires* – here you have it – read.
>   *P.* Libels and *Satires!* lawless Things indeed!
> But grave *Epistles*, bringing Vice to light,
> Such as a *King* might read, a *Bishop* write,
> Such as Sir *Robert* would approve –
>   *F.*   Indeed?
> The Case is alter'd – you may then proceed.
> In such a Cause the Plaintiff will be hiss'd,
> My Lords the Judges laugh, and you're dismissed.   (lines 143–56)

Negative response to *Fortescue* tended to fall into four overlapping classes: objections to Pope's politics and political allies; dislike of his partial and harsh satire; disgust with the man behind such a work and its influence on other poets; and rejection of his notion, or joke, that Sir Robert could approve of him or his satire. Most of these reponses were by ministerial allies, though at least one in the last group was by a writer who seems to have shared Pope's attitude towards Sir Robert and his world.

"It is time for [Pope] to retire, for he has made the town too hot to hold him," Lord Bathurst wrote to Swift shortly after *Fortescue* appeared.[10] One reason for such heat was Pope's praise of Bolingbroke, the opposition's shadow first minister, and the administration's detested enemy. "TO VIRTUE ONLY and HER FRIENDS, A FRIEND" (line 121) was fertile ground for hostile comments. The author of *An Epistle to the Little Satyrist of Twickenham* (30 March; London 1733), for example, quotes that offending line with contempt (p. 8).[11] On 16 June 1733 the Walpolean newspaper the *Daily Courant* does the same, and asks, "Can St. John's *Treasons* feast a Patriot-Soul?"[12] On 4 March 1735 Thomas Bentley's *Letter to Mr. Pope* (London) also berates the satirist for his "almost treasonable!" praise of Bolingbroke, who has no virtue; Pope has "but little." What Pope really means, Bentley argues, is *"To my self only and my Friends a Friend"* (p. 12).

The *Muse in Distress: A Poem Occasion'd by the Present State of Poetry* (3 November; London, 1733) is dedicated to Sir William Yonge, a Walpole loyalist. The unknown author both mentions Pope's poem and quotes several of its politically noisome lines. He urges Pope and like-minded colleagues to abandon their petulance, political spleen, and ill-chosen idol.

> St. John with them ne'er knew the Guilt of Treason,
> *He is the Flow of Soul the Feast of Reason.*
> *Judges* are Hangmen, *H*— cannot write,
> And who but *M*—, now alive can fight? (pp. 12–13)

Such a poet can have few friends or happy readers, for in spite of his demonstrable talent and his once pleasing verse, he is blinded by party zeal that encourages his unjustified anger rather than praise. The perpetrator of *The Muse in Distress* thus claims that if Pope really would *"sweetly flow thro' all the Royal Line,"* as Fortescue had suggested, his satire might be regarded as virtuous and as an ally of mankind – which it clearly is not, and so we cannot "think Mankind and He were *Friends*" (p. 13). The writer of the *Little Satyrist of Twickenham* also mourns Pope's lost reputation due to his political and satiric involvements, and warns Pope with his own words: "*Satire* [is] *your Weapon;* if you will attack, / Be careful that the Scandal don't fly back" (p. 6). He equates Pope's angry response with Walpole's, in a line again borrowed from the poem he is attacking:

> To Anger prone you've own'd yourself before;
> *But touch me, and no Minister so sore:*
> 'Tis natural, the Proverb does evince,
> The Horse that's gaul'd when touch'd will surely wince. (p. 9)

The poem proceeds by granting Pope's own admitted weak points, and by denying his claims to virtue. Consequently, Pope cannot be secure in his grotto, for his assumptions concerning his virtuous serenity and retirement are false.

> Thus vainly your Opinion you belye,
> Lay Claim to Virtue, and your Vice deny.

> For he that's good shou'd start at ev'ry Wind,
> Of Vice be conscious, to his Virtue blind;
> Not think that *all the Din the World can keep*
> *Rolls o'er his Grotto and but soothes his Sleep:*
> For he so lost will live, in endless Fame,
> An everlasting Monument of Shame;
> For if such horrid spots as these appear,
> How does it prove *the Medium must be clear?* (p. 10)

Part of Pope's shame was traceable to his influence on lesser men who already were following his bad example. The *Daily Courant*'s attack on Pope, for instance, also was an attack on Paul Whitehead and his *State Dunces, Inscrib'd to Mr. Pope* (7 June; London 1733). It seems reasonable to assume that threatened punishment of Whitehead was a hint to Pope as the teacher of satiric murder. Accordingly, *The Muse in Distress* warns the scion of "This envious *Bard*" that he is unprotected, and lacks the trappings of wealth and power that Pope displays in *Fortescue*:

> Thou hast no *Quincunx*, Thou no *Vines* to prune,
> May'st sleep in Peace from *January* to *June;*
> Thy Rest no *Great Ones* with their Visits break,
> None who will risque a Shilling for thy sake;
> Cease then to murder with thy *Rhyming Saw*,
> And dread th' avenging *Myrmidons* of *Law*. (pp. 13–14).

These authors have rejected many of Pope's political, personal, satiric, and, we might say, speluncular assumptions. Lady Mary and Lord Hervey are comparably unwilling to grant Pope's arguments, and in fact add some new objections, including a denial that Pope's connections can protect him from deserved punishment. Their exquisitely vulgar *Verses Address'd to the Imitator of the First Satire of the Second Book of Horace* (8 March; London 1733) stress Pope's impertinence in pretending to imitate Horace, Pope's ugly body as an image of his ugly soul, his satanic qualities as an enemy of mankind, and, as they warm to their task, his vulnerability and their power to harm him when they please: "whilst you *bruise* [the human race's] *Heel*, beware your Head," and especially beware, since "if thou drawst thy Pen . . . / Others a Cudgel, or a Rod, may draw." Pope's "wretched little Carcass" is merely "yet . . . / Unwhipt, unblanketed, unkick'd, unslain" (p. 6). If he is safe, it is because the world despises and laughs at his satiric as it does his sexual impotence. "Is this the *Thing* to keep Mankind in awe, / *To make those tremble who escape the Law?*" Resolutely no. So far from being the country squire courted by the great, Pope is the assassin of his brother, the Cain whose back is God's avenging mark and a sign that Pope shall "Wander like him, accursed through the Land" (p. 8).[13]

Another group of responses challenges the view that the lawyer Fortescue is metamorphosed from "*adversarius* . . . into coadjutor." Indeed, these poets quickly borrow the legal metaphor and characterize Pope as the loser not the winner of his case since, as all knew, Sir Robert disapproved. Accordingly, on 26 February 1733 Mr. "Guthry" completed his "First Satire of the Second Book of Horace Imitated. In a Dialogue between Mr. Alexander Pope, and the Ordinary of Newgate."[14] He invites the reader to compare it to Pope's effort of 15 February, so that he will at once see that Pope has already been jailed, is awaiting graver punishment for his libel of mankind, yet still wishes to write more to purge his spleen. The Ordinary, replacing Fortescue but using his words, says, "*You could not do a worse Thing for your life*" (p. 83). Pope himself will reserve the praise of virtue (not the dispraise of vice) for the next age, knows that "Both High and Low wish me the shortest *Date*" (p. 86), and that "hang'd I shall be, if my *Judge* be P—" (p. 88). Far from being the brave conqueror of a death sentence through misapplied law, Pope embodies the vile fury over which death and law must triumph. The Ordinary says:

> *Alas, young Man! your Days can ne'er be long,*
> In Flow'r of Age you'll dangle for a Song.
> *Ralph, Cooke, Concanen, Henly,* and his *Wife,*
> Will club their Testers, now, to take your Life!   (p. 89)

Pope, who hates Walpole, knows that nothing can keep him from death – "methinks I feel the Bow-String in *my Sleep.*" Having already condemned himself from his own mouth, this "Pope" could not have been surprised by the Ordinary's response to his "*What* thinks my Rev'rend Father of *my Cause?*" Very little. Pope will be hanged for his infamous poems:

> *Libels* and *Satires, – lawless Things Indeed!*
> Had I been just, set Virtue's Deeds *to Light,*
> *Such as a* King *might read, a* Bishop *write,*
> Such as Sir *Robert* would approve –
> ORDINARY
>   Indeed?
> *Alter'd* had been *your Case: –* But to proceed.
> Fatal is now your Doom, you will be Cast,
> And your *first* Psalm, I fear, will be your *last.*   (p.92)

Guthry has imitated *Fortescue* from a ministerial point of view and, by his poem's appearance on 2 March, denied the basis of Pope's apparent victory.

Four days later, the pseudonymous Patrick M'Doe-Roach published his *Sequel of Mr. Pope's Law Case: Or, Farther Advice thereon* (6 March; 2nd ed., London, 1733), purporting to be from a fledgling lawyer who is aware that "The Point is not, Did you right, – or wrong?" (p. 8) but whether he knows "How stands the Great-Man? Does he appear? / (Not against, but for you: I mean, be sure!)" (p. 5). Pope's present lawyer is useless, since only if one can do a variety of legally irrelevant things like "trot the long Dance" or talk nonsense, "There might be some Hopes, – to succeed" (pp. 6–7). The trial itself will either be a farce or "a bitter Jest," and will conclude with

Gaol or Pillory,
Unless Death or Money makes Matters easy.
A Fine of Ten Marks by *P-pe* rich and great;
A Trifle back of his Subscription-Cheat.   (p. 9)

M'Doe-Roach's counsel is simple and glosses a key description of Pope's grotto as a retreat, a place of rest, retirement, and on political grounds, a failure: "take Advice, – indulge Retreat" (p. 9) and "spare the Great Man!" (p. 10) – though M'Doe-Roach himself shows little inclination to follow his own advice.[15]

I cannot pretend to have exhausted the answers to Pope's satire which was, after all, commented upon throughout the 1730s, and often discussed with his other imitations rather than as a separate poem.[16] But I believe that I have cited the large majority of the responses appearing in 1733 and shortly thereafter, and have provided representative reactions of a few friends and most of the administration, its nominally aristocratic fellow-travelers, its hired drudges, and others simply offended by Pope's attacks, claims, religion, politics, or person. Even some of those sharing Pope's vision of Walpole's government had difficulty accepting the appropriateness of the fantasy conclusion in the actual world As M'Doe-Roach says, "How stands the Great-Man? . . . be sure!" And as Guthry argues, "*Alter'd* had been *your Case*" in the improbable event of Sir Robert's approval. Instead, "Fatal is now your Doom," the threatening voice of reality says.

✳

These published reactions suggest that Pope's enemies were angry rather than annihilated. Indeed, in this instance Pope received more than he gave in the exchange with his tormentors, and had to wait until *An Epistle to Dr. Arbuthnot* (1735) before evening the score, and in the process showing how badly hurt he had been. Moreover, many readers not already persuaded, or outside of Twickenham and its circle of unemployed grandees, rejected Pope's values and his grotto as "a viable alternative" for administration politics, since Bolingbroke had long been regarded as a Jacobite stalking-horse. Sir Robert himself, I suspect, would have encouraged Pope and the opposition to be as viable as they pleased, so long as the vias were enshrouded in a distant grotto and not nearby Parliament. One major, and elegiac, point of Pope's dark salon des refusés is that it united the worthy, neglected, and defeated, not the triumphant. Pope's poem actually shows Walpole's power not his own.

After all, Pope can gain Sir Robert's approval only under the most managed of circumstances. *If* Sir Robert approves, "you may then proceed." If he does not approve, we are back in a world of "Beware!" and "A Man was hang'd for very honest Rhymes." Of course the administration never does hang Pope, or inflict on him any of the several unpleasant punishments still legally possible for libel.[17] Nonetheless, on 4 June 1737 its *Daily Gazetteer* argues that opposition satire should be restrained by law; on 16 July the *Gazetteer* urges a restoration of the Augustan Roman Law of the XII Tables that decreed death to anyone defaming *"another Man's good Name"*; and on 27 October 1738 the same newspaper bluntly states that "a late Satyrist" should be among those "clubb'd or rather bastinadoed" to death in accordance with that law. Perhaps such intimidation is one reason why Pope soon ended his career as a formal verse satirist and why he or Warburton added a pessimistic note to the second dialogue of the *Epilogue to the Satires* (1738): "bad men were grown so shameless and so powerful, that Ridicule was become as unsafe as it was ineffectual" (p. 327). In 1740 Pope wrote, but did not publish, a fragment of a jeremiad in which he claimed that "The plague is on thee, Britain, and who tries / To save thee in th' infectious office *dies*" (p. 336; lines 75–76).

Fortescue's political context suggests an obvious but important point: satire, and especially Pope's, demands that we reclaim a high degree of specific information. A theory of "the poem as a poem" has clear limitations in analysis of satire, as indeed does any approach that excludes the contemporary and concrete external referents on which the satire is built. Percy Bysshe Shelley is free to tell us how he falls upon the thorns of life and bleeds. We do not pity the poor madman reluctantly subject to the laws of gravity; instead, we assume that in a self-referential romantic lyric the poet soon realizes that the west wind can not lift him as if he were a wave, leaf, or cloud, and that he had better change his metaphor – say, to one in which the wind can scatter the leaves of his book rather than his weightier body. Alexander Pope, on the other hand, is writing a satire that is both personal and public, that provides known characters able to confirm or deny the actions or words attributed to them. To be sure, Pope enjoys his limited personal triumph within the confines of the poem, where Sir Robert's approval could not be tested; Pope embodies exalted values in exalted verse; he elevates comic satire and its frail champion to the heroic; he dents Fortescue's legal armor with weapons forged in the smith of morality, not law; he provides formidable impetus and a splendid example for other opposition poets; he convinces many of us, long beyond the heat of battle, that he is the defender of Virtue, his nation at large, and his retired world in little. As a result, we wish Pope the conquest he seems to have earned, and are all the more saddened and impressed with the odds against him; we again realize that his life and letters may depend on the permission and approval of the man he is attacking; and we may even admire his wit and lingering courtesy in attributing to Sir Robert enough grace to accept the joke (and grim compliment regarding his power) and laugh with him. Yet even in the poem, such triumph as there is remains fragile, and unbelieving readers rushed into print to inform Pope that he was wrong on several counts. So far from silencing *"the Clamour raised"* (p. 3) by his ethic epistles, Pope raised yet more clamor from foes and concern from friends, apparently including Fortescue himself,[18] who knew that an answer from Sir Robert was likely to be more potent, ominous, and persuasive than an answer from Horace. Modern readers of Pope's *Fortescue* may still wish to argue that by the end of the poem the adversarius becomes an aide-de-camp, Walpole is defeated, and Pope and his values are victorious and have a real place in the real world of 1733. If so, however, they must account for evidence that contradicts their hypothesis: Pope himself, his friends, and his lawyer feared for his safety as a result of *Fortescue*; those presumably vanquished rejected virtually all of Pope's points and the modern judgment regarding papal supremacy; in answering-poems as in life, Sir Robert was seen to disapprove of Pope's satire; and, finally, the government which such satire was intended to intimidate or reform grew progressively stronger in the near future, used its most important newspaper to threaten Pope's life, and thereafter silenced him as a formal verse satirist. Would not triumph have been made of sterner stuff?

9 · THE CONVENTIONS OF CLASSICAL SATIRE AND THE PRACTICE OF POPE

THE EIGHTEENTH-CENTURY satirist, like any writer in any genre at any time, was faced with a series of literary choices. These would include such banal matters as the nature of his topic, the expectations of his several audiences, the relevant verse form, and the tone most appropriate for his particular satiric end. The satirist in and near the 1730s, however, had more choices than most other satirists before or after him. Pope and his contemporaries inherited fully developed, communicated, and appreciated traditions of Roman, French and, perhaps to a lesser degree, English formal verse satire, traditions generally understood as well by their victims as their friends. Fruitful use of such traditions meant neither worshipping nor breaking of icons. At his best and most characteristic the eighteenth-century poet is emulative not imitative, and comprehensive not exclusive in his uses of the past, a past he is more likely to see as an opportunity for his own improvement rather than debility, a past which must be understood and digested in the present before it can be valuable to the future. To grovel before one's sources of imitation is un-British servility; to ignore or not comprehend them is all-too-British duncery. Hence Pope describes the votaries of dullness as having "Less human genius than God gives an ape." They offer "Small thanks to France, and none to Rome or Greece," and produce "A past, vamped, future, old, reviv'd, new piece."[1]

A theory of coherent but independent use of an earlier model was long part of British practice. As William King argued in 1709, "An Imitator and his Author stand much upon the same Terms as *Ben* does with his Father in the play [Congreve's *Love for Love*]: '*What tho' of he be my Father, I an't bound Prentice to 'en.*'"[2] William Clubbe noted retrospectively (in 1795) that Swift and Pope generally "imitated (and that loosely) such parts of him [Horace] only as suited the purposes of their own immediate satire."[3] What was true for particular poems also was true for the more general adaptations of history and literary models. The modern, Bolingbroke urged, should adapt only "the spirit and force," only "the particular graces" of the best of what was relevant for his own culture or needs. That adaptation must be "according to the idiom of our own tongue," and useful to contemporary experience.[4] These remarks suggest that eighteenth-century satirists were more eclectic than, say, the limiting tags "Horatian" or "Juvenalian" imply, since those terms brought with them political, moral, and literary contexts that were subject to redefinition, modification, and approval or disapproval at different times. There is good reason to expect Pope to blend the different "particular graces" of each kind, add to his own satire's "immediate purposes," and write a poem demonstrably in a Roman tradition while demonstrably British and his own. Whatever accuracy the notion of a supposed "anxiety of influence" has for the putative romantics and their heirs, it is a perfectly useless description of the typical literary and psychological procedures of Pope and his generation.

In discussing those procedures, I shall focus on Pope's three main satiric legacies – the Roman formal verse satires of Horace, Persius, and Juvenal, and the ways they were perceived both by poets and commentators. I hope to clarify some of the choices before Pope, to indicate the received conventions and reputations of the Roman satirists, and then to suggest how Pope used his inheritance to create his own and greater estate in his imitation of Horace's first satire of the second book.

The Horatian Voice

For the eighteenth century, the Horatian voice often is comfortable, secure, harsh when necessary, but normally inclusive and conversant with the age's great men, to whom it speaks as a moral equal. His satires offer gentle philosophy, avuncular guidance, an understanding of fallibility, and a willingness to correct it where possible and endure it where necessary. This view was well expressed by the Abbé Charles Batteux in his widely known and conveniently unoriginal *Course of the Belles Lettres*, which appeared in English in 1761. He says that Horace's satire shows "the sentiments of a polite philosopher, who is concerned to see the absurdities of mankind." He sometimes "diverts himself with" those absurdities and berates them through "general portraits of human life." If he occasionally becomes particular it is not to offend but "to enliven the subject, and put the moral . . . into action." His characters generally are fictitious: real persons named are those "only who were universally decried, and had no longer any pretence to reputation." Horace's genius was neither malicious nor morose, but that of

a delicate friend to the true and the good; taking mankind as it found them, and esteeming them oftener rather objects of compassion, than of hatred or ridicule . . . His style is plain, delicate, sprightly, and full of moderation and gentleness; when he corrects a fool, a fop, or a miser, he does it in so nice a manner, that the wounded hardly feels any smart.[5]

At least some details of this portrait of Horace may be seen in his first satire of the second book, an apologia which Pope was to imitate – with significant differences – in 1733. Horace begins by addressing the supremely distinguished lawyer Trebatius, a man who first was a friend of Cicero and then a friend and advisor to Julius and Augustus Caesar. Augustus would in fact do nothing regarding law without consulting him.[6] Trebatius tells Horace that if he wishes to avoid charges of satiric brutality, he should either not write at all, or sing Caesar's martial praises and gain appropriate rewards. Horace laments that he cannot produce the requisite epic verse, associates himself with his superior Lucilius as a satirist who defends Rome by attacking its enemies with his harsh verse, and insists that whatever happens, even if death threatens him, he must write. To Horace's adamant "Scribam" (line 59) Trebatius offers a wordly and paternal "O puer" (line 60) a friendly warning of consequences, and a willing ear when Horace again asserts the Lucilian pattern of attack on the wicked, including leaders of the nation if necessary, and praise of the virtuous. All the seeming outrage, however, never becomes Juvenalian. In Batteux's words, Horace is diverting himself, enlivening the subject and showing himself a friend of the good while being sprightly and moderate. The moderation is induced by Trebatius' own presence as a powerful muscle in the legal arm of the Augustan court, and equally powerful evidence that Horace does in fact have the approval of the great (line 76) as he claims. It thus is fitting to have Trebatius say in lawyerly evaluation of Horace's outburst, "I can't find anything to disagree with" (line 79). The satire ends with Horace's witty turn on Trebatius' final advice regarding "mala . . . carmina" (line 82) – that is, libellous verse. Horace ignores this as a legal description and turns it, instead, into a qualitative matter. In the process he accepts Trebatius' earlier counsel, as he implied he would (lines 17–20), that he praise Caesar and receive his rewards. "What if I write good verses and Caesar's judgment praises them? And if I have only attacked those who deserve it, while being untainted myself?" In such a case, Trebatius concludes, the legal slate will be wiped clean and he is free.

The poem clearly supports the moral and governmental status quo. Lucilius, for example, is now very different from the pre-Augustan rough versifier and vilifier of Horace's *Satires* i.iv and i.x. Instead, he is described as the friend of the great Scipio Africanus and Laelius, a testament to their worth and a companion of their private moments – an ideal for Horatian life and letters. Lucilius has been changed from scourge of scoundrels to implicit prop of the new Augustan order. Moreover, the establishment's favorite lawyer is, finally, a friend of Horace's satire. The satirist lives in a world in which the politically great are his allies and only the envious are his enemies. He is willing to attack evil men in power, but does not need to, since those in the highest reaches of the Augustan dispensation, even the princeps himself, read and praise his verse. The enemy is routed, the general's tent is colored with imperial purple, and the satirist has shown the unbelievers that their prudence, if not virtue or taste, should suggest finding another opponent. This satire is a triumph of wit, threat, and dubiously moral suasion that both helps Horace's personal case and that of the government, here portrayed as guided by the exquisite hand of a martially unvanquished, poetically literate and judicially wise emperor.[7] *Satires* II.i was justly admired during the eighteenth century – but its political values would not have been accepted by Alexander Pope, however "Horatian" he may be thought.

Horace is of course often described as the darling of eighteenth-century satire. Actually, he is the interloper of the late seventeenth century who must break into the consciousness of the English satirist long used to the blunter modes of Juvenal and Persius. Once that Horatian option is established, he is hard to uproot, and his equable tones become indelibly associated with the glittering world of Julius Caesar Octavianus Augustus after the death of Antony, when the savagery of the triumvirate and its genocidal proscriptions were ended and Rome's propagandists depicted a city and a literature changing from brick to marble. Such a vision often was questioned and denied by classical as well as eighteenth-century readers,[8] but it had its appeal, part of which was the example of a manly, confident Horace writing satire in the Augustan age, even writing at Augustus' own invitation, sharing the stage with Maecenas and Virgil and embodying the proper relation between throne and letters.

Horace's satires also offered dialogue, use of letters addressed to the great and near-great, a sense of the proximity of his literature and knowledgeable audience involved with, or understanding, both the social and political world of the court and the appeal of retirement from that court to the simple but civilized country, where one's spirit rather than career might flourish. Horace was attractive to a nation barely becoming urban and long accustomed to harangues against the trials and concerns of the perfidious court. But Horace, unlike Pope, does not attack the court itself – merely, as in *Satires* I.ix – the grotesquely unworthy aspirers who seek entrance to it. Such affirmation of a deserved moral stability and punishment of the threats to it endeared Horace to monarchists of several generations, especially since they often considered Augustus the paradigmatic ruler. The Tory Laurence Echard describes Augustan government as a transference of "all the Power of the People and the Senate" to the princeps himself. The occasional "Assemblies of the people" passed "nothing of Importance" that was "contrary to the Pleasure of the Emperor," who skilfully preserved his authority while seeming to share it.[9] Support for such clever management would be thought virtuous only so long as such monarchic absolutism itself was thought virtuous. The death of English absolutism cannot be precisely dated, though it was hardly enhanced by the definitive beheading of Charles I, the virtual forced abdication of James II, Parliament's invitation of William III, the Act of Protestant Succession, and the beginning of the Hanoverian dynasty. With deviation from the remnants of absolutist doctrine came a related deviation from the new satiric gospel, one which, by the later seventeenth century, was either respectably second to Juvenal's or, for some, comparable and for a few others superior.

Hence in 1698 Joseph Addison writes that there "has been long a Dispute among the Learned, whether that Keenness and Bitterness of . . . JUVENAL . . . or HORACE's more jocose *Lampoons* are most agreeable to the End of Satire." Addison's answer is clear: "Both of them, allowing for the different Manner of their Writing, are perfect Masters in their several Ways; in the one shines the *Ridicule*, in the other the *Severe*."[10] Addison, however, leaves out an important part of the equation, the role that Horace had to play in supporting the Augustan throne, a throne coming to be seen as built on the rubble of the great republic and its constitutional balance destroyed by Augustus. Hence in 1717 Mr. Wickstead contrasted his benevolent George I and the malevolent Augustus in their different encouragement of the arts. The British king nurtures art and liberty, the Roman emperor art and tyranny. He helped his poets and was in turn helped by them.

> Their Harps with flattering Sounds repay'd
> Th'Imperial Patron's skillful Cost;
> But whilst th'applauded Artists play'd,
> The *Roman* Liberty was lost.[11]

In 1728 the virulently anti-Augustan Thomas Gordon makes even clearer that Horace and Virgil supported the imperial despot for personal gain. For Gordon, to admire those "charming poets" is to admire Augustus, "who was so generous to them, and is the chief burthen of their Panegyricks." These words come as part of the long prefatory matter to Gordon's translation of a resolutely anti-absolute Tacitus, the historian who, as Sir Ronald Syme put it, "arraigns the whole moral and social programme of the Princeps, a failure when it was not deleterious."[12]

Moreover, in the severe eighteenth-century judgment, Horace need not have been so compliant, so willing to buttress that infant tyranny. In 1759 James Grainger honored Tibullus because no distresses "could ever induce him to praise those powerful but wicked Men, who had subverted the Liberties of his Country," however much contemporaries like Horace offered "the most extravagant Adulation." Tibullus, Grainger later says, was also unlike Horace in being independent from the Augustan court and thus was "a true Patriot."[13]

This is a small sample of the contemporary hostility to Augustus, Horace, and Horatian satire. One can predict that the opposition to Sir Robert Walpole, and in some cases the administration as well, would see Horace as the miserable ally of a miserable butcher. In 1740 the indignant author of *Plain Truth* is conventional when he says that Horace and Virgil are "*Weeds*" that ornament the "*Tyrant's Nest*" of Augustus.

> They serve to *lull and blunt the Pain*,
> Of *vilest Crime*, still hide such Stain,
> In Luxury, they thrive amain,
> Of *Tyranny bear up the train*.[14]

Here is a significant influence upon the choice a satirist of the 1730s must make in employing literary models: should his tone be Horatian and support the government and its leaders, or at the very least be gentle, general and compassionate in attacks upon it and those supporting it? Many administration friends – George Bubb Dodington and the writers for the *London Journal* and the *Gazetteer* among them – asked precisely for that kind of satire.[15] The opposition and zealots for "liberty" and "patriotism" came up with a resounding *no*, a word that echoes in Pope's denunciation of Horace as a fawning court toady in the first *Dialogue* of the *Epilogue to the Satires* (1738, lines 11–22), and in his own epitaph, where he contrasts his refusal to praise heroes and kings with Horace's and Virgil's flattery of them: "Let Horace blush, and Virgil too," he concludes.[16] Horace of course continued to be read, admired, translated and imitated; but he was suspected of moral equivocation, the worst of sins for a satirist, and thus had grave imperfections, especially when seen through anti-absolute or anti-Walpole spectacles.

Where, then, would Pope, or indeed Johnson or Whitehead or others sympathetic to the opposition, go for a model and literary norm to fit his satiric purposes? The answer, I believe, is divided into three parts, none of which is from Gaul. He would go to the Horatian devices and even the poems themselves while redefining them for his own purposes; he would go to the philosophic, gloomy, but often indignant voice of Persius that seemed to resist the coming darkness of Nero; and he would go to the great model of opposition courage and symbolic protest – Juvenal and the cry in his first satire that it is difficult *not* to write satire at such a time (line 30). I shall deal with these in reverse order.

An Answer from Juvenal

In 1751 John Hill agreed that most of Juvenal's "Admirers think him an angry Writer, whose Subject required him rather to tear to the Bone, than to play about the Imagination."[17] Such violence could be accepted only in the best of causes, and so his partisans were careful to define the nature of that subject in elevated terms – the resistance to tyranny, attack on its agents, and affirmation of the political, moral, and economic values that built the Roman Republic before the Caesars and its own internal weaknesses destroyed it. This libertarian vision was emphasized as early as 1616 in Nicholas Rigault's – Rigaltius – widely known essay on Juvenal and Roman satire in which Juvenal is characterized as the preserver of old Roman virtues. Specifically, the end of his fourth satire shows the satirist using "free and forthright words" which encouraged brave men to curse "their terrible bondage" under Domitian. His pose also demanded the courage to resist the enemy: "He kept on writing," Rigault says in words that Pope could have adopted as his own motto, "in an age corrupted by the vices of the Caesars, an age when laws were vanishing along with the throttled voice of magistrates, an age when that one time Roman courage grew feeble in an almost death like sleep."[18]

This bold enemy of oppression was attractive to other seventeenth-century commentators in Latin, French, and English. Barten Holyday's Juvenal, for instance, emerges as "a Lover of the Liberty of . . . the *Roman Common-wealth*" and a hater of the Caesars who "by force and fraud mastered their own Country."[19] The implicit contrast with Horace's accommodating spirit is made explicit in Dryden's influential discussion of the two satirists in 1693, a discussion so well known that in 1721 John Dennis was to complain that the generality of readers prefer Juvenal because Dryden does. Horace, Dryden says, "as he was a courtier, complied with the interest of his master," and was not as critical as he should have been, especially since he himself "was dipped in the same actions" as Augustus and hence could not draw their ugliness. Juvenal, however, is properly indignant against vice. He is sharper and has "more of the commonwealth genius; he treats tyranny" and its attendant vices with "the utmost rigour: and consequently, a noble soul is better pleased with a zealous vindicator of Roman liberty than with a temporizing poet, a well-mannered Court slave, and a man . . . who is ever decent, because he is naturally servile." For the exalted Juvenal, Dryden continued, "oppression was to be scourged instead of avarice [as in Horace]: . . . the Roman liberty was to be asserted."[20]

This judgment and the evidence for it were known and respected by schoolboys, university students, and common and specialist readers for over one hundred years thereafter. Two earlier eighteenth-century remarks are representative. In 1711 Joseph Trapp tells his students at Oxford that Juvenal is the biting, noble, tragic satirist whose smiles differ from those of Horace: "they are not the genteel ones of a Courtier, but mix'd with Gall and ill Nature" against the vicious sinners he attacks. Fifteen years later Lewis Crusius argues that "Satire seems to have arrived to its highest perfection" in Juvenal, who is "a true generous spirited *Roman*, a friend to liberty and virtue." If Horace were "a worse courtier, he would have been more serious" – that is, better.[21]

To be Juvenalian, then, is to resist oppression, to punish those who aid corruption of manners, virtue or politics, and to embody high standards of bravery in the face of the enemy's hordes. Since Juvenal could see that those hordes already had won, his tones became not only biting but "epic" or "tragic" and thus more sublime and compelling than the Horatian comic satire and its play on words – the latter a kind of feeding on garbage, Dryden claimed. Hence Walter Harte characterizes Juvenal in terms of the reader's response to the poet's magnetic vigor:

> See his strong Sense, and Numbers masculine!
> His Soul is kindled, and he kindles mine:
> Scornful of Vice, and fearless of Offence,
> He flows a Torrent of impetuous Sense.

John Brown uses even more lofty language in describing Juvenal's "exalted page" and "ardent eloquence" which "aw'd corrupted *Rome*." Indeed, "Not lofty Epic soars a nobler flight."[22]

Juvenal offered yet another convention unavailable or less noticeable in Horace – the principle of strict organization along the lines of praise of a particular virtue that is the opposite of the vice attacked. This pattern, Dryden claimed, was followed by Persius and Juvenal and not by Horace, and was the pattern of the best formal verse satire. In 1737 the young author of *Four Satires* found this useful advice, and so tells the audience no doubt eagerly waiting to read his Juvenalian poems that, with one exception, "In the Conduct of my Satires, I have observ'd Unity of Design, and confin'd myself to a single Subject." Far later in the century William Boscawen argued that the "regularity of Method" that characterized modern (and Juvenalian) satire is not to be found in Horace's "familiar Satire."[23]

There are two apparently disparate traits of style that conclude my examination of Juvenalian conventions. The first is the expected one of intermittent vulgarity and harshness of tone that may produce jagged rhythms. These blemishes were neither overlooked nor, for many, forgiven; but they were often thought of as being virtuous because the product of an impassioned response to vice. Barten Holyday claimed that such a man is "set on fire" by villains, and is so transported by his fury that he has no time "for the placing or displacing" of particular words. The satirist and his poems are "uneven, rough and furious ... in this poetical perturbation." Rigault, indeed, had already argued that such fury was a conscious act of stirring up the smut in order to wake Rome from its morally debilitating apathy.[24]

Though Juvenal could be rugged, he also could be polished. Gibbon read Juvenal for the first time in 1763 and recorded his largely positive reactions. They included praise for Juvenal's unique post-Augustan "love of liberty, and loftiness of mind," and also praise for his style, which is "superior to that of most of the Latin poets. Managed by him, the Roman language loses all its roughness." Samuel Johnson summed up the spirit of several of these observations in this synoptic remark: "The peculiarity of Juvenal is a mixture of gaiety and stateliness, of pointed sentences, and declamatory grandeur."[25]

Juvenal, then, offers a set of perceived conventions obviously different from those of Horace. We hear his monologues, often in sublime epic or tragic tones; his resistance to Caesarian absolutism and praise of republican greatness, each of which requires severity of satire and applause for opposition; his organization of satire into coherent design of praise and blame; his speaker's courage in refusing to be silent in the face of personal or official corruption; and the stylistic ability to be rough or polished, sprightly or grand as the situation required. In 1778 young Vicesimus Knox looked back upon his country's satiric production and said: "The English seem to have copied the manner of Juvenal rather than of Horace. Our national spirit is indeed of the manly and rough kind, and feels something congenial with itself in the vehemence of the sullen Juvenal."[26] Some of the Juvenalian ethos would have been reinforced by the satires of his predecessor, the least comely of the three Roman satirists, but nonetheless important as a model and, I believe, as the final weight that turns eighteenth-century satire dominantly toward the Juvenalian rather than Horatian side of the satiric spectrum.

The Persian Leaven

The *Satires* of Persius were translated or imitated in whole or large part at least thirteen times between the earlier seventeenth and earlier nineteenth centuries. There also were numerous imitations and translations of individual poems and adaptations of his presumed style and manner. These generally reduced themselves to two dominant modes, one somber "philosophic," weighty, and contemplative; the other snippy, politically involved, hostile to the ruling scoundrels, and concerned with the decay of literary standards. These models sometimes overlapped, and were subject to interpretation as to which was most representative; but the first and fourth satires tended to be regarded as dominantly political and the other three as dominantly philosophic.

A useful instance of the melancholic and marginally political Persian mode is John, Lord Hervey's *A Satire in the Manner of Persius: In a Dialogue Between Atticus and Eugenio. By a Person of Quality* (London, 1739). It is a bitter, melancholic, disillusioned, quasi-Christian, and stoic poem. For our purposes, however, it is most interesting in two ways: its use of dialogue as essential to Persius' manner; and its immediate assumption that the speakers are "quality" and educated, as befits the highest born and most academic of the three great Latin satirists. But Persius' dialogue had a significant difference from Horace's and especially Pope's, where it is an emblem of dialectic, of the thrust, counter-thrust and resolution of argument. Neither Persius nor Hervey offers substantial growth and interplay between the speakers. Instead, we have characters enunciating set pieces with general rather than particular targets (a veiled Nero excepted). But Persius' dialogue, if not Hervey's conception of it, did in fact offer Pope an apparently unique convention. As John Aden notes, Persius alone among his colleagues uses "an adversary between whom and the satirist there exists genuine tension or opposition, and he is the only one to make his adversary notably naive or intellectually corrupt."[27] That device, we know, characterizes much of Pope's dialogue form.

The other Persian mode is well exemplified in five different adaptations, imitations, or translations between 1733 and 1740, each of which makes overt the perceived similarity between Juvenalian and this kind of Persian satire.[28] For example, in 1740 Benjamin Loveling imitates the first satire and turns it into a piece of opposition propaganda that clarifies the presumed *"Obscurity"* of the poem by means of cleverly attacking the court and administration and praising Pope and the opposition. Loveling's Persius ridicules "Bad Poets . . . Bad Orators, and . . . the depraved Taste of Rome, in admiring the wretched Performance of Nero and his Nobles" (sig. A1ʳ). He also dislikes "what *Cibber* sings" and *"Grubstreet* Swans [who] delight the Ear of Kings" (p. 5). *Gazetteers* are the mere "Beings of a Day" (p. 7), and though he purports to admire George II, he knows that he himself is the lone soldier fighting barbarism (p. 7) and that he can have no praise if he does not write a Birthday Ode, those "Songs by the Court and vulgar Great admir'd" (p. 11). Predictably, in such a depraved world revered opposition leaders have no place, and so Stair and Cobham, "Sick of the Fool's and Parasite's Resort, / Retire, illustrious Exiles from a Court!" (p. 13). The poem is punctuated with references to stage licensing, Fanny, poor Jenkins' lost ear, echoes of Pope, and praise of him as the "sworn Foe to Knave and fool" who assailed Timon, Chartres, Peter, Ward, and Balaam (p. 19).

Loveling's posture may have been influenced by the splendidly intemperate attack (perhaps by Paul Whitehead) one year earlier, which credits Juvenal and Persius as being the joint authors of a mélange called *The State of Rome Under Nero and Domitian.* That is of course a collapsing state, and one shown to be through the poem's imitations of parts of Persius I and IV, and Juvenal I, III and VII, each of whose supporting Latin appears at the foot of the page. Juvenal–Persius says that "Fierce Indignation boils within my Veins" (p. 5) because of the political and literary corruption around him. He supports Pope's attacks on the administration and berates Walpole's manipulation of George II and his "depending, gaping, servile Court" (p. 14).

Persius shared political outrage and sympathies with Juvenal; he was even more concerned with the fate of literature. Here is part of Thomas Brewster's Argument to his translation of Persius' first satire, a poem, like the rest of Brewster's Persius, so accommodated to aspects of Pope's style and concerns, that the collected volume of 1741 was printed with Pope's name on the title page. Literary worth aside, that error is understandable, since this argument could serve to gloss much of Pope's imitation of the first satire of Horace's second book and his *Epistle to Dr. Arbuthnot*:

We may suppose the Author to be just seated in his Study, and beginning to vent his Indignation in Satire. At this very Juncture, comes in an Acquaintance, who, upon hearing the first Line, dissuades him, by all Means, from an undertaking so perilous; advising him rather, if he needs must write, to accommodate his Vein to the Taste of the Times, and to write like other People.

PERSIUS acknowledges that this, indeed, were the readiest Method to gain Countenance and Applause; but then adds, that the Approbation of such Patrons as this Compliance would recommend him to, was a Thing to be desired on no Terms at all; much less, upon Terms so shameful . . . The only Readers whose Applause *he* covets, must be Men of Virtue, and Men of Sense.[29]

The "Men of Virtue, and Men of Sense" – naturally from the opposition – reappear in Pope's *Fortescue*, and they suggest how the Juvenalian and Persian conventions combined and helped Pope to turn an Horatian poem in praise of the Augustan court and its values, into an opposition poem in defiance of the new Augustan court and its values. In the process, Pope abandons allegiance to the poet he is supposedly imitating: he takes Horace's first satire of the second book, and much of its context, language, and devices; but he borrows from Persius and Juvenal as well, so that the Horatian poem virtually becomes a double palimpsest, with the original certainly not erased, but certainly not dominant either.

Pope and the Mingled Muse

There are several obvious ways in which Pope's poem is genuinely Horatian. Horace supplies the framework, the original imitated on the facing page and peering at us with its italics, roman type, solid caps and empty spaces as the occasion requires. If we are to read Pope properly we must read Horace as well, and see that Horace's poem did, as Pope put it, hit his circumstances.[30] Like Horace, Pope must defend himself and his genre and show that both are part of accepted satiric procedures. By giving such an historically dignified "answer from Horace," often with Horace's own words Englished, Pope places himself in a familiar and already justified tradition, and places his detractors in an equally familiar and defeated position. By implication, their arguments are even more tired and unconvincing in 1733 than they were over 1,700 years ago. Similarly, Pope's dialogue and dialectic, his adversarius as a distinguished lawyer associated with the court, the frequent tones of civilized banter and wit play, and the adversarius' ultimate acceptance of Pope's case, all have deep roots in Mediterranean soil. The same may be said of Pope's brilliant use of his "own" voice and personality, a device adapted from Horatian precedent. As Jean Dusaulx would say in 1777, "Autant Juvénal, s'est caché dans son livre, autant Horace s'est montré dans le sien."[31] Consequently, many eighteenth-century and modern readers believe that Pope has in fact captured the spirit of Horace.

But these similarities often call forth their differences, and suggest manifestly un-Horatian, often anti-Horatian, techniques that were noticed by Pope's enemies. In 1734, for example, Mr. Gerard is unhappy about *Fortescue* and writes a hostile *Epistle to the Egregious Mr. Pope*. There the unoriginal, ugly, ungrateful Pope is seen "measuring swords" in open combat with Horace.[32] Gerard does not say whether Pope had allies in the fight, though Persius and Juvenal were, I believe, protecting his vulnerable flanks. Pope's Persian qualities emerge in a variety of ways. Fortescue was Pope's friend and aid, and could not be seriously attacked; but he does function as an amiable vehicle of administration values and does encourage standards that corrupt literature.

He joins his Roman ancestor in urging his "client's" abandonment of satire altogether. But "if you needs must write, write CAESAR's Praise: / You'll gain at least a *Knighthood*, or the *Bays*" (lines 21–22). Later, upon hearing the name of Sir Robert Walpole, he knows that all resistance is foolish, since one cannot quarrel with what he seems to approve. Horace's Trebatius is the friend of a wise and moral court that disarms the poet's misguided enemies; Pope's Fortescue is the friend of a shrewd but immoral court that arms and rewards the poet's enemies. The Persian corrupt adversary is paramount in Pope's bitter *Epilogue to the Satires* in 1738; but its seeds were planted in 1733.

The decline of literature as a function of the decline of political virtue again is Persian, as is the pose of the lonely satirist resisting the many vulgar poets encouraged by vulgar noble patrons. Horace cannot offer Augustus the epic praise he deserves; but he does command Augustus in a more familiar idiom, and makes him part of the moral center of the poem. Pope, on the contrary, urges that George II has done nothing to deserve praise. Those who offer it are either incompetent, sycophantic, or both. The laureate Cibber is the paradigm of one who accepts Fortescue's advice to sing Caesar's virtues and be rewarded. Pope is unable to cite a poet other than himself who criticizes bad politics and literature, and he later realizes that he is nearly alone as a defender of church and law and is threatened in body and spirit. As a rough parallel to this stand, listen to the final lines of Brewster's argument to Persius' first satire:

he takes occasion to expose the wretched Taste that prevailed then at *Rome*, both in . . . Verse and Prose; and informs us what abominable Stuff . . . noble Poetasters not only scribbled themselves, but encouraged in others. Of these miserable Attempts in the way of Poetry, the Author exhibits to us a small Specimen: At the same Time lamenting, that he dares not speak out with the Freedom allowable in former Times, and practiced by his Predecessors in Satire, *Lucilius* and *Horace*. He then concludes, expressing a generous Disdain for all worthless Blockheads whatever. (pp. 3–4)

For Pope, the free Lucilius of Persius' first satire replaced the more docile though still belligerent version in Horace. There Lucilius certainly attacked the praetors and consuls where necessary. But he is on excellent terms with the noble Scipio and Laelius, and it is that aspect of Lucilius' character with which Horace associates, and in fact with which the administration associates Horace. Persius was not so happy, and thus gives us a portrait of a savage Lucilius that Pope was to borrow in part from Dryden's translation.

> old *Lucilius* never fear'd the times;
> But lash'd the City, and dissected Crimes.
> *Mutius* and *Lupus*, both by Name he brought;
> He mouth'd 'em, and betwixt his Grinders caught.
>
> . . .
>
> Cou'd he do this, and is my Muse controll'd
> By Servile Awe? Born free, and not be bold?[33]

No indeed – and even less so for Pope, who redefines Horace's Lucilius. Pope neither places himself below his satiric ancestors nor approves of their closeness to the courts of their rulers, as Horace had done in each case. Instead, he urges that he is superior to the courtly Boileau and Dryden and, by extension, to Lucilius and Horace. We recall that Grainger praised Tibullus over Horace as "a true Patriot" for divorcing himself from the court – that is precisely the praise Pope wished to have. Horace says that *Lucilius* was a friend only to virtue and her friends, virtue here exemplified by two great men in authority. Pope speaks that line of *himself* and in the process affirms his Persian genealogy of freedom, boldness, and absence of awe and servility. He will be

> arm'd for *Virtue* when I point the Pen,
> Brand the bold Front of shameless, guilty Men,
> Dash the proud Gamester in his gilded Car,
> Bare the mean Heart that lurks beneath a Star;
>
> .   .   .
>
> Could pension'd *Boileau* lash in honest Strain
> Flatt'rers and Bigots ev'n in *Louis'* Reign?
> Could Laureat *Dryden* Pimp and Fry'r engage,
> Yet neither *Charles* nor *James* be in a Rage?
> And I not strip the Gilding off a Knave,
> Un-plac'd, un-pension'd, No Man's Heir, or Slave?
> I will, or perish in the gen'rous Cause.
> Hear this, and tremble! you, who 'scape the Laws.   (lines 105–18)

This elevated and rhetorical passage also has much Juvenalian force behind it, and reminds us that Pope too could be both witty and declamatory. Juvenal's Lucilius, even more than Persius, was a proud "out" who had no intention of being politically "in," and served primarily as a scourge of the wicked – with results that would have pleased Pope as he read them in Dryden's translation of Juvenal's first satire.

> But when *Lucilius* brandishes his Pen,
> And flashes in the face of Guilty Men,
> A cold Sweat stands in drops on ev'ry part.   (lines 251–53)

One must at least suspect that these and not Horatian lines are father to Pope's "I point the Pen / [to] Brand the bold Front of shameless, guilty Men" (lines 105–6). Pope looks beyond court satirists for his most exalted conventions – to the terrifying Lucilius of the republic as seen in Persius' and in Juvenal's rather than in Horace's apologia. The opposition Bolingbroke and Peterborough, "Chiefs, out of War, and Statesmen, out of Place" (line 126), are Pope's equivalents of Horace's Scipio and Laelius.

Mention of Pope's friends makes clear that he is abandoning Horace's satiric and personal as well as political values. Pope is anything but, in Batteux's terms, without malice, unwilling to name real persons, and willing to be gentle and take mankind as it is, so that "the wounded hardly feels any smart." Blackmore, Cibber, Bond, Scarsdale, Walter, Chartres, the royal family, and Sir Robert are among those specifically mentioned, often in rude language that tormented the administration. On 27 October 1738, for example, the *Gazetteer* savagely attacked Pope's satire and hunchbacked body, and insisted that however good a rallier Horace was, "he never took the Liberty to turn Persons of Consular Dignity into Ridicule." And even Boileau agreed that satirists "must not offend the *State*." Since for Pope and the opposition, Walpole was becoming both the consul and the state, not to offend him meant not writing satire at all – as Fortescue advised. Under such circumstances it is preferable (in the poem at least) to risk exile or death with Juvenal than share silence or general satire with Horace.

Juvenal even more than Persius depicts the hordes of successful wicked men victimizing the few defenders of virtue. Hence his third satire shows us a humble Roman first metaphorically and then literally buried and crushed to pieces by the new Rome (lines 257–61). Only extraordinary courage can resist such force; and that is what Pope shows in his insistence that "What-e'er my Fate" (line 92), "In Durance, Exile, Bedlam, or the Mint" (line 99) he shall attack highly placed knaves "or perish in the gen'rous Cause" (line 177). Pope is fighting government becoming progressively more powerful and dangerous to the health of the nation and of Pope himself. In the poem of 1733 Fortescue predicts that some of the offended great will conspire and take Pope's life (line 104). On 12 June and again on 27 October 1738 the *Gazetteer* threatened Pope with a fatal beating for his satires.[34] Because Pope is the emblem of genuine poetry, a threat to him also is a threat to the besieged republic of letters. The violence in Horace's satire remains "comic" because fenced by the protective armor of Augustan order. The violence in Pope's suggests the tragic and the Juvenalian because there is no protective order other than that of his own verse, the moral world of Twickenham, and Sir Robert Walpole's court – the latter a protection of perhaps dubious stability. Pope's poem includes a variety of ominous words addressed to him and by him, and reminds us that the satire's happy ending could easily have taken another turn. The poem includes a portion of friendly and positive remarks as well, for this is not apocalyptic but formal verse satire, in which there is hope for a relapse into virtue, and the models for such virtue must be plain. And they are, more so than in Horace's satire, which lacks the perfect coherence of opposition vs. administration, country vs. court. But one is aware of the tenuous success of Pope's defense of himself, one made legally convincing only because Pope fantasizes that Walpole will like his satire and because under those circumstances prosecution is pointless.[35] Yet both satirist and adversarius are aware that Pope now is poetically, and could be literally, put on trial for his opposition verse, as Paul Whitehead was in 1739 for his relatively mild poem *Manners*. As Fortescue puts it, "have a care," since a man may be "hang'd for very honest Rhymes" (lines 144, 146). And so Pope says, in an appropriately legal term, and after a noble summation that includes his own merits of character and politics: "This is my Plea, on this I rest my Cause" (line 141).

Whatever the momentary success, Pope continued to need defense well before the *Gazetteer*'s threats of 1738. In 1735 Thomas Bentley's *A Letter to Mr. Pope* accuses him of being "almost treasonable!" in his praise of Bolingbroke in the *Essay on Man*. And he insists that in *Fortescue* itself Pope's proclamation of his own friendship to virtue in capital letters is nonsense, since Bolingbroke could not possibly be virtuous. "You have but little your self," he tells Pope, and concludes that what Pope really means in his un-Horatian imitation is *"To my self only and my Friends a Friend"* (p. 12). No wonder Thomas Newcomb later portrayed the administration ally Horace indignantly saying to his imitator: "If you quote more – I must protest, / And swear your Sense is none of mine."[36] It was, I think, Juvenal's sense that Pope was adapting.

One final example of the Juvenalian convention of exalting the virtuous heroes of the past may be instructive. Pope urges the impossibility of praising George II, but he is eminently capable of praising those who could regain British glory if not for Walpole's debilitating peace policy and the Hanoverian banishment of Stuart luminaries. Pope thus sings Charles Mordaunt, Earl of Peterborough, Queen Anne's conqueror of Barcelona and Valencia in 1705 and 1706, and now a denizen of the old virtuous England epitomized at Twickenham. That is, I believe, an elegant parallel to Juvenal's third satire, where lingering republican virtues are preserved in the country far from the corrupt city and its imperial degradation. Horace cites the Augustan court as a norm; Juvenal skips several generations of time and several miles of space to cite his republican norm. Pope's practice is similar to Juvenal's, as we go from Hanoverian to Stuart, and London to Twickenham when settling on Peterborough for praise as the living exemplar of what Britain can and should do to the offending Spaniards (lines 129–32).

Some Implications

If this essay has been convincing, it has implications for the study of Pope and of eighteenth-century satire in general. We should further expand our generally monolithic view of Pope's satiric genealogy, for it now allows us to believe that *Fortescue* ends with what one recent commentator has called "the burst of curative laughter that it is the end of true satire to produce."[37] A study of Pope's imitations that assumes one kind of "true satire" and thus one "true" response cannot transcend the Horatian mode of satire and cannot be faithful to Pope's view of his art or politics. Moreover, the related conventions of Persius and Juvenal that Pope used tilt the satiric balance away from administration and Horatian satire, and towards an opposition, indignant, minority bias that characterizes so much verse satire of the 1730s – indeed, much of the eighteenth century. Perhaps, too, we should reconsider the beatification of a genteel, mythic, Pope who wished to make at Twickenham a Christian–Palladian Sabine farm so that a modern Flaccus the Second could reign like Flaccus the First. As Pope's contemporaries, especially his victims, testified, he was more eclectic, hostile, and both sublime and vulgar than such an approach suggests. And it hides us from what I think a truth of Pope's conception of his satire: he turned to Juvenal and Persius because Horace was an inadequate guide, and by the mid 1730s often was regarded as morally and politically offensive, though his supreme artistry continued to give pleasure and practical instruction. Only the full panoply of classical satirists could have begun to satisfy the needs of Pope's emulative imagination and to offer the abundance of literary and moral "choices" he needed. As a young man in 1717 Pope said that "All that is left us is to recommend our productions by the imitation of the Ancients."[38] That may be the only libel for which he should have been prosecuted.

10 · PERSIUS, THE OPPOSITION TO WALPOLE, AND POPE

Persius has generally been considered far less attractive than Horace or Juvenal, and thus far less important as a contributor to the history of British satire. Indeed, the few modern studies of Persius' relevance for the eighteenth century suggest an advanced case of anorexia, a willful starvation and withdrawal of nourishment rather than a healthy leanness.[1] Most earlier readers also placed Persius beneath Horace and Juvenal, though still in their qualitative group, and still of great interest and significance. His dark, rough, grave poems were essential for the ongoing Renaissance view of what satire should be, and his other conventions mingled well with those of Juvenal to create a satirist of immediate utility for Pope and the opposition to Walpole – the biting, hostile, somber, virtuous outcast who attacked a society rotting from the top down.

Some of his attraction can be documented in the list of English translations from 1616 to 1817: Holyday (1616), Dryden (1693), Eelbeck (1719), Sheridan (1728), Senhouse (1730), Stirling (1736), Brewster (1733–42), Burton (1752), Madan (1789), Drummond (1797), anonymous (1806), Howes (1809), and Gifford (1817).[2] Oldham acknowledges his debt to Persius for the Prologue of his *Satyrs upon the Jesuits* (1679); F. A. imitates the third satire in 1685; Tom Brown tries his hand at the Prologue and part of the first satire in 1707; six different imitators emerge between 1730 and 1740; Thomas Neville imitates most of the satires in 1769; Edward Burnaby Greene follows suit in 1779; an unknown author applies the fourth satire to Pitt in 1784; William Gifford's *Baviad* (with its title-page motto from Juvenal 1.1–4) massively expands the first satire in 1791; and George Daniel's *Modern Dunciad* performs a similar task in 1814.[3] Persius was of course commented upon in numerous encyclopedias, manuals, discussions of Roman satire, and Latin editions of his works, and was often translated in France, where he again was regarded as the least exalted of the elevated three. No doubt this is a partial list, since the voluminous miscellanies and collected poems must harbor other individual efforts. One may say, erring on the side of conservatism, that from the earlier seventeenth to the earlier nineteenth century in Britain, Persius enjoyed a minimum of thirteen complete translations, two nearly complete groups of imitations, eleven imitations or translations of individual satires, and much commentary, controversy, and pedagogical application. Multiple English, Continental, and Latin editions, many known in Britain, would swell this list substantially. Reclamation of Persius' conventions and reputation suggests that his influence must have been virtually inevitable, and inevitably in the direction of Juvenal and Pope.

Perceptions of Persius

The eighteenth century's Persian inheritance probably begins in 1605, with Isaac Casaubon's *Prolegomena* and edition of the satires which – together with his revolutionary *De Satyrica Graecorum et Satira Romanorum* – became loci classici of the study of Persius and formal verse satire. To Casaubon goes the credit for permanently forcing Persius into the same circle as Horace and Juvenal, vigorously resisting Scaliger's attacks upon Persius, and establishing his reputation as a dominantly political satirist. From Dacier and Dryden to Drummond and Howes, most roads lead to and from Casaubon.[4]

His *Prolegomena* insists that the three Roman satirists must be examined with respect for their different individual contributions and for their "nearly equal . . . diverse virtues," each of which he describes in familiar terms.[5] Casaubon's defense implies that he prefers Persius to his brother-satirists, but he nonetheless concludes modestly "that there is no one of these who was not superior to the rest by a certain virtue peculiar to himself; and, again, that there was no one who was not inferior to the rest for some reason" (p. 294).

Obscurity was one of the points on which Persius needed defense. Casaubon turns that apparent fault into an asset, and characterizes Persius as a courageous and clever satirist in the face of political intimidation: "In Persius what spirit? What ardor? What stimulus? For indeed his outspokenness was so great that he could not be induced even by fear of death to spare Nero" (p. 293). Since Persius was not foolhardy and did not court the separation of body from soul before its proper time, he intentionally wrote obscure verse "out of fear of that most cruel and bloodthirsty of tyrants against whom" his satires were written. The source of this wisdom was his tutor Cornutus, "who as an old man repeatedly whispered to him the words, 'be obscure.' Although Probus, or whoever is the writer of the life, does not say this explicitly, he nevertheless reports matters from which we ought to infer this much" (p. 296). These and comparable remarks would echo throughout the next 200 years.

After 1605, in fact, nearly everyone agreed that Nero was Persius' main target in several of his six satires. In England translators from Holyday to Howes, from 1616 to 1809, tell British readers that, as Senhouse puts it, Persius "aims particularly at [Nero] in most of his Satirs."[6] This opinion appears in France as well, and even though the formidable Pierre Bayle, later joined by the Abbé le Monnier in 1771, characteristically doubts that received truth, he admits that his is a minority opinion. "I should never have done," he says, "if I undertook to quote all the Authors who imagine that" Persius attacks Nero's unfortunate taste and poetry by citing four lines from his presumed, and bad, tragedy.[7] These commentators also tend to follow Casaubon in explaining Persius' obscurity. As Holyday says, difficulty in reading Persius proceeds in part "from the want of Libertie, which in his desperate times, was altogether lost."[8] Far later Senhouse confirms that "the Fear of his Safety under *Nero*, compell'd him to this Darkness in some Places" (sig. A4[r]). In 1736 John Stirling offers a similar commonplace to his schoolboy audience: though Persius aimed at Nero in nearly all of his satires, he was "prudent enough not to arraign him openly and plainly."[9]

For some critics, the veil of obscurity extended beyond the grave. According to M. Selis in 1776, Persius' satires appeared after his death because only in that way of self-censorship could he be secure in attacking Nero. He thus joined caution to courage. 'Il eut la sagesse de retenir son Ouvrage, & il mourut dans son lit." Since Cornutus had comparable affection for his own life, he refused to edit the satires, surrendering them instead to Caesius Bassus. Selis is confident that Persius' consistent attacks upon Nero are clear enough so that haters of the tyrant would recognize them, and obscure enough so that the tyrant himself could not understand them. No courtier would dare to explicate such satire in order to illumine his master's darkness. Apparently, for courtiers as well as poets, "il falloit être obscur ici, sous peine de la vie."[10]

Nero was a target because of his own corrupt taste and character and their influence on his subservient aristocrats, for, as a bad poet, the emperor encouraged a perverse emulation of incompetence. According to Senhouse, in Satire 1 "*Persius* covertly strikes at *Nero*, some of whose Verses he recites with Scorn and Indignation. He also takes notice of the Noblemen and their abominable Poetry, who in the Luxury of their Fortune, set up for Wits and Judges" (p. 6). John Stirling adds that "as a Friend to true Learning," Persius sharply lashed "the corrupt and degenerate Taste both of the Poets and Orators of his Time" (sig. A3[r]), and especially the poetry of Nero. Persius thus appeared to Pope's ancestors and contemporaries as a poet concerned with the decay of letters and with the imperial cause of that decay. "Indignation breaks out more and more because they would make such base and affected Verse," Eelbeck observes of Satire 1.[11]

These cultural and political poses evoked a variety of related satiric conventions, four of which are especially useful for our purposes: disguise, dialogue, the nature of the adversarius, and irony.

John Stirling discusses the consequence of Persius' politically enforced obscurity – disguise, or what we might call the use of a persona for the poet, and historical label or analogue for his victim. Persius, Stirling claims, "was oblig'd to strike at [Nero] under borrowed Names, the better to evade his cruel Resentment" (sig. A3[r]). Comparable remarks pervade the criticism of

Persius throughout the seventeenth and eighteenth centuries. According to Dryden, such role-playing begins in the Prologue itself, which hoped to conceal its author's name and station. "He liv'd in the dangerous Times of the tyrant *Nero*; and aims particularly at him, in most of his Satyrs. For which Reason, though he was a *Roman* Knight, and of a plentiful Fortune, he wou'd appear in this Prologue, but a Beggarly Poet, who Writes for Bread."[12] In 1728 Thomas Sheridan observes that in Satire I "it is very probable that *Persius* levels at *Nero* under this covert Name" of Polydamus. Sheridan also joins previous commentators and anticipates later ones in saying that in Satire IV Persius "levels at *Nero* under the name of *Alcibiades*, for presuming to undertake the Administration of publick Affairs, without sufficient Qualifications for so great an Undertaking."[13] Just two years thereafter John Senhouse offers virtually the same argument and traces its provenance to Casaubon, who "made it apparent, that the Sting of this Satir was particularly aim'd at *Nero*" (p. 97).

The many shifts of speaker were another reason for the apparent obscurity of Persius. According to Casaubon, because of satire's "affinity with the plots of drama, it is complicated by the shifts of personae" (*Prolegomena*, p. 297). De la Valterie dutifully concurs in 1680 and says that because satire is a species of comedy, there are frequent changes of voice in Persius' poems. "La première est toute de cette sort. . . C'est un Dialogue perpetuel."[14] These shifts were thought to have been largely sorted out by the eighteenth century, and so readers knew who was speaking to whom. The dialogue between them, however, is quite different from that of Horace and the Pope of *Fortescue* and *Arbuthnot*, where dialogue represents both argument and resolution of argument. Persius does not offer a sense of growth and interplay between speakers. Instead we have unchanging characters enunciating noble or ignoble set pieces, and, often, with general rather than particular targets. Edward Burnaby Greene observes something along these lines when, in 1779, he says that Horace portrays "*living* Characters" in action, whereas Persius is busy "'teaching the passions to move' in the higher circle of *Personification*" and that his dialogues were closer to "the spirit of Epic Poesy" than to the conflict between "the human puppets of the *Horatian Drama*."[15] More than forty years later William Gifford would complain that Persius "drew his ideas of mankind from the lessons of his preceptor, and looked upon human actions in the abstract; not modified and controlled by conventional circumstances, but . . . independent of all extrinsick influence."[16]

I suspect that Burnaby Greene and Gifford have overstated the degree to which disembodied voices palaver in the thin air of Persius' poems; but there is a satirically and aesthetically sound reason for such relatively non-terrestrial conflicts; namely, the participants are so morally distant that they cannot hear or influence one another. Eighteenth-century readers knew that the Monitor who tried to dissuade Persius from writing shared the values of

Nero's court and courtiers. When he warns Persius that the doors of the great may be closed to him and that he will be in danger if he continues to write, the Monitor is not trying to protect Persius, but the objects of Persius' satire (lines 107–10). In a comparable situation Horace was able to move Trebatius to his side, for the emperor and his aristocratic friends were Horace's allies (*Satires* II.i). Persius, on the other hand, has created an adversarius who is unchanging in his support for the corrupt values that a decent man would abandon. John Aden accurately points out that Persius is the only one of the three Roman satirists to use such a device.[17] Horace reforms, dismisses, or shares values with his adversaries; Juvenal's occasional real – rather than nonce – adversarius normally is on his side or is scarcely vocal enough to ruffle the poem's rhetorical monologue; Persius alone gives us a corrupt or uneducable foil to the morally triumphant but defeated satirist. Because the satirist cannot refute someone incapable of understanding his own folly, Persius invited his readers to see the adversarius discredit himself. Pope, I shall argue, was among those who recognized this device, and saw, as Francis Howes remarks, that "the objector is represented as sliding imperceptibly into self-ridicule till he exposes his own cause."[18]

As a result of the impenetrable dullness before him, Persius sometimes must retreat behind the protection of both masked and revelatory irony. Henry Eelbeck observes that the fourth satire's apparent attack upon Alcibiades really is "an Ironical Oration, vehement and very sharp," that labels Nero an unprepared ruler "intirely ignorant, either to condemn the Guilty, or to defend the Innocent" (p. 43n). The sixth satire includes "A Satyrical Irony in the Person of some third Speaker" (p. 80 n1). In 1752 Edmund Burton praises the politics and political irony in Satire I, for the satirist could not openly attack his emperor as a bad poet. Indeed, most auditors praised Nero's verse, "it being his constant custom to bribe people into an approbation of his ridiculous writings."[19] Hence, Burton says, in a passage that illuminates Persius' use of political opposition, disguise, and irony,

The following five lines [from line 59] are beautifully couched under a strong irony, and the greater pains we take to discover their beauties, the greater will be the pleasure which results from a true knowledge of their meaning. By the word *Iane* [*Janus*] we are to understand *Nero*, as by the words *Patricius sanguis* [*blue-blooded patricians*] following, is meant the *Roman* nobility. By this subtle irony *Persius* seems to be paying *Nero* a great compliment; whereas those three lines mean quite the reverse of what they seem to import. (p. 20)

Similarly, when the Monitor warns Persius not to be so critical, or he will be in professional and personal danger, Persius immediately plays the docile poet and says: "Well, well, have your way; I will paint everything white henceforth. Bravo! Bravo! You shall all be paragons of creation. Will that please you?" (lines 110–11).[20] Whether it pleased the Monitor we cannot say, though the wit did please Burton: "This is an ironical concession . . . This is said with a masterly sagacity, to appease the person he is speaking to here, who cautions him against writing too fully" (p. 30).

Commentators and readers were also interested in the man behind "Persius," and found that he was both like and unlike his satiric mask. Barten Holyday praises Persius' prudent bravery, political virtue, consequent anger at those without it, and the punishment he must therefore inflict. Such a reincarnation of Brutus and his now dead Roman virtues shall take his purer fire and burn out "th' envenom'd fogges of Vice" from their seat of infection.

> And then inflame
> Them, that they may be lights to their own shame;
> Which as a Comet, may affright the Earth
> With horror, at its own prodigious birth;
> And, with its darting tail threatening dread
> Vengeance, point-out to wrath each guilty Head.

F. A., in 1685, relates Persius' bravery to the poet's own virtue, which must overcome all. He thus has the tutor, thought to be a persona for Persius in the third satire, tell his student: "*Dare* to be good; – and *Vertue* be thy Guide; / No way to daring *Vertue* is deny'd."[21] Henry Eelbeck, on whose list of "Encouragers and Subscribers" Dr. Arbuthnot appears in 1719, characterizes Persius as scorning the vulgar opinion of his Monitor who discouraged his writing of satires. He would vigorously soldier on, "notwithstanding all the Vengeance that might befal him either from *Nero* the Emperor, or any Nobleman at *Rome*" (p. 3). And, as Senhouse insists, Persius, who "is of a free Spirit, breaks through all these Difficulties, and boldly arraigns the false Judgement of the Age in which he lives" (p. 7).

Prudent bravery, good taste, and animosity to bad taste clearly bring with them other important traits of personal and literary character. In the first satire Persius describes himself as a teller of harsh truths (lines 56–57, 120–23) and a man whose petulance and spleen ("sed sum petulanti splene," line 12) burst forth in response to miserable art, for he knows true passion and can be moved only by it (lines 90–91). This indignation easily can be, and was, praised as necessary for the opponent of imperial vice. It also could be seen as unpleasant. In his *Poetices* (1561) Julius Caesar Scaliger labels Persius "morosus." By 1674 René Rapin tells readers in France and England that Persius is grave, vehement, obscure, and "speaks not but with *sadness*, what by *Horace* is said with the greatest mirth imaginable, whom sometimes he wou'd imitate; his moroseness scarce ever leaves him . . . and he never sports, but after the most serious manner in the world." Boileau calls Persius "un Philosophe chagrin"; the Abbé Batteux regards him as grave, serious, and "ever melancholic"; the *Encyclopédie* thinks him "un peu triste," as indeed does Edward Burnaby Greene, who remarks Persius' "gloom of severity due to the collapse of learning and morals in his age."[22]

Persius' indignation and sadness could be matters for reasoned evaluation, one group arguing that outrage and unhappiness are the appropriate responses to vice, the other arguing that the speaker seems to enjoy being hurtful and gives no pleasure with his solemnity, especially since the generic source of satire is comedy, not tragedy. But there was no difference of opinion regarding the essential morality of Persius the man. Many of his editors were schoolmasters who naturally were moved by the admiring and respectful relationship between the young satirist and Cornutus who, as John Stirling says, taught Persius to abhor the vices of Nero and the decline of learning. Stirling also admires the "unparallel'd Gratitude to his Master *Cornutus*" (sig. A3ʳ). Moreover, Persius was exemplary in other ways as well, and morally superior to either Horace or Juvenal. Like other commentators, Pierre Bayle draws his kind words from Probus' life of Persius.

He was a Roman Knight, and related both by blood and marriage to persons of the highest rank . . . He was a good friend, and a better son, brother and relation. He was perfectly chaste, though a very handsome man; he was sober, gentle as a lamb, and modest as a young virgin: so true it is, that we must not always judge of a man's morals from his writings, for Persius's *satyrs* are very licentious, and full of rancour and gall.   (7:324–25)

Such beneficence was praised throughout the seventeenth and eighteenth centuries. Bishop Gilbert Burnet frequently was cited as having recommended Persius' satires as excellent quasi-Christian sermons.[23] In 1705 Thomas Jaffray also notes that Persius' morality often was Christian, and one year later in France, le Noble argues that Persius was a wiser and more accomplished philosopher than Horace or Juvenal, as his spiritually Christian fifth satire makes clear. Stirling thus is conventional when he observes that Persius "had a sincere Veneration for Religion, as may be discover'd by his Writings" (sig. A3ʳ). Near mid century "Sir" John Hill is aware of Persius' many weaknesses – including his insults rather than more pleasing laughter – but, he tells a noble lord no doubt interested in such matters, "he is worth the pains: his sense is worth the search. His virtue is a point in which he excels all the rest of the satyrists, and to me his eminence in this compensates for all and would compensate for more than all his faults."[24]

During the Restoration and eighteenth century, then, there was one nearly unchallenged view of Persius: he was the brave, prudent, serious satirist who attacked moral, political, and literary vice, especially as exemplified by the tasteless, wicked, bribing Nero and his court. Since open attack would have meant death, he resorted to masks, irony, a self-refuting, self-condemning, and uneducable adversarius, and the obscurity his friend and tutor urged upon him; he even refused to publish his satires until after his death, thus assuring that he could be reasonably satirical during his lifetime. The decay around him both angered and saddened him, but did not affect his personal ethics, family life, or religious views, all of which were excellent, in spite of the severity and occasional vulgarity in his poems. Though probably not so great a satirist as Horace or Juvenal, he was their moral superior, and certainly in their approximate qualitative rank.

With these traits and conventions before us, two remarks must be made.

First, as many readers knew, in spite of Persius' use of some Horatian techniques, his satiric vision includes more of Juvenal's declining world than Horace's stable one, and thus includes more bitterness than equanimity. Late in the century William Boscawen was among those who had made the connection between Persius and Juvenal. Post-Horatian times

> Saw angry Satire, wak'd by daring crimes;
> When from the Stoic school grave Persius brought
> The rigid lore her ancient sages taught,
> And ardent virtue with sublimer rage
> Inspir'd fierce Juvenal's indignant page.[25]

The choice of satiric options thus was heavily weighted on the side of a satirist portraying himself as the outnumbered, brave, hostile enemy of daring crimes in the state, crimes commonly inspired by monarchic and aristocratic precedent. Second, Persius, like Juvenal himself, was therefore adaptable for the needs of Alexander Pope and his colleagues in the outraged, gloomy, disaffected, "patriot" opposition to Sir Robert Walpole.

Persius and Opposition

As early as 1685 an angry adapter of Persius struck what would become a familiar pose. The tutor, confident of the power of "daring *Vertue*," speaks to his student and hopes that the "Great *Sovereign* of the Skies" will vouchsafe "To scourge the Pride of Tyrants" by showing them the face of goodness and the felicity they have lost. So punished, they will "*turn pale*, and pine away, and dye."[26] Whether this satire was read in the 1730s is doubtful, and irrelevant, for it nevertheless shows Persius' lashing and contemplative mode and makes plain that he was known to poets as well as commentators for his dialogue, praise of virtue, insistence on close human relationships, and immediate involvement in the resistance to tyranny.

Several of these traits were blended with Persius' melancholic and, in this case, marginally political mode in John, Lord Hervey's unsigned *A Satire in the Manner of Persius: In a Dialogue Between Atticus and Eugenio. By a Person of Quality.*[27] Atticus at first is indignant regarding man, and his friend Eugenio is sadly disillusioned: "I thought Men worthless, now I've prov'd 'em so," he laments (p. 10). Since Atticus already has that knowledge and is aware of the "Senate's sinking Fame" and Britain's mere "Shew of Freedom dwindled to a Name," lashing the wicked age is appropriate (p. 6). After this Juvenalian outburst Atticus goes on to offer quasi-stoical advice and urges Eugenio to laugh at men's follies before he weeps at their faults. If the wicked prosper,

> submit, for Prudence lies
> In suffering well – 'Tis equally unwise
> To see the Injuries we won't resent,
> And mourn the Evils which we can't prevent.   (p. 8)

In spite of Eugenio's efforts, he cannot take this sound advice, and regretfully says that he is immune from disappointments, because immune from the vain hopes of joy: "Repuls'd, I strive; betray'd I trust no more" (p. 9). After several complaints, lashings, and reluctant acceptance of the world's miserable condition – "What Joy for Truth, what Commerce for the Just?" (p. 14) – Atticus praises his friend's early wisdom and refusal to be seduced by secular tinsel. He consoles us with a Christianized stoic vision and an orthodox answer to a familiar question regarding the existence of evil, for man's dim sight cannot see God's just plan:

> undeserv'd he ne'er inflicts a Woe,
> Nor is his Recompence unsure, tho' slow.
> Unpunish'd none transgress, deceiv'd none trust,
> His Rules are fix'd, and all his Ways are Just. (p. 17)

The manner of Persius is reflected in the stoical but also bitter personal and political tones of the educated and aristocratic speakers appropriate for the highest born and most academic of the three great Latin satirists.

Hervey's commitment to Walpole's government made it difficult for him to portray too corrupt a political world, for that would reflect upon those from whom he still hoped to gain rewards. Most of the poem thus is general and laments the human, not Walpolean, situation. But Walpole's literary enemies were quick to realize that the general could be made particular, Zeno could be altered to Cobham, the tyrants of the mind replaced by the tyrants of the court, and that Nero could evoke George II, Walpole, or both. Historical parallels were popular with the opposition in part because of the legal camouflage they supplied. In 1741 the anonymous author of *The Art of Poetry* (London) ironically tells his antiministerial readers that

> Old *Roman Names* your Characters suit best;
> Secure, as if in *Roman* Armour drest.
> Happy the Author whose Performance shines
> With living *Nero*'s, living *Catilines*! (p. 9)

At least five such occasional well-armored efforts suggest that, in varying degrees, the opposition was in league with Juvenal and Persius and generally found Horace irrelevant or antithetical for its purposes. Indeed, as the "progress" of these poems suggests, the imitations get harsher, more overtly political, more Juvenalian, and more indebted to Pope as the decade advances.

The first is a relatively muted anonymous adaptation of the fourth satire and its attack upon Nero. In *Advice to an Aspiring Young Gentleman of Fortune* (London, 1733) that unpleasant emperor has been replaced by his modern equivalent, the author's "*garter'd* Friend . . . / To whom an injur'd Nation Vengeance owes." The court is a place "of *well-invented* Lies" where the "Dangers of *Excise*" must be slurred over (p. 5), where the corrupt rich thrive, where purchased coronets abound, and where flattery, and not achievement, will "fit you for *Preferment* in a trice" (p. 10). It is best, the honest speaker urges, to leave the ticklish helm of government "to —*y*'s saving Hand" (p. 10). That line surely supports replacement of Walpole with Pulteney, is hostile to the gartered knight, and commissions Persius as a Roman officer in the opposition's British army.

One year later the pseudonymous Griffith Morgan D'Anvers is less subtle than his predecessor. D'Anvers' *Persius Scaramouch: Or, a Critical and Moral Satire on the Orators, Scriblers, and Vices of the present Times* (London, 1734) imitates Persius' first satire and dedicates it to Pulteney, without benefit of nonobfuscating dashes. D'Anvers, in dialogue with Henley, immediately opposes the "ministerial Crew of profligate Scriblers" (p. iii) who try to defame Pulteney, aligns himself with Juvenal, who also had to say, "Semper ego auditor tantum nunquamne reponam?" (p. iii), and labels himself "a Man of a true old *British* Spirit and Integrity." D'Anvers also alludes to, and approves of, Pope's earlier and potential attacks on the administration. He himself offers his political and moral enemies "a little present and gentle Chastisement"; but he is assured that their miserable characters "will be transmitted to Posterity with all the Infamy they deserve, by a Person of as great a Genius as this, or perhaps any other Age hath produc'd" (p. iv).

For some the mask of Persius has a partially downturned tragic mouth; for many others it has bared teeth and satyr's horns by which the administration was not amused, and which it hoped its own writers could obviate. In *Persius Scaramouch*, for instance, Sir Robert is mocked as inviting hacks to "caper nimbly o'er [his] Stick," and to sing "Not to their own, but to his Honour's Notes" (p. 7). Similarly, the named "W–p–le's Gold and Coxcomb's Praise" have also allowed "worthless Scriblers" to usurp the laureateship (p. 13). Juvenalian qualities in the Persius poem, however, consist of more than opposition and attacks on the Robinocracy by a nonaristocratic speaker; they also include both personal bitterness of tone and a cultural theory of causation, each related to the political climate induced by Walpole. Hence the main speaker stresses his *"British* Mind" (p. 9), refusal to compromise with corruption (pp. 9, 11, 13 and passim), persecution because of his poverty and virtue (pp. 9, 17), and consequent anger, gall (p. 9), and spite (p. 19). This imitation could have as its motto the Juvenalian tag "Who cannot write satire in such an age?" One of the reasons he must write far transcends personal deprivation: Wherever he looks he sees decay. "How ripe for Ruin is the present Age!" the poem begins (p. 9), in a more than free rendering of Persius' "O Curas hominum! O quantum est in rebus inane!" to which D'Anvers' facing line refers. Commons, peers, courts of law, bishops, and most groups in society are corrupt in a world where "Who can be wickedest Men seem to strive" (p. 11). The reason for such ruin is made clear in the attack on the poet laureate appointed by the prime minister.

> Some *Cibber*'s Works peruse, and some rehearse
> Thy Flights *Blancoso* in *Miltonick* Verse.
> No wonder therefore, if the younger Fry,
> Unable to distinguish, read and try
> To write pert Nonsense, like the *London* Spy.   (p. 15)

The British people, like British virtues, are banished, "since *Frenchmen*, like a mighty Flood, / O're-spread the Land" and "belie our Father's Reins" (p. 17). Pope again must be the scourge who "roastedst well the Witlings of our Isle" (p. 19). D'Anvers, told by Henley that a surly Welshman like himself will never get past the great man's door, where only courtiers and Henleys prosper (p. 17), must retreat to the privacy of his close-stool for release from his spleen and spite. There he "Shall tear some Trifler's Works whene'er I sh–te" (p. 19).

By 1739 one Mr. Dudley, with better control of his bowels, had also turned the *First Satire of Persius* (London) to opposition use. His translation is dedicated to the Society of Antient Free Catonians, since there is a "near Affinity . . . in the respective Characters and Principles of our Satirist" and Cato. Each man enjoyed an abstemious severity in the cause of virtue and freedom: "If *Cato* scorn'd and detested *Caesar* on Account of his Tyranny and Usurpation; *Persius*, animated with the same Godlike Spirit, disdain'd to be the Slave of *Nero*, and held that Monster of Impiety in a like Abhorrence" (p. iv). The Argument of the poem also indicates that Persius hated the bad taste of Nero and his nobles, and emphasizes that Nero was "the Patron of every mean Pretender" to wit (p. 9), a man, the reader might suspect, perhaps something like Sir Robert. This Persius is the Juvenalian–Popean noble adversary of the horde of bad, court-encouraged poets, even though his prudent friend urges him to "desist. Invidious Truths conceal" (p. 11). For Dudley's Persius, if "none dare their Follies to disclose," his own "warm indignant Zeal" shall act: "Be mine the Province," he claims as protector of poetic virtue. "What can I do? My Spleen is too severe, / Such sordid Scribblers urge the scornful Sneer" (p. 11). In so doing, he is consciously in the great tradition of Lucilius, who "lash'd the latent Vices of the State" (p. 25), and of "subtle *Horace*," who slyly and politely destroyed foibles. "Shall I be cow'd, / Nor dare to whisper what they spoke aloud?" (p. 27). Clearly not, though Dudley is threatened with hanging by his ungentle adversarius (p. 25).

Even fuller antiministerial suggestions in the first satire were not to wait long before being plucked from the politicized classics. In 1740 Benjamin Loveling published his *First Satire of Persius Imitated* (London), the third known version in six years, and abandoned even the pretense of being deliberative, general, or stoic. He offers sheer opposition propaganda that clarifies the "Obscurity" of the poem. He attacks the court and Walpole, and of course praises Pope and the opposition. Loveling's Persius is a product of what the commentators long had taught. He ridicules "Bad Poets . . . Bad Orators, and . . . the depraved Taste of Rome, in admiring the wretched Perform-ances of *Nero* and his *Nobles*" (sig. A1ʳ). His modern counterpart implicitly compares the Neronian and Georgian dispensations, for he rejects both "what *Cibber* sings" and Grubstreet's bad poets who "delight the Ear of Kings" (p. 5). Writers of gazettes, like their journals, are mere "Beings of a Day," and though he pretends to praise George II, he is aware of his own role as the lone opponent of barbarism (p. 7) and of his adversarius' role as one of those many who hope to be "By Kings rewarded, and by Nobles prais'd" (p. 9). These grandees would want him to write Cibberian birthday odes, those "Songs by the Court and vulgar Great admir'd" (p. 11). The few opponents of such values are willing exiles from a corrupt world:

> *Stair* and *Cobham*, Names to *Britain* dear,
> Names which the Virtuous and the Wise revere,
> Sick of the Fool's and Parasite's Resort,
> Retire, illustrious Exiles from a Court! (p. 13)

The satire includes familiar opposition hostility to stage licensing, Fanny, Jenkins' unavenged lost ear, allusions to and echoes of Pope's satires, and consequent celebration of him as "sworn Foe to Knave and Fool" like Timon, Chartres, Peter, Ward, and Balaam (p. 19). The imitation has plucked the fig leaf of obscurity from Persius' satire upon "Nero," and left itself covered only by the shadow of a column from Cobham's opposition seat at Stowe, a world far different from the one Loveling sees in Walpole's London, where Truth is anathema:

> Feign but a Senate where Corruption reigns,
> And leads her courtly Slaves in golden Chains,
> Where one directs three hundred venal Tongues,
> And owes his Grandeur to a People's Wrongs;
> To —'s Favour can the Bard pretend?
> *No* Hints he cries, the Minister's my Friend;
> And for the *Sock* the Stage is never free,
> For draw a Blockhead —'s Death! the Dog means me! (p. 15)

In contrast, "'Tis Noise and Froth that *Young* or *Blackmore* sings, / Tho' both were favour'd with the Smiles of Kings" (p. 17). Not surprisingly, by now this modern Persius is unwilling even to pretend to keep his harsh satire in the secure privacy of his book. His heroes are not Lucilius and Horace but Dryden and the hostile Pope,[28] and his poetical enemies are all those including Boileau and Prior, who praise kings. By 1740 Loveling's Persius has eschewed even the transparent irony of earlier masks and insists on speaking out. His satirist will remain undaunted in the cause of virtue, and "Yes, I will sneer the Follies of Mankind" (p. 19).

This indignant opposition Persius is a close kinsman of Pope and Juvenal, as Paul Whitehead makes clear in his unsigned *The State of Rome, Under Nero and Domitian: A Satire. Containing, A List of Nobles, Senators, High Priests, Great Ministers of State, &c. &c. &c.* (London, 1739). This bitter poem pretends to be written "by Messrs. Juvenal and Persius" and imitates scattered sections of Persius, *Satires* I and IV, and Juvenal, I, III, VII, and VIII, whose patchwork quilt of supporting Latin appears beneath the English. The amalgamated satirist asks, "What Ribs of Iron can my Gall contain?" (p. 4), and proclaims that "Fierce Indignation boils within my Veins" (p. 5) at the political and consequent literary corruption around him. He thus turns to Pope for support in his Juvenalian–Persian poem and alludes to his satires as another natural ally in the resistance to corrupt government and a corrupt nation in which "No social Virtue meets one Friend at Court" (p. 7). Accordingly, in this emotive rhetorical monologue, Messrs. Juvenal and Persius virtually become Pope and proclaim with him, in lines stemming from *One Thousand Seven Hundred and Thirty Eight* and the *Epistle to Dr. Arbuthnot* (1735),

> Spread, Satire, spread thy Wings, and fearless fly
> To seize thy Prey, tho' lurking ne'er so high.
>
> . . .
>
> Here *Sporus* live – and once more feel my Rage,
> Once and again I drag thee on the Stage;
> *Male–Female* Thing, without one Virtue made,
> Fit only for the *Pathick*'s loathsome Trade. (pp. 5–9)

Walpole's "depending, gaping, servile Court," his manipulation of George II (p. 14), and the consequent degradation of Britain appear in uncomplimentary Roman dress. Britain is a land in which an absolute Nero refuses to accept advice (p. 16), and which, like an overlarge dead fish long out of water, stinks and rots just below its surface (p. 17).

Several important points should emerge from this review of Persius' role in what was largely a drama cast and directed by the opposition to Walpole. As is obvious, he is far closer to Juvenal than to Horace and shares many of his conventions and tones. The familiar Horatian device of dialogue is transmuted by this Juvenalian spirit of hostility to the dim adversarius who wishes only to gain official praise, even at the expense of truth and virtue. The imitations of Persius become more hostile to Walpole as the decade advances; along the way they also become more Juvenalian and allied with Pope, the frequent parent of their invective and one probable source for their own notion of how "Persius" should write. Horace, as perceived in the seventeenth and eighteenth centuries, was the only Roman satirist to support his government. By the mid 1730s, however, that government was already seen as the corrupt father of Nero's and Domitian's tyrannies against which Persius and Juvenal were forced to complain, just, indeed, as Pope was forced to complain about his own Augustan tyranny.[29]

Persius and Pope

Pope alludes to Persius' satires at several places throughout his career. The first seems to be in 1704, in his youthful pastoral "Summer." Thereafter, he and his commentators note two allusions to the Prologue, six to the first satire, and two to the third satire in Pope's other works.[30] He mentions Dryden's notes to Persius' sixth satire and quotes *Satires* v.41–44, in a letter to Cromwell on 12 October 1710; and he quotes the same Latin lines when writing to Broome on 24 April 1724. On 12 October 1728 he thanks Thomas Sheridan for the gift of his Persius; on 26 July 1734 he makes clear to Dr. Arbuthnot that he accepts the standard interpretation of Persius as an enemy of Nero and in the process associates his own age with Nero's and Persius with Juvenal. He also refers to Persius' description of Horace in Satire I, lines 116–17 in the summer of 1739 and again in April of 1742.[31] Pope thus both has a general knowledge of Persius' satires and at least two major translations of him; and he joins his eighteenth-century colleagues in reacting more strongly and most frequently to Persius' first satire, the dialogue which shows outsider and insider in futile exchange and which laments the collapse of literature, national virtue, and political morality under Nero.

We may reasonably hypothesize that many of the general and presumed Horatian traits of Pope's satires also have roots in Persius. For instance, the contemplative, sometimes abstract qualities of the *Essay on Man* (1733–34) may adapt Persian gravity and religious thoughtfulness as well as Horatian ethics. Pope's warm adherence to Bolingbroke in that poem and elsewhere as a guide, philosopher, and friend at the very least parallels Persius' affection for Cornutus in Satire v.[32] Similarly, the use of dialogue, so important in Pope's poems, has its primary source in Horace but includes as a supplementary and differentiating source Persius' hostile and uneducable adversarius. Pope's *One Thousand Seven Hundred and Thirty Eight* is "Something like" Persius as well as Horace. Pope's insistence upon his affectionate family relations, his essential goodness, his inner drive to write satire and speak out against the vicious also suggest models other than Horace and, in the latter case, Juvenal. Pope's concern with the world of letters often is closer to Persius than to Horace as well, for Pope is more concerned with the decline than the prosperity and continuity of thriving literary traditions. And in Persius, more than in either of his fellow Romans, one is aware of a persona who is consciously and obviously made as a foil to the satirist; someone who, as Persius says, he has made to speak as an adversarius, but who then takes on a fictive life of his own ("Quisquis es, o modo quem ex adverso dicere feci" [line 44]). The opponent exemplifies the values of the hated Nero, who provided one of the many unpleasant historical parallels and labels the opposition tacked on to George II and Walpole.[33]

These similarities in general effects also suggest similarities in specific settings and uses of conventions. In at least one case the combination of these perhaps led the printer Bettenham and the bookseller Cooper to place Pope's name on the title page of Thomas Brewster's collected *Satires of Persius* in 1741. Indeed, Brewster's Argument to Persius' first satire could serve as a gloss for much of *Fortescue, Arbuthnot*, and even *One Thousand Seven Hundred and Thirty Eight*, and suggests how congenial Persius could be for Pope. The Argument points out uses of personae, dialogue, and conflict with the adversarius, an attempt to stifle satire, a divorce from the values of the debased and debasing court, the isolation of the satirist, and the collapse of modern freedoms as contrasted with the unshackled, thriving past.

We may suppose the Author to be just seated in his Study, and beginning to vent his Indignation in Satire. At this very Juncture, comes in an Acquaintance, who, upon hearing the first Line, dissuades him, by all Means, from an undertaking so perilous; advising him rather, if he needs must write, to accommodate his Vein to the Taste of the Times, and to write like other People.

Brewster goes on to say that Persius would not seek fame or patronage under such shameful terms, that he in fact exposes the wretched literary taste of Roman nobles and their followers, and that he laments how "he dares not speak out with the Freedom allowable in former times, and practised by his Predecessors in Satire, *Lucilius* and *Horace*. He then concludes, expressing a generous Disdain for all worthless Blockheads whatever: The only Readers whose applause he covets, must be Men of Virtue, and Men of Sense."[34]

Brewster's gloss demands that we focus on the dramatic relationship between the moral satirist and his incorrigible opponent. That is one of Pope's characteristic devices, one, we recall, with scant parallel in Horace and none in Juvenal. Pope hints at such a dubious relationship in *Fortescue*. That lawyer offers darker implications than Horace's Trebatius, who agreed that any legal action against Horace would be quashed when once he affirmed his satiric virtues and, more important, aristocratic friends. Fortescue, however, says:

> Alas young Man! your Days can ne'er be long,
> In Flow'r of Age you perish for a Song!
> Plums, and Directors, *Shylock* and his Wife,
> Will club their Testers, now, to take your Life!

Fortescue later reminds Pope that "in *Richard*'s Times / A Man was hang'd for very honest Rhymes."[35]

Whether this grim interpretation of the court's possible decision was influenced by Persius' first satire is difficult to say. Pope was, after all, well aware of ministerial annoyance with dispraise and needed no classical precedent to learn of his own frailties. Nonetheless, as we have seen, Persius' adversarius in a comparable situation heard the growling guard dogs at the great man's gate, and Mr. Dudley in 1739, perhaps himself influenced by Pope, appreciated the administration's ability to intimidate those it could not buy. The Monitor in Dudley's imitation of Persius' first satire says:

> Yet the Resentments of the Great are strong,
> And if they snarl, they snap before 'tis long:
> Hold in your Hand, avert the pointed Sting,
> Or you may chance to starve, if not to swing. (p. 25)

Dudley's warning of the gibbet has no counterpart in Persius, just as Pope's has no counterpart in Horace: the modern satirists are closer to each other than to their sources, but each is closer to the perceived spirit of Persius' uncertain world than Horace's stable one. The adversarius is the unchanging voice of the government's values. He triumphs over the satirist in practical terms, for he is incapable of feeling the shame that might bring reform, and is quite capable of threatening him with physical force, loss of audience, and literary seclusion. As a result, Persius must retreat into irony, appear to praise what he despises, and to destroy his own satire.

Pope's adversarii are more complex than Persius'. The Monitor hopes to silence Persius because his satire is vexing to Rome's delicate ears; he wishes to protect not Persius from the court but the court from Persius. Dr. Arbuthnot, on the other hand, is concerned with the vulnerable, hostage, body of his sick friend, and not with the court, which he too "could," and later will, satirize:

> No Names – be calm – learn Prudence of a Friend:
> I too could write, and I am twice as tall,
> But Foes like these! (lines 102–4)

Pope's reply immediately acknowledges the doctor's scarcely hidden point: "It is the Slaver kills, and not the Bite" (line 106). By the end of the poem Arbuthnot agrees with Pope and seconds his apologia; but it is a tenuous victory, for the ominous external world may temporarily have been intimidated, but it has not been converted. The full-blown court disciple thus appears with frightening confidence in the two dialogues of *One Thousand Seven Hundred and Thirty Eight*, a poem that is Horatian in its familiar repartee, Juvenalian in its rage, and Persian in its dialogue with a deaf man and the satirist's consequent retreat. When the hostile "Friend" tells Pope to mute his satire and "charitably comfort Knave and Fool" (Dialogue 1, line 62), he is adapting the advice of Persius' Monitor in Satire 1, and evokes a similar response, as Pope cries:

> Dear Sir, forgive the Prejudice of Youth:
> Adieu Distinction, Satire, Warmth, and Truth!
> Come harmless *Characters* that no one hit,
> Come *Henley*'s Oratory, *Osborn*'s Wit!
>
> .   .   .
>
> So – Satire is no more – I feel it die –
> No *Gazeteer* more innocent than I!
> And let, a God's-name, ev'ry Fool and Knave
> Be grac'd thro' Life, and flatter'd in his Grave.[36] (lines 63–66, 83–86)

The later outburst ("Not to be corrupted is the Shame," line 160) leaves Persius standing in his tracks, as Pope rushes to an apocalyptic Juvenalian conclusion in which "Nothing is Sacred now but Villany" (line 170). But it returns to the Persian dense adversarius in the second dialogue's first line, as the Friend complacently says, "Tis all a Libel – *Paxton* (Sir) will say." Yet more complacently, it ends with the same adversarius, morally torn asunder by Pope and his own lack of perception and principle, still muttering:

> Alas! alas! pray end what you began,
> And write next winter more *Essays on Man*.   (lines 254–55)

In several instances Pope's general tone (indignation against the government) and specific conventions (dialogue with a corrupt friend) have parallels in Persius' satires and, I suspect, draw their initial sustenance from fertile Persian lands. This is true as well in a particular passage in *Arbuthnot*, whose possible and richly allusive source is the accepted commentary on comparable lines in Persius' first satire. We recall that at least from 1605 the poem was regarded as an attack upon Nero, his tragedy, and his nobles for their collective abuse of poetry. Since such mockery could not go too far without an invitation to open veins in a warm bath, Cornutus prevailed upon Persius to change and soften a key line that drew upon the familiar story of Midas, the king of Phrygia who was granted the wish that everything he touched be turned to gold. More important here is Midas' poor taste in music, for he preferred the music of Pan to Apollo, who promptly punished Midas by giving him asses' ears. Midas hid his shame beneath his cap, but his barber discovered the ears, and was bursting with his knowledge. He thus dug a hole in the earth, told it, refilled the hole, and both relieved his burden and kept the secret – he wrongly thought, for on that place a reed grew and whispered its secret to the world.[37]

Persius revitalizes the second part of the myth. At line 8 he cries, "Who is there in Rome who is not ... " He cannot yet say what demands to be said, and so waits until line 121, when he asks, "Who is there who has not the ears of an ass?" – "auriculas asini quis non habet?" According to the old scholiast, whose remark was broadly accepted by Pope's ancestors and contemporaries, this line originally was "Auriculas asini Mida rex habet" – King Midas has asses' ears, or, as Cornutus feared that everyone would understand it, Emperor Nero has asses' ears and thus has the taste, talent, and intelligence of the ass he resembles. For Romans the word *rex* also was a virtual synonym for tyrant, and so the line had to be generalized and made apparently unimperial in its attack. Students of Persius in Pope's generation probably would read the line about Midas' ears and recall both the Midas myth and Persius' putative original use of it as an attack upon Nero and bad poetry.[38] That being so, is it not probable that "Midas" in other satires hostile to a court would also evoke that same association? Is it not more likely still if that association is helped along by the word *king* and by a particular action that associates the modern king with an ass? Here is *Arbuthnot*'s conflation of Persius' Midas section:

> 'Tis sung, when *Midas*' Ears began to spring,
> (*Midas*, a sacred Person and a King)
> His very Minister who spy'd them first,
> (Some say his Queen) was forc'd to speak, or burst.   (lines 69–72)

Arbuthnot dismisses Pope's plight with "Tis nothing," and hears the outraged echo, "Nothing? if they bite and kick?" (line 78). He then blurts out the secret which Persius held for 111 more lines and which he would make even more overt in his imitation of Horace, *Epistles* i.i (1737), where "a Minister's an Ass" (line 96):

> Out with it, *Dunciad!* let the secret pass,
> That Secret to each Fool, that he's an Ass:
> The truth once told, (and wherefore shou'd we lie?)
> The Queen of *Midas* slept, and so may I.   (lines 79–82)

Pope is casting Arbuthnot in the role of the dissuading, protective Cornutus, for as soon as Midas appears the worried Doctor urges Pope to forbear and not "name Queens, Ministers, or Kings" (line 76). As "Out with it" may suggest, Pope is bringing the scholiast's meaning from its limbo of censorship, telling his adversarius that he will not be a docile pupil and abandon satire, and asserting his bravery in labeling King Midas an ass during his own lifetime and not thereafter. Indeed, to carry the Cornutus–Arbuthnot analogy one step further, when Arbuthnot himself becomes a satirist and lashes Sporus as a "mere white Curd of Ass's milk" (line 306), Pope makes clear that in such a world even a friendly dissuader must become actively involved with the protection of virtue and battle against vice.

Moreover, as Maynard Mack has shown, the word *kick* connoted the fierce anger of George II and his "savage temper which could only be relieved by kicking somebody or something." Hence on 16 July 1737 *Fog's Weekly Journal* portrays Augustus Caesar *cum* George II kicking a football and then his flattering courtiers. This derogatory number "with its audacious parallel," as an eighteenth-century reader called it, goaded the government into arresting the printer.[39] Pope also incriminates Walpole (and Queen Caroline) by insisting that the first minister, and not a mere barber, sees the king's folly and no doubt shares it.[40] In fact, since Midas gained his asses' ears for offending the god of poetry, Walpole emerges as an accomplice, as the man who brought bad judgment in poetry – the selection of Cibber as poet laureate for example – to the king. At the same time, however, Pope adopts Persius' prudence in the face of powerful enemies by veiling much of this meaning and having the possible recourse of claiming Boileau's ninth satire (1667) as his innocent source, for Boileau there writes that "Midas, le roi Midas a des oreilles d'âne."[41] If Louis XIV took no umbrage, surely, one might argue, George II should not as well. Pope also adopts at least part of Persius' printed, uncensored version by generalizing onto the literary world: each London and Roman fool is an ass, for in literary, moral, and asinine matters the principle of *ad exemplum regis* extends down the social scale. I believe that Pope bases his Midas passage on Persius' printed text and the commentary upon it, and in the process intensifies its impact by condensing, enriching, and making plain the theory of causation presumed implicit in Persius' "auriculas asini quis non habet?" Neither Persius nor Pope has such beastly organs, and they become progressively lonelier in their sadly normal states, and progressively more endangered. The asses "bite and kick" as well as taunt Pope by perking their ears in his face (lines 78, 74); unlike their antique royal paradigm, they lack even a sense of shame for their ears and the reason for their presence. The world is worse than worst, it seems under King Midas II. Pope's magnifying rage sees "a bursting World" (line 88) that demands satire, however ineffectual and dangerous it might be. In the process he becomes the informing barber, the speaking rushes, the Persian satirist, the tutor of Cornutus, and the British scholiast-hero undaunted by friendly or courtly pressures.

I cannot claim that contemporary readers recorded their awareness of the *Mida rex* analogue; but several eighteenth-century readers were aware of mingled and Persian qualities in Pope's satires, and in *Arbuthnot* in particular. In 1753 the Abbé Yart includes Pope's poem as part of his *Idée de la Poësie Angloise* (1749–56), and observes that *Arbuthnot* contains a great number of facts concerning Pope, his friends, and enemies. Over and above these facts, the poem offers

des morceaux admirables, écrits avec la force & la véhémence de Juvénal, la légèreté & la finesse d'Horace, la précision & la noblesse de Perse. M. Pope semble avoir affecté en quelques endroits de prendre non-seulement le ton & les Dialogues de ce dernier Poëte, mais encore son air mystérieux & son obscurité, pour dérober aux yeux de ses ennemis dangereux ou puissans, les traits qu'il leur lançoit.

Yart goes on to say that when dealing with Pope one must remember that he was, among other things, "un Philosophe chagrin & sévère"[42] – that is the term that Boileau had used to characterize Persius.

The humblest member of the triumvirate of classical satirists deserves the praise that Pope himself surely would have offered, perhaps in words similar to those of Martin Madan in 1789: "However the comparative merit of *Persius* may be determined, his positive excellence can hardly escape the readers of his Satires."[43] The evidence suggests that at least some of these excellences escaped neither Pope nor the opposition to Walpole. He provided conventions that were borrowed and generously repaid – in part by associating Persius with the more vigorous Juvenal and the braver Pope, with the defense of Britain from its apparent Neronian threats, and with a resurrected Cornutus now willing to join him in battle. Persius, in short, was both useful in his own specific satires adapted by the literary opposition, among others, and for specific conventions that could be blended with the conventions of other satirists, as the Abbé Yart saw so clearly in the *Epistle to Dr. Arbuthnot*. Pope's shade could not have been surprised by Yart's comments. Nor, I think, should we.

11 · JOHNSON'S *LONDON* AND JUVENAL'S THIRD SATIRE

THE COUNTRY AS "IRONIC" NORM

THE AFFIRMATION of Johnson's distinction as a poet has renewed interest in *London* (1738), his first major poem and the first work that brought him literary reputation. The Juvenalian texts that he used have been meticulously traced; much of the poem's political background and satiric and rhetorical techniques have been discovered; and its successes and failures have become the object of lively, if not always enlightened, controversy.[1] This last issue has an importance beyond that of simple evaluation, for in the case of *London* that evaluation is linked to the larger question of how to read an imitation. We have learned that knowledge of the parent-poem is necessary for understanding of the imitation; but historical reclamation often surrenders to modern impressionism, the Loeb text replaces that of Heinsius or Casaubon, and we read Horace or Juvenal as if they were our rather than Pope's or Johnson's "contemporaries."[2] The reader of *London* needs to know both how Johnson would have read Juvenal's third satire and how to acquire such information. The assumption that Johnson read Juvenal as we do leads to inappropriate methodology and mistaken literary criticism. Specifically, according to several recent critics, Johnson failed to see that in Juvenal's third satire the poet was ironic and not serious in praising the country, missed part of his point, some of his resonance and, it would seem, some of his greatness as well.

As far as I can tell, this view first reached print in 1959, when Mary Lascelles told the readers of her "Johnson and Juvenal" that Juvenal's

real theme is not country pleasures but the mingled attraction and repulsion exercised by the great cosmopolitan city . . . The two men [Umbritius and Juvenal] are represented as going together to the point of departure from Rome, the gate on the Appian Way. There, Umbritius urges his friend to follow his example; but in much of what he says ironic overtones can be heard: in his allusions, for example, to the insignificant, depopulated village where he means to settle, or the even more desolate regions which Juvenal ought to prefer to Rome's tawdry splendour. These wry hints are surely but the echo of Juvenal's own thoughts: of his inmost certainty that, if life in Rome is disagreeable, dangerous, degrading, outside Rome there is nothing to be called life, at all.[3]

She illustrates Johnson's frail understanding of Juvenalian irony in his portrait of the country seat. When Umbritius describes the place of his retreat, he names little hill towns (romantic, perhaps, to us, but for him uncouth, cold, and dull); towns in which, for the price of a Roman garret, you can have the best house there is, with a little patch of kitchen-garden – a *very* little patch: there will be room enough merely to raise the vegetables on which you will have to subsist, with a lizard for livestock . . . But Johnson turns *hortulus* into a country estate, and Juvenal's sour acceptance of a countryman's life into a little pastoral . . . In such a mood, [of loneliness and anger in London, Johnson] might perhaps miss the irony in Juvenal's tale of country pleasures, yet find the denunciation of Rome (to which [the country scenes] had been a merely conventional foil) heartily congenial.[4]

Lascelles concludes that "Johnson's *London* has not the brilliance of its original, because it lacks the lightning flash of its irony."[5]

A few years later her view of Juvenal's irony was quoted, approved, and elaborated upon by John Hardy[6] who, in turn, was praised by William Kupersmith. Hardy, Kupersmith says, argues "rightly, that Juvenal's praise of the country is ironic," and he himself insists that it is certainly "wrong to take Juvenal's jokes in 229 and 231 [the 100 Pythagoreans as guests and the single lizard as subject] as serious descriptions of rural pleasures." More recently still, Ian Donaldson has seconded Lascelles' "shrewdly observed" ironic interpretation.[7]

Such a view of Juvenal's poem, however, has little to recommend it. The statements above have no evidence, contemporary or otherwise, to support them. There is hardly much reference to Juvenal's poem. Instead, we merely have four critics who congenially borrow from and support one another on the strength of *ipsa* and *ipse dixit*. In spite of their arguments on authority, they have not considered the important reading of the third satire by William S. Anderson. He argues that Juvenal's poem is about the loss of Roman values in Rome and their preservation in the country. Aquinum has a variety of pleasant associations – friendship, divinities, and closeness to the land – whereas Rome is stripped of all pleasant connotations and is filled with faults and degeneration from virtue. By the end of the satire, Rome's

traditional values have abandoned it, and it remains an empty shell, a glittering façade which conceals its total rejection of the past, its complete subjection to foreign and debased practices. In Rome, men violate Nature; in Cumae she constitutes the only immediate attraction . . . The natural state of things possesses a freshness, an innocence, that can exist only in the country; in Rome, innocence can only be violated, so that the cheap decoration of the fountain [of Egeria] symbolizes the whole scale of tawdry values of the city. As the Satire proceeds, the innocence of Nature comes to represent the original Roman character, and, in the charm of the country, Juvenal sets former Roman customs, Roman clothes, and Roman values now discarded in Rome itself. Since the country really constitutes the last stronghold of the Roman character, Umbricius must withdraw to Cumae, because there alone a true Roman will find satisfaction.[8]

The non-ironic reading of the third satire's country scenes appears to be literal minded but in fact is profoundly symbolic. That Johnson might have been aware of this interpretation is suggested in his (unsuccessful) attempt to relate the attack on the city to praise of the old virtues of British strength, poverty, defiance of foes, and control of the sea.[9] The ironic interpretation and the implied criticism of Johnson's deafness in not hearing it are denied by one of the best classicists writing on the subject.

Since it is possible that even the best and the brightest can be wrong, however, we should establish criteria for a permitted ironic reading that exists independent of such authority. Let me, then, suggest four ways to determine whether Johnson could or should have read the third satire as being ironic: (1) What was Juvenal's characteristic attitude towards the presumed subject of irony in other poems? (2) Does the third satire itself demand or exclude an ironic reading of its apparent norms? (3) Is there a tradition of ironic interpretation of Juvenal which Johnson is likely to have accepted? (4) What was Johnson's attitude towards and use of irony in general at the time he wrote *London* and, in particular, did he discuss irony in Juvenal's poem?

(1) Juvenal does not often write about the country, but when he does it is appreciative, lyrical, and wholly like the non-ironic country of his third satire. Congreve translated the eleventh satire for Dryden's 1693 version of Juvenal and Persius, and there tenderly communicated Juvenal's praise of rural life that provides wholesome, humble food: a suckling kid, asparagus, large eggs, rich grapes, and pears. The country farm represents the old Roman values,

> When the good *Curius* thought it no Disgrace,
> With his own Hands, a few small Herbs to dress;
> And from his little Garden, cull'd a Feast,
> Which fetter'd Slaves wou'd now disdain to taste.[10]

John Dryden Junior's translation of the fourteenth satire again emphasizes that the country is the home of the true old Roman values:

> Give me, ye Gods, the Product of one Field,
> As large as that which the first *Romans* Till'd;
> That so I neither may be Rich nor Poor,
> And having just enough, not covet more.
>   'Twas then, Old Souldiers cover'd o'er with Scars,
> (The Marks of *Pyrrhus*, or the *Punick* Wars,)
> Thought all past Services rewarded well,
> If to their share at last two Acres fell:
>
> . . .
>
>   Yet, then, this little Spot of Earth well Till'd,
> A num'rous Family with Plenty fill'd;
> The good old Man and thrifty Housewife spent
> Their Days in Peace, and fatten'd with Content.
> Enjoy'd the Dregs of Life, and liv'd to see
> A long-descending Healthful Progeny.
> The Men were fashion'd in a larger Mold;
> The Women fit for Labour, Big and Bold.
> Gygantick Hinds, as soon as Work was done,
> To their huge Pots of boiling Pulse wou'd run:
> Fell too, with eager Joy, on homely Food;

> And their large Veins beat strong with wholesom Blood.
> Of old, two Acres were a bounteous Lot,
> Now, scarce they serve to make a Garden-Plott.   (pp. 299–300)

Juvenal's vision of the country in Satires III, XI, and XIV is substantially the same: serious, non-ironic, lyrical, and patriotically early Roman.[11]

(2) Let us also look carefully at the poem itself, and especially at lines 229 and 231 which – we are told – are jokes. Since Dryden has eliminated a key word (the Circus becomes the playhouse), here is Madan's literal translation of 1789:

> Could you be plucked away from the Circenses, a most excellent house
> At Sora, or Fabrateria, or Frusino, is gotten
> At the price for which you now hire darkness for one year.
> Here is a little garden, and a shallow well, not to be drawn by a rope,
> It is poured with an easy draught on the small plants.
> Live fond of the fork, and the farmer of a cultivated garden,
> Whence you may give a feast to an hundred Pythagoreans.
> It is something in any place, in any retirement,
> To have made one's self master of one lizard.[12]

The presumed ironic jokes are the hundred Pythagoreans ("Unde epulum possis centum dare Pythagoraeis")[13] and the single lizard ("Unius sese dominum fecisse lacertae"). Throughout the poem, however, Umbritius pictures the formerly free Roman enslaved by his own poverty, the heartless oppression of the rich and ambitious, the illicit triumph of immoral foreigners, and the decay and dangers of life in Rome. At strategic points he places the exiled Roman in a true Roman setting, where he may attain humble poverty, hospitality, love of the land and its products and, most important, control over his own life. It is pitiful that a Roman must leave his city and define proper mastery as lord of a lizard; but it is nonetheless preferable to non-Roman slavery in the Greek city still called Rome.

Moreover, the poet behind Umbritius highlights the contrast between city servitude and country sovereignty. In the country one can feast 100 vegetarian Pythagoreans from his garden, in which his sole subject is a lizard; in Rome we see 100 humble clients and their servants coming from a great man's elaborate dole ("Nonne vides quanto celebretur sportula fumo? / Centum convivae; sequitur sua quemque culina": lines 249–50).[14] Each servant has the food resting upon a chafing dish heated by live coals; the dish, in turn, rests upon his head as he marches to the master's home. The Roman, metaphorically enslaved to the rich, also enslaves the "Servulus infelix" (line 253) whose lot is even worse than his master's. There is thus no joke in being lord of a single lizard and humble host of 100 invited and equal Pythagoreans: it is, in fact, a position morally superior to the urban Roman who is one of the 100 faceless dependents of a rich man and merely putative master of his own overworked slave. Insistence upon the loss of real Roman liberty is again made clear late in the poem where the drunken bully beats the poor Roman and gives him the "liberty" ("libertas pauperis haec est": line 299) of begging to keep a few teeth in his head. The poor man can only hope that the bully will not also bring him before a magistrate and charge him with assault. As a free country resident Umbritius will be master of a lizard; as an enslaved city resident he will be tyrannized by all. That may be black humor, but Juvenal surely means us to take seriously the emblematic sovereignty over a lizard and the projected invitation to 100 guests.

(3) There is, then, no warrant either in Juvenal's other discussions of the country or in the poem itself for concluding that the country in the third satire is presented as anything but a positive norm. Nor is there justification for such a reading in any Latin edition and commentary or English translation or imitation from the early seventeenth to the early nineteenth century or in the work of Boileau and his compatriots in France. I have not been able to examine every possible Latin commentary, but I have seen most of those that Johnson might have seen and will here report on those of Britannicus and Curio (1627), Schrevelius (1648, 1671 ed. quoted), and Prateus (1684, 1736 ed. quoted). None of these, or any other commentator, sees ironic undercutting of the country anywhere in the poem. Though such scholars are not famous for their wit, they nonetheless were able to see and label irony when they thought it appeared. Prateus, for instance, reading Juvenal's praise of the divine poetry of Codrus (III.207), says: "This is ironic; in fact he called Codrus raucous in Satire I" ("Ironice, Raucum enim Codrum dixit Sat. I" [p. 55]). Britannicus and Curio comment upon the opening of the poem and Umbritius' decision to go to Cumae. If they had noted irony, here would surely be a place to mention it. Instead, they tell us that Juvenal introduces Umbritius

who is prepared to quit the city because of its moral depravity: He presents his own account of the city's most outstanding horrors: Therefore the poet says: Though I am not unmoved because my friend Umbritius is leaving the City, yet because it is all thought out in his mind, I praise his resolution since, leaving Rome behind, he has decided to go to Cumae.[15]

Schrevelius' discussion of the opening is substantially the same and also laments the loss of his dear friend to Cumae, the very ancient city in Campania and the home of the Sybil of Cumae ("Cujus dulci consuetidune & familiaritate mihi carendum").[16] Prateus similarly remarks that Umbritius attacks Rome and is leaving to go to Cumae, the home and shrine of the Sybil.[17] These commentators cannot find anything wrong with Cumae, or the towns Juvenal mentions later in the poem; nor can they see irony in the 100 Pythagoreans or single lizard. Schrevelius, borrowing from Lubin, includes this gloss on the lizard: "Migrating from the city to whatever place may receive you, that is considered the best home, where you may have a house and garden so small that hardly a single lizard itself can run about."[18] However small the land, it is nonetheless preferable to life in Rome and is "optimum putato domicilium."

The English translations, imitations, and commentaries were of course influenced by the Latin and would have reinforced Johnson's literal reading of the rural virtues. In 1682, for example, Oldham imitates the third satire, praises the country in the several expected places, and says that in Kent, or Surrey, or Essex,

> Had I the smallest Spot of Ground, which scarce
> Would Summer half a dozen Grasshoppers,
> Not larger than my Grave, tho hence remote,
> Far as St. *Michaels Mount*, I would go to 't,
> Dwell there content, and thank the Fates to boot.[19]

Dryden, who has not often been accused of lacking an ear for irony, is no less explicit in his translation of 1693. He portrays Umbritius as going to "quiet *Cumae*"

> Where, far from noisie *Rome* secure he lives,
> And one more Citizen to *Sybil* gives.
> The Road to *Bajae*, and that soft Recess
> Which all the Gods with all their Bounty bless.   (p. 31)

Dryden becomes more lyrical when he describes the "Sweet Country Seats" and their "Crystall Streams" that water "all the pretty Spot of Ground."

> There, love the Fork, thy Garden cultivate,
> And give thy frugal Friends a *Pythagorean* Treat.
> 'Tis somewhat to [be] the Lord of some small Ground
> In which a Lizard may, at least, turn round.   (p. 48)

In 1763 Edward Burnaby Greene's loose imitation attacks the Scottish triumphs in England and shows their power in banishing the English to the barren hills of Scotland.[20] But that is the only such negative use of the country within the more than 200 years I have surveyed. It is, I suspect, the exception that proves the rule, since Greene's inversion of country values can best be appreciated only when set against the received interpretation of a positive and revivifying country.

One later-eighteenth-century comment upon the lizard will characterize the attitude of the century as a whole. In 1789 Madan says:

The poet means, that, wherever a man may be placed, or wherever retired from the rest of the world, it is no small privilege to be able to call one's self master of a little spot of ground of one's own, however small it may be, though it were no bigger than to contain one poor lizard. This seems a proverbial or figurative kind of expression.

Madan's remark is supported both by a note in the Casaubon edition of 1695 and by Smith's more modern Latin *Dictionary*. There, under *lacerta* we see the line from Juvenal's third satire, see also that it is "Prov." and that it means "to get a place of one's own, however small."[21]

Furthermore, no less a satiric ironist than Boileau annotated and adapted

Juvenal's third satire. Although he does see ironic lines in the poem, he fails to see them in the country scene and glosses "Cumae" by saying: "Cumes est un passage pour aller à Baies, un rivage fort agréable, une solitude charmante."[22] In 1701 he read and corrected Pierre Le Verrier's commentaries upon his work and thus provided a gloss upon his own first and sixth satires and Juvenal's third satire. With slight modifications, the commentary passed into the major editions by Brossette (1717) and Saint-Marc (1747) as the "Avis sur la I. Satire" of Boileau:

C'est une imitation de la troisième Satire de JUVÉNAL, dans laquelle est aussi décrite la retraite d'un Philosophe qui abandonne le séjour de Rome, à cause des vices affreux qui y regnoient. *Juvénal* y décrit encore les embarras de la même ville; & à son exemple, Mr.
  Despréaux, dans cette première Satire, avoit fait la description des embarras de Paris.[23]

This is a sample of the nearly unanimous view of the commentators, translators, and imitators of Juvenal's third satire on the Continent, in England, and in America from about 1600 to 1800:[24] they agree that the country as Juvenal presents it is the norm of a poem in which Rome is an anti-norm. There is, in short, no tradition of reading which could have shown Johnson that Cumae or the other country retreats were unpleasant.

(4) Nevertheless, when faced with so independent a reader as Samuel Johnson, especially the young Sam Johnson, the lack of such a tradition need not exclude the possibility that he could have found irony in the relevant scenes. The preponderance of evidence – so great that it virtually amounts to proof – is that he in fact did not hear Juvenal's irony because it is not to be heard. We should remember, after all, that Johnson's "Swiftian" political pieces *Marmor Norfolciense* and *A Compleat Vindication of the Licensers of the Stage* were published in 1739 and that *London* itself is filled with ironies – of those who "vote a patriot black, a courtier white" (line 53),[25] of Frenchmen who use industry to escape industry (line 113), and of a great man whose palace is destroyed by Heaven and restored in abundance by men (lines 194–209). At this point in his literary career Johnson's ear was as finely tuned to irony as it ever was.

Moreover, the opening of the poem makes clear that we are to see Thales' departure as intelligent and thoughtful. The first speaker echoes Juvenal and insists: "Yet still my calmer thoughts his choice commend, / I praise the hermit, but regret the friend" (lines 3–4). Johnson revised the first edition's reading of the following two lines in order to stress Thales' wise decision. He changed the couplet which began "Who now resolves from vice and London far" to "Resolved at length, from vice and London far, / To breathe in distant fields a purer air."[26] And as A. D. Moody has shown, Johnson also revised the country scenes in order to make them more attractive.[27]

Perhaps, it might be argued, Johnson really did find irony in the poem but chose to ignore it, since it did not suit his purposes. Though we cannot reclaim Johnson's exact attitude in 1738, we do have several of his subsequent remarks regarding Juvenal's third satire. On 8 March 1758 he wrote to

Bennet Langton: "I am satisfied with your stay at home, as Juvenal with his friend's retirement to Cumae: I know that your absence is best, though it be not best for me." He then quotes the first three lines of Juvenal's third satire – Boswell's note to the *Life* adds the first eight of *London* – and adds: "*Langton* is a good *Cumae*, but who must be Sibylla? Mrs. Langton is as wise as Sibyl, and as good; and will live, if my wishes can prolong life, till she shall in time be as old."[28] Near the end of 1770 when the Reverend Dr. William Maxwell was to return to Ireland, Johnson, Maxwell reports, told him that "he knew, it was a point of *duty* that called me away. – 'We shall all be sorry to lose you,' said he: '*laudo tamen*'" (2:133) – that is, from the second line of Juvenal's poem as Johnson rendered it, "Yet still my calmer thoughts his choice commend" (line 3). And, finally, on 9 April 1778, Boswell, Johnson, and others discussed the erstwhile lizard without hinting at ironic meanings:

> One of the company asked him the meaning of the expression in Juvenal, *unius lacertae*. JOHNSON. "I think it clear enough; as much ground as one may have a chance to find a lizard upon."
> Commentators [Boswell adds] have differed as to the exact meaning of the expression by which the Poet intended to enforce the sentiment contained in the passage where these words occur. It is enough that they mean to denote even a very small possession, provided it be a man's own.[29]   (3:255)

Let me now sum up the findings of the four points regarding irony in Juvenal and its perception, or lack of it, in Johnson: (1) in his other satires Juvenal is consistently favorable to the country and uses it as an emblem of the old Roman values; (2) the third satire itself insists that the 100 Pythagoreans and mastery of a single lizard in the country be contrasted with the 100 dinnertime dependents and metaphorical enslavement in Rome; (3) English, Latin, and French commentators, translators, and imitators – including some conspicuous ironists – for over 200 years regard the country sections as serious norms that are not undercut; (4) Johnson was particularly sensitive to irony during 1738 and is not likely to have missed something that was in the poem. His own work on *London* and his subsequent comments as late as forty years thereafter indicate that he regarded the praise of the country as clear, positive, and, in its opening at least, warm and touching.

Several obvious but neglected points emerge from this review. In general, an undefended modern interpretation should not be foisted upon an ancient poem; if that poem is the model for an eighteenth-century imitation the student should attempt to reclaim the contemporary reading. In particular, it is misleading to apply a hitherto unknown interpretation of Juvenal's third satire to show Johnson's benighted understanding of his parent-poem; and it is similarly misleading to suggest that Johnson's ignorance can explain the comparatively diminished brilliance of *London* or explain aspects of the poem that other hypotheses fail to do. There are many obstacles in the way of "proper" reading of an eighteenth-century imitation: perhaps the first is acceptance of the tautology that it is an eighteenth-century imitation.

12 · NO "MOCK DEBATE"

QUESTIONS AND ANSWERS IN
THE VANITY OF HUMAN WISHES

"THEY WHO ARE demanded by others, instantly rouse themselves with eagerness to make a reply; so this Figure of question and answer leads the hearer into a persuasion, that what is the effect of study is conceived and uttered without any premeditation." So Longinus says when discussing Demosthenes' use of questions, and when summing up much of this aspect of rhetorical theory among the ancients. He adds that "the spirit and rapidity of the question and answer, and the Orator's replying upon himself, as if he was answering another, not only ennoble his oration, but give it an air of probability."[1] In *The Vanity of Human Wishes* (1749) Johnson's own questions also achieve this sense of immediacy and exchange, of vigorous involvement between narrator and reader; they also help to make his poem convincing and to engage us in our own schooling.

Johnson's poetic technique is as firmly rooted in contemporary psychology and pedagogy as in ancient rhetoric. Questions, Johnson says in July 1738, allow "the reader the satisfaction of adding something that he may call his own, and thus engage his attention by flattering his vanity." They encourage us to respond with our own thoughts, and summon our "different faculties of memory, judgment, and imagination." In the Preface to Dodsley's *Preceptor* (1748) Johnson shows how graduated questions can lead to the student's expanded vision and understanding through dialogue with and guidance by his benevolent master. The student should not merely answer the question with its own words, since that may be a limited and limiting act of memory. Instead, "it is always proper to vary the words of the question, to place the proposition in different points of view, and to require of the learner an explanation in his own terms, informing him, however, when they are improper. By this method the scholar will become cautious and attentive, and the master will know with certainty the degree of his proficiency." Exchange, education, and pleasure therefrom are also present in Johnson's definitions and illustrations of the verb "To question," and also suggest that these traits were associated with the concept of questioning. The word means "1. To enquire ... 2. To debate by interrogatories." The illustration of "To enquire" is drawn from Bacon's essay "Of Discourse": "He that *questioneth* much shall learn much, and content much; but especially if he apply his questions to the skill of the persons whom he asketh. For," Bacon adds in a sentence not quoted, "he shall give them occasion, to please themselves in Speaking, and himselfe shall continually gather Knowledge."[2]

In such a process, both teacher and student, poet and reader, must be willing to seek and share knowledge. In 1759 Edmund Burke states his procedure in the *Enquiry* into the sublime and beautiful, one related to Johnson's own practice:

> I am convinced that the method of teaching which approaches most nearly to the method of investigation, is incomparably the best; since not content with serving up a few barren and lifeless truths, it leads to the stock on which they grew; it tends to set the reader himself in the track of invention, and to direct him into those paths in which the author has made his own discoveries, if he should be so happy as to have made any that are valuable.[3]

Burke's "method" obliquely describes one of Johnson's important techniques in *The Vanity of Human Wishes*, one that is in the manuscript of the poem and thus is his own, and not a compositor's. Johnson's generous poetics of reciprocity uses questions to help his speaker enlarge both the dramatis personae and the historical and chronological sweep of his poem. He also directly questions the reader and engages him first in an assumed and then in a more vocal dialogue. As the poem progresses, he allows us to try on different psychological roles (the harsh, the sympathetic), as well as choices of life (the statesman, scholar, hero), to see the weaknesses in each, and to enter into the poem ourselves, either in our own voice or a voice that could be ours and is spoken for us by the perceptive speaker who knows how we will reply. He leaves us with the most likely series of questions a proper coinvestigator, or perhaps fellow student in a Socratic dialogue, would have arrived at, for he has come to "the stock on which" spiritual truths grow: "Where then shall Hope and Fear their objects find?" (line 343).[4] The clear discrimination between kinds of questions, some of which are scarcely veiled imperatives, nonetheless has an obvious and necessary common denominator – interrogation itself, and its consequent dialogue, energy, probability, education, and pleasure.

A recent commentator on the poem has argued that the *Vanity* "derives its structure from a search for a point of view" through questions.[5] That useful remark needs modification: it is not the poem or its narrator that seeks a point of view, but the reader, the questioner, the very object of keen but good-humored satire who is seeking what the poem already has, and who must learn to dismiss his own pernicious wishes for earthly success.[6] As Edward Young says in 1719, "he that asks the guilty person a question, makes him, in effect, pass sentence upon himself."[7] As Young could not have known, however, "the guilty person" in the *Vanity* also finds the way to help redeem and reprieve himself, and thereby to "learn much, and content much," and he does so in part by means of the accusatory questions themselves. I shall examine, seriatim, the *Vanity*'s different questions in order to see how they help us to move from frantic worldly to calming celestial wisdom.

✳

The *Vanity* opens with a massive overview by Observation with extensive view, a personification that remarks and watches man's strivings for happiness, and then says how we make a difficult job worse by our folly and vain human wishes. History (line 29) soon joins Observation and tells of the dangers to those in high places. The vassal, however, is appreciably safer than his lord; the simple farmer, with nothing worth having, is secure as "confiscation's vulturs hover round" (line 36) his betters and feast on the carrion that is their estate. "The needy traveller," the itinerant rather than stable poor man, is equally "secure and gay" (line 37) on his path across the dangerous and perhaps thief-infested heath.

That is the context of Johnson's first question and of the first role he chooses for us to investigate. Why, after all, should the ignorant and socially inferior hind be happier than his industrious and ambitious master? Why should those of us apparently blessed with the ability to serve the nation be victims of "anxious toil" and "eager strife" (line 3) while the useless underling "sings his toil away" (line 38)? Johnson gives his reader the unpleasant power to remove that happiness by allowing us to give the poor man wealth, and by assuming that he would accept the offered prize. "Does envy seize thee? crush th' upbraiding joy, / Increase his riches and his peace destroy" (lines 39–40). Fears in dreadfully ranked order "invade" (line 41) his mind, and pain and alarm follow naturally. The "wild heath" (line 38), which previously reflected the serenity of the traveler's song, now reflects his anxiety as both "rustling brake . . . and quiv'ring shade" alarm him (line 42).

The vassal's joy may be crushed, but the human condition has not changed; we have, after all, learned nothing from this resentful aggression in a continuously restless world, for "gain and grandeur [still] load the tainted gales" (line 46). Perhaps, however, someone wiser than ourselves or the ignorant traveler, someone with a classical genealogy, can change the situation through the mockery it deserves. Johnson thus invokes Democritus (*c.* 400 B.C.) as an enlargement of our own lack of sympathy for our fellows. Observation and History merely relate the facts; Democritus responds to those facts with the sardonic laughter that much of Juvenal's tenth satire has for its victims. Democritus scorned his own relatively innocent culture; he would do more in the face of modern "motly life" (line 51):

> How wouldst thou shake at Britain's modish tribe,
> Dart the quick taunt, and edge the piercing gibe?
> Attentive truth and nature to descry,
> And pierce each scene with philosophic eye.
> . . .

174

All aid the farce, and all thy mirth maintain,
Whose joys are causeless, or whose griefs are vain.　　　　(lines 61–68)

This passage has often been taken as Johnson's own voice wrongly adopting an inappropriate Juvenalian tone.[8] I suggest, instead, that Johnson is offering the reader another vantage point – overtly by means of the sort of question he raises on Democritus' behalf, but covertly on the reader's behalf. Is man in fact the subject of a farce worthy of laughter? Are his joys causeless and griefs vain? Does this pagan with his savage arsenal of taunts, darts, and piercers offer a path to truth and nature that a modern Christian would find acceptable? Juvenal's Democritus was placed next to Heraclitus, the weeping philosopher, as alternate ways of coping with the world. Juvenal chooses to ignore tears in favor of harsh mockery, and adopts Democritean tones thereafter. Johnson was not likely to have been as favorably impressed with the Greek philosopher, or to have allowed his readers to think that Democritus was the stock of his own truths. He eliminates both Juvenal's praise of Democritus as evidence that a wise man could come from a land of dunces, and all references to Heraclitus. Johnson replaces the choice between mockery and tears with a choice between mockery and love; he moves from Democritus and Heraclitus to Democritus and Johnson with the benevolent God behind him.

Johnson's abnegation of Democritus is predictable enough. Though Democritus was often given high praise, he was associated with Epicurus' and Lucretius' atheistic theory that the universe was created by the accidental union of atoms; he denied that the soul was incorporeal and immortal, and insisted that it perished with the body; he preferred retreat and speculation to practical experience, may have blinded himself, and even shut himself up in a tomb the better to meditate and test the strength of his imagination; he allowed suicide for those frustrated in the world; he seemed to have starved himself to death in his weariness of old age; and he claimed that "All Man is from his very Birth a disease" without hope of cure.[9] Lest we forget or be ignorant of those facts, or lest we remain willing to destroy another's peace, Johnson as speaker adds an implied question of his own, a question that is without precedent in his parent-poem, and is not directly answered now because we must do so ourselves, and will have done so with a silent negative by the time the poem ends.[10]

Such was the scorn that fill'd the sage's mind,
Renew'd at ev'ry glance on humankind;
How just that scorn ere yet thy voice declare,
Search every state, and canvass ev'ry pray'r.　　　　(lines 69–72)

Democritus is a philosopher who detaches himself from humanity, whose scornful mind merely glances at the world as he confuses the part with the whole,[11] and who assumes that incorrigible man must forever be a subject of jest and a character in a farce (lines 52, 67). We are invited to join the Christian narrator, who also invites Observation, its extensive view, and History to help us in our examination of the external – every state – and internal – every prayer, so that we can try to change and to earn a part in God's divine comedy. Johnson's questions and our response make us skeptical of Democritus' philosophy as a norm, for his harsh view is as useless as the envious one we ourselves have just abandoned.[12] The conclusion of the poem will make clear the inferiority of pagan isolation and severity. There, religion will lead us to "love, which scarce collective man can fill" (line 361), and to celestial wisdom, which calms rather than agitates the mind (line 367). Indeed, it would be logically impossible for Johnson to regard Democritus' views as "just" if he is to begin his final paragraph with another question and a sign of the continuing search: "Where then shall Hope and Fear their objects find?" (line 343). And it would be theologically inconsistent in the poem and in his larger thought to hold that philosophy or reason, and not religion, could give the comfort which the reader is seeking. In Sermon 25, for example, written for the funeral of his wife (1752), Johnson urges that in the face of death few could "solace their passage with the fallacious and uncertain glimmer of philosophy." Religion is "our only friend in the moment of distress, in the moment when the help of man is vain." The reflections of "the voice of truth" offer "that comfort which philosophy cannot supply, and that peace which the world cannot give."[13]

Moreover, even two apparently normative words regarding Democritus might have evoked a context foreign to the values. He is supposed to have "chearful wisdom and instructive mirth" (line 50), neither of which is in Juvenal. Granting his "chearful" quality in the face of human suffering, "instructive mirth" is nonetheless tainted praise, and offers instruction different from that Democritus intended. Johnson defined the adjective "instructive" simply as "Conveying knowledge"; he illustrated the word with a conflation of a slightly longer line in Addison's *Spectator*, No. 179 (1711): "I would not laugh but in order to instruct; or if my mirth ceases to be *instructive*, it shall never cease to be innocent." It seems reasonable to assume that Johnson reread the *Spectator* in the months immediately preceding the writing of the *Vanity* in the fall of 1748, and that Addison's "Mirth ceases to be Instructive" (as the *Spectator* had it) was either the evocative source or clear analogue of Johnson's invention of a Democritean "instructive mirth." Mr. Spectator, certainly a friend to good humor, also insisted that his humor must be "Innocent," and suppress "Stroaks of Raillery" and "glances of Ill-nature."[14] Democritus' "instructive mirth" came trailing sentimental clouds uncongenial to a pagan's mind filled with scorn, the justice of which already is doubtful.

Questions have allowed us to test and discard or suspect different roles, and thus to "reply" to the speaker. Johnson continues this approach in his discussion of the fallen statesman, who is a microcosm of all those who "mount, . . . shine, evaporate, and fall" (line 76); but he also is a particular instance of our vain wish to rise and succeed in this world. Johnson thus poses a question on the statesman's behalf and phrases it so that it may come from the reader and represent a familiar defense mechanism – namely, is there not a mistake? Will the nation rectify the error? If it does not, the nation, alas, is utterly corrupt. Like most other modern students of the poem, I have considered this passage an expression of Johnson's own attitude towards British politics in 1749.[15] It now seems to me that he is presenting the dismissed statesman's own point of view and is showing that it is either hyperbolic or solipsistic. Johnson also is showing the statesman's vanity both in being suppliant to Preferment and to Fortune and in blaming anyone but himself for the consequences.

> But will not Britain hear the last appeal,
> Sign her foes' doom, or guard her fav'rites' zeal?
> Through Freedom's sons no more remonstrance rings,
> Degrading nobles and controuling kings;
> Our supple tribes repress their patriot throats,
> And ask no questions but the price of votes;
> With weekly libels and septennial ale,
> Their wish is full to riot and to rail.   (lines 91–98)

These intemperate remarks do not characterize the severe but generally sympathetic voice in *The Vanity of Human Wishes*. If the speaker's question is correct, his wish to be a highly placed statesman would not be vain, for he would then return to (say, Walpolean?) ministerial power at the head of a prudent nation, and that opposes Johnson's intention in the poem. If the declarative sentence is correct, the statesman was foolish to wish to lead such a people in the first place. Moreover, there is no evidence in the portrait to suggest that he was or deserved to be Britain's favorite; we know only that he hoped to rise, not that he deserved to rise. The glowing inference is the statesman's about the statesman, and we need not accept it. Of course the British, as we often hear in the poem, ask far more "questions but the price of votes." Finally, the speaker's separation of himself from those he satirizes is precisely what Johnson hopes we will learn to avoid. "Our supple tribes repress *their* patriot throats" and "*Their* wish is full to riot and to rail" are un-Johnsonian satiric thrusts in a poem that finally insists upon our collective responsibility for vice and our collective potential for God's love.

Since the portrait of a fallen, unregenerate Wolsey exemplifies the transient power of the statesman, the corrected reader will dismiss such a choice of life; he has learned the danger of public exposure and public greatness. Johnson thus takes a new tack with the fourth set of questions. Hitherto we have temporarily tried the roles of powerful envier, of Democritus, and of statesman, and seen how each was inadequate. By now the questioning reader is ready to enlarge his share in the debate and perhaps reconsider the previous role of humble poor man, the role he envied and tried to destroy; but we are educated, perhaps are gentlemen, and so must raise our expectations. After the portrait of Wolsey, the reader is presumed to be more active than before, and is prepared for a new role and a new question, one that bears its own dangers.

> Speak thou, whose thoughts at humble peace repine,
> Shall Wolsey's wealth, with Wolsey's end be thine?
> Or liv'st thou now, with safer pride content,
> The wisest justice on the banks of Trent?
> For why did Wolsey near the steeps of fate,
> On weak foundations raise th' enormous weight?
> Why but to sink beneath misfortune's blow,
> With louder ruin to the gulphs below?
> What gave great Villiers to th' assassin's knife,
> And fixed disease on Harley's closing life?
> What murder'd Wentworth, and what exil'd Hyde,
> By kings protected, and to kings ally'd?
> What but their wish indulg'd in courts to shine,
> And pow'r too great to keep, or to resign?   (lines 121–34)

We are encouraged to say – no, Wolsey's wealth and end will not be mine; or we are not likely to say more than the answers above couched as questions in the final couplet of each paragraph. We may add – perhaps the pleasures of rural peace, safer pride, and wisest justice are what we should wish to have after all; let us retire to private life. Accordingly, Johnson moves us to the relative obscurity but intellectual brilliance of the academy, where the "fever of renown" (line 137) breaks out in the desire to publish learned tomes for a learned university. Yet here too he challenges us with a question: "Are these thy views?" (line 141). This instance of safer pride still tortures the unwary, who must "Deign on the passing world to turn thine eyes, / And pause awhile from letters, to be wise" (lines 157–58). Such wisdom shows us that the earlier views were radically myopic and led to poverty or, if successful as in Laud's case, precisely the dangers of eminence that the private life was to obviate. The human condition, in our present cast of mind, is such that we invariably do repine at humble peace, cannot have safe pride, and seek control of others and the world's superlatives of any sort ("wisest justice") at a high price.

This is nowhere more apparent than in the portrait of Charles of Sweden, the most magnetic and destructive military hero of his age and a man, Johnson told Boswell, vastly more attractive than the civilized and cerebral Socrates.[16] The "universal charm" of such martial fame (line 184) evokes the reader's uncomprehending response to the decline of Charles from "Unconquer'd lord of pleasure and of pain" (line 196) to the "needy supplicant" who waits "While ladies interpose, and slaves debate" (lines 213–14) on his behalf. The reader has temporarily lost control of his own life and is drawn to

Charles' "resistless" tale (line 178), just as Charles is drawn to the resistless charms of conquest.[17] As such readers we are astounded at his collapse, and either break into the poem or hear our probable questions raised by the narrator. A created or a nonce "we" ask the questions; Johnson, "replying upon himself," supplies the answers that already are part of our expectations.

> But did not Chance at length her error mend?
> Did no subverted empire mark his end?
> Did rival monarchs give the fatal wound?
> Or hostile millions press him to the ground?
> His fall was destin'd to a barren strand,
> A petty fortress, and a dubious hand;
> He left the name, at which the world grew pale,
> To point a moral, or adorn a tale.   (lines 215–22)

The rejection of the epic end for the epic hero further demonstrates the flimsy foundation of the warrior's pride. It also answers one of Johnson's own muted questions regarding Charles, and invites us to recollect a comparable question regarding Democritus. Then we heard:

> How just that scorn ere yet thy voice declare,
> Search every state, and canvass ev'ry pray'r.   (lines 71–72)

Now we hear:

> On what foundation stands the warrior's pride,
> How just his hopes let Swedish Charles decide.   (lines 191–92)

The two passages have implied and parallel questions and answers that reinforce one another: Democritus' unjust scorn and its contempt for mankind are all too like the unjust martial hopes of Charles and his contempt for mankind. The negative and prompt answer regarding Charles reinforces our sense of the inadequacy of Democritus as a norm. Johnson has offered us the heroic option, let us join other men trapped by it, shown us its vanity, and in the process invited us to recall and enlarge upon the less destructive but still hostile ("Dart . . . taunt . . . edge . . . piercing" [line 62]) and vain approach of the pagan philosopher.

The different questions allow us to see how the poem and its audience "grow," how we move from having the narrator question us, to the point at which we seem to or could raise our own questions, whose answers remind us of the vanity of human wishes. There is another change in the next question, the framing of which again suggests that we see the insufficiency of the Democritean option – in fact, our presumed compassion for Laud and the enthusiastic young scholar already leads us in this direction. Specifically, we abandon the destructive for the sympathetic, as we wish not enviously to crush a poor man's peace (much less that of a poor country), but lovingly to extend an innocent good man's life. He is

> The gen'ral fav'rite as the gen'ral friend:
> Such age there is, and who shall wish its end?   (lines 297–98)

Not I, each of us must say. The aggression of "Increase his riches and his peace destroy" has been discarded in favor of benevolence, which Johnson would say, in Sermon 19, stems from God's dictates, is celebrated in all nations, and is "the most amiable disposition of the heart, and the foundation of all happiness" (*Sermons*, p. 208). But the world's act of destruction is as powerful as ever, for even the wish to have a peaceful and healthy age may be pernicious. If we do not punish the happy man, the human condition itself will, as "ev'n on this her load Misfortune flings" (line 299). The aging man sees his family and friends die, and feels his "joy" (line 306) drop from life ("crush th' upbraiding joy" [line 39], we were told when involved in a punitive role; laugh at those "Whose joys are causeless" [line 68], Democritus believed). He sees himself superfluous and forgotten, and waits only "Till pitying Nature signs the last release" (line 309), just as the statesman, defeated by his briefly fulfilled wish, waited fruitlessly for Britain to "Sign her foes' doom, or guard her fav'rites' zeal" (line 92). The virtuous, lonely man is indeed among the lucky ones. Misfortune, unlike the reader, does not repent of its severe role and shows us that even the most exalted of men collapse in the face of the body's frailty.

> In life's last scene what prodigies surprise,
> Fears of the brave, and follies of the wise?
> From Marlb'rough's eyes the streams of dotage flow,
> And Swift expires a driv'ler and a show.   (lines 315–18)

The reader's acceptance of sympathy is emphasized in the last question before the poem's concluding great paragraph. Johnson enlarges the range of his audience by adding female concerns and by showing how the daughter pays for the mother's pride. He juxtaposes the old man's death with the familiar wish of "The teeming mother, anxious for her race," who begs that her daughter be beautiful (lines 319–20) and prosper accordingly. A similar offspring had been a threat to the scholar's success, for the narrator hoped that "Beauty [would] blunt on fops her fatal dart, / Nor claim the triumph of a letter'd heart" (lines 151–52). This is one of the several instances of the poem's interlocking portraits which expand the objects of the poem's satire and our concern for those, like ourselves, sharing dangers in life's treacherous mist. Indeed, for all the obvious differences between the scholar and the beauty, both are victims of fulfilled vain human wishes. The clever young man must "pause awhile from letters, to be wise" (line 158); the radiant young woman's pleasure "keeps [her] too busy to be wise" (line 324). We no longer wish unhappiness for such fragile joy, and so we ask an elegiac question on the young woman's behalf; we also see that the martial imagery that permeates the poem is as important and destructive for the dancing maiden as for the epic hero.

> What care, what rules your heedless charms shall save,
> Each nymph your rival, and each youth your slave?
> Against your fame with fondness hate combines,
> The rival batters, and the lover mines. (lines 329–32)

Soon "none the pass defend" (line 337) and "beauty falls betray'd, despis'd, distress'd, / And hissing Infamy" (lines 341–42) proclaims her social and moral ruin. What care can save her? None, for we have come closer to the narrator's own vision and now appreciate his earlier judgment:

> Fate wings with ev'ry wish th' afflictive dart,
> Each gift of nature, and each grace of art. (lines 15–16)

The beautiful young woman who can "smile with art" (line 327) is inviting her own seduction just as surely as, in the larger sphere, "nations sink, by darling schemes oppress'd" (line 13).

We started the poem as uncommitted recipients of knowledge; we soon become agents of our own nastiness; we then become active or at least comprehending questioners and saddened viewers of the world we have made and inhabit. The questions allow us to move from the role of malevolent to sympathetic actor and asker; from classical philosophic scorn to modern military achievement; from active participant in the nation's highest public offices of church and state to private scholar in the university; from surprise at the aged good man's senile end to sorrow at the fall of the young beauty. By now Johnson need not encourage us to inquire regarding many other classes. Presumably, we understand the point of this debate by interrogatories and see how each different role ends in unhappiness because it is a vain human wish. The response of the serious investigator is likely to be either despair or redefinition, either abandoning or rechanneling the earthly energy that motivates our "eager strife" (line 3). That is just what the reader indicates in the poem's four final questions. We have been set in Johnson's own track of invention and are on the verge of his own discoveries. The reader clearly wishes to resist the option of despair, to use his native energy to bring him closer to God. "Faith is opposed to infidelity, and *hope* to despair," Johnson reports in an illustrative quotation from Bishop Jeremy Taylor (*Dictionary*). The speaker thus becomes an intrusive and benevolent narrator who plays upon our potential for goodness, so well demonstrated by our refusal to persevere in aggression or Democritean severity. He also builds upon our discoveries, human vitality, desire for free will, and need to ask questions and to receive answers; and he offers the one option hitherto unexamined, the one that responds to several of the questions raised earlier.

> Where then shall Hope and Fear their objects find?
> Must dull Suspence corrupt the stagnant mind?
> Must helpless man, in ignorance sedate,
> Roll darkling down the torrent of his fate?
> Must no dislike alarm, no wishes rise,

No cries attempt the mercies of the skies?
Enquirer, cease, petitions yet remain,
Which heav'n may hear, nor deem religion vain.   (lines 343–50)

The final couplet quoted makes clear that the reader is actively involved in the poem as a vocal inquirer and eagerly uses language on his own behalf. We no longer need to be urged to participate, as in "Speak thou" (line 121); but we do need the narrator's guidance – "nor deem religion vain" – and do need to know that religion is "Virtue, as founded upon reverence of God, and expectation of future rewards and punishments" (*Dictionary*).[18] Wolsey and Laud were nominally men of God, but actually men of this world and its power. To be sure, Wolsey's "last sighs reproach the faith of kings" (line 120); but that faith was secular, not religious, and was broken with Wolsey rather than with God. Genuine religious petitions bring us to a world of spiritual, not human, wishes, where questions disappear, for the debate has been resolved. Now the historical characters and indiscriminate masses everywhere else in the poem are replaced by our personal relationship with a timeless God. Each of the following points refers to an earlier vain wish and redefines it. For example, "Unnumber'd suppliants" futilely appealed to Preferment (line 73; see also lines 12, 112, 213, 256); with religion we

Still raise for good the supplicating voice,
But leave to heav'n the measure and the choice.   (lines 351–52)

Earlier we were betrayed (line 7) and confused in the misty (line 9) and "clouded maze of fate" (line 6); we foolishly prayed for long life (line 255); we were tottering in a world where "wealth, nor truth nor safety buys" (line 27; see also lines 31–32); we ourselves were restless (lines 20, 105), and saw Wolsey denied his "refuge of monastic rest" (line 118). Similarly, the misguided mother "Begs" (line 320) – a synonym for implores – her daughter's beauty; Xerxes' "pow'rs" (line 233) were unreliable and led to the death of thousands; and Wolsey's smile, it wrongly seems, "alone security bestows" (line 104). Johnson alludes to all of these, as well as the earlier martial imagery, in his new evocation of *safety, power, perception, prayer, implore, rest,* and *security.* We are

Safe in his pow'r, whose eyes discern afar
The secret ambush of a specious pray'r.
Implore his aid, in his decisions rest,
Secure whate'er he gives, he gives the best.   (lines 353–56)

The tack is quite the same when Johnson considers how best properly to channel man's energy, need to transcend his limitations, and wish to escape from solipsism. "Infinite wisdom . . . has not created minds with comprehensions never to be filled" (*Sermons*, p. 135), we hear in Sermon 12,[19] which also urges that revelation promises us the happiness we seek and does not leave us in the state of permanent disease in this world, and permanent soullessness in the next, as Democritus believed. The healthful mind replaces the senile mind; "Obedient passions, and a will resign'd" (line 360) replace restless passions that alienate a father's will (line 282) and make our moral will alien to God's; God's love replaces love as attachment to a rising career (line 79), or as a trivial emotion the hero ignores (line 195), or as sexual love that destroys the beauty (lines 329–42); patience reigns over the ills that must come to all of us and, if viewed correctly, can prepare us for the next world; faith in God replaces Wolsey's reproach of the temporal "faith of kings" (line 120). The material possessions that we had so avidly sought have been changed from gold, mortgages, and buildings to spiritual coin one may keep. Laws that were unreliable and easily perverted by man are made immutable, and the wisdom that the scholar and beauty had to seek is transmuted from the secular to the celestial. The empiricism with which the poem began and by which it is guided reemerges, as a superior divine empiricist works to ease the unhappiness of those who try to find her.

> These goods for man the laws of heav'n ordain,
> These goods he grants, who grants the pow'r to gain;
> With these celestial wisdom calms the mind,
> And makes the happiness she does not find.   (lines 365–68)

Such exalted answers are a direct result of the questions we have been urged to ask, of the roles we have been asked to evaluate by means of questions, of the inadequacies we have seen in those roles, and of the wisdom and generosity of the poem's narrator. He teaches us through serious debate and appears to investigate with us, though his own such job was long done. "What is the effect of study" seems to be "uttered without any premeditation."[20]

It may be useful briefly to contrast Johnson's with Juvenal's relevant poetic methods and moral assumptions. Johnson's characters do not speak to one another – as Juvenal's do in largely uncomplimentary ways (lines 67–72) – so much as to the narrator himself and to other readers who are improved in the process. Juvenal, on the other hand, makes Democritus a consistent norm and adopts his hostility to his fellows throughout the poem: the people are the "turba" or mob, or derogatory "populus," the rabble (lines 73–74). Indeed, we are all basically hostile, since even those of us who do not want to kill are willing to have the power to do so: "Et qui nolunt occidere quemquam, / Posse volunt" (lines 96–97). Aggression is a permanent part of human nature, is apparent in Juvenal's narrator himself, and is unmitigated by the religious comparison in Johnson's poem. Hannibal illustrates the vanity of human wishes; he also illustrates the folly of attempting to conquer Rome and Rome's ultimate vengeance for the disgrace of Cannae. For Juvenal, Hannibal is quite frankly "demens" (line 166) and encourages our pleasure at his humiliation rather than, as with Charles of Sweden, disbelief at a fall that might have been ours and that we briefly thought would be conventionally heroic. Dryden's translation captures Juvenal's mockery, without any of the grandeur that Johnson saw:

> Ask what a Face belong'd to this high Fame;
> His Picture scarcely wou'd deserve a Frame:
> A Sign-Post Dawber wou'd disdain to paint
> The one Ey'd Heroe on his Elephant.
> Now what's his End, O Charming Glory, say
> What rare fifth Act, to Crown this huffing Play?
>
> . . .
>
> Poyson, drawn through a Rings hollow plate,
> Must finish him; a sucking Infant's Fate.
> Go, climb the rugged *Alps*, Ambitious Fool,
> To please the Boys, and be a Theme at School.[21]   (lines 252–72)

When we near the end of the poem, we ask Juvenal's advice only once, in contrast to our fourfold request to Johnson: is there nothing we should pray for ("Nil ergo optabunt homines?" [line 346])? This counsel is not that of a speaker with affection for the audience he has been respectfully debating and guiding for the last 348 lines; it is the counsel of someone who continues to be Democritean, to debunk our wishes *and* the notion of dependence upon something external to ourselves. We may ask for a wife and children; but the gods know better and will not give us those dubious blessings if we leave the choice to them. But if you must go through all the nonsense of sacrificing a little white pig's entrails and sausage meat, ask for all the happy ramifications of a sound mind in a sound body, which that man-made divinity Fortuna cannot give you in any case (lines 365–66). You can give those to yourself through a life of virtue (lines 363–64).

Juvenal, then, asks many questions of his readers and has them ask the wrong questions of one another and their gods; he assumes an audience and narrator perhaps morally static and certainly capable of less growth than their Johnsonian posterity. The Roman poem culminates, not in a necessary looking upward towards celestial wisdom, but looking inward towards a stoic self-reliance that includes contempt for or detachment from other human beings and their wishes. The questions and answers between Johnson and his audience ultimately imply questions to and from a benevolent God. As we have seen, "nor deem religion vain" leads to an inversion of the insecurity, selfishness, crowded loneliness, and spiritual myopia of earlier vain human wishes. The questions and answers between Juvenal and his audience imply an earth-bound wisdom that Johnson would think atheistic, a contradiction in terms, and an insult to those capable of sympathy, not hostility, when led to virtue by the right guide. "Sympathy," he said in Sermon 11, is "the great source of social happiness" (*Sermons*, p. 120).[22] Johnson's poem begins with Observation and History as the masters in our empirical quest; they show us, among other things, "How rarely reason guides the stubborn choice" (line 11), and so Johnson as severely corrective but good-humored and sympathetic narrator takes on that role. In the process, he becomes like the walking abstraction Reason in "The Vision of Theodore" (1748) who points the way to heaven but wisely surrenders to Religion thereafter. Reason says that

there are asperities and pitfalls, over which Religion only can conduct you. Look upwards, and you perceive a mist before you, settled upon the highest visible part of the mountain; a mist by which my prospect is terminated, and which is pierced only by the eyes of Religion. Beyond it are the temples of Happiness, in which those who climb the precipice by her direction, after the toil of their pilgrimage, repose for ever. I know not the way, and, therefore, can only conduct you to a better guide.[23]   (*Works*, 9, 168–69)

Hence at the end of the *Vanity*, celestial wisdom replaces the personified secular Observation and Johnson's own reason, and thus more than any other force "calms the mind, / And makes the happiness she does not find." As James Grainger said in 1759, "The truth is, Virtue is the sole Parent of Happiness. See Mr. Johnson's admirable Poem, intitled the Vanity of Human Wishes."[24] As such a Parent, Celestial Wisdom can *make* where Observation merely could *see* and History merely *tell*; the capacity for change is directly related to Johnson's Christian, public, and religious as opposed to Juvenal's pagan, private, and stoical views. All this is rendered possible not by the chimerical Fortuna,[25] but by Johnson's willingness to ask, attribute, encourage, and hear our questions. These enable us to assume and to test a variety of roles, to see their weaknesses, and to see the strengths of the narrator who, in turn, like Adam at the end of *Paradise Lost*, finds his and our answers from above, and subjects himself to God at the right time, so that we will be encouraged to do so as well. As Johnson urges in Sermon 11, no "greater benefit [can] be conferred, than that of settling doubts, or comforting despair, and restoring a disquieted soul to hope and tranquillity" (*Sermons*, p. 124). In the *Vanity* Johnson knows more profoundly than Bacon how "He that *questioneth* much shall learn much, and content much; but especially if he apply his questions to the skill of the persons whom he asketh."

13 · POPE, HIS SUCCESSORS, AND THE DISSOCIATION OF SATIRIC SENSIBILITY

AN HYPOTHESIS

THE DIRECTION OF Pope's career aş a formal verse satirist is from an essentially Horatian ethic epistle like *Burlington* (1731), to mingled satire with a variety of Horatian, Juvenalian, and Persian emphases, to the overwhelmingly Juvenalian–Persian elevation and gloom of the *Epilogue to the Satires* (1738). Both Pope's poems and his contemporaries' reception of them indicate that his career was progressively less, not more, of "an *Imitatio Horatii*," and that Horace's "place to stand" was progressively less, not more, attractive for him;[1] it was sapped and then replaced by the conventions of Persius and Juvenal, which Pope himself welcomed.

One may, however, raise certain questions regarding the satiric method I have attributed to Pope. Why did he continue to imitate the satirist he was supposedly rejecting? Should he not have imitated poems of Juvenal and Persius as well? Some answers to these questions are implied in the poems imitated themselves – imitating Donne's Renaissance Horace, for example, is imitating a surrogate Juvenal. There are other answers as well, since in spite of Horace's several inadequacies, he and his special achievements were necessary for Pope's own purposes.

Why Horace?

Pope's imitations of Horace are part of his campaign to refine English verse. Early in his career he adapted the Ovidian epistle and the Virgilian country poem, and as he matured he looked to the third member of that distinguished group to continue his task. Horace insisted that his own generation burnish the rusty knives of Lucilius; Pope had a comparable attitude regarding the satire of Donne and his successors. Horace also offered greater modulation of tone than Juvenal or Persius. Horace's varied voice sings secure retirement or refutes attacks on his poetry; it affectionately praises Maecenas as father or Horace's biological father; it considers literary traditions of which Horace is a part or political traditions of which Augustus is a part; and it engages in epistolary or present dialogue with the princeps or a servant. Such a persona suggests a practical pose of flexibility and mature wisdom rather than rigid patriotism or withdrawn stoicism, and it does so in a context of decent values in a decent state and, often, from a country retreat and *locus amoenus*.

This polished, complex voice offered Pope many advantages, including the few biographical and historical similarities that appeared to suggest a (tenuous) link between the two Augustan ages. Most obviously, the Sabine farm is paralleled in Twickenham, the circle of Augustus in Pope's eminent friends and Prince of Wales, post-revolutionary imperial Rome in post-revolutionary Britain taking its place among nations famous for arts and arms. Consequently, by putting on the mask of Horace, Pope could adapt him for satiric attacks upon the administration and attempt to make him a literary Trojan Horse. The sophisticated conversation appropriate between gentlemen might, however infrequently, bring Pope a hearing with those he wished to reform; by preserving the façade of civilized discourse, he briefly seemed a member of the club. Thereafter, he was freer to add intimations of political mortality that would have been rejected at once if he were too gloomy or elevated in angry monologue. Alternatively, Horace was useful for Pope's "patriot" ends, since the opposition's political program included the creation of a court of Bolingbrokean tincture at St. James's. Pope in his grotto could create a shadow cabinet or government in exile, in which his lowered voice would be listened to more intently. Cobham and Bathurst were no less peers for being in opposition, and no more likely than, say, the administration's Dodington to encourage what James Beattie called the "vindictive zeal of the unmannerly Juvenal."[2] The opposition program also was linked to the country and its landed gentry, and again found a sympathetic voice – if, ultimately, unsympathetic values – in Horatian respect for retirement and affection for rural rather than urban charms. Juvenal's country is a lingering enclave of otherwise moribund Roman virtues. Horace's country nourishes many of the best Romans and returns them to the city with renewed moral energy for the support of the thriving nation. Horace thus offered the norms of corrigible humanity, functioning government, and poets able to speak to their rulers in a manly and educational way. Much of this, Pope came to believe, was wishful thinking, or simple duplicity and collusion by Horace; but such mythology deserved preservation as a standard that Persius and Juvenal were less able to invoke as an active force in their own lives, cultures, or poems.

Horace could be invoked not only as a lost norm in *Arbuthnot* but as an inadequate norm in *Fortescue* (from Horace, *Satires* II.i) and other poems. When Maecenas becomes Bolingbroke in Pope's imitation of the first epistle of the first book, Horace's union with the throne is, metaphorically, a noble ruin on the facing page; but the substitution also suggests that Horace lacked both moral and political judgment in supporting such a throne. Pope's Juvenalian implications are the clearer when placed in their Horatian frame. Hence Pope's rejection of Augustan tyranny is more striking when set against the flattery on the verso of the *Epistle to Augustus*; Pope's concern with licensing and government manipulation of the arts is more impressive when, in the same poem, we see Horace's willingness to accept and encourage such censorship; and Horace's insinuating voice is more dangerous when we see that in the *Epilogue to the Satires* it complies with the court's desire to turn satire into polite smiles and screening of corruption in the name of good manners. Pope is being consistent and commonplace when he says in his own epitaph, "Let Horace blush, and Virgil too" for profiting from flattery of their tyrant.[3]

The relevance of aspects of polished verse, modulated tone, miscellaneous devices, biography, politics, topography, and myths – these and the consequent opportunities for rejection, modification, and parody – all help to explain why Pope could imitate Horace and not necessarily identify with his values; in many cases hostility to those values is more nearly the case, as Pope's contemporaries often saw. We can add to these reasons the characteristic eighteenth-century wish to engage in a contest to excel the original, and the awareness that modern satire is a product of many individual talents within an evolving tradition. Though Horace was Pope's first companion in formal satire, he was joined by others who suggested different paths; he absorbed their several directions and arrived at a "place" far from the Sabine farm.

Perhaps this description of Pope's synthesizing muse will evoke related, useful speculation. The excellence of Pope's satires, for example, in part stems from the breadth of their form; they catch what Aaron Hill called both "the acrimony of *Juvenal*" and "the *Horatian* air of ease and serenity," so that he is "raised and familiar at once." This complexity helps to recall the complexity of life – or so Samuel Johnson thought in 1765 when he praised Shakespeare's tragicomedies because they imitate nature, not critical rules. "The two modes of [dramatic] imitation, known by the names of tragedy and comedy," were so designed "to promote different ends by contrary means, and [were] considered as so little allied" that no Greek or Roman writer attempted both. Shakespeare, however, knew that "the mingled drama may convey all the instruction of tragedy or comedy ... because it includes both ... and approaches nearer than either to the appearance of life." His plays thus are "compositions of a distinct kind; exhibiting the real state of sublunary nature, which partakes of good and evil, joy and sorrow, mingled with endless variety of proportion and innumerable modes of combination."[4] Johnson's conception of Shakespeare's "mingled drama" at the very least parallels John Brown's, and others', conception of Pope's mingled satire.

Indeed, Johnson's "Prologue Spoken at the Opening of the Theatre in Drury-Lane, 1747" is also relevant for the study of evolving genres in the eighteenth century.[5] He characterizes Shakespeare as the coherent product of learning, imagination, truth, and passion; this fruitful union allowed him personal immortality and his auditors instruction and pleasure. Thereafter, in the poem's chronology, Ben Jonson limits himself to academic learning, the

Restoration wits imitate not nature but their own vice, early eighteenth-century tragedians use boring rules and declamation, and mid-century authors succumb to exotic farce and mere spectacle. Johnson begins his poem with Shakespeare's inclusive form and shows it atomized and decayed. The new theater, fortuitously opening with *The Merchant of Venice*, promises a new age which can return to Shakespearean nature and truth, communicated in a form that combines "useful mirth, and salutary woe" (line 60), and to a dramatic mode that imitated both real "many colour'd life" and "imagined" life (lines 3–4). Shakespeare's practice signals comprehensive vision and successful mimesis; the debased or monolithic form signals meager and transient art that imitates the part rather than the whole.

Something like this unhappy progress in formal verse satire may offer one reason for the genre's lamented decline. I offer a tentative hypothesis, which requires abundant testing before it can be accepted, modified, or perhaps rejected – namely, that though Pope's influence is as varied as his practice, later formal verse satire tends to become either excessively Horatian or excessively Juvenalian, loses its modulation of voice and response, and suffers as a result. Such dissociation of satiric sensibility can even be useful for describing poems somewhat beyond the limits of formal verse satire, though of course it cannot "explain" all of the strengths and weaknesses of, say, Robert Lloyd's *The Progress of Envy* (1751), or Burns' "Holy Willie's Prayer" (1785, 1799), any more than it can "explain" Marvell's *Last Instructions to a Painter* (1667) or Rochester's "On Poet Ninny" (1680). Each of these, and numerous other satires between about 1660 and 1800, is different from classical models and Pope's amalgamation of them.

Extended speculation of this sort can take us beyond the borders of this book and into realms of literary psychology and aesthetics, for which more than a tourist's visa is necessary. Johnson's remarks and their implications nonetheless suggest that Pope's satiric practice is part of an ongoing development in the relationship of modern to ancient literary forms and of art to reality, and that in his synthesis he was doing for his genre what Shakespeare and, in different ways, Milton had done for theirs.

Dissociation of Satiric Sensibility

Several of Pope's followers also tried his mingling of modes,[6] but they could not scale his steeps, nor incorporate his model as Pope incorporated and altered Horace's, Persius', and Juvenal's; instead, they generally turned to and exaggerated one or the other of Pope's chief models. Perhaps this is to be expected. *Paradise Lost* is the culmination and graveyard of traditional epic poetry, though few would have seen that at the time; a similar remark may be made regarding the offsprings of Pope's satires from 1731 to 1738. Much formal and some other verse satire after Pope's tends to be either Horatian or

Juvenalian in the worst sense – either socially elegant with the satirist in control of an essentially trivial satiric subject, or bloated, hyperbolic, and rhetorical in a world of monsters whom the satirist hopes to knock down with his loud voice. One reason for Pope's malleable satire is his malleable speaker, who allows his tone to be determined by his satiric object. In *Arbuthnot* alone, we know, he adapts himself to Horatian, Persian, and Juvenalian targets. Many of Pope's successors reverse that process, allow their predetermined tone to define their satiric object, and banish complexity of form with complexity of response. They either refuse to see dangers or see only dangers, and in either case they eliminate the attractive and varied voice both within and behind Pope's poems. As Donald Taylor observes, for example, Chatterton as a satirist engages in "a search for evil commensurate with his anger."[7] We can see some of this dissociated satiric sensibility in the later eighteenth century by contrasting the "mingled" attack on homosexuality in Pope's *Arbuthnot* with the trivializing Horatian attack in Garrick's *Fribbleriad* (1761), and the extravagant Juvenalian attack in Churchill's *The Times* (1764). Garrick's poem is not, strictly speaking, a formal verse satire, but it is sufficiently and consciously linked to Pope to qualify for its pseudo-Horatian role, and thus suggests that some traits of formal satire were carried into other satiric species.

Specifically, Sporus, the male whore of Nero, is unnatural, a violator of the divine order, and demonstrably satanic as a tempting toad "at the Ear of *Eve*" (line 319).[8] Pope so wishes this allusion recognized that his note in 1735 drew the reader's attention to Book 4, line 800, of *Paradise Lost*. The corruption of Eve is the corruption of Queen Caroline as ordered by Walpole who breathes the venom that puppet Sporus finally spits abroad. The portrait transcends its genesis in Hervey's personal insult and Pope's punitive satire, and reaches the highest moral fervor. In punishing Sporus, Pope wields the revealing, now satiric, spear of Ithuriel (*PL* 4, 811–13) and defends his readers as he defends himself against the forces of disorder; he is the ally of God's original plan and the lingering decency of His world, which is threatened by agents of darkness near the throne. The name Sporus also suggests a shift from the Augustan and Horatian to the Neronian and Persian. Protection of the satirist is replaced by hostility to the satirist, especially if he opposes the sexual deviance that is an emblem of political deviance. The poem that was Pope's own "Bill of Complaint" becomes an effort to stop the sodomizing of Britain; it can do this only with abandonment of desired Horatian satire in "Atticus," and with acceptance of Juvenalian indignation and Miltonic and Christian allusion in the service of the nation's unappreciative governors. Pope is only a small reason for his apologia, and Sporus' Master–Miss ambiguity is vile not before Pope alone but before God.

Garrick's *Fribbleriad* is an attack upon Thomas Fitzpatrick, called Fitzgig, for his hostile pamphlet *An Enquiry into the Real Merit of a Certain Popular*

Performer (1760).[9] Garrick knew the *Epistle to Dr. Arbuthnot* and clearly was aware of Pope's precedent in this sort of attack. The Fribble is "like a toad" who vents his "venom" (lines 42–43), and the speaker asks his muse to "Say for what cause these Master-Misses / To Garrick such a hatred bore" (lines 98–99). The poem also imposes a Miltonic frame – but there the similarity ends. Indeed, the use of Milton suggests a major difference from Pope. Garrick's *Fribbleriad* is both a mock-epic and a mock-Horatian poem in which the satirist controls a fool who mistakenly attacked his better and is punished with severe but amused contempt. Fitzgig remains Garrick's enemy, not Britain's, and the guiding structure of the council scene in Book 2 of *Paradise Lost* accentuates the piddling rather than the ominous quality of the person and his sexual preference. The scene is held at a noisy public room of a déclassé inn, is dubbed Panfribblerium in lieu of Pandaemonium, and includes mincing, dainty, stereotypical characters with names like Lord Trip, Sir Cock-a-doodle, Baronet, and of course Fitzgig, who, poor fellow, is elected Satan to attack the god Garrick. The hero is drawn "With stretch'd-out fingers, and a thumb / Stuck to his hips, and jutting bum" (lines 211–12). Pope's symbol of political and moral corruption, whose name and character both were attacks on the court, here is metamorphosed into an Irish upstart who is the "COCK FRIBBLE" (line 405).

The difference between Pope's concern with genuinely threatened institutions, and Garrick's concern with his undeservedly attacked but secure reputation, is made clear in lines Sir Cock-a-doodle speaks of Fitzgig himself:

> "Would you have one can smile, be civil,
> "Yet all within a very devil –
> "Lay pretty schemes, like cobwebs spin 'em,
> "To catch your hated foes within 'em,
> "Let him a thousand times break thro 'em,
> "The *ingenious creter* shall renew 'em.   (lines 199–204)

The antithetical smiling devil probably comes from Pope's Sporus, or at the very least is analogous to him in the comic way of the *Fribbleriad*. The cobweb image also comes from *Arbuthnot*, and also suggests the difference between public and private concerns. Pope laments that he cannot adequately destroy the bad poet; the laughable Sir Cock mindlessly praises Fitzgig for being an industrious bug – whom Garrick finally does destroy. Pope speaks to his friend:

> Who shames a Scribler? break one cobweb thro',
> He spins the slight, self-pleasing thread anew;
> Destroy his Fib, or Sophistry; in vain,
> The Creature's at his dirty work again;
> Thron'd in the Centre of his thin designs;
> Proud of a vast Extant of flimzy lines.   (lines 89–94)

Fitzgig aims at mischief (line 205); Sporus aims at God's plan. Garrick deals with an impertinent who, in the way of this Horatianism, he seems easily to manipulate and defeat. Pope deals with a force so ominous that he must abandon modest satire and collect his harsher talents to flap, break, and expose the great adversary. For one satirist, homosexuality is a silly and superficially elegant aberration, for the other it epitomizes national decay at its presumed center of value.

Garrick's personal, "Horatian" poem was shaped by the fragmented presence of Pope and Milton. Churchill's poem exemplifies the hyperbole of a poet who ignores the satirist's concern with his function in society. Churchill's knowledge of varied satiric modes and his choice of the one most suitable for his temperament is clear in his *Apology* of 1761.[10] Heaven designed the satiric muse's role as one "To please, improve, instruct, reform mankind" (line 315) and to make oppressed Virtue rise above "splendid Vice" (line 317). The task of subduing Vice to Virtue is not one for those who speak softly or tickle gently:

> Now arm'd with wrath [the muse], bids eternal shame;
> With strictest justice brands the villain's name:
> Now in the milder garb of Ridicule
> She sports, and pleases while she wounds the Fool.
> Her shape is often varied; but her aim,
> To prop the cause of Virtue, still the same.
> In praise of Mercy let the guilty bawl,
> When Vice and Folly for Correction call;
> Silence the mark of weakness justly bears,
> And is partaker of the crimes it spares.   (lines 320–29)

Like many earlier satirists, Churchill insists that he will not polish his vigorous lines for the sake of softness and sound. "Perish my Muse," he orates, "If e'er her labours weaken to refine / Th' gen'rous roughness of a nervous line" (lines 352, 354–55).

This satiric manifesto suggests that for Churchill satire's varied shapes were irrelevant, for he saw his life as a series of encounters with different persecutors, none of whom could humble him: "Ne'er will I flatter, cringe, or bend the knee, / To those who, Slaves to ALL, are slaves to ME" (lines 274–75), he claims in the *Apology*. The generalized sense of outrage often seems unearned, monotonous, excessive, and, perhaps above all, to lack an enemy who is a threat to anyone but the speaker's career and consequent self-image. That image is related, not to the harmonious working of the poet within the order of divine, social, and poetic institutions, but to the poet as his own subject.[11] Churchill incorporates Juvenalian rage for apparently personal slights; he lacks the theory of causation that made Pope's satires so impressively urgent; and he cannot accept the mellifluence of Garrick's, or even Pope's, verse, since that would imply an enemy whom one can defeat without benefit of "Virtue's awful frown" (line 319). Excess is the bone and marrow of Churchill's satire, and is well illustrated in one of his own attacks on the presumed decline of heterosexuality, *The Times* (1764), a poem far more concerned with the outraged satirist than with the outrages to the nation that Juvenal saw in his second and ninth satires on a comparable subject.

The opening of the poem immediately establishes the angrily nostalgic contrast of past and present that soon discloses its grandparents' lineaments. "The Time hath been," and "Time was," and "Time was" (lines 1, 13, 33) that all virtues were active and vices controlled, when the shunned vicious at least tried to hide their shame and exalted scoundrels could be reformed because no one could be bribed to help them. Now, in this infinitely corrupt age, all this is reversed, and Churchill adapts the final paragraph of Juvenal's first satire to help find a model for his world:

> We begin,
> Where our Sires ended, and improve in Sin,
> Rack our invention, and leave nothing new
> In vice, and folly for our sons to do.   (lines 105–8)

He quickly reconsiders a key word in that last line. "Sons" denotes procreation, which denotes the coupling of male and female, which seems no longer to be performed in a nation so uniformly depraved (lines 109–18). Britain robs the world to import and perfect foreign vices, and performs sins beyond the reach of God's grace (lines 265–66). In Pope's final satires he was the agent of an angry God; Churchill is the master of God, as he declares:

> Be Grace shut out, be Mercy deaf, let God
> With tenfold terrours arm that dreadful nod
> Which speaks them lost and sentenc'd to despair;
> Distending wide her jaws, let Hell prepare
> For Those who thus offend amongst Mankind,
> A fire more fierce, and Tortures more refin'd.   (lines 273–78)

The monsters who control Sodom must be punished hereafter, since "On Earth, alas! They meet a diff'rent fate" (line 280), and are forgiven their sins, or are joined in them by hordes of like-minded chums.

A simple paraphrase of the remaining dreadful consequences indicates Churchill's method. Hard-working whores cannot earn a decent living any more. Woman, who excited the normal male till his "whole body [was] tingling with desire" (line 326), is discarded in favor of some beastly Ganymede or Hylas (lines 332–33). Women waste their luscious youths as men seek male whores. Apicius, an aging aristocrat, behaves like a lovesick adolescent who loses his appetitte. Why? Not because he lusts after a reluctant wench, or because his wife remains unfaithful, or for any other reason compatible with traditional upper-class debauchery: "His cause of grief behold in that fair Boy; / APICIUS dotes, and CORYDON is coy" (lines 429–30). Poor child – if only he could be saved from his vanity and leave Apicius' service, for that atheist lord surely will seduce and abandon him. But where can he go? The churches, and academies, the young, the old, the seeming rake, the married man – all are Apicius with different masks:

> Would'st Thou be safe? Society forswear,
> Fly to the desert, and seek shelter there,
> Herd with the Brutes – they follow Nature's plan –
> There's not one Brute so dangerous as Man.   (lines 495–98)

On the other hand, if you wish to live in society, "Amongst the monsters of AUGUSTA's breed' (line 508), dress like a woman, "Put off the Man, from Men to live secure" (line 510). Being a transvestite for virtue's sake is better than being one for vice's sake. At least that way you won't be propositioned in the street, though you may be beaten. Women themselves no longer have to be careful, as in the good old days when only a castrated priest would be allowed into the house that included daughters. Now, even if females wished to be whores, there isn't a man around "Who thinks it worth his while to make them so" (line 536). Propagation is in danger (line 554). All the well-known studs are dead or dying. Pimps and whores have nothing to do. Concupiscence and lechery are in disgrace. Wise mothers pray for daughters, who, though rejected by men, will at least keep her company, whereas a handsome boy will become a pathic's plaything by the time he is sixteen. Want to keep him sound? Tell the world "That He is coarse, indelicate, and brown" (line 622) or Sodom's hordes will get to him. And of course keep male servants, tutors, priests, brothers, and even his father away from him. No one who is male can be trusted. Surround him with pretty, young, and willing maids, and count yourself lucky, and be indulgent, if "He chance to get some score . . . with child" (line 654). After all, "To have a bastard is some sign of grace" (line 658) – a grace the sodomites were refused.

I suspect that I am not alone in finding this hyperbole comic and therefore not likely to rouse my alarm or fears for the future of the race. Like Churchill's contemporary reviewers, however, I do not think most of the humor intentional. After the last tirade, Churchill offers the conventional Juvenalian apologia and a Persian insistence on telling the truth about Midas. Here the poet must speak out all the more in order to associate himself with the stallion not the gelding or mare.

> Born in such times, should I sit tamely down,
> Suppress my rage, and saunter thro' the town
> As one who knew not, or who shar'd these crimes?
> Should I at lesser evils point my rimes,
> And let this Giant Sin, in the full eye
> Of Observation, pass unwounded by?   (lines 659–64)

> Born in such times, nor with that patience curst
> Which Saints may boast of, I must speak, or burst.   (lines 679–80)

Churchill concludes with regrets if he has offended the Fair, an assurance that he actually is writing for them – "The Cause of Woman is most worthy Man" (line 688) – and insistence that he will continue to write so long as a single sodomite prowls the land. He will track down and banish such deviants, until either God destroys them and their loathed city, or they reform, beg pardon of women, "And learn to honour them, as much as I" (line 702).

The moral ambiguities of the poem hardly need elaboration. For example, whether one wishes to hold up even the tainted norms of lechery, pimping, whoring, and bastardy on behalf of the beloved, luscious female sex is perhaps doubtful. The oceanic verbal virility of the poem helps one temporarily to overlook those blemishes while reading. One does not overlook the incessant anger, improbable solutions, lack of focus, absence of specific causation, usurpation of the divine function, and the paucity of recognizable particulars which allow us to believe that a genuine enemy has performed genuinely offensive acts, that he is part of a larger coherent pattern of demonstrable corruption, and that he must be punished for the sake of the commonweal. The modern reader is likely to join the reviewer in the *London Chronicle* who said of Churchill's effort: "every one must applaud the Poet's indignation; but it would certainly have had a stronger effect, had it been less indiscriminate and *outré*" (Grant, p. 550). Garrick is so civilized that his satire causes twitters rather than concern; Churchill is so strident and excessive that in spite of his announced affection for the sex with which he prefers to copulate, we discount his claims and may not put on skirts to save our manhood. Pope is the most successful of the three in part because of his native talent, and in part because that talent – as in *Arbuthnot* and "Sporus" – was benevolently synthetic.

I do not wish either to ride the Horatian–Juvenalian hypothesis too hard or to insist that it offers the sole paradigm for the development of formal or other satire after mid century. Both Johnson's *Vanity of Human Wishes* (1749) and Arthur Murphy's *Seventeen Hundred and Ninety One: A Poem in Imitation of the Thirteenth Satire of Juvenal* illustrate a redefined Juvenal without Churchill's lack of proportion. Garrick's *Fribbleriad*, however, suggests that the devolution of satiric kinds also may illumine some of the weaknesses in later satires different from Pope's, for here too we often see extreme Horatian or Juvenalian modes that actually abandon their neglected parents. When Pope does reemerge as a model, he becomes a source not for mingled but for grimly Juvenalian satire.

The Horatian impetus may be seen in the satires of Richard Owen Cambridge. Their frugal meal includes several imitations of Horace, adaptations of his techniques, and an affinity with Satire's comic mask. In one poem that alludes to Pope's *Epilogue to the Satires* Cambridge uses Horatian dialogue to indicate that Horatian satire itself is unmannerly and suspect – that is, in "The Danger of Writing Verse; A Dialogue between a Young Poet and his Friend. Addressed to Sir Charles Hanbury Williams, Knt. Occasioned by his satirical Ode upon Mr. Hussey's Marriage with the Duchess of Manchester; which gave so much personal offence" (1746). As in many satiric dialogues, the Friend tries to dissuade the Poet from writing satire. For Cambridge, however, the dissuader is not an arm of the ominous state, or an aristocrat offended by attacks, or a court hireling deaf to the song of virtue; instead, he is the exemplar of civility who hopes to aid society and the poet by blunting satire's barbs. The satirist's friends, for example, fear that his unforgiving foes will harm him and that the satirist soon will attack them. Indeed, Horace himself is generally enjoyed not merely because of his excellent verse but because his antiquity makes him safe for us. In any case, satire is read by the malicious, who enjoy seeing their fellows attacked. That is not the way human beings should deal with one another, the Friend insists, and he concludes with the salutary admonition that were Horace alive, "I should think it, tho' loth, / My duty to give this advice to you both."[12]

In this mid-century dialogue the Friend-and-adversarius embodies not the wrong but the right dissuasion from satire, deservedly has the last word, and rejects Horace because his satire offends. That Cambridge was not alone in recommending a subdued form of subdued satire, one ultimately traceable to certain Horatian devices and assumptions, is made clear in Christopher Anstey's *New Bath Guide* (1766), which reached its twelfth edition in 1784, and which in many ways embodies popular and amiable satiric flaccidity.

The *New Bath Guide* is written in a series of epistles with some precedent in Horace.[13] The writer and recipient, however, are not Rome's polished satirist and powerful aristocrat but the naive members of the well-connected B[lunde]R[head] country family writing to their audience at home. The poem's tones and intention appear in Miss Jenny's first letter, which praises the "wholesome satire" that "much enhances / The merit of our best romances" as well as modern plays. The other letters in the series are also opposed to the "base and unjust accusations" that "Arise from the malice and spleen of mankind" (p. 78), as Mr. Simkin B–n–r–d puts it in Letter 12. Only "the meanest" of the poetic band take "satire's thorny road" (p. 110).

Nonetheless, there is satire aplenty here, though it is so gentle that in 1771 Smollett's *Humphrey Clinker* takes many of the same scenes and, from Matt Bramble's point of view, puts them in a hostile Juvenalian perspective of the decline of civilized values. But for Anstey, the only relevant model is a wholly toothless satirist with a significantly altered but recognizable lineage. The first line of Anstey's "Epilogue" below probably comes from Horace's first satire of the second book and Pope's *Fortescue*; the second comes from Anstey's apparent desire not to cause any alarm by invoking those walkers among thorns; the third and fourth show that he is dealing with the most unthreatening sort of weaknesses in unthreatening folk:

> There are who complain that my verse is severe,
> And what is much worse – that my Book is too dear:
> The Ladies protest that I keep no decorum
> In setting such patterns of folly before 'em.   (p. 105)

Anstey's version of a defensive Horace need not fret about his adversaria in such a world, since she – the change is worth noting – is simply a creature of the fashionable moment and not an offended grandee able to bruise one's corpus of bones or words. The satirist-Guide argues that he never intended any harm to religion or virtue and that, like Horace, he is imitating nature. As in Cambridge's earlier poem, this Horatian apologia is found wanting because it is found unfriendly – now by a judge perhaps less than fully informed. The Second Lady rejects even Horace of the *Ars Poetica* if he justifies satire at all.

> Prithee don't talk to me of your HORACE and FLACCUS,
> When you come like an impudent wretch to attack us.
> What's *Parnassus* to you? Take away but your rhyme,
> And the strains of the bell-man are full as sublime. (p. 107)

The women in this epilogue remain unconvinced and, like their male counterparts in Horace and Pope, continue to urge an end to satire – but now with a major difference. "Pray," the Guide says to the ladies, "tell a poor poet what's proper to do." The First Lady knows the answer: "Why if thou must write, thou hadst better compose / Some *novels*, or elegant letters in prose," and do so "In epistles like PAMELA's chaste and devout – / A book that *my family's never without.*" The other women request an appropriate hero with delicate feelings, taste, passion, and "some incidents" in an amusing and pleasurable novel "Fit for modest young ladies" (pp. 116–17). Earlier synthesizing or Juvenalian satirists associated hostility to satire with hostility to culture, decency, and exposure of evil. Anstey sees the death of satire in the call for novelistic amusements and is annoyed rather than apocalyptic. In earlier battles for satire's life, Horace conjured up Lucilius, and Pope adapted Lucilius, Horace, and Juvenal. Anstey raises the shade of the actor Quin, an adversarius willing to justify the satiric urge. "I come not to accuse / The motley labours of the mirthful Muse" (p. 119), he reassures the quaking mortal. Quin finally gives the Guide full permission to write on and to "Take the mask from [woman's] d–mned hypocritical face" (p. 122). The Guide, helped by the ghost whose harshness to women he cannot accept, gives his own speech in defense of satire:

> Come on then, ye Muses, I'll laugh down my day,
> In spite of them all will I carol my lay;
> But perish my voice, and untun'd be my lyre,
> If my verse one indelicate thought shall inspire:
> Ye angels! who watch o'er the slumbering fair,
> Protect their sweet dreams, make their virtue your care!
> Bear witness, yon moon, the chaste empress of night!
> Yon stars, that diffuse the pure heavenly light!
> How oft have I mourn'd that such blame should accrue
> From one wicked letter of pious Miss PRUE! (p. 123)

Pope had elevated the apologia that Anstey diminishes. In *Fortescue* Pope tells his lawyer that, whatever the odds, he will "strip the Gilding off a Knave" or "perish in the gen'rous Cause" (lines 115, 117); in *Arbuthnot* he tells his doctor that "Curst be the verse, how well soe'er it flow, / That tends to make one worthy Man my foe" (lines 283–84). Pope's Juvenalian anger is transmogrified into Anstey's laughter; his "perish" as death becomes "perish" as polite satiric voice; his man of moral worth becomes a woman of fashion. In *Fortescue* that lawyer says "if you needs must write, write CAESAR's Praise" (line 21), and implies that the king remains an active source of reward. Anstey's woman says, "Why if thou must write, . . . compose / Some novels." Pope justifies his satire with moral imperatives borrowed from Horace and given backbone by his brother-satirists. Anstey justifies his satire by rejecting even mild Horace and insisting that – in the proper sort of female at Bath – virtue already is guarded by angels. In such a comfortable world, no wonder that the Second Lady can insist, "don't talk to me of your HORACE and FLACCUS," for Anstey anticipates her sternest demands and removes the arrows that the comic satirist once used.

Apollo, no doubt aware of the principle of *discordia concors*, saw fit to redress that balance and gave those barbs to Juvenal's later heirs. John Wolcot's invention of his generally raucous Peter Pindar well illustrates the other one-note version of satire that scarred the later eighteenth century, and which Peter himself called "volcanic."[14] Peter's satire includes energetic vulgarity, amusing scandal, and appealing abuse. Much of it has the compromised and compromising charm of a Rowlandson or Gillray print, in which the world seems to be populated by grotesques of whom we disapprove, but by whom neither we nor the artist are threatened. We laugh at such verbal cartoons in which the superiority of contempt replaces the insecurity of isolated outrage. Instead of Pope's ominous George II, we see Wolcot's ridiculous George III. The *Lousiad* (1785–95), for example, shows the king falling from his horse during the hunt: "all the Nobles deem'd their Monarch dead; / But luckily he pitch'd upon his head" (line 196). Wolcot abounds with this vivacious and surly wit; but he also abounds with hostility to the corrupt powers, fear of collapsing institutions, and, as Britain reacted to the French Revolution, fear of suppression or worse. His satire thus burns, scalps, kills, tears, blasts, lashes, cannonades, and pierces. It performs these acts with a sword, tomahawk, cannon, whip, or other weapon suitable for the blunt additive art of Peter's satire, which is "eagle, falcon, kite, / Hawk" (1:404). Peter of course subjects much of his nation to his lash; in the process he incorporates several other genres in his broad net. Odes, elegies, jeremiads, mock-heroics, and epistles share approximately the same waspish tones, and so, as Peter says in an ode, he must praise the virtuous abroad "Because I cannot find them . . . *at home*" (1:439). In the gospel according to Peter, Horatian satire is not sly, polite, and insinuating, but is once again the product of rage, as it was thought, to be in the Renaissance: "As brother Horace has it – *tumet jecur.* / Nor in her angry progress will I check her" (1:89). Consequently, when Peter adapts the *nil admirari* tradition of Horace's sixth epistle of the first book, he turns away from modest disclaimer of the world's attractions and towards his own more vigorous attack – here upon Bishop Porteus and Hannah More.

There are several reasons for Peter's anger. One is that he waves a banner inscribed with Juvenal's *facit indignatio versum*: "Shock'd at th' abuse, how rage inflames my veins! / Who can help swearing when such wights he sees?" (1:90). Another is that Wolcot's admittedly egotistical persona (5:173) frets about how the world treats him. His "Jeremiad," for instance, "pathetically lamenteth the fallen state of ONE of OUR MOST *admired* POETS, *videlicet*, MYSELF!" (5:62). He also offers the commonplace that the British character demands ferocity, "truth," and repudiation of flattery, courts, and kings. In one ode, "Satire" asks the receptive Peter: "Where is the glorious freedom of our Isle, / If not permitted to call names?" (1:86). In another poem, Peter talks with the laureate Thomas Warton, who grouses that Peter does not fear kings, whom he regards as "merely *common* folks" (1:434). Peter himself rejects all "crouching courtiers, that surround a throne" (1:440) and tells Warton that he must turn his back on a king who would "disgrace thy lay," must be like a bristling porcupine, and must not trade his soul for mere sustenance (1:442).

Anger and satire are predictable when Peter looks at this apparently unredeemable world in which his poetic weapons slay fewer than he hoped and endanger himself. Accordingly, in "Liberty's Last Squeek," Peter complains that because of Pitt "there is death in the joke / That squinteth at Queen or at King" and folly must therefore "go *free*." Such freedom means political and satiric slavery:

> Yes, FOLLY will prattle and grin
>   With her scourges OPPRESSION will rise,
> Since Satire's a damnable sin,
>   And a sin to be virtuous and wise.   (5:70)

In the second part of his poem, his "Ode to Jurymen," Peter hopes that his persecutors will not invoke "Dame INJUSTICE," throw him in jail, and hang him (5:80). And in "Out at Last" he envies the poet Isaiah, who freely satirized "the Babylonian Monarch"; but "Were *I* to talk so of a *British King*, / What were my fate? Alas! a string!" (5:115).

By the end of the eighteenth century, Wolcot's Peter Pindar comes to live in a world even more rigorously hostile than that of Juvenal, who was merely banished, not executed, for his impertinence to the court. Peter turns to Pope for what may be his most eloquent response to that world, and makes his own George III and Pitt as dangerous to civilized Britain as Pope's George II and Walpole. Wolcot's title announces his genealogy and foreshadows his intention, as we recall Pope's two dialogues of *One Thousand Seven Hundred and Thirty Eight* in Wolcot's two dialogues of *One Thousand Seven Hundred and Ninety Six*.

Wolcot indeed echoes several of Pope's satires and devices in this poem. In *Bathurst*, for example, Pope writes that after the unworthy Balaam is knighted, "lo! two puddings smoak'd upon the board" (line 360); in Wolcot's second dialogue Peter says that "The JUDGES' venison smoak'd upon the board!" (5:29). Pope's second epistle of Horace's second book characterizes London poets' displacement of their betters: "Call *Tibbald Shakespear*, and he'll swear the Nine / Dear *Cibber*! never match'd one Ode of thine" (lines 137–38); Wolcot's Tom claims, "Call MASON, SHAKESPEAR; *Mister* HAYLEY, POPE, / Their jaws with sudden inspiration ope" (5:18). Such examples can be multiplied; but they are most significant, not as evidence to support one's intuitive response to Wolcot's poem, but because in certain ways they undergo a sea-change and significantly darken Pope's shading. Thus in *Arbuthnot*, Pope insists that "Curst be the Verse, how well so'er it flow, / That tends to make one worthy Man my foe" (lines 283–84). Wolcot's bitterly Juvenalian Tom sees no good man at all and turns Pope's couplet against a flatterer: "Curs'd be the period, whether verse or prose, / That round a worthless head a glory throws" (5:17). Similarly, Arbuthnot asks "Who breaks a Butterfly upon a Wheel?" (line 308), but Tom sees a larger creature who needs rough strokes: "Who with a velvet lash would flog a Bear?" (5:30). This depraved world offers no support from the throne or its aristocrats. Pope told Burlington that he could "Erect new wonders, and the old repair," and "Jones and Palladio to themselves restore" (lines 192–93). His ideas inspire the kings who will "Bid Harbors open, public Ways extend, / Bid Temples, worthier of the God, ascend" (lines 197–98). In Peter's normless world the satirist himself must assume the royal mantle, fantasize that if he had "GEORGE's millions" (5:15) or, better still, if he were king, "palaces should rise," not for court sycophants, as now, but for "lab'ring GENIUS" and Taste. He would renew the world with great artists and "Bid . . . Palladios spring" (5:15).

Wolcot's effort in the genre of the satiric calendar enlarges Pope's scenes in another grim way. *One Thousand Seven Hundred and Thirty Eight* shows that even in its decadent world the satirist wields God's "sacred Weapon" (*Dialogue* 2.212), and that ultimately Vice shall be known and labeled and Virtue loved and protected – if only in the hereafter, where Virtue's "Priestess Muse forbids the Good to dye, / And ope's the Temple of Eternity" (lines 234–35). "Truth guards the Poet" and sanctifies his verse (line 246), because whatever happens during this age, God will not let His servants be thwarted when all books are closed. For Pope, a distant "success" is possible so long as God is possible. In Wolcot's resolutely secular poem, wit and liberty are dead, the arts are in disgrace, and omnivorous ministers devour the country.

All this gloom is placed in a frame of energetic, sometimes clever exchange between Tom and Peter. Tom is a young college-bred satirist yearning to inflict himself upon the many who deserve his falchion, thunder, lightning, broadsides, and comparable weapons from the magazine of outrage. Peter is the jaded satirist cast in the unfamiliar role of dissuading adversarius and apparent advocate of Horatian ridicule. This heightened exercise in Pope's dialogue form is a virtual confrontation between apparently competing approaches to satire, and it shows that in so unhappy a time both rage and ridicule are useless. Unlike their poetic predecessors, Wolcot's satirist and adversarius agree regarding the need to punish those responsible for the malign world about them; and unlike their predecessors, his satirist and adversarius have only one another to speak to and are ignored by Pitt's minions, who nonetheless can destroy them. Hence when Tom fumes that he will "make a charming little *hell* for COURTS," Peter replies with "Heav'ns! TOM, be cooler; take advice" (5:13), and later, "Fie, fie, TOM – really you are too severe" (5:30). Tom, in turn, scolds with "For shame! – by *ridicule* you ward each stroke, / And make the Ruin of the State a *joke!*" (5:32), and "Misplac'd indeed is all your ridicule, / That means to thwart my plans by calling *fool*" (5:33). Since the speakers are friends and share the same dark vision of the world, they finally agree and Tom is finally educated. He realizes that Peter's rough laughter is a good man's attempt to protest the world he cannot defeat.

> TOM
> So, then, you laugh at hopes of *Reformation?*
> PETER
> PITT finds a tame old *Hack* in our *good* NATION:
> Safe through the dirt, and ev'ry dangerous road,
> The BEAST *consents* to bear his galling LOAD;
> And spite of all that we can *sing* or *say,*
> FOOLS will be FOOLS, and MINISTERS – *betray.* (5:35)

This is the ridicule of despair, not the ridicule of the satirist confident that laughter is appropriate in a nation whose ministers, like Maecenas, reflect a benevolent poet-prince to whom a poet-citizen can speak and expect to be heard.

This poem also shows a government potentially fatal to the satirist. From the start, Peter warns Tom that Truth is dangerous and cannot screen him: "The MUSE that tells plain truth, with edge-tools sports" (5:8), that his song's "note is *death*" (5:9), and that, perhaps alluding to Juvenal's banishment, Horace's *Satires* II.i, or both, Tom can succeed no better than a more famous opponent of Pitt's:

> But what says PITT? will PITT thy rage allow?
> Believe me, TOM, the blunderbuss of Law
> Makes a long shot – an engine form'd to *awe* –
> By this has many a bird of Satire bled –
> Be prudent, therefore, and revere the *lead.*
> Think of thy banish'd *Namesake!* (5:24)

Horace had used a comparable scene to argue on the authority of Lucilius – if he then was protected by the state in his just satire, so should Horace be now; Pope adapted this to argue that if the sycophants Boileau and Dryden could satirize freely then, so should Pope now. In Wolcot's scene, the argument on authority is an argument on punishment – Tom the satirist shall, he thinks, gain strength from the example of opposition punished by the court:

> What! TOM PAINE?
> I *like* the Man – should boast to *hold his train*:
> TOM PAINE speaks boldly out; and so I dare
> Strike at Court Slaves, nor sex nor order spare;
> Spread o'er my quarry VICE, my eagle wings,
> Nor dread the conflict, though opposed by *Kings*! (5:24)

Thus far we have seen Wolcot elevating scenes or devices from Horace, Juvenal, and Pope. He does the same with Persius. We remember that in his first satire the court's dissuading Monitor warned Persius that there is a snarling dog guarding the great man's door if he approaches. Pope may allude to this when, in *Bathurst*, Old Cotta's "gaunt mastiff growling at the gate, / Affrights the beggar whom he longs to eat" (lines 197–98). Wolcot's Tom may be alluding to both, and again heightening both, when he laments the decline not of hospitality but of aristocratic patronage in general, and the contempt with which art is held by the court:

> How is fair ART, and SCIENCE, in disgrace!
> What Patron meets them with a smiling face?
> See, like a shadow, GENIUS, limping, poor,
> In supplication at a GREAT MAN's door! –
> And see with insolence his lacquey treat him;
> And were he fat enough, the *Dog* would eat him. (5:23)

Though Peter immediately begs for Taste and Reason to return to Britain, he knows this is impossible so long as George III, Pitt, and their minions continue to reject and starve art and the satirists who hope to correct them: "Ere long [Pitt] leaps on PETER's dove-like strains; / And should the MUSE be ravish'd, what remains?" (5:25). Like Pope before him, Wolcot exaggerated the dangers to the resilient nation and confused the discomfort of the part with the ruin of the whole. Along the way, however, he reflected and contributed to the process of bifurcation that formal and some other satire were undergoing through much of the later eighteeenth century. Wolcot is most at home strutting and raging among ruins, and would be least at home in Pope's social, "artificial" grotto and gardens, where affection induces belief in anger, and literary form tries to suggest the complexity of human response.

The monist satiric practices of Cambridge, Garrick, and Anstey on the one hand, and Churchill and Wolcot on the other, highlight Pope's own plural or mingled formal verse satire; this (relatively) new kind, as Johnson said of Shakespeare, and Dryden said of Milton, improves on the ancient patterns because it includes their separate strengths. Pope used Horace, Persius, and Juvenal in the proportion his occasion demanded.[15] His ability to combine every poet's power in one would have been lessened without his eclectic imagination and ability to compartmentalize, to accept and adapt certain literary devices and political postures in these poets while rejecting others. Pope's character, individual talent, and historical moment, including the prior example of Boileau, offered the perfect receptacle for the satiric traditions he inherited. Others thereafter tried to follow both his separate and synthetic roads; but they did so with less distinction and, more often, I believe, took the disparate paths that leave Pope's comprehensive achievement as impressive in its way as *Paradise Lost* is in its. Each is a monument to the highest level of a composite art shaped by a personal voice.

NOTES

Introduction: The Achievement of Dryden's "Discourse on Satire"

1 The Works of John Dryden, vol. 2, *Poems 1681–1684*, ed. H. T. Swedenberg, Jr. (Berkeley: Univ. of California Press, 1972), p. 3 in italics. *The Medal* is quoted from the same edition, p. 43.

2 The Works of John Dryden, vol. 4, *Poems 1693–1696*, ed. A. B. Chambers, William Frost, and Vinton A. Dearing (Berkeley: Univ. of California Press, 1974), p. 71. Subsequent citations are given in the text.

3 *The Poems of John Dryden*, ed. James Kinsley (Oxford: Clarendon Press, 1958), 3:1182.

4 I have discussed some of these matters in "Historical Criticism, Hypotheses, and Eighteenth-Century Studies: The Case for Induction and Neutral Knowledge." This paper was presented at the Georgetown University, Graduate School, conference, "The English Eighteenth Centuries: Theory and Method," and will appear in the volume of that name.

1. The Pattern of Formal Verse Satire

1 *PQ* 21 (1942): 369, 373. Miss Randolph refers to two studies which discuss this structure in classical satire: Augustin G. C. Cartault, *Etude sur les satires d'Horace* (Paris, 1899), p. 347, and Oscar E. Nybakken, *An Analytical Study of Horace's Ideas* (Scottsdale, Pa.: The Mennonite Press, 1937), p. 12. See also the Yale diss. by Arthur H. Weston, *Latin Satirical Writing Subsequent to Juvenal* (Lancaster, Pa.: New Era Printing Co., 1915), p. 5.

2 Randolph, *PQ* 21 (1942): 374–75.

3 Ibid., pp. 383–84.

4 See: Maynard Mack, "The Muse of Satire," *Yale Review* 41 (1951): 80–92; John Butt, *The Augustan Age* (London: Hutchinson House, 1950), pp. 68–70; Robert W. Rogers, *The Major Satires of Pope*, Illinois Studies in Lang. and Lit., 40 (Urbana: Univ. of Illinois Press, 1955), 83; Rebecca Price Parkin, *The Poetic Workmanship of Alexander Pope* (Minneapolis: Univ. of Minnesota Press, 1955), pp. 126, 166–68. See also: Alvin B. Kernan, *The Cankered Muse* (New Haven: Yale Univ. Press, 1959), pp. 11–32, and passim; Robert C. Elliott, *The Power of Satire* (Princeton: Princeton Univ. Press, 1960), pp. 109–12. For an earlier study of Pope's satiric method, see Elder Olson's "Rhetoric and the Appreciation of Pope," *MP* 37 (1939–40): 13–35.

5 *The Essays of John Dryden*, ed. W. P. Ker (Oxford: Clarendon Press, 1926), 2: 282–83; see also Randolph, p. 383.

6 See, for example, "To Matthew Prior, Esq.; Upon the Roman Satirists" (1721), in *The Critical Works of John Dennis*, ed. Edward Niles Hooker (Baltimore: The Johns Hopkins Press, 1943), 2:218, 220.

7 It was included in Charles Gildon's *Miscellany Poems* and as an appendix to René le Bossu's *Treatise of the Epick Poem, to which are added an Essay Upon Satyr by Mons. D'Acier and*

   a Treatise on the Pastoral, by Mons. Fontenelle (London, 1695; 2nd ed. London, 1719), and in the first volume of *The Works of Mr. Thomas Brown, Serious and Comical* (London, 1707); 9th ed. (London, 1760). Brown is probably the translator of the essay in Gildon's *Miscellany*; see Benjamin Boyce, *Tom Brown of Facetious Memory* (Cambridge, Mass: Harvard Univ. Press, 1939), p. 38.

8 See Collier's *The Great Historical, Geographical, Genealogical and Poetical Dictionary, . . . Collected from the best Historians, Chronologers, and Lexicographers . . . but more especially out of Lewis Morery* [*Moréri*], *D. D. his 8th ed . . .* (2nd ed., London, 1701). Collier remarks about satire: "*Satyr* amongst the *Latins*, is, in a large sence, applicable to all Discourses that recommend Vertue, and explode Vice: But the Word, as it is now commonly used with us, only signifies a stinging piece of Poetry, to lash and expose the Vices of Men." Collier closely follows Moréri's *Grand Dictionnaire historique* which, in turn, closely follows Dacier. See the "Préface sur les satires d'Horace," in *(Œuvres d'Horace en Latin, traduites en françois . . . par M. Dacier* (Paris, 1691), 6: **6^{r-v}. Collier might have seen the same passage translated in Brown, *Works*, 2nd ed. (London, 1708), 1:25, and in Dryden's "Discourse," *Essays*, 2:67. Trapp paraphrases the same passage. See the English translation of his *Praelectiones: Lectures on Poetry Read in the School of Natural Philosophy at Oxford* (London, 1742), pp. 223–24.

9 *The Works of Horace*, 3rd ed. (London, 1750), 2:li. Watson often refers to Dacier in his "Critical Dissertation on the Origin and Progress of Lyrick Poetry and Satire amongst the Ancients." See especially, 2:vii, xlvi–xlvii. Although called the "third edition," this is the first edition of the complete *Works*. The first volume, *The Odes, Epodes, and Carmen Secularae*, was printed separately in 1741, and again in 1747, and the *Works* reprinted in 1760 (4th ed.) and 1792.

10 Quoted from *The Complete Art of Poetry*, in A. F. B. Clark, *Boileau and the French Classical Critics in England (1660–1830)*, "Bibliothèque de la Revue de Littérature Comparée," 19 (Paris: E. Champion, 1925): 287. For other English allusions to Dacier, see pp. 286–88.

11 *Oeuvres d'Horace*, 6: sig. **8^{r}–9^{r}; spelling has been modernized.

12 Ibid., sig. **9^{v}. Watson translates much of this passage: *Works of Horace*, 2:xlvi–xlvii.

13 For examples of Dacier's praise of Horace's method of inculcating virtue, see his remarks on *Satires* i.i, *Oeuvres d'Horace*, 6:23; *Satires*, i.ix, 6:558; and *Satires*, ii.vii, 7:510–11.

14 Dacier, *Oeuvres d'Horace*, 8: sig. A3^{r}; original is italicized throughout.

15 Ibid., sigs. A3^{v}–A5^{r}; italics and roman type inverted in text. Watson also translates this passage: *Works of Horace*, 2:li–lii. It is likely that Dacier's view was a commonplace of continental Renaissance thought. For example, in his second *Discorso sopra le epistole* appended to his translation of the *Epistles* of Horace (1559), Lodovico Dolce observed that the satires and epistles had complementary functions: "In the satires it was his intention to remove the vices from the breast of men, and in [the epistles] to plant there the virtues." See Bernard Weinberg, *A History of Literary Criticism in the Italian Renaissance* (Chicago: Univ. of Chicago Press, 1961), 1:143.

16 London, sigs. A4^{r}–A5^{r}; italics and roman type inverted.

17 *Essays*, 2:100, 102.

18 John Dryden et al., *The Satires of Decimus Junius Juvenalis . . . Together with the Satires of Aulus Persius Flaccus* (London, 1693), p. 2. The original is italicized throughout.

19 Ibid., pp. 87–88; italics and roman type inverted.

20 Ibid., p. 146.

21 Dryden's indebtedness to the Renaissance commentators is mentioned in *Essays*, 2:43–44, 282–85. However, there is no thorough study of Dryden's sources in the "Discourse." The theories of Casaubon, Heinsius, and Rigaltius are discussed in Chester Hubbard Cable's "Methods of Non-Dramatic Verse Satire 1640–1700" (unpubl. diss., Univ. of Chicago, 1948), pp. 9–31.

22 *A Translation of Juvenal and Persius into English Verse*, 2nd ed. (London, 1786), pp. iii–iv, xiv–xvi, 195–96.

23 *Boswell's Life of Johnson*, ed. George Birkbeck Hill and rev. by L. F. Powell (Oxford: Clarendon Press, 1934–50), 4:38.

24 *The Satires of Decimus Junius Juvenalis* (London, 1802), pp. 1, lx–lxvi.

25 *Essays upon Several Subjects* (London), pp. 224–25.

26 *Critical Works*, 2:218.

27 Essays, 2:26; Edward Young, *Love of Fame, The Universal Passion. In Seven Characteristical Satires*, 2nd ed. (London, 1728), sig. A4ᵛ.

28 Père Dominique Bouhours, *The Arts of Logick and Rhetorick, Illustrated by Examples taken out of the best Authors . . . To which are added [by John Oldmixon], Parallel Quotations Out of the Most Eminent English Authors* (London, 1728), pp. 360–61.

29 *Works of Horace*, 2:xl.

30 Allen Lyell Reade, *Johnsonian Gleanings . . . Part V: The Doctor's Life 1728–1735* (London: privately printed for the author by Percy Lund, Humphries & Co., 1928), 5:225. Johnson's knowledge of Dryden's work remained with him. Late in his life he called Dryden the father of English criticism, and both praised and blamed his translation of Juvenal and Persius. See *Lives of the English Poets by Samuel Johnson*, ed. George Birkbeck Hill (Oxford: Clarendon Press, 1905), 1: 385, 446–47.

31 Lewis Freed, "The Sources of Johnson's Dictionary" (unpubl. diss., Cornell Univ., 1939); Dryden, p. 57; Pope, p. 73; Shakespeare, p. 76. Freed has tabulated all the illustrations in the first volume and a few – an unspecified number – from the second.

32 See Dryden's Juvenal and Persius, p. 4 of "The Satires of Aulus Persius Flaccus" (new pagination and title page after p. 316 of Juvenal): "The Reader may observe that our Poet was a Stoick Philosopher; and that all his Moral Sentences, both here, and in all the rest of his Satyrs, are drawn from the Dogma's of that Sect"; original is italicized throughout. Note too that Joseph Nicol Scott, in his 1755 revision of Bailey's *A New Universal Etymological Dictionary*, borrowed Johnson's illustrations for *underpart, arraignment,* and *declamatory.*

33 Reade, 5:115; *The Letters of Samuel Johnson*, ed. R. W. Chapman (Oxford: Clarendon Press, 1952), 1:6 n. 2; James L. Clifford, *Young Sam Johnson* (New York: McGraw Hill, 1955), pp. 156–57.

34 James H. Sledd and Gwin J. Kolb, *Dr. Johnson's Dictionary* (Chicago: Univ. of Chicago Press, 1955), p. 107.

35 *Life*, 1:188 n. 2. Powell epitomizes the remarks of Dr. Thomas Percy. Note too that a remark of Johnson's in Sermon 6 also suggests knowledge of Dryden's concept of satire: "every argument against any vice is equally an argument in favour of the contrary virtue; and whoever proves the folly of being proud, shews, at the same time, *that with the lowly there is wisdom.*" See *Sermons on Different Subjects, Left for Publication by John Taylor, LL.D.*, 2nd ed. (London, 1790), 1:137. Maurice J. Quinlan places this sermon "in the last ten years" of Johnson's life: *Samuel Johnson: A Layman's Religion* (Madison: Univ. of Wisconsin Press, 1964), p. 97.

36 *Characteristics of Men, Manners, Opinions, Times* (London, 1711), 1:9.

37 *The Satyrs of Persius* (London), p. xi.

38 (London), p. 10.

39 *The Correspondence of Alexander Pope*, ed. George Sherburn (Oxford: Clarendon Press, 1956), 4:112.

40 2nd ed. (London, 1738), p. iii. Hill did not sign the work.

41 Ibid., pp. vii–viii; italics and roman type inverted.

42 In addition to the remarks of Shaftesbury quoted above, see his "Essay on the Freedom of Wit and Humour" (1709), in *Characteristics*, 1:141; see also Addison's *Spectator*,

No. 209 (1711), Greene's *Satires of Juvenal Paraphrastically Imitated and Adapted to the Times* (1763), pp. v, vii, xvi, and Owen, *Juvenal and Persius*, pp. 213–14, 221–22.

43 *The Works of Alexander Pope Esq.*, ed. William Warburton (London, 1751), 3: 229–30, 263.

44 Ruffhead, *Life of Pope* (London, 1769) p. 289.

45 Ibid., p. 302.

46 Ibid., pp. 305–6. Here, and throughout his *Life of Pope*, Ruffhead is probably indebted to Warburton. See W. L. MacDonald, *Pope and his Critics* (London: J. M. Dent & Sons, 1951), pp. 251–82.

47 Ruffhead, *Life of Pope*, p. 360.

48 Ed. by W. Carew Hazlitt (London, 1871), 4:409.

49 For the contrasting sections of praise and blame, see lines 173–79, the attack on Shaftesbury, and lines 69–78, the praise of the conservative Tories. The virtues of the moderate Tory and the vices of the extreme Whig are neatly set forth in the portrait of Edward Seymour (lines 899–913). For a similar view of the poem, see C. V. Wedgwood, *Poetry and Politics under the Stuarts* (Cambridge: Cambridge University Press, 1960), p. 168.

50 *Satire* 1, pp. 14–15.

51 Ibid., pp. 15–18.

52 *Satire* 7, p. 168. This satire was published in 1726 as "Satire the Last," but was followed by Satires 5 (1727) and 6 (1728).

53 *Satire* 7, p. 172. The three kinds of Ambition are discussed on pp. 170–72, and the king characterized on pp. 172–75.

2. History, Horace, and Augustus Caesar

1 *The Roman History, from the Building of the City to the Perfect Settlement of the Empire, by Augustus Caesar* (London, 1695), p. 430.

2 For these see *Astraea Redux*, lines 320–23; *Windsor Forest*, lines 335–36, and passim; *Hop Garden*, in *The Collected Poems of Christopher Smart*, ed. Norman Callan (London: Routledge & Kegan Paul, 1949), 1:151 (the context is warmly pro-Augustan); *The Bee*, in *Collected Works of Oliver Goldsmith*, ed. Arthur Friedman (Oxford: Clarendon Press, 1966), 1:198.

3 David L. Evans, "*Humphry Clinker*: Smollett's Tempered Augustanism," *Criticism* 9 (1967):257.

4 Reuben Brower, *Alexander Pope: The Poetry of Allusion* (Oxford: Clarendon Press, 1959), p. 176.

5 Sanford Budick, "The Demythological Mode in Augustan Verse," *ELH* 37 (1970): 391.

6 For a few of these observations see, on proscription, Samuel Clarke, *The Life and Death of Julius Caesar . . . As Also the Life and Death of Augustus Caesar In whose Reign our Blessed Lord, and Soverein Jesus Christ was borne* (London, 1665), pp. 56–57; on his sexual misadventures, see Nathaniel Lee, *Gloriana or the Court of Augustus Caesar* (London, 1676), p. 27 and passim, and John Dryden, Preface to *Ovid's Epistles* (1680) in *John Dryden: Of Dramatic Poesy and other Critical Essays*, ed. George Watson (London and New York: Dent and Dutton, 1962), 2:263–64, *Monthly Review* 44 (1771):528; on cowardice, Robert Jephson, *Roman Portraits* (London, 1794), pp. 176–77; on inferiority to Jesus, Clarke, *Life and Death of Caesar*, p. 93, and [Joseph Wilcocks] *Roman Conversations* (London, 1763), 1:218–19 (for a far earlier example see – with thanks to Dr. Robert Brawer – the portrayal of Caesar Augustus in the medieval cycle of Towneley Plays, IX); on Tiberius, Thomas Blackwell, *Memoirs of the Court of Augustus* (Edinburgh, 1755, 1763), 2:185, 3:503; on similarities and differences from Louis XIV, [Wilcocks] *Roman Conversations*, 2:256, and Jerom Alley, *Historical Essays on the Lives of Augustus Caesar; and Lewis XIV* (Dublin, 1782),

p. 86. Much of the information in these works comes from the Roman historians, especially Tacitus and Suetonius.

7 "English Vergil: The *Aeneid* in the XVIII Century," *Philologica Pragensia* 10 (1967): 1–11. For other recent studies of the eighteenth century's mixed reaction to Augustus, see Jay Arnold Levine, "Pope's *Epistle to Augustus*, Lines 1–30," *SEL* 7 (1967): 427–51; Manuel Schonhorn, "The Audacious Contemporaneity of Pope's *Epistle to Augustus*," *SEL* 8 (1968): 431–44; J. W. Johnson, *The Formation of English Neo-Classical Thought* (Princeton: Princeton Univ. Press, 1967), pp. 16–30; Howard Erskine-Hill, "Augustans on Augustanism: England 1655–1759," in *Renaissance and Modern Studies* 11 (1967):55–83; Ian Watt, "Two Historical Aspects of the Augustan Tradition," in *Studies in the Eighteenth Century: Papers Presented at the David Nichol Smith Memorial Seminar Canberra 1966*, ed. R. F. Brissenden (Toronto: Univ. of Toronto Press, 1968), pp. 67–88; M. M. Kelsall, "What God, What Mortal? The *Aeneid* and English Mock-Heroic," *Arion* 8 (1969): 359–79; Howard D. Weinbrot, "Augustan Imitation: The Role of the Original," in *Proceedings of the Modern Language Association Conference on Neo-Classicism*, ed. Paul J. Korshin (New York: AMS Press, 1970), pp. 53–70. Addison Ward's essay is also of interest: "The Tory View of Roman History," *SEL* 4 (1964): 413–56. Sir Ronald Syme's brilliant *The Roman Revolution* (Oxford: Clarendon Press, 1939), remains the best introduction to the complexities of the rise of Augustus.

8 *Alexander Pope: Imitations of Horace*, The Twickenham Edition of the Poems of Alexander Pope, vol. 4, ed. John Butt, 2nd ed. (London and New Haven: Methuen and Yale Univ. Press, 1953), p. 3. Subsequent references to this edition are cited in the text.

9 *Oeuvres d'Horace en latin et en français, avec des remarques critiques et historiques, par monsieur Dacier* . . ., 3rd ed. (Paris, 1709) 1: lxxxii. See also the remarks of Dusaulx and his English translator, note 28, below.

10 For a positive view of Augustus, see Marguetel de Saint-Denis, "*Of* Augustus, *his Government, and his Genius*," in *Miscellaneous Essays: By Monsieur St. Evremond. Translated out of French. With a Character, By a Person of Honor there in England. Continued by Mr. Dryden* (London, 1692), 1:96–98. For the negative remark quoted above, see "A Discourse upon the word VAST, to the Gentlemen of the Academy," ibid., 1:303.

11 "To Monsieur the Marshall de Créqui, Who ask'd the temper of my Mind, and my Thoughts of things in general," *Miscellaneous Essays* (1694), 2:9–10.

12 *The Works of Henry Fielding, Esq.*, ed. Leslie Stephen (London, 1882), 4:390, the final paragraph of ch. 9. Fielding's view of Echard, however, did not deter Mrs. Western from reading his *Roman History* (*Tom Jones*, Book 1, ch. 6).

13 *Monthly Review* 44 (1771), 529. The remark appears in Gilbert Stuart's important review of Voltaire's *Questions sur l'encyclopédie*. For the attribution, see Benjamin Christie Nangle, *The Monthly Review First Series 1749-1789: Indexes of Contributors and Articles* (Oxford: Clarendon Press, 1934), p. 105.

14 The play was reprinted in 1734 – separately from Lee's *Works* of that year – and since it apparently was not performed, may have been an attack upon George II. The opening couplet is spoken by Ovid, and is worthy of *Tom Thumb*: "Vast are the Glories, *Caesar*, thou has won, / To make whose Triumphs up, the World's undone." If the play was involved in political squabbles, it would not have been the first time for Lee's efforts, since *Lucius Junius Brutus* (1680) was "silenc'd after the third Day of acting it; it being objected, that the Plan, and Sentiments of it had too boldly vindicated, and might enflame Republican Principles" (*An Apology for the Life of Colley Cibber*, ed. B. R. S. Fone [Ann Arbor: Univ. of Michigan Press, 1968], p. 188).

15 Watson edition (see note 6), 2:133–35. Subsequent references will be cited in the text.

16 *The Works of Tacitus . . . Containing the Annals. To which are Prefixed Discourses upon that Author* (London, 1728), 1:50. See also 1:49, where Gordon berates flattery by Virgil and

Horace, and urges that "every admirer of those charming Poets, is an admirer of AUGUSTUS, who was so generous to them, and is the chief burthen of their Panegyricks." The *Craftsman*, No. 220 (1730), borrows Gordon's views of Tacitus and Augustus. There Humphry Oldcastle berates "the Usurpation of *Augustus*," praises "the glorious *fourth* and *fifth Centuries* of the Republick of *Rome*," and urges Caleb D'Anvers to "Advise [Osborne] to learn better notions of Government from Mr. *Gordon*'s excellent Discourses, prefix'd to his Translation of *Tacitus*; in which He will find his Favourite Augustus set in a true Light, and prov'd to be an infamous *Tyrant*, though somewhat more artful than his Successors." See also *Craftsman*, No. 117 and the Postscript to No. 122 (1728).

17 *The Roman History, From the Building of Rome to the Ruin of the Commonwealth* (London, 1771), 4:363n. Hooke has in fact quoted Middleton (note 19), and adds that "this historian greatly paid his court to the reigning family" by softening Augustus' "odium," however little the softening now appears.

18 The subscribers to Middleton's work included Ralph Allen, Burlington, Colley Cibber, Samuel Johnson, Esq. (probably not *the* Johnson?), Lyttelton, Uvedale Price, Pope, Sir Robert Walpole (five large paper books), William Warburton, and Daniel Wray. The Royal Family subscribed for the large paper edition, and John, Lord Hervey subscribed for twenty-five large paper sets.

19 *The History of the Life of Marcus Tullius Cicero* (London, 1741), 2:499-500. For an ironic "defense" of Augustus' proscription of Cicero – Antony promised to spare him – see "A Dialogue Between Augustus Caesar, and Cardinal Richelieu," in *The Works of John Sheffield, Earl of Mulgrave, Marquis of Normanby, and Duke of Buckingham* (ed. Alexander Pope), 2nd ed. (London, 1729), 2:161-62.

20 *The Works of George Lord Lyttelton*, ed. George Edward Ayscough, 3rd ed. (London, 1776), 2:157-58. At least one (unknown) commentator, however, believed that Lyttelton's Dialogue gave Messala the better of the argument: see *Candid and Critical Remarks on the Dialogues of the Dead* (London, 1760), pp. 38-39.

21 *The Works of Cornelius Tacitus* (London, 1793), 1:6. Subsequent references are cited in the text.

22 Similar points are made throughout the work sometimes attributed to Tacitus (sometimes to Quintilian, and sometimes to the younger Pliny), and translated in Murphy's vol. 4, "A Dialogue concerning Oratory, or the Causes of Corrupt Eloquence." Murphy's translation was praised by Robert Jephson in his *Roman Portraits*, pp. 264-65, and remained the standard translation through much of the nineteenth century.

Seneca's remark is the basis for the *Craftsman*, No. 4 (1726), an attack upon Augustus for perverting the law and for setting an example for Tiberius "to prosecute the most *innocent Books*, and destroy entirely that *just liberty*, which is the greatest Blessing of a free People." Nos. 117, 122 (1728), and 182 (1729) add further relevant comment.

23 4th ed. (Lyons, 1687), 1:388-89.

24 *Reflections on the Causes of the Grandeur and Declension of the Romans* (London, 1734), p. 132. Montesquieu makes clear that he is using the word "tyrant" to apply to Augustus only as one "who had subverted a Democracy, for in all other particulars, *Augustus* was a lawful Prince, after the Law enacted by the People" (p. 132n).

25 *Encyclopédie, ou dictionnaire raisonné des sciences, des arts et des métiers* (Neufchastel, 1765), 14:334, s.v. "Romain Empire."

26 *Observations on the Romans* (London, 1751), p. 94.

27 (Geneva [?], 1770-72), 2:351-52. In the early nineteenth century such attacks were commonplace in France: see Eusèbe Salverte [Anne-Joseph Eusèbe Baconnière] *Horace et l'empereur Auguste* (Paris, 1823), passim. The *Questions* were published in London in 1771, again in 1771-72, and were read in England: see R. S. Crane, "Diffusion of Voltaire's Writings in England," *MP* 20 (1923):267. To this should be added Gilbert

Stuart's sympathetic review of the *Questions* in the *Monthly Review* 44 (1771):525-33. Stuart seconds Voltaire's hostility to Augustus.

28 *Satires de Juvénal*, 3rd ed. (Paris, 1789), 1:lxxxvj and xlvij, respectively. The second edition, 1782, added the discourse concerning the Latin satirists. R. C. Whitford notes that Dusaulx's Juvenal "was well known in England during the half-century" ("Juvenal in England 1750-1802," *PQ* 7 [1928]: 12, n. 16). Since the first edition appeared in 1770, Whitford overstates, but his general point is well taken. In his commentary upon Juvenal, for example, William Gifford gratefully acknowledges his debt to Dusaulx, but nevertheless attempts to correct his excessive zeal for freedom. He points out that though everyone agrees with Dusaulx that Augustus smothered the last breath of Roman liberty, this had actually been accomplished long before: "What liberty was destroyed by the usurpation of Augustus?" (*The Satires of Decimus Junius Juvenalis* [London, 1802], p. li n). He translates Dusaulx on pp. li–liv. Gifford did not believe that this part of the discourse "ever appeared in English"; but much of it was in fact in the *Literary Magazine* for 1791.

For further reaction to Dusaulx and Gifford on Juvenal, see Dr. Charles Burney's review of La Harpe's *Lycaeum, or Course of Lectures on Antient and Modern Literature*, *Monthly Review*, 2nd ser. 34 (1801):518 and Christopher Lake Moody's review of Gifford's Juvenal, ibid., 40 (1803):8–9. Moody concurs with Gifford's "character of *Horace* as a satirist": "he must have been the *enfant gâté* in the palace of Augustus" (ibid., p. 9). For the attribution of the reviewers, see Benjamin Christie Nangle, *The Monthly Review Second Series 1790-1815: Indexes of Contributors and Articles* (Oxford: Clarendon Press, 1955), pp. 234, 148, respectively. Nangle believes that Dr. Burney the elder reviewed La Harpe; considering the classical subject matter, however, I wonder if it was not Dr. Burney the younger.

29 *Literary Magazine and British Review* 7 (1791):441–43. The "Parallel" is identified only as "Translated from the French." For an additional anti-Augustan remark, see ibid. 9 (1792):461.

30 *The Works of Virgil, Englished* (Birmingham, 1766), p. 12. Andrews' main concern is with Virgil. Blackwell's *Memoirs of the Court of Augustus* (1755) 2:355-57, 436, uses a similar argument for Horace and Virgil.

31 For Jephson, see *Roman Portraits*, pp. 256–57, and for Shelley, see *Mary Shelley's Journal*, ed. Frederick L. Jones (Norman: Univ. of Oklahoma Press, 1947), pp. 30, 73. I am indebted to Professor Susan L. Brisman for the latter reference. Jephson includes these lines regarding Augustus: "In him combin'd the extremes of sense and vice, / Consummate art, and cruel cowardice" (p. 172).

32 (1763), 3:376. Subsequent quotations are cited in the text. Reconsideration of the specifically "Augustan" quality of the Emperor's great men of letters had taken place before Blackwell and would go on after him. See St. Evremond's remarks (1692, 1694) above, p. 23, and notes 10 and 11; Jean Baptiste du Bos, *Réflexions critiques sur la poésie et la peinture* (1719; trans. into English by Thomas Nugent, 1748), 6th ed. (Paris, 1755), 2:193–94; George Turnbull, *A Treatise on Ancient Painting* (London, 1740), p. 107, which quotes du Bos (I am indebted to Professor Eric Rothstein for these references); Joseph Warton, *Essay on the Genius and Writings of Pope* (vol. 2, 1782), 5th ed. (London, 1806), 2:341n; and Warton, *The Works of Alexander Pope, Esq.* (London, 1797), 4:146–47n.

33 Johnson's review appeared in the *Literary Magazine* 1 (1756):41–42, 239–40. See also *The Works of Samuel Johnson* (Oxford, 1825), 6:9–16. Since Blackwell's style, sources, and theme are the same for all three volumes, Johnson's strictures upon volume 2 would almost certainly stand for 3 as well. In 2:362, for instance, Blackwell argues that after the Peace of Miseno the remaining republicans returned to Rome and, in effect, "gave up all Thoughts of again taking arms in defence of LIBERTY." They "submitted to the Ruins of their Fortunes, and sate tamely down in that *Shadow* of a SENATE . . . a strange

ROMAN SENATE it was!" Augustus, as chief of the Triumvirs and final source of power, remains the villain.

34 (London, p. 13. The subtitle tells us that the author will include "Some Critical Thoughts concerning *Horace* and *Virgil*."

35 Pp. 15, 19, respectively. In a note to the last phrase, the author says: "Not only *Horace*, who shews his fulsome Flattery to *Augustus* in several of his Odes, but even also Virgil in his *Bucolicks* and *Georgicks*, as most particularly in his *Aeneid*. *Vide* the Description there of *Aeneas* his *Armour*, made by *Vulcan*."

36 *An Ode to the Right Honourable the Earl of Huntingdon* (London, 1748), p. 11.

37 (London), 3:55–56. I owe this reference to Professor William Park.

38 *Boswell's Life of Johnson*, ed. George Birkbeck Hill, rev. L. F. Powell (Oxford: Clarendon Press, 1934–50), 2:234.

39 Joseph Spence, *Observations, Anecdotes, and Characters of Books and Men Collected from Conversation*, ed. James M. Osborn (Oxford: Clarendon Press, 1966), 1:229–30; probably July–August of 1739. Pope also tells Spence that Virgil was "as slavish a writer as any of the gazetteers" (ibid.). See also Edmond Malone's remarks on Pope and Virgil, in *The Critical and Miscellaneous Prose Works of John Dryden* (London, 1800), 3:454–58 n. 1. On p. 449 of this edition, Dryden uses Virgil's praise of Cato (Uticensis, he thinks) to argue that Virgil "was still of republican principles in heart," T. W. Harrison's essay is particularly valuable for this view of a "political" Virgil: see n. 7, above.

40 *Alexander Pope: The Poetry of Allusion*, pp. 163–64.

41 *A Dissertation Upon the Most Celebrated Roman Poets* (in Latin, 1692), trans. Christopher Hayes (London, 1718), p. 49. Joseph Trapp made a similiar remark in the Preface to his translation of the *Aeneid* (London, 1718), 1:ix, as did John Dennis in his discussion of the Roman satirists (see n. 47, below). See also Ephraim Chambers' *Cyclopaedia* entry for *Poet*, in which Horace is said to excel as a lyric poet, "And Juvenal, Persius, Regnier, Boileau, Dryden, & Oldham, as satiric *Poets*," 6th ed. (London, 1750); and the *Monthly Review* 2nd ser. 19 (1796):176: "In Satire [Horace] surpassed Lucilius, and divides the palm with Juvenal." The remark appears in Alexander Geddes' review of Gilbert Wakefield's edition of Horace: see Nangle, *The Monthly Review Second Series*, p. 141.

It is worth pointing out that however equivalent in talent, the two poets were far apart in years, Horace living between 65 and 8 B.C., and Juvenal, whose dates are uncertain, between about A.D. 55 and 131. He published satires from 110 on, though he read them in public several years earlier.

42 For Boileau, see Dryden's "Discourse concerning . . . Satire," *Essays*, 2:81; Brossette's letter in 1700, in *Correspondance entre Boileau-Despréaux et Brossette*, ed. Auguste Laverdet (Paris, 1858), pp. 47–48; and Edward Young's *Love of Fame, The Universal Passion*, 2nd ed. (London, 1728), sig. A4ᵛ. For Pope see William Warburton, *The Works of Alexander Pope* (London, 1751), 4:36–37; Edward Burnaby Greene, *The Satires of Juvenal Paraphrastically Imitated* (London, 1763), p. xxi; Warton, *Essay on the Genius and Writings of Pope*, 2:266–67; William Boscawen, *Progress of Satire* (London, 1798), in *Poems by William Boscawen* (London, 1801), p. 136. Boscawen says that Pope's satire is "soft as the music of th' Horatian lyre, / Sublime as Juvenal's more vigorous fire."

43 *The Spirit of the Laws*, trans. Thomas Nugent, 5th ed. (London, 1773), 1:467.

44 *An Essay on . . . Pope*, 2:48–49. Warton uses a different translation – perhaps his own.

45 *The Letters of Philip Dormer Stanhope 4th Earl of Chesterfield*, ed. Bonamy Dobrée (London: Eyre and Spottiswoode, 1932), 3:1067, letter No. 1486, from London, 11 December, O.S., 1747. Thanks to Professor Claude Rawson for this reference.

46 For a discussion of Smollett's use of classical learning in that novel, see Charles Knapp, "The Classical Element in Smollett, *Roderick Random*," *Classical Weekly* 23 (1929):9–11, 17–19.

47 "To Matthew Prior, Esq., Upon the Roman Satirists," in *The Critical Works of John*

Dennis, ed. Edward Niles Hooker (Baltimore: The Johns Hopkins Univ. Press, 1943), 2–218.

48 3rd ed. (London, 1753), 1:162–63. Subsequent references are cited in the text.

49 *Essay towards Fixing the True Standards of Wit, Humour, Raillery, Satire, and Ridicule* (London, 1744), pp. 50–51.

50 *Essay on Satire: Occasion'd by the Death of Mr. Pope* (London, 1745), pp. 25, 26.

51 "Extraits de mon Journal," in *Miscellaneous Works*, ed. John, Lord Sheffield (London, 1796), 2:103. Gibbon also includes praise of Virgil, Horace, and Augustus here and in other places but nonetheless says of the latter: "Tyran sanguinaire, soupçonné de lâcheté, le plus grand des crimes dans un chef de parti, il parvient au trône, et fait oublier aux républicains qu'ils eussent jamais été libres" (*Essai sur l'étude de la littérature*, ibid., p. 493). See also ibid., pp. 494, and 494, note‡, "Recueil de mes observations," ibid., pp. 381–83, and "Extrait de trois mémoires de M. l'Abbé de la Bleterie," ibid., 3 (1815):75. It is not surprising that in ch. 3 of the *Decline and Fall* (1776) Gibbon finds the origin of the decay in Augustus' corruption of the Senate and his solidification of all power in his own less than tender hands. "The principles of a free constitution are irrecoverably lost, when the legislative power is nominated by the executive," he says in that chapter (*The History of the Decline and Fall of the Roman Empire*, ed. J. B. Bury [London, 1900], 1:60. In manuscript notes somewhat later, he lamented that he had not made clearer the implications of Augustus' changes: "Should I not have deduced the decline of the Empire from the tyranny which succeeded the reign of Augustus? Alas! I should" (ibid., p. xxxv n). Gibbon's anti-Augustan stance was entirely conventional by 1776.

52 *Polymetis* (London), pp. 18, 85–86 and *Remarks and Dissertations on Virgil; With Some other Classical Observations; By the late Mr. Holdsworth, Published with Several Notes, and Additional Remarks, by Mr. Spence* (London, 1768), pp. 208, 217, 227 and passim. In 1730 Spence also wrote essays on the *Aeneid* as a "party-piece." At least two were read to his Oxford audience as part of his duties as Professor of Poetry. See BM Add. MS 17281, especially Lecture 9 "On Virgil's Aeneid. That it was a Political Poem."

53 The Twickenham Edition of the Poems of Alexander Pope, vol. 6, *Minor Poems*, ed. Norman Ault and John Butt (London and New Haven: Methuen and Yale Univ. Press, 1954), p. 376. The date of publication is 1738; the date of composition is unknown.

54 See, for example, his remark to Spence in *Observations*, 1:160–61, and lines 182–84 of the second Dialogue of the *Epilogue to the Satires*, in which Pope proclaims that courtly flattery turns his stomach and is excrement.

55 For Cicero's reference to Damasippus, see *Ad Atticum* XII.29, 33, and *Ad familiares* VII.23. Pope is also adapting another remark of Damasippus – so far as the English court sees, Pope is not writing poetry at all. Pope told Warburton that he "thinks he cou^d make something of the *Damasippus*, and intends to do it" (*Imitations of Horace*, p. 327n).

56 See *Quinti Horatii Flacci Opera. Interpretatione & Notis, Illustravit Ludovicius Desprez* (London, 1722), pp. 446, n. 1, and especially p. 448, n. 24, and *Oeuvres d'Horace*, ed. Dacier, 7:194–97, and especially 208: "Avant que de s'attacher à cette Secte [stoics], il s'étoit ruïné à acheter & à revendre des statuës, & toutes sortes d'Antiques."

It is also possible that Pope remembered the Damasippus of Juvenal's Satire VIII.185–86, especially since he apparently knew and commented upon George Stepney's manuscript translation, and its edited version in Dryden's Juvenal of 1693. In that poem the newly impoverished Damasippus "Is forc'd to make the Stage his last retreat, / And pawns his Voice, the All he has, for Meat" (*George Stepney's Translation of the Eighth Satire of Juvenal*, ed. Thomas and Elizabeth Swedenberg, Publications of the William Andrews Clark Memorial Library [Berkeley: Univ. of California Press, 1948], pp. 46–47). See pp. 9–10 for the evidence of Pope's knowledge of the manuscript and printed translations.

57 *The Poems of John Dryden*, ed. James Kinsley (Oxford: Clarendon Press, 1958), 2:749. Subsequent quotations are cited in the text.

58 *Imitations of Horace*, p. vii. Warburton and Warton would share my objections. See their remarks, as indicated in n. 42 above. Note, too, that the *Craftsman*, No. 7 (1726) and No. 10 (1727), also imply the Horace–Walpole parallel. No. 182 (1729), however, discusses Horace and the Damasippus in more favourable terms.

59 Thomas E. Maresca, *Pope's Horatian Poems* (Columbus: Ohio State Univ. Press, 1966), p. 30. The same remark might be made of Juvenal.

60 W. B. Carnochan, "Satire, Sublimity, and Sentiment: Theory and Practice in Post-Augustan Satire," *PMLA* 85 (1970): 260. Professor Carnochan also observes: "Oldham can probably be read out of the Augustan ranks on the grounds of his insistent Juvenalian manner" (ibid.). For further discussion of this essay, see William Kupersmith, "Juvenal as Sublime Satirist," *PMLA* 87 (1972): 508–11, and ibid. 88 (1973): 144. See also Thomas Gilmore, "The Politics of Eighteenth-Century Satire," ibid. 86 (1971): 277–79, and Professor Carnochan's replies, ibid., pp. 279–80 and ibid. 87 (1972): 1125–26. Kupersmith also offers valuable remarks on eighteenth-century satire and some of its modern students in "Pope, Horace and the Critics: Some Reconsiderations," *Arion* 9 (1970): 205–19. Howard Erskine-Hill makes good distinctions between the Horatian and Juvenalian Pope in his *Pope: Horatian Satires and Epistles* (London: Oxford Univ. Press, 1964), pp. 12–13.

61 Isaac Watts twice urges the value of Horace's *Odes* as a fertilizing force for the Christian poet: "Amongst all the rest of the *Pagan* writers, I know none so fit for this service as the odes of *Horace*, as vile a sinner as he was" (Remnants of Time, XII, "Heathen Poesy Christianized" [1736], in *The Works of the Late . . . Isaac Watts* [London], 1953, 4:608)". See also his *Horae Lyricae*, 8th ed. (London, 1743), p. xxi. Octavio van Veen's *Emblemata Horatiana* (Amsterdam, 1684), uses Horatian tags to illustrate its moral emblems, but cites the *Odes* 66, the *Epistles* 40, the *Satyres* 32, and the *Ars Poetica*, obviously less applicable, 4 times.

62 Professor Maresca cites some of these (pp. 27–28); the "Christianizing" of Juvenal, especially Satire x, had already taken place. Many of these theologians, however, still make clear that there is an essentially unbridgeable gap between pagan and Christian knowledge. Henry More's *Enchiridion Ethicum* (1667; English, 1681, 1690) fairly bristles with supportive quotations from Pythagoras, Aristotle, Cicero, Horace, and others. Yet More insists that religion must "not be defrauded of her due Honour," and declares that all the wisdom of the "Renowned Heathens" comes either from the precedent, inspired, Jewish Church, or from "the *Eternal* Son, that *Logos*, or WORD *of God*" *(An Account of Virtue . . . Put into English* [London, 1690], p. 267). By 1721 the berating of heathens had become so fashionable in the pulpit – perhaps including Swift's own sermon on "The Excellency of Christianity in Opposition to Heathen Philosophy" – that Swift reminded a novice clergyman of the value of pagan philosophy as a gloss upon those parts of the Bible not dealing with revelation (*A Letter to a Young Gentleman, Lately Enter'd into Holy Orders* [London, 1721], pp. 18–19). H. R. Swardson is probably correct in arguing that "by the time of the Augustans" (presumably the early eighteenth century) any real contest between the pagans and Christians was clearly resolved in favor of the latter, and that "the great mass of classical or mythological reference is merely incidental, a kind of literary swank or slang, innocent of any uniform affective significance" (*Poetry and the Fountain of Light: Observations on the Conflict between Christian and Classical Traditions in Seventeenth-Century Poetry* [Columbia: Univ. of Missouri Press, 1962], p. 36). Nevertheless, the issue was sufficiently alive for Johnson to be troubled by *Lycidas*, and for Uncle Toby to be troubled by Walter Shandy's numerous references to Venus, Jupiter, and Dione. "Pray brother," he says, " . . . what has a man who believes in God to do with this?" (8:33; 1765). As late as 1785 the devout Cowper urged that "All truth is from the

sempiternal source / Of light divine. But Egypt, Greece and Rome, / Drew from the stream below" (*The Task*, 2:499–501). See also the remainder of that verse paragraph, through line 544, and 6: 232–38.

63 Herbert Davis, "The Augustan Conception of History," in *Jonathan Swift: Essays on his Satire and Other Studies* (New York: Oxford Univ. Press, 1964), p. 278.

64 Edward Wortley Montagu, who believes that "Augustus rivetted [the chains of slavery] beyond a possibility of removal," also argues that James II "at one stroke disarmed the people, and established a large standing army" (*Reflections on the Rise and Fall of the Ancient Republicks. Adapted to the Present State of Great Britain*, 4th ed. [London, 1778], pp. 264, 384). The illustrations to Dryden's *Aeneid* show Aeneas – a surrogate Augustus – as a hooknosed warrior, very much resembling William III. It is likely that in this commercial publishing venture Tonson thus wished to flatter William. Dryden, however, has several unflattering comments upon usurpation, and thereby slaps at both Augustus and William. The latter has been noticed by L. Proudfoot, *Dryden's Aeneid and its Seventeenth Century Predecessors* (Manchester: Manchester Univ. Press, 1960), pp. 201–2, 206. For further discussion of William, Aeneas, and Dryden, see George Watson, "Dryden and the Jacobites," *TLS* 16 March 1973, pp. 301–2.

65 The quotation – a few lines above a paragraph beginning "*Juvenal*, of Satyrists is the best" – is probably from the third edition (London), p. 89, ch. 10, Of Poetry. This edition contains information concerning blazonry which Johnson quotes at other places in the *Dictionary*. I am grateful to Mr. and Mrs. Herman W. Liebert for this information.

66 *The Life of Samuel Johnson, LL. D.* (Dublin), p. 472.

67 (Edinburgh), p. 212.

68 The student of Augustanism may wish to pursue its modern windings in the following places: Howard D. Weinbrot, *Augustus Caesar in "Augustan" England: The Decline of a Classical Norm* (Princeton: Princeton Univ. Press, 1978); Howard Erskine-Hill, *The Augustan Idea in English Literature* (London: Edward Arnold, 1983), and Howard D. Weinbrot, "The Emperor's Old Toga: Augustanism and the Scholarship of Nostalgia," *MP* 83 (1986): 286–97.

3. Masked Men and Satire and Pope

1 The most important of the essays regarding the persona are Elder Olson, "Rhetoric and the Appreciation of Pope," *MP* 37 (1939–40): 13–35; (especially) Maynard Mack, "The Muse of Satire," *YR* 51 (1951): 80–92, and Robert C. Elliott, "Swift's I," ibid. 52 (1973):372–91. On the other side, Irvin Ehrenpreis begins serious counterattacks in his "Personae," in *Restoration and Eighteenth-Century Literature: Essays in Honor of Alan Dugald McKillop* (Chicago: Univ. of Chicago Press, 1963), pp. 25–37. A special number of *Satire News Letter* 3 (1966):88–153, includes eighteen contributions to a symposium on "The Concept of the Persona," together with H. T. Greany's "Satiric Masks: Swift and Pope," pp. 154–59. Studies in support of Ehrenpreis' position have been written by Gardner D. Stout, Jr., "Speaker and Satiric Vision in Swift's *Tale of a Tub*," *ECS* 3 (1969):175–99; Ulrich C. Knoepflmacher, "Impersonations of Alexander Pope: Current Views Within a Nineteenth-Century Perspective," *MLQ* 34 (1973):448–61; John Traugott, "In-House Hullaballoo," *Scriblerian* 5 (1973):73–75; and Howard Erskine-Hill, *The Social Milieu of Alexander Pope* (New Haven: Yale Univ. Press, 1975). The debate continues, with other efforts promised, and with the battleground spreading to Swift's *Verses on the Death of Dr. Swift*. See, for instance, Arthur H. Scouten and Robert D. Hume, "Pope and Swift: Text and Interpretation of Swift's Verses on His Death," *PQ* 52 (1973):205–31, and David M. Vieth, "The Mystery of Personal Identity: Swift's 'Verses on His Own Death,'" in *The Author in His Work: Essays on a Problem in Criticism*, ed. Louis L. Martz and Aubrey Williams (New Haven: Yale Univ. Press, 1978),

pp. 245-62. (This volume honors Maynard Mack.) For further aspects of the context of the argument, see Niall Rudd, "Theory: Sincerity and Mask," in *Lines of Enquiry: Studies in Latin Poetry* (Cambridge: Cambridge Univ. Press, 1976), pp. 145-81, and Phillip Harth, "The New Criticism and Eighteenth-Century Poetry," *Critical Inquiry* 7 (1981):521-37, especially pp. 528-35. I gratefully borrow several of the classical citations below from Rudd, who, in turn, quotes from Charles Garton, *Personal Aspects of the Roman Theatre* (Toronto: A. M. Hakkert, 1972), pp. 3-40. Robert C. Elliott's *The Literary Persona*, which appeared too late for me to benefit from its findings, should be consulted for further discussion of the theory and practice of the persona.

2 For some of these synthesizing efforts, see Thomas R. Edwards, *This Dark Estate: A Reading of Pope* (Berkeley: Univ. of California Press, 1963), p. 110; Maynard Mack, *The Garden and the City: Retirement and Politics in the Later Poetry of Pope 1731-1743* (Toronto: Univ. of Toronto Press, 1969); Leon Guilhamet, *The Sincere Ideal: Studies on Sincerity in Eighteenth-Century English Literature* (Montreal: McGill-Queen's Univ. Press, 1974), pp. 136-51; and Dustin Griffin, *Alexander Pope: The Poet in the Poems* (Princeton: Princeton Univ. Press, 1978).

3 For Chamaeleon and Quintilian (*Institutes* x.i.100), see Rudd, "Theory", p. 169, n. 65. For Cicero on the lawyer's emotions, see *De Orator* ii.xlv.189. The words from Quintilian, paraphrased from the *Institutes* iii.26-36, are in Rudd, p. 173. Horace, *Ars Poetica*, lines 102-3, is quoted from *The Satires, Epistles, and Art of Poetry of Horace*, trans. David Watson and Samuel Patrick (London, 1743), p. 370. Longinus is in section 13 of Boileau's translation (1674) and eighteenth-century English versions, normally indebted to Boileau. The quotation is from Leonard Welsted's "Longinus's Treatise Concerning the Sublime," (1712, 1724), in *The Works in Verse and Prose of Leonard Welsted*, ed. John Nichols (London, 1787), p. 347. This is section 15 in modern editions of Longinus.

4 *Tusculan Disputations* iv.2.55, as in Rudd's "Theory", p. 171. See also the reference to Cicero in n. 32, below.

5 Ovid *Tristia* ii.353-54; Martial *Epigrams* i.iv.8 (also cited by Ausonius); Apuleius *Apologia* xi; Ausonius *Cento* cxxx, Catullus xvi.5-6 (also cited by Apuleius). See Rudd, "Theory", pp. 174-75, and p. 175, n. 79. The matter of "sincerity" has recently been studied by Rudd, in the essay cited, as well as by Rachel Trickett, *The Honest Muse: A Study in Augustan Verse* (Oxford: Clarendon Press, 1967), and Guilhamet, *The Sincere Ideal*.

6 *The Tatler*, ed. George A. Aitken (London, 1899), 4:234.

7 *Two Epistles to Mr. Pope, Concerning the Authors of the Age* (London), p. 29.

8 *Q. Horatii Flacci Epistolae Ad Pisones et Augustum: With an English Commentary and Notes* (1757), 4th ed. (1766), 1:97. See also 1:96. Fielding approvingly repeats Horace's lines in *Tom Jones*, Book 9, ch. 1.

9 For Shaftesbury, see Anthony Ashley Cooper, third Earl of Shaftesbury, *Characteristics of Men, Manners, Opinions, Times*, ed. John M. Robertson, rpt. (Indianapolis: Bobbs-Merrill, 1964), 2:283. For Steele, see *The Englishman: A Political Journal by Richard Steele*, ed. Rae Blanchard (Oxford: Clarendon Press, 1955), pp. 32-33.

10 YE vol. 5, *The Rambler*, ed. W. J. Bate and Albrecht B. Strauss (New Haven: Yale Univ. Press, 1969), pp. 317-18. For further discussion of the persona and the periodical essay, see Arthur H. Scouten's contribution in *Satire News Letter* 3:134; Richmond P. Bond, "Isaac Bickerstaff, Esq.," in *Restoration and Eighteenth-Century Literature*, pp. 103-24, and Robert Donald Spector, "The *Connoisseur*: A Study of the Function of a Persona," in *English Writers of the Eighteenth Century*, a volume in honor of James L. Clifford, ed. John H. Middendorf (New York: Columbia Univ. Press, 1971), pp. 109-21.

11 Boswell's *Life of Johnson*, ed. George Birkbeck Hill, rev. by L. F. Powell (Oxford: Clarendon Press, 1934-50), 3:251, and 4:42, and 4:42 n. 6, respectively. Jean H. Hagstrum discusses Johnson's attitudes towards the poetic mask and "sincerity" in *Samuel Johnson's Literary Criticism* (Minneapolis: Univ. of Minnesota Press, 1952), pp. 44-47.

12 *Critical Essays on Some of the Poems of Several English Poets, with an Account of the Life and Writings of the Author by Mr. Hoole* (London), pp. 46, 51. See also Robert Potter, *An Inquiry into Some Passages in Dr. Johnson's Lives of the Poets* (London, 1783), p. 3.

13 For these illustrations, see the frontispieces to CE, vol. 4, ed. A. B. Chambers, William Frost, and Vinton A. Dearing (Berkeley: Univ. of California Press), *Poems 1693–1696*, *Q. Horatius Flaccus*, ed. Richard Bentley, 3rd ed. (Amsterdam, 1728), and *D. Junii Juvenalis . . . Satyrae*, ed. Henricus Christianus Henninius (Utrecht, 1685). I am indebted to Professor A. B. Chambers for drawing this illustration to my attention. The engraving for John Brown's *Essay* is reproduced and discussed by Donald E. Eddy in "John Brown: 'The Columbus of Keswick,'" *MP* 73 (1976): S 76–S 77 (a special number in honor of Arthur Friedman). The illustration was designed by John Bernard Gilpin, and etched by William Gilpin. For Pope, see *The Works of Alexander Pope Esq.* (London), facing 4:231, plate 18. This is the small octavo edition of the *Works*.

14 *D. Junii Juvenalis, et Auli Persii Flacci Satyrae*, ed. Cornelius Schrevelius (Leyden, 1671). See also *Oeuvres Diverses de S' Boileau Despréaux* (Paris, 1701), 2, facing p. 1, and the frontispiece and "Explication de l'Estampe" in *Satires de Perse*, trans. Abbé le Monnier (Paris, 1771), p. xxiij.

15 I quote from Peter E. Medine's valuable "Isaac Casaubon's *Prolegomena* to the *Satires* of Persius: An Introduction, Text, and Translation," *English Literary Renaissance* 6 (1976):297. Persius' importance for eighteenth-century satire has been generally ignored. For suggestions regarding his popularity and relevance for Pope and his contemporaries, see William Frost, "English Persius: The Golden Age," *ECS* 2 (1968):77–101; Cynthia Dessen, "An Eighteenth-Century Imitation of Persius, Satire I," *Texas Studies in Language and Literature* 20 (1978):433–56. See also "The Conventions of Classical Satire and the Practice of Pope," and "Persius, the Opposition to Walpole, and Pope," in this volume, and Weinbrot, *Alexander Pope and the Traditions of Formal Verse Satire* (Princeton: Princeton Univ. Press, 1982), pp. 59–76, 121–29.

16 De la Valterie, *Les Satyres de Juvenal et de Perse* (Paris), 2:sigs. Lij^v–Liij^r; Le Monnier, *Satires de Perse* (1771), p. viij; Boscawen, *The Satires, Epistles and Art of Poetry of Horace* (London, 1797), p. ix.

17 Dacier, *Oeuvres d'Horace en Latin et en François* (1681–89), 3rd ed., (Paris, 1709), 6:33; Holyday, *Decimus Junius Juvenalis, and Aulus Persius Flaccus* (Oxford, 1673), p. 56, n. 30; Owen, *The Satires of Juvenal . . . Also Dr. Brewster's Persius* (London, 1785), 1:37.

18 Watson, *The Satires, Epistles, and Art of Poetry of Horace*, p. 124; Blackwell, *Memoirs of the Court of Augustus* (Edinburgh, 1753–63), 3:71. Volume 3 was completed, from Blackwell's papers, by John Mills.

19 Dryden, *Poems 1693–1696*, p. 293, italics and roman type are reversed in the text; Eelbeck, *A Prosaic Translation of Aulus Persius Flaccus's Six Satyrs* (London), p. 30 (see also pp. 46 and 78); Gifford, *The Satires of Decimus Junius Juvenalis, and of Aulus Persius Flaccus* (London), 2:xiii.

20 Holyday, *Juvenalis, and . . . Persius*, p. 245, n. 13; Dryden, *Poems 1693–1696*, p. 91, the original is italicized; Owen, *Juvenal . . . Also Persius*, 2:108 n. 92; Saint-Marc, *Oeuvres de M. Boileau Despréaux*, (Paris, 1747), 1:168.

21 *Les Satires de Boileau Commentées par Lui-Même et Publiées Avec des Notes par Frédéric Lachèvre: Reproduction du Commentaire Inédit de Pierre Le Verrier avec les Corrections Autographes de Despréaux* (Courménil, 1906), p. 85. These remarks were "approved" by Boileau.

22 Dryden, *Poems 1693–1696*, p. 265; Sheridan, *The Satires of Persius*, 2nd ed. (London, 1739), p. 15; Owen, *Juvenal . . . Also Persius*, 2:90n.

23 Medine, "Isaac Casaubon's *Prolegomena*," p. 296.

24 Dryden, *Poems 1693–1696*, pp. 255, 311; italics and roman type are reversed in the text.

25 *The Satires of Persius* (1741–42), 2nd ed. (London, 1751), p. 93n.

26 *The Works of Monsieur Boileau. Made English from the Last Paris Edition By Several Hands*

(1711-13), 2nd ed. (London, 1736), 1:clvi. Des Maizeaux also quotes Steele's *Tatler* No. 242 to support his case: 1:clviii–clix. For further discussion of the satirist's self-defense, see P. K. Elkin, *The Augustan Defense of Satire* (Oxford: Clarendon Press, 1973).

27 *Samuel Johnson: The Rambler*, p. 318.

28 *The Letters of Atticus, as Printed in the London Journal. In the Years 1729 and 1730, on Various Subjects* (London, 1731), p. 12.

29 The "Answer" is in the Advertisement of Pope's *Imitations of Horace*, in The Twickenham Edition of the Poems of Alexander Pope, vol. 4, *Imitations of Horace*, John Butt, 2nd ed., corr. (London and New Haven: Methuen and Yale Univ. Press, 1961), p. 3. Subsequent quotations from Pope are from this edition and are cited in the text. For further discussion of reactions to *Fortescue*'s conclusion, see "'Such as Sir Robert Would Approve'? Answers to Pope's Answer from Horace," in this volume.

30 Anon., *A Hue and Cry After Part of a Pack of Hounds, which Broke Out of their Kennel in Westminster To which is Added, Modern Characters By Another Hand*, p. 28.

31 Newcomb's poem appeared in the *Gazetteer* for 16 June 1738, No. 1244, and is called "Q. HORATII FLACCI ad CURIONEM Epistola. Or, *An Epistle from Horace* in Elizium to CURIO in England, *faithfully translated into* English, *from* the Elizian *Copy. By J. M. of the Inner-Temple*, Barrister." It also appears in Newcomb's *A Miscellaneous Collection of Original Poems* (London, 1740), pp. 52–56. One line of his, and the administration's, recognition of the difference between Pope and Horace is quoted below on p. 47.

For discussions of eighteenth-century law and its relevance for satire and the opposition, see Lawrence Hanson, *Government and the Press, 1695-1763* (London: Oxford Univ. Press, 1936); C. R. Kropf, "Libel and Satire in the Eighteenth Century," *ECS* 8 (1974–75):153–68; Robert Halsband, "Pope's 'Libel and Satire,'" ibid. 8 (1975): 473–74; Robert Halsband, "Libels and Satires! Lawless Things Indeed!" ibid. 475–77; and Donald Thomas, "Press Prosecutions of the Eighteenth and Nineteenth Centuries," *The Library*, 5th ser., 32 (1977):315–32.

32 By 1755 some of these terms were part of conservative lexical wisdom. See Johnson's *Dictionary* and the noun "Person," definitions 8, 9, 10, the verb "To Personate," which is "from *persona* Latin," and the noun "Personation." The illustrative quotations are of course helpful, as, for example, in "Person, n.s.," definition 8, "Man or woman represented in a fictitious dialogue." According to Hooker the apostle speaks "in the *person* of the Christian gentile," and according to Baker, Cicero speaks "under the *person* of Crassus."

33 For an excellent discussion of opposition rhetoric and its meager ability to effect change, see Bertrand A. Goldgar, *Walpole and the Wits: The Relation of Politics to Literature, 1722-1742* (Lincoln: Univ. of Nebraska Press, 1976).

34 [Lady Mary Wortley Montagu, and John, Lord Hervey], *Verses Address'd to the Imitator of the First Satire of the Second Book of Horace. By a Lady* (London, 1733), p. 3; *Characters: An Epistle to Alexander Pope Esq; and Mr. Whitehead* (London), p. 11. For later comments upon Pope's Persian and Juvenalian, rather than Horatian, qualities, see Warburton, *Works of Alexander Pope, Esq.*, 4:36–37. For an apposite French comment see the Abbé Yart, *Idée de la poësie Angloise, ou traduction des meilleurs poëtes Angloises* (Paris, 1749–56), vol. 3 (1753):96. With the possible exception of Johnson's *Life of Pope* (1781), the Abbé Yart's is the most important commentary upon Pope in the eighteenth century.

35 Howard Erskine-Hill, "Augustans on Augustanism: England, 1655–1759," in *Renaissance and Modern Studies* 11 (1967):74.

36 *Lives of the Poets*, ed. George Birkbeck Hill (Oxford: Clarendon Press, 1905), 3:211.

37 *Lives*, 3:206.

4. The Swelling Volume

1 *Eighteenth-Century English Literature*, ed. Geoffrey Tillotson, Paul Fussell, Jr., and Marshall Waingrow (New York: Harcourt, Brace, & World, 1969).

2 I have dealt at greater length with these distinctions in *The Formal Strain: Studies in Augustan Imitation and Satire* (Chicago: Univ. of Chicago Press, 1969), pp. 86–94. I use the term apocalyptic not in the biblical sense of destruction of the evil old world and the beginning of the purged new but as prophetic revelation of darkness. Of course each mode of satire might appear in verse, prose, or the mingled Menippean kind. Since poetry is generally the medium of the best eighteenth-century satires which show a functioning norm, I have chosen to deal only with formal *verse* satire at this time. I should also reiterate that some of the conventions of the three satiric kinds discussed here may be shared with one another. Apocalyptic satire, for instance, is often punitive, but it punishes an age (or a culture, or a nation) rather than an individual.

3 *The Complete Poems of John Wilmot, Earl of Rochester*, ed. David M. Vieth (New Haven: Yale Univ. Press, 1968), p. 141. Subsequent quotations are from this edition.

4 For a fuller analysis of this poem, see "The 'Allusion to Horace': Rochester's Imitative Mode," in this volume.

5 Thomas H. Fujimura, "Rochester's 'Satyr against Mankind': An Analysis," *SP* 55 (1958):590.

6 For the former see Anne Righter, "John Wilmot, Earl of Rochester," in *Proceedings of the British Academy* 53 (1967):55: "Artemisia [as in Pinto's spelling] herself, the woman composing the Letter, is a kind of seventeenth-century Elizabeth Bennet. Witty and self-aware, both amused and exasperated, delighted and saddened by the follies she describes, she is the sister of Jane Austen's heroines." For the latter see Vivian de Sola Pinto, *Enthusiast in Wit: A Portrait of John Wilmot Earl of Rochester 1647–1680* (London: Routledge & Kegan Paul, 1962), pp. 121, 124; Vieth, *Complete Poems*, pp. xl–xli; and James Sutherland, *English Literature of the Late Seventeenth Century* (Oxford: Clarendon Press, 1969), pp. 171–72. Some aspects of the dialogue, devices, and characters do have analogues in Restoration comedy, but these seem to me subsumed under the larger satiric, revelatory, intention.

7 George Williamson shrewdly observed that "For all his agnostic wit, Rochester's best love poems are haunted by ideas of religion": *The Proper Wit of Poetry* (Chicago: Univ. of Chicago Press, 1961), p. 126. The same can be said about his two major satires as well, even though such a reading does not conform to the conventional view of pre-Burnet Rochester as atheist-libertine. Rochester, we know, sought out Burnet, not Burnet Rochester.

While discussing the dialectical cast of Rochester's mind, V. de Sola Pinto quotes this tale Rochester told Robert Parsons:

> One day at an Atheistical Meeting, at a person of Qualities', I undertook to manage the Cause, and was the principal Disputant against God and Piety, and for my performances received the applause of the whole company; upon which my mind was terribly struck, and I immediately reply'd thus to myself, Good God! that a Man, that walks upright, that sees the wonderful works of God, and has the use of his senses and reason, should use them to the defying of his Creator!

The rest of Rochester's discussion of his reaction to the "Atheistical Meeting" is also instructive:

> But tho' this was a good beginning towards my conversion, to find my conscience touched for my sins, yet it went off again. Nay, all my life long, I had a secret value and reverence for an honest man, and loved morality in others. But I had formed an odd scheme of religion to myself, which would solve all that God and conscience might force upon me; yet I was not ever well reconciled to the business of

Christianity, nor had that reverence for the Gospel of Christ as I ought to. (*A Sermon Preached at the Funeral of the Right Honourable John Earl of Rochester . . . August 9* [1680] [London, 1772], p. 26).

Pinto observes that "Rochester was always 'replying to himself'. His celebrated conversion to religion was no sudden volte-face; it was the culminating point of a dialectical process which had been going on in his mind for years": *Enthusiast in Wit*, pp. 185–86.

8 See Edward Topsell, *The Historie of Foure-Footed Beastes. Describing the true and lively figure of every Beast, with a Discourse of their several Names, Conditions, Vertues* . . . (London, 1607), pp. 3, 10–13. Topsell translates much of Konrad Gesner's *Historia animalium* (1551). The 1658 edition – eleven years after Rochester's birth – was "Revised, Corrected, and Inlarged" by John Rowland, and includes the same information and illustrations. Topsell, other contemporary and later naturalists, and lexicographers use the term *ape* to include a variety of monkeys as well. See, for example, the definitions in Johnson's *Dictionary* (1755) and the varied translations of "una ximia de bronze" in Part 2, Book 4, ch. 39 of *Don Quixote* (Madrid, 1615), p. 149. Philips, Motteaux, Ozell, Smollett, and Jarvis translate *ximia* as "monkey," Shelton and Stevens as "ape."

For other seventeenth- and eighteenth-century references or discussions, see *II Henry IV* (1600; III.ii.338–39); *Othello* (1622; III.iii.402–3); Donne's *Progresse of the Soule* (1601; stanzas 46–49); Locke's *Essay concerning Human Understanding* (1690; 3, 6, 23); and Edward Tyson's "A Philological Essay concerning the Satyrs of the Ancients," in *Ourang-Outang. Sive Homo Sylvestris* (1699), Eric Rothstein, *Restoration Tragedy: Form and the Process of Change* (Madison: Univ. of Wisconsin Press, 1967), p. 71. H. W. Janson's *Apes and Ape Lore in the Middle Ages and the Renaissance* (London: The Warburg Institute and the University of London, 1952), supplies an abundance of relevant information.

9 John Harold Wilson, however, regards the poem as "the longest and mildest of Rochester's satires against women," and observes that "The moral is clear; poor, weak, silly woman is capable of incredible monstrosities. Only the man of wit can escape her ravagings": *The Court Wits of the Restoration: An Introduction* (Princeton: Princeton Univ. Press, 1948), p. 131.

10 Artemis is the Greek name of Diana, the perpetually celibate goddess of the chase who presided over child-birth, was identified with the moon, and in a many-breasted statue at Ephesus, symbolized the productive forces of nature. Artemisia, the Queen of Caria and daughter of Lygdamis, had masculine courage, performed heroically for Xerxes at Salamis, and later was so in love with Dardanus that, when he slighted her, she put out his eyes while he slept. Artemisia Queen of Caria, daughter of Hecatomnes and wife of Mausolus, immortalized herself by preserving her husband's memory in the magnificent mausoleum at Halicarnassus, lived two years after her husband's death, and was reported to have died of grief and melancholy. These tales of Artemisia were recorded in Moréri's and Bayle's encyclopedic dictionaries, first published, respectively, in 1674 and 1697. In Moréri, Artemisia the wife of Mausolus received the most attention, and it is possible that if Rochester has either model in mind as a norm, it is that of tender rather than brutal love. The masculine achievements of the Queen of Caria, however, may have inspired Rochester to have his Artemisia succeed in masculine poetry. Since the two earthly Artemisius were often mingled, both could easily supply background for Rochester. Bayle reports that "It would be too tedious to point out all those, who have confounded the two *Artemisia's. Ravisius Textor* . . . and the Authors of the *Thesaurus Fabri* are of this number. *Olivier*, who wrote a *Commentary on Valerius Maximus*, is also one of them." For fuller discussion of the classical and Renaissance and later seventeenth-century contexts of these names, see Des Maizeaux's edition of *The Dictionary Historical and Critical of Mr. Peter Bayle*, 2nd ed. (London, 1734), 1:522–25.

11 The apocalyptic quality does not deny the comic aspects of *Artemisia*, any more than it

does that of *A Tale of a Tub*, *Gulliver's Travels*, and *The Dunciad*. Indeed, one might argue that their ultimate effect is enhanced by the comedy, which serves as a comfortable entryway to terror. The Fine Lady's "conversation" with the monkey, for example, is amusing until one realizes that it becomes an emblem of upper-class depravity, just as the childish urinating contest in *The Dunciad* is raucous until one sees that the contestants include a gonorrheal publisher who is polluting his London audience. An intensive study of the intermingling of comic, tragic, and satiric modes and conventions would be of great value.

5. The "Allusion to Horace"

1 For relevant works concerning Augustan imitation, see William Francis Galloway, "English Adaptations of Roman Satire, 1660–1800" (unpublished Ph.D. Diss., University of Michigan, 1937); William K. Wimsatt, Jr., "Rhetoric and Poems: The Example of Pope," in *English Institute Essays 1948* (New York: Columbia Univ. Press, 1949), p. 183; Harold F. Brooks, "The 'Imitation' in English Poetry, Especially in Formal Satire Before the Age of Pope," *RES* n.s. 25 (1949):124–40; Ian Jack, *Augustan Satire* (Oxford: Clarendon Press, 1952), pp. 97–114, 135–45; Reuben A. Brower, *Alexander Pope: The Poetry of Allusion* (Oxford: Clarendon Press, 1959); TE vol. 4, *Imitations of Horace*, ed. John Butt, 2nd ed. (London, 1961), pp. xxvi–xxx; Butt, "Johnson's Practice in the Poetical Imitation," in *New Light on Dr. Johnson*, ed. Frederick W. Hilles (New Haven: Yale Univ. Press, 1959), pp. 19–34; Mary Lascelles, "Johnson and Juvenal," ibid., pp. 35–55; G. K. Hunter, "The 'Romanticism' of Pope's Horace," *EIC* 10 (1960):390–404; John M. Aden, "Pope and the Satiric Adversary," *SEL* 2 (1962):267–86; Aubrey L. Williams, "Pope and Horace; *The Second Epistle of the Second Book*," in *Restoration and Eighteenth-Century Literature: Essays in Honor of Alan Dugald McKillop*, ed. Carroll Camden (Chicago: Univ. of Chicago Press, 1963), pp. 309–21; Thomas E. Maresca, *Pope's Horatian Poems* (Columbus: Ohio State Univ. Press, 1966); Jay Arnold Levine, "Pope's *Epistle to Augustus*, Lines 1–30," *SEL* 7 (1967):427–51; M. N. Austin, "The Classical Learning of Samuel Johnson," *Studies in the Eighteenth Century*, ed. R. F. Brissenden (Toronto: Univ. of Toronto Press, 1968), pp. 285–306; John Hardy, "Johnson's *London*: The Country versus the City," ibid., pp. 251–68; Manuel Schonhorn, "The Audacious Contemporaneity of Pope's *Epistle to Augustus*," *SEL* 8 (1968):431–44; Leonard A. Moskovit, "Pope and the Tradition of the Neoclassical Imitation," ibid. 445–62; Howard D. Weinbrot, *The Formal Strain: Studies in Augustan Imitation and Satire* (Chicago: Univ. of Chicago Press, 1969); John M. Aden, *Something Like Horace: Studies in the Art and Allusion of Pope's Horatian Satires* (Nashville, Tenn.: Vanderbilt Univ. Press, 1969); Aden, "Bethel's Sermon and Pope's Exemplum: Towards a Critique," *SEL* 9 (1969):463–70; Maynard Mack, *The Garden and the City: Retirement and Politics in the Later Poetry of Pope 1731–1743* (Toronto: Univ. of Toronto Press, 1969); P. J. Köster, "Arbuthnot's Use of Quotation and Parody in His Account of the Sacheverell Affair," *PQ* 48 (1969): 201–11; Köster, "Means and Meanings: Translation as a Polemic Weapon," *Echos du Monde Classique: Classical News and Views*, 14 (1970): 13–20; William K. Wimsatt, "Imitation as Freedom, 1717–1798," *New Literary History*, 1 (1970):215–36; Weinbrot, "Augustan Imitation: The Role of the Original," in *Proceedings of the Modern Language Association Conferences on Neo-Classicism, 1967–1968*, ed. Paul J. Korshin (New York: AMS Press, 1970), pp. 53–70; R. L. Selden, "Dr. Johnson: A Problem in Critical Methods," *CL* 22 (1970):289–302; Edward A. and Lillian D. Bloom, "Johnson's *London* and its Juvenalian Texts," "Johnson's *London* and the Tools of Scholarship," *HLQ* 34 (1970):1–23, 115–39.

2 The conventional procedure in eighteenth-century France and England was to note the author's imitation of Horace or Juvenal and praise or blame him regarding the individual passage. This technique is particularly clear in the edition of Boileau by

Claude Brossette in 1717, and M. de Saint-Marc in 1747. On 6 July 1700, Brossette wrote to Boileau regarding his projected edition of the works, "avec des notes, et surtout avec la conférence, et le parallèle des endroits d'Horace et Juvénal que vous avez imités." *Correspondence entre Boileau Despréaux et Brosette*, ed. Auguste Laverdet (Paris, 1858), pp. 47–8. Warburton performs a similar task – a sort of piecemeal comparison and contrast – for Pope in 1751. This practice may probably be traced to the habit of reading commentators for particular lines and phrases, and is severely criticized by Joseph Spence in *Polymetis* (London, 1747), p. 287.

3 *Of Dramatic Poesy and Other Critical Essays*, ed. George Watson, (London and New York: Dent and Dutton, 1967), 1:270.

4 Dryden, *Essays*, 1:271.

5 Ibid.

6 Bishop Gilbert Burnet relates that "*Boileau* among the *French*, and *Cowley* among the *English* Wits were those Rochester admired most." See *Some Passages of the Life and Death of . . . Rochester* (London, 1680), p. 8. I briefly discuss Rochester's free adaptation of Boileau's third and eighth satires in *The Formal Strain*, pp. 46–9.

7 As quoted in Harold F. Brooks, *RES* n.s. 25:132.

8 For the dating of these works, see David Vieth, *The Complete Poems of John Wilmot, Earl of Rochester* (New Haven: Yale Univ. Press, 1968), pp. 194, 201–2, and 207 respectively; quotations are from this edition.

9 London, sig. A2ᵛ. Rochester also uses the word in (apparently) the narrower sense of reference to part of a poem in "An Epistolary Essay from M. G. to O. B. upon their Mutual Poems" (1680). The dim-witted M. G. proclaims: "But why am I no poet of the times? / I have allusions, similes, and rhymes." *Complete Poems*, p. 146.

10 In Part 3 of the second edition (London, 1705), Bysshe includes *A Collection of the Most Natural, Agreeable, and Sublime Thoughts. viz. Allusions, Similes, Descriptions and Characters of Persons and Things that are in the Best English Poets*, and adds: "I have inserted not only Similes, Allusions, Characters, and Descriptions; but also the most Natural and Sublime Thoughts of our Modern Poets on all Subjects whatever" (sig. F4ᵛ).

11 *Dictionarium Anglo-Britannicum*, 2nd ed. (London, 1715).

12 *The New World of Words* (London, 1720).

13 *Dictionarium Britannicum* (London, 1730).

14 6th ed. (London, 1750).

15 For the full context of the remark, see TE vol. 5, *The Dunciad*, ed. James Sutherland, 3rd ed. (London and New Haven: Methuen and Yale Univ. Press, 1963), p. 9.

16 See David Vieth, *Attribution in Restoration Poetry* (New Haven: Yale Univ. Press, 1963), pp. 386–90.

17 In, for example, *The Works of the Right Honourable the Earls of Rochester and Roscommon*, 3rd ed. (London, 1709), p. 15, and *The Works of the Earls of Rochester, Roscommon, Dorset, the Duke of Devonshire, &c.* (London, 1721), p. 10.

18 See *Poems by John Wilmot, Earl of Rochester*, ed. Vivian de Sola Pinto, 2nd ed. (Cambridge, Mass.: Harvard Univ. Press, 1964), p. 192. In spite of this and the poem's publication as a translation in *The Odes and Satyrs of Horace that Have Been Done into English by the Most Eminent Hands* (London, 1715; 1717, 1721, 1730; Dublin, 1730), I must disagree with Brooks' judgment that the poem "belongs to the English line of imitations that were also translations" (*RES* 25:133). The subsequent analysis should make clear the grounds of this view. See also my comment on David Vieth's observation in n. 35, below.

19 For Moore see "The Originality of Rochester's *Satyr Against Mankind*," *PMLA* 68 (1943):398–99, and for Johnson, *Lives of the English Poets*, ed. G. Birkbeck Hill (Oxford: Clarendon Press, 1905), 1:224. James Osborn believes that this remark was prompted by Johnson's knowledge of Pope's opinion: "Rochester has very bad versification sometimes. (He instanced this from his tenth satire of Horace, his full rhymes, etc.)."

Joseph Spence, Observations, Anecdotes, Characters of Books and Men, ed. James M. Osborn (Oxford: Clarendon Press, 1966), I, 202. As I hope to show shortly, Johnson's remark is misleading, not only because of Rochester's different treatment of his main target, but also because of his barely Horatian conception of harsh satire. He told Bishop Burnet: "A man could not write with life unless he were heated by Revenge: For to make a Satyre without Resentment, upon the cold Notions of *Phylosophy,* was as if a man would in cold blood, cut mens' throats who had never offended him: And he said, the Lyes in these Libels came as often as Ornaments that could not be spared without spoiling the beauty of the Poem." *Some Passages of . . . Rochester,* p. 26.

20 Valuable discussions of the relationship between Lucilius and Horace may be found in George Converse Fiske, *Lucilius and Horace: A Study in the Classical Theory of Imitation,* Univ. of Wisconsin Studies in Lang. and Lit., no. 7 (1920), pp. 25–63, 219–368, *passim;* Eduard Fraenkel, *Horace* (Oxford: Clarendon Press, 1957), pp. 128–35; Niall Rudd, *The Satires of Horace* (Cambridge: Cambridge Univ. Press, 1966), pp. 61–131.

21 *The Odes, Satyrs, and Epistles of Horace,* tr. Thomas Creech (London, 1684), p. 416. Subsequent references are to this edition and are cited in the text.

22 See Rudd, *The Satires of Horace,* pp. 118–24, especially his brief summation on pp. 123–24.

23 The line represented a minor interpretive crux. Jacobus Cruquius argues: "Ego certe propter epitheton optimus [in *Octavius optimus*] potius iudiciarium hic signari Octavius Augustum, qui mansuetudine & morum facilitate mirabiliter ab omnibus commendatur & poeta fuit non incelebris." *Q. Horatius Flaccus* (Leiden, 1597), p. 405. Ludovicius Desprez says: "Optimus nempe is poeta historias etiam scripsit. Cave, lector, ne Augustum accipias." *Quintus Horatii Flacci, Opera . . . In Usum Serenissimi Delphini* [1691] (Philadelphia, 1814), p. 428n. And thus William Baxter: "Ego plane sentio cum Jacobo Cruquio *Octavium optimum* non fuisse alium quam ipsum Augustum, etsi vir doctus Ludovicus Desprez hoc caveri jubeat." *Q. Horatii Flacci, Eclogae* (London, 1701), p. 310n. Somewhat later, both Dacier and Sanadon believe that Octavius is the poet, not the Emperor: see the *Oeuvres d' Horace* (Amsterdam, 1735) 5.428–9. The little controversy is not yet dead, as witnessed by *Oeuvres d'Horace . . . Satires publiés par Paul Lejay* ([first ed., Paris, 1911] Georg Olms Verlagsbuchhandlung: Hildesheim, 1966), p. 280n.

24 *Horace,* pp. 131–32.

25 Johnson defines the verb *embroider* in this way: "To border with ornaments; to decorate with figured works; to diversify with needlework; to adorn with raised figures" (1755).

26 By the later 1670s Dryden was exposed to such innuendo, as well, in the anonymous *An Exclamation against Julian, Secretary to the Muses; with the Character of a Libeller. By a Person of Quality* (London, 1697): in "Bed-rid Age" Dryden "has left his Sting upon the Stage" (p. 1).

27 These remarks are often regarded as sincere praise of Dryden: see John Harold Wilson, *The Court Wits of the Restoration* (Princeton: Princeton Univ. Press, 1948), p. 188, and Vivian de Sola Pinto, *Enthusiast in Wit: A Portrait of John Wilmot Earl of Rochester, 1647–1680* (London: Routledge & Kegan Paul, 1962), p. 99.

28 Ironically, the argument that Rochester adapts from Horace has been applied to Rochester himself. David Hume observes: "The very name of Rochester is offensive to modest ears; yet does his poetry discover such energy of style and such poignancy of satyre, as give grounds to imagine what so fine a genius, had he fallen in a more happy age and followed better models, was capable of producing. The adroit satyrists often used great liberty in their expressions, but their freedom no more resembles the license of Rochester than the nakedness of an Indian dress does that of a common prostitute" (*The History of Great Britain* [London, 1757], 2:453).

29 Of course this raises a troubling problem regarding analyses of specific imitations. How can we determine whether the earlier poet has read the poem imitated in the way we

suggest? In Pope's case the job is made easier through his reproduction of the classical poem, with certain key words drawn to our attention, on the facing page. Since Rochester does not do this, one's interpretation is on weaker grounds. A contemporary and conventional reading of Horace, *Satires* 1.10, however, makes clear that much of the reading discussed above would have been known to Rochester. Lewis Crusius observes:

> Horace . . . has not fail'd to censure [Lucilius] on . . . account [of his extravagance]; and excuses the liberty he took in doing so to one, who was his master in Satire, by that which *Lucilius* himself had taken to find fault with *Ennius*. . . *Horace* therefore in gratifying his own good taste, by condemning this style of *Lucilius*'s, pleas'd his prince's at the same time.
>
> *Besides* these faults, *Lucilius* had a particular affectation of mixing Greek words with the Latin, which absurd as it was, found many admirers. This oblig'd that excellent writer to condemn him for it, and ridicule so absurd a mixture. Nevertheless, he readily grants, that he not only exceeded *Ennius*, and those that preceded him in his art, but would have been correct himself, had he lived to the *Augustan* Age (*Lives of the Roman Poets*, 3rd ed. [London, 1753], 1:xv–xvii; the first edition was published in 1726.)

Crusius insists that his views are drawn from the authors' texts and "*the most* judicious Critics *concerning the* Roman Poets, *whose Labours I am much beholden to*" (sig. A4ʳ); many of these critics wrote prior to, or contemporary with, Rochester.

30 Compare, for example, the opening of Rochester's poem with that of Creech's below:

> Well, Sir, I grant, I said *Lucilius*, Muse
> Is uncorrect, his way of Writing loose,
> And who admires him so, what Friend of his
> So blindly doats as to deny me This?
> And yet in the same Page I freely own,
> His Wit as sharp as ever lash't the Town;
> But This one sort of Excellence allow'd,
> Doth not infer that all the rest is good:
> For on the same Account I might admit
> *Labenius* Farce for Poems and for Wit.   (p. 415)

31 James Osborn observes that "despite Pope's disapproval of Rochester's versification, this poem . . . influenced Pope's own imitations of Horace. It is notable that this is one of Horace's satires that Pope did not choose to imitate." *Observations*, 1:202. For Pope's other praise and blame of Rochester, see *ibid*.

32 *The Critical Works of Thomas Rymer*, ed. Curt A. Zimansky (New Haven: Yale Univ. Press, 1956), p. 81. Rymer may have been aware of Bishop Burnet's similar remarks: "Sometimes other mens' thoughts mixed with his Composures, but that flowed rather from the Impressions they made on him when he read them, by which they came to return upon him as his own thoughts; than that he servilely copied from any. For few men ever had a bolder flight of fancy, more steadily governed by Judgment than he had." *Some Passages of . . . Rochester*, p. 8. The "originality" of Rochester's imitative poetry was a commonplace: see, for example, the comments of St. Evremond, Robert Wolsely, Anthony à Wood, Robert Parsons, and Bishop Burnet in *The Works of the Earls of Rochester, Roscommon, Dorset, The Duke of Devonshire, &c*, pp. xx, xxix, xxxii, xxxv, xxxviii, respectively.

33 *Imitations of Horace*, p. 3.

34 On this point, see Levine, *SEL* 7, and Weinbrot, *Proc. MLA Neo-Classicism*, n. 1. To these should be added Ian Watt, "Two Historical Aspects of the Augustan Tradition," in Brissenden, *Studies in the Eighteenth Century* pp. 67–88; J. W. Johnson, *The Formation of English Neo-Classical Thought* (Princeton Univ. Press, 1967), pp. 16–30; Howard Erskine-

Hill, "Augustans on Augustanism: England 1655–1759," *Renaissance and Modern Studies* 9 (1967):55–83.

35 I hope that the pages above have made clear the grounds of my disagreement with Professor Vieth regarding the "Allusion." He states:

> This poem is an "imitation" in the same sense as Pope's "Imitations of Horace" and is apparently the first such work in the English language. Based on Horace, *Satires* I.x, it requires a close knowledge of the Latin original so that the reader will be aware not only of clever adaptations of Roman circumstances to English ones, but of ironic discrepancies between the two. (*Complete Poems of Rochester*, p. 120n)

36 None of the manuscript titles of the poem mention Boileau or offer the first line, as do comparable texts for Horace and the "Allusion." But the 1707 edition of the *Works* of Rochester and Roscommon (and subsequent reprints) says that the *Satyr* is "Imitated from Monsieur Boileau" (p. 1). See Vieth, *Attribution*, pp. 370–75. Contemporary readers were far more aware of the freedom of the *Satyr* than of the "Allusion": see the prefatory comments on the former poem in Rochester's *Poems on Several Occasions* (London, 1680), sigs. A4ᵛ–6ʳ. I have discussed several aspects of the relationship between imitation and translation in *The Formal Strain*, pp. 14–30.

6. "Natures Holy Bands"

1 For some studies celebrating this point of view, see Bernard Schilling, *Dryden and the Conservative Myth* (New Haven: Yale Univ. Press, 1961), pp. 48, 281; Alan Roper, *Dryden's Poetic Kingdoms* (New York: Barnes & Noble, 1965), pp. 185–86, 191; Earl Miner, *Dryden's Poetry* (Bloomington: Indiana Univ. Press, 1967), pp. 115–22; Leon Guilhamet, "Dryden's Debasement of Scripture in *Absalom and Achitophel*," *SEL* 9 (1969): 409; Bruce King, "*Absalom and Achitophel*: A Revaluation," in *Dryden's Mind and Art*, ed. Bruce King (New York: Barnes & Noble, 1970), pp. 68–69; Steven N. Zwicker, *Dryden's Political Poetry: The Typology of King and Nation* (Providence, Rhode Island: Brown Univ. Press, 1972), p. 88; George deForest Lord, "*Absalom and Achitophel* and Dryden's Political Cosmos," in *Writers and their Background. John Dryden*, ed. Earl Miner (London: G. Bell & Sons, 1972), p. 171; Thomas E. Maresca, "The Context of Dryden's *Absalom and Achitophel*," *ELH* 41 (1974): 341; Zwicker, *Politics and Language in Dryden's Poetry. The Arts of Disguise* (Princeton: Princeton Univ. Press, 1984), p. 93. In addition to the antidotes cited below, see George McFadden's valuable and suggestive chapter on *Absalom and Achitophel* in *Dryden the Public Writer 1660–1685* (Princeton: Princeton Univ. Press, 1978), pp. 227–64.

2 "Beyond the Polemics: A Dialogue on the Opening of *Absalom and Achitophel*," *The Critical Survey* 5 (1971): 145.

3 "A Reading of *Absalom and Achitophel*," *Yearbook of English Studies* 6 (1976):53.

4 "Fathers and Sons: The Normative Basis of Dryden's *Absalom and Achitophel*," *Papers on Language and Literature* 17 (1981):363. See also Roper, *Dryden's Poetic Kingdoms*, p. 193; Maresca, "The Context of *Absalom and Achitophel*," pp. 347, 349, 357; Sanford Budick, *Poetry of Civilization. Mythopoeic Displacement in . . . Dryden, Pope, and Johnson* (New Haven: Yale Univ. Press, 1975), pp. 88–90.

5 See Robinson, "Reading," p. 54, and Donnelly, "Fathers and Sons," pp. 375, 376–79. Donnelly's essay is most insistent, and most useful, on the poem's filial structure.

6 Barbara Lewalski's distant judgment remains largely accurate: "There is now general critical agreement in referring *Absalom and Achitophel* to the heroic genre despite the elements of satire and wit." "*David's Troubles Remembered*: An Analogue to *Absalom and Achitophel*," *Notes and Queries*, n.s. 11 (1964): n. 6. Steven Zwicker has more recently argued that the poem's genre is a confusion of epic, satire, prophecy, and history. *Politics and Language in Dryden's Poetry*, pp. 88–89, and pp. 220–21n.

7 *John Locke. Two Treatises of Government*, ed. Peter Laslett, 2nd ed. (Cambridge: Cambridge Univ. Press, 1967), p. 198, Treatise I, ch. 6, section 55. Praise of matriarchal authority may also have alluded to Queen Elizabeth as an alternative to Stuart patriarchy. See Larry Carver, "*Absalom and Achitophel* and the Father Hero," in *The English Hero, 1660–1800*, ed. Robert Folkenflik (Newark: Univ. of Delaware Press, 1982), p. 36, and pp. 44–45 n. 3. H. T. Swedenberg, Jr., observes that Dryden's own passage on government does not employ Filmer's arguments. CE, vol. 2, *Poems 1681–1684*, ed. Swedenberg (Berkeley: Univ. of California Press, 1972), p. 271. This is the text from which I quote *Absalom and Achitophel*.

8 *Two Treatises*, p. 226; II.9.90.

9 *Two Treatises*, pp. 329–30, II.6.66. For Schochet, see *Patriarchalism in Political Thought . . . Especially in Seventeenth-Century England* (Oxford: Basil Blackwell), 1975, p. 201, with specific reference to James Tyrell.

10 Here and elsewhere, dates cited are those by Narcissus Luttrell, whose annotated copies I have seen or have found recorded in Hugh MacDonald's *John Dryden. A Bibliography of Early Editions and of Drydeniana* (Oxford: Clarendon Press, 1939). Pordage's attack on *Absalom and Achitophel* here refers to the Popish Plot; the others in this paragraph refer to the Rye House plot.

11 Roper, *Dryden's Poetic Kingdoms*, pp. 186, 191.

12 *The Complete Poems of John Wilmot, Earl of Rochester*, ed. David M. Vieth (New Haven: Yale Univ. Press, 1968), pp. 60–61, lines 14–15, 18–19. For some other attacks on Charles's seminal generosity and its consequences, see *Poems on Affairs of State. Augustan Satirical Verse . . . 1660–1678*, ed. George deForest Lord (New Haven: Yale Univ. Press, 1963), pp. 228–29, 243–44, 278; *Poems on Affairs of State . . . 1678–1681*, (1965), ed. Elias F. Mengel, Jr. 2:147, 155–56, 158 (in the latter two he is called "Priapus"), 200, 202, 208, 220–21; *Poems on Affairs of State . . . 1682–1685* (1968), ed. Howard H. Schless, 3:30–31, 253, 478–79, 567. The Restoration's energetic vulgarity towards its monarchs renders suspect – and in my judgment denies – the anachronistic theory of "the king's two bodies," which absolves the monarch of responsibility for his personal actions. That medieval theory of kingship often is used in support of *Absalom and Achitophel*'s presumed apology for Charles' behavior.

13 The text is reproduced in *The Works of John Dryden*, ed. Walter Scott (London, 1808), 9:205–7, p. 206 for this quotation.

14 *A Commentary upon the Historical Books of the Old Testament* (1694), 5th ed. (London, 1738), 2:306. Subsequent citations are given in the text. For some relevant aspects of these books, see Thomas Jemielity, "Divine Derision and Scorn: The Hebrew Prophets as Satirists," *Cithara* 25 (1985): 47–68.

15 *The Dictionary Historical and Critical of Mr. Peter Bayle*, (1697) trans. Pierre des Maizeaux, 2nd ed. (London, 1735), 2:607–8 n. F. For further discussion, see *The David Myth in Western Literature*, ed. Raymond-Jean Frontain and Jan Wojcik (West Lafayette, Indiana: Purdue Univ. Press, 1980), and Allan J. Gedalof's informative review of this volume in *Eighteenth-Century Studies* 15 (1982): 356–59.

16 Attacks on Dryden are discussed by Hugh MacDonald, "The Attacks on Dryden," in *Essential Articles for the Study of John Dryden*, ed. H. T. Swedenberg, Jr. (Hamden, Conn.: Archon Books, 1966), pp. 22–53; MacDonald, *John Dryden. A Bibliography*, passim; and John Robert Sweney, "Political Attacks on Dryden, 1681–1683," unpublished Ph.D. dissertation, University of Wisconsin, Madison, 1968.

17 "Legends no Histories: The Case of *Absalom and Achitophel*," *Studies in Eighteenth-Century Culture*, ed. O M Brack, Jr. (Madison: Univ. of Wisconsin Press, 1975), 14:13–29. Harth also notes Dryden's attempts to influence external action. "Dryden's Public Voices," in *New Homage to John Dryden*, ed. Alan Roper (Los Angeles: William Andrews Clark Memorial Library, 1983), pp. 6–7, 13–14, 18. In the preface to his translation of

the *Aeneid* (1697), Dryden himself insisted on the poet's educational function for his ruler. He there uses the familiar argument that the idealized portrait of Aeneis was designed to educate the cruel Augustus into the true manners of a prince. See "Dedication of the Aeneis," in *Essays of John Dryden*, ed. W. P. Ker (New York: Russell & Russell, 1961), 2:174.

18 As quoted in Schochet's *Patriarchalism in Political Thought*, p. 196, with comparable references cited by Locke, Tyrell, and Thomas Hunt in n. 16. For a royalist version, see John Wilson, *A Discourse of Monarchy* (London, 1684): "the people had no more right to chuse their Kings, than to chuse their Fathers" (p. 15).

19 For a relevant summary of Bethel's reputation, see Swedenberg, *Dryden, Poems 1681–1684*, pp. 262–63.

20 "Fathers and Sons," p. 371.

21 He calls *The Sodomite* "An abusive thing on Oates, Pilkington, & c" and *Dr. Oates Last Farewell to England* (together with "fourscore Bums to Attend his Sir-Reverence") a "scandalous libell." Each annotated work is at the William Andrews Clark Memorial Library in Los Angeles.

22 For the relevant sons, see Scott's *The Works of John Dryden*, 9:250, 298; and for Ossory's defence of his father, see 9:295–97. For other parallels and contrasts in the poem, see Eric Rothstein, The Routledge History of English Poetry, vol. 3, *Restoration and Eighteenth-Century Poetry 1660–1780* (Boston and London: Routledge & Kegan Paul, 1981), pp. 17–18.

23 Barbara Lewalski observes that Jotham is from "the period of the Judges" rather than of David; Sanford Budick adds that Jotham parallels Dryden himself. Lewalski, "The Scope and Function of Biblical Allusion in *Absalom and Achitophel*," *English Language Notes* 3 (1965): 34, and Budick, *Poetry of Civilization*, p. 87.

24 As quoted in Howard H. Schless, "Dryden's *Absalom and Achitophel* and *A Dialogue Between Nathan and Absolome*," *PQ* 40 (1961):141.

25 *Lives of the Poets*, ed. George Birkbeck Hill (Oxford: Clarendon Press, 1905), 1:437.

26 Dustin Griffin provides an attractive revisionist discussion of the final speech in "Dryden's Charles: The Ending of *Absalom and Achitophel*," *PQ* 57 (1978):359–82.

27 For the traditional view of Virgilian association with *Aeneid* IX.106 and X.115, see Lord, "*Absalom and Achitophel* and Dryden's Political Cosmos," p. 187.

7. *The Rape of the Lock*

1 These are from, respectively, Ian Jack, "A Complex Mock-Heroic: *The Rape of the Lock*," in *Augustan Satire: Intention and Idiom in English Poetry 1660–1750* (Oxford: Clarendon Press, 1952), p. 78; Reuben A. Brower, "Am'rous Causes" in *Alexander Pope: The Poetry of Allusion* (Oxford: Clarendon Press, 1959), p. 144; Earl R. Wasserman, "The Limits of Allusion in *The Rape of the Lock*," *Journal of English and Germanic Philology* 65 (1966): 428. They are conveniently gathered in *Twentieth Century Interpretations of The Rape of the Lock*, ed. G. S. Rousseau (Englewood Cliffs, N.J.: Prentice-Hall, 1969), pp. 39, 53, 72. By 1969, indeed, even several of Clarissa's friends had doubts regarding her wisdom. See the remarks by Rousseau (1969) and Brower (1959), *Interpretations*, pp. 9–10, 66, and J. S. Cunningham, *Pope: The Rape of the Lock*, Studies in English Literature no. 2 (Great Neck, NY: Barron's Educational Service, 1961), p. 45.

2 Apparently there are two genealogical lines in such criticism. One descends from the Ur text, Rebecca Price Parkin's *The Poetic Workmanship of Alexander Pope* (Minneapolis: Univ. of Minnesota Press, 1955), pp. 127, 171 (the first quotation above), and extends to John Trimble, "Clarissa's Role in *The Rape of the Lock*," *Texas Studies in Literature and Language* 15 (1974), 673–91; Ellen Pollak, "Rereading *The Rape of the Lock*: Pope and the Paradox of Female Power," *Studies in Eighteenth-Century Culture* 10 (1981): 442 (the second

quotation above), and her amplification in *The Poetics of Sexual Myth: Gender and Ideology in the Verse of Swift and Pope* (Chicago, Univ. of Chicago Press, 1985), pp. 80–82, 85–86; and C. N. Manlove, "Change in the *Rape of the Lock*," *Durham University Journal*, n.s. 45 (1983):48–49. In this critical branch the old new criticism and its perceptions of irony and ambiguity abounding is transmogrified into the new ideological criticism and the politically incorrect abounding. The other branch is self-generating in the manner of unmoved movers. It includes John P. Hardy, *Reinterpretations. Essays on Poems by Milton, Pope and Johnson* (London: Routledge & Kegan Paul, 1971), pp. 56–58; James Reeves, *The Reputation and Writings of Alexander Pope* (London: Heinemann; New York: Barnes & Noble, 1976), pp. 148–49; Sheila Delany, "Sexual Politics in Pope's *Rape of the Lock*," in *Weapons of Criticism: Marxism in America and the Literary Tradition*, ed. Norman Rudich (Palo Alto, Cal.: Ramparts Press, 1976), pp. 188–89; Robin Grove, "Uniting Airy Substance: *The Rape of the Lock*," in Howard Erskine-Hill and Anne Smith, eds., *The Art of Alexander Pope* (London: Vision Press, 1979), pp. 52–88, especially p. 83 (the third quotation above); and Kelly Reynolds, "*The Rape of the Lock*: Love Match. The 'Earthly Lover' vs. The 'Birth-night Beau'," *Schola Satyrica* 6 (1980):3–11. Leaves from either branch share common markings. Clarissa is a prude, tactless, hypocritical, haughty, inferior to Thalestris, unctuous, exploitive, devious, self-interested, insidious, a moral imperialist and opportunist, Belinda's enemy and sexual rival who wishes to destroy her, mischievous, a huntress of the baron, and "chauvinized." The change in vision is perhaps a function of Ovid redivivus or some other theology.

3 Ogilby, *Homer his Iliads Translated* (London, 1669), sig. A1ᵛ; the original is italicized; Fiddes, *A Prefatory Epistle Concerning some Remarks To be published on Homer's Iliad; Occasion'd by The Proposals of Mr. Pope towards a new English Version of that Poem. To the Reverend Dr. Swift* (London, 1714), pp. 18, 112 (Danger); Parnell, "An Essay on the Life, Writings, and Learning of Homer," in TE, vols. 7–8, *The Iliad*, ed. Maynard Mack, *et al.* (London: Methuen & Co.; New Haven, Conn.: Yale Univ. Press, 1967), 7:80. Subsequent citations are from this edition and will be cited in the text by Twickenham volume (TE) and by the book of Pope's *Iliad*.

4 Desmarets, *Clovis ou la France Chrestienne. Poème héroïque* (Paris, 1657); "Discours pour prouver que les sujets Chrestiens sont les seuls propres à la poésie héroïque," in *Clovis*, 3rd ed. (Paris, 1673). For some specific remarks, see *La Defense du poème héroïque* (Paris, 1674), pp. 4, 9, 12–19, among others; Gueret, *Le Parnasse reformé. Nouvelle edition* (1671; Paris, 1674), p. 5; Perrault, *Parallèle des anciens et des modernes* (Paris, 1688–97); Houtar, *A Critical Discourse upon Homer's Iliad*, trans. Lewis Theobald (London, 1714). Houtar says, for example, that "the whole *Iliad* is but a piece embroider'd with Pride, Anger and Revenge" (p. 10). These disagreeable arguments in France were of the highest importance both within their own country and for the moderns in England with whom, we shall see, Pope shared several assumptions. The best introductions to the "querelle" are by H. Rigault, *Histoire de la querelle des anciens et des modernes* (Paris, 1856); A. Lombard, *La Querelle des anciens et des modernes. L'Abbé du Bos* (Neufchâtel, 1908); Noémi Hepp, *Homère en France au XVIIᵉ siècle* (Paris: Librairie C. Klincksieck, 1968); A. Owen Aldridge, "Ancients and Moderns in the Eighteenth Century," in *Dictionary of the History of Ideas* (New York: Charles Scribner's Sons, 1968), 1:76–87: and Kirsti Simonsuuri, *Homer's Original Genius: Eighteenth-Century Notions of the Early Greek Epic (1688–1798)* (Cambridge: Cambridge Univ. Press, 1979). Joseph M. Levine attempts to offer some new perspectives in "Ancients and Moderns Reconsidered," *ECS* 15 (1981): 72–89, and "Edward Gibbon and the Quarrel between the Ancients and the Moderns," *The Eighteenth Century* 26 (1985):47–62. In spite of its severity, the debate in France was conducted at a higher level than in England, Bentley's and Wotton's contributions only excepted.

5 "A Discourse on Criticism and the Liberty of Writing," in *Poems on Several Occasions* (London, 1707), sigs. A4ʳ⁻ᵛ.

6 St. Evremond, "Of Antient and Modern Tragedy," in *The Works of Monsieur de St. Evremond*, trans. Pierre des Maizeaux (London, 1728), 2:102; Bayle, *A General Dictionary, Historical and Critical* (1697, French), trans. and ed. Thomas Birch, *et al.* (London, 1735), 2:266; Terrasson, *A Discourse of Ancient and Modern Learning* (1715, French), trans. Francis Brerewood (London, 1716), p. lxv (Perrault and Aristotle), p. lxviij (Homer). This work later appeared as *A Critical Dissertation Upon Homer's Iliad*, (London, 1722). Homer as a bad model for battles, below, appears there in 2:306. Jean-François De Pons, *Oeuvres [1738] suivies de Lettre à Madame Dacier sur son livre des causes de la corruption du goust* [1715] (Geneva: Slatkin Reprints, 1971), "Dissertation sur le poème épique," pp. 95–145; "Lettre à monsieur * * * sur l'Iliade de Monsieur De La Motte," pp. 288–314; "Observations sur divers points, concernant la traduction d'Homère," pp. 333–54; and "Lettre à Madame Dacier" (two letters, with new pagination), pp. 1–48.

7 "A Comparison of Homer and Virgil" (1666, French), in *The Whole Critical Works of Monsieur Rapin*, trans. Basil Kennet, 2nd ed. (London, 1716), 1:144. Subsequent citations are given in the text.

8 François Hédelin, Abbé D'Aubignac, *Conjectures académiques ou dissertation sur l'Iliade*, ed. Victor Magnien (Paris, 1925), pp. 108 (chien et fou), p. 114 (goinfrerie), p. 118. Subsequent citations will be given in the text. The work was written during the 1670s and published posthumously in 1715.

9 Le Bossu, *Monsieur Bossu's Treatise of the Epick Poem* (London, 1695), p. 218; Vico, *Principi di una scienza nuova* (Naples, 1725), "Search for the True Homer," in *The New Science*, trans. Thomas G. Bergin and Max H. Fisch (Ithaca, New York: Cornell Univ. Press, 1984), from the 3rd ed. of 1744, p. 302; Houtar, *A Critical Discourse upon Homer's Iliad* (n. 4 above); Saint-Hyacinthe, Hyacinth Cordonnier, known as Chevalier de Themiseul de, "Une Dissertation sur Homère et sur Chapelain," as in *Le Chef d'oeuvre d'un Inconu . . . Par M. . . . Chrisostome Matanasius* [pseud.], new pagination for the Dissertation (The Hague, 1714), pp. 9–10; Ramsay, "A Discourse upon Epick Poetry, and the Excellency of the Poem of Telemachus," in François Salignac De La Motte Fenelon, Archbishop of Cambray, trans. Isaac Littlebury and Abel Boyer (London, 1719), 1:13.

10 Wesley, "Essay on Heroic Poetry," prefatory to *The Life of our Blessed Lord & Saviour Jesus Christ. An Heroic Poem*, 2nd ed. (London, 1697), The Augustan Reprint Society Series 2, Publication no. 5 (Los Angeles: The William Andrews Clark Memorial Library, 1947), p. 17; Bayle, *A General Dictionary, Historical and Critical* (London, 1734), 1:178.

11 *Homeros, Homoros. The Third Book of Homer's Ilias Burlesqu'd* (London, 1722), unsigned sigs. A2^{r-v}, with the title page as A1; sig. B1^r (paultry). Cornwall also believes that Homer does "an unconceivable deal of Harm; *viz.* by corrupting the Innocence, and Purity of our most Holy Discipline: and tainting the Minds of Men, with Heathenish, and Anti-christian Trumpery" (B1^v).

12 For some of these views see the second century A.D. Claudius Aelian, *Varia historia*, XIII. 14, which also appeared in Rome, Basle, Leiden, Leipzig, and London. The latter is in Thomas Stanley, trans., as *Claudius Aelianus his Various History* (London, 1665). Charles Perrault alludes to Aelian and others who shared his notion: *Parallèle des anciens et des modernes* (Paris, 1692; n. 4 above), 3:32–36: "beaucoup d'excellens Critiques soutiennent qu'il n'y a jamais eu au monde un homme nommé Homère, qui ait composé" the *Iliad* and the *Odyssey*. These poems "ne sont autre chose qu'un amas, qu'une collection de plusieurs petits Poëmes de divers Auteurs qu'on a joints ensemble" (pp. 32–33). See also Samuel Wesley, *The Life of Our Blessed Lord & Saviour Jesus Christ. An Heroic Poem*, 2nd ed. (London, 1697), sig. A3^v (partial refutation), and in the poem itself, p. 201 (partial acceptance); the Abbé D'Aubignac, *Conjectures académique . . . sur l'Iliade* (n. 8 above), pp. 51–53, 56, 58, 60, 62, 74, 118; Richard Bentley, *Remarks Upon a Late Discourse of Free-Thinking* (London, 1713), p. 18; John Oldmixon, ed., *Poems and Translations by Several Hands* (London, 1714), p. 245; Vico, *The New Science* (n. 9 above), pp. 318–28; Charles

Cornwall, *Homeros, Homoros,* (n. 11 above), sigs. A2^{r-v}. Some aspects of the controversy have been discussed in the introductory and bibliographic essays in the valuable *F. A. Wolf. Prolegomena to Homer, 1795,* trans. Anthony Grafton *et al.* (Princeton: Princeton Univ. Press, 1985).

13 Thomas Burnet and George Duckett, *Homerides: Or, A Letter to Mr. Pope Occasion'd by his intended Translation of Homer. By Sir Iliad Doggrel* (London, 1715), p. 10. Subsequent citations are given in the text.

14 Scudamore, *Homer A la Mode. A Mock Poem Upon the First and Second Books of Homer's Iliads* (Oxford, 1664), pp. 53–56; Ninnyhammer, *Homer in a Nut Shell: Or, The Iliad of Homer In Immortal Doggrel* (London, 1715), p. 44. An early reader of the British Library's copy of Scudamore has placed asterisks next to some characterizations of gross Greek manners, including drunken vomits (p. 55), and farting Jove (p. 60): shelf-mark 11315 b. 12.

15 *Deuteripideuteron: The Second Part of the Second Part of Homer Alamode. Or, a Mock-Poem on the Ninth Book of the Odysses* (London, 1681), p. 33.

16 Fitzcotton, *A New and Accurate Translation of the First book of Homer's Iliad* (Dublin and London, 1749), p. 21; *Homer A la Mode. The Second Part in English Burlesque: Or, a Mock-Poem upon the Ninth Book of Iliads* (London, 1681), p. 16.

17 *A Burlesque Translation of Homer* (London, 1772), pp. 188, 196. Bridges began to publish his efforts in 1762. His translation also includes anger regarding the Greek "thick scull'd sons of bitches" who "In mighty wrath kept boxing on, / And knock'd the foremost Trojans down" (p. 530). A comparable degree of deflation of the gods and discontent with epic values seems to me present as well in Samuel Wesley's *The Iliad in a Nutshell: Or, Homer's Battle of the Frogs and Mice. Illustrated with Notes* (London, 1726).

18 *An Enquiry into the Life and Writings of Homer* (London, 1735), p. 28. Blackwell also observes that "Peace, Harmony and good Order which make the happiness of a people, are the *Bane* of a Poem that subsists by Wonder and Surprise" (p. 27). William Melmoth makes a similar argument regarding oratory, which flourishes during turbulence and signals national and personal loss: "the superior eloquence of Cicero" could not "make him any amends for his sad catastrophe." *Letters on Several Subjects. By the Late Sir Thomas Fitzosborne, Bart.* (London, 1748), 2:333.

As Pope knew from Virgil's *Georgics* and Homer's relevant similes, a miniature world need not denote diminished human values. Small things, Pope says of Homer, "give Lustre to his greatest Heroes." Pope quotes Eustathius' confirming wisdom: by comparing soldiers to flies Homer does not diminish "his Heroes by the Size of these small Animals, but . . . [raises] his Comparisons from certain Properties inherent in them, which deserve our Observation" (TE, 8:254–55n; *Iliad,* XVI.314).

19 TE, vol. 2, *The Rape of the Lock and Other Poems,* ed. Geoffrey Tillotson, 3rd ed. (London: Methuen & Co.; New Haven, Conn.: Yale Univ. Press, 1962), Canto 2, line 32. Subsequent citations to this edition are given in the text by canto and line.

The baron's offerings include trophies of his former loves and reflect further modern adaptations of epic behavior. In *Iliad,* XIV.359–72, Jupiter proves his lust for Juno "by the Instances of its Warmth to other Women." Though this seems strange, "Perhaps a Man's Love to the Sex in general may be no ill Recommendation of him to a Particular. And to be known, or thought, to have been successful with a good many, is what some Moderns have found no unfortunate Qualification in gaining a Lady, even a most virtuous one like *Juno*" (TE, 8:180n). On this hypothesis, the baron's reputation attracts Belinda; the hypothesis gains support if one assumes, rightly I believe, that her morning billet-doux was from him, and that her response was in part the suggestive card game.

20 See, for example, Pope's note to *Iliad,* XI.565: "I must confess I am not altogether pleas'd with the Railleries [Homer] sometimes uses to a vanquish'd Warrior, which Inhumanities if spoken to the dying, would I think be yet Worse than after they were dead" (TE, 8:59n). See also TE, 8:475n to *Iliad,* XXII.467.

21 One commentator has even found a five-act dramatic structure. See James L. Jackson, "Pope's *Rape of the Lock* Considered as a Five-Act Epic," *PMLA* 65 (1950): 1283–87.

22 As a gloss upon the ribbon and Belinda's danger, see the "Dialogue between Surly and Beau. By a Person of Quality," in [John Oldmixon, ed.] *Poems and Translations. By Several Hands* (London, 1714):

> Under his Left Arm a Bamboo,
> Ribbon dangling at his Sword;
> Tells you all he has, or can do,
> And whom last he laid on Board.
>
> Well he knows th' Intrigues of *London*,
> Which he whispers round the Room;
> What believing Maids are undone;
> Where they Lay in, and by whom. (p. 39)

For further sense of the woman's social and sexual danger, see n. 27, below.

23 For some aspects of trade and *The Rape of the Lock*, see Louis A. Landa, "Pope's Belinda, the General Emporie of the World, and The Wondrous Worm," and "Of Silkworms and Farthingales and the Will of God," in *Essays in Eighteenth-Century English Literature* (Princeton: Princeton Univ. Press, 1980), pp. 178–98, 199–217. See also Madame du Boccage's letter of 14 April 1750 from London, which includes these "Verses upon Ranelagh":

> Trade, which connects each distant shore,
> Which makes men various climes explore,
> To all the gifts this land affords,
> Adds *Chinese* Tea to crown their boards;
> Coffee of Moca, which bestows
> Tranquillity and calm repose;
> And the black *Indian* bev'ridge fam'd,
> *Ambrosia* by the *Spaniard* nam'd.

Letters concerning England, Holland, and Italy . . . Translated from the French (London, 1750), 1:20.

24 TE, 8:65–66; *Iliad*, xi.668, translated in xi.681 as "the slow Beast with heavy strength indu'd." Though Pope admires the simile, he records several objections to it and omits "the mention of the word Ass in the Translation" out of respect for "the Taste of the Age in which he lives" (8:64n).

25 *Madame Dacier's Remarks upon Mr. Pope's Account of Homer, Prefixed to his Translation of the Iliad. Made English from the French, By Mr. Parnell* (London, 1724), p. 4. Curll mischievously published this translation. The Parnell who wrote the "Essay on . . . Homer" prefatory to Pope's *Iliad* died in 1718. For Pope's response to Madame Dacier's *Remarks*, see *The Correspondence of Alexander Pope*, ed. George Sherburn (Oxford: Clarendon Press, 1956), 2:157–58. Pope's notes to Homer include several disagreements with Madame Dacier's comparable interpretations. On 1 September 1718 he thus tells the Duke of Buckingham: her efforts are too often borrowed from Eustathius without acknowledgement; she is inferior to her husband as a classicist; in general he respects her learning without sharing his grace's high opinion of her; and on rhetorical and poetic grounds Houtar de la Motte has much the better of the argument with Madame Dacier (*Correspondence*, 1:492–93; see also 1:485–87).

26 See especially Aubrey Williams, "The 'Fall' of China and *The Rape of the Lock*," *PQ* 41 (1962):412–25.

27 Compare Pope's note to *Iliad* xvi.468–69, "(When guilty Mortals break th' eternal Laws, / And Judges brib'd, betray the righteous Cause)." Pope adapts "*Homer*'s indirect and oblique manner of introducing moral Sentences and Instructions . . . We have

Virtue put upon us by Surprize, and are pleas'd to find a thing where we should never have look'd to meet with it" (TE, 8:261n). Giles Jacob also saw the potential seriousness and danger in Pope's poem. His unsigned *Rape of the Smock* (1717) shows a suitor, Ambrosio, seriously wounded in a duel, and the woman, Celia, trading her virtue to Philemon in order to reclaim the appearance of virtue – her own stolen smock. The seriousness of a mock epic appears as well in another poem indebted to Pope but far kinder to women than Jacobs': *Modern Fashions. A Poem address'd to the Ladies* (London, 1745), especially pp. 2, 5, 10, 13–15. The final pages contrast the benevolent female victor in the battle of the sexes, "whose kindness banishes *Despair*," with the malevolent female tyrant who "calmly sees the Conquer'd die" (p. 14). The contrast recalls that between Thalestris and Clarissa, as does the consequence of "mutual Good" (p. 15) for man and woman if the proper advice is taken.

28 For Pope's contrast of the ancient and modern Beauty at her toilette, see TE, 8:169n; *Iliad*, XIV.203n; and for one view of why Belinda is so well armed, see TE, 8:184n; *Iliad*, XIV.442n from the beginning of Plutarch's *Life of Pelopidas*: "the bravest and stoutest of [Homer's] Warriors march to Battel in the best Arms."

29 For the epic challenger's normative mixed tone of challenge, see TE, 7:367n; *Iliad* VII.79, regarding Hector's boast to the Greek champions: "If he seems to speak too vainly, we should consider him under the Character of a Challenger, whose Business it is to defy the Enemy. Yet at the same time we find a decent Modesty in his manner of expressing the Conditions of the Combate." Robert Williams points out that confident Belinda "plays a military game with 'Let Spades be trumps' (from Italian *spada*, a sword)." "Fate and the Narrative of the *The Rape of the Lock*," *Sydney Studies in English* 11 [1985–86]:34.

30 *Oeuvres diverses du sieur D * * *, Avec le traité du sublime* (1674) (Amsterdam, 1674), 2:39. See also *The Works of Mons' Boileau Despreaux*, ed. Nicholas Rowe et al. (London, 1711–12), 2:7–8, 37–38; new title page and pagination for *A Treatise of the Sublime*.

31 See "Remarks on Mr. Pope's *Rape of the Lock*" (written 1714, published 1728) in *The Critical Works of John Dennis*, ed. Edward Niles Hooker (Baltimore: The Johns Hopkins Press, 1967), 2:342, and [Charles Gildon] *New Rehearsal, or Bays the Younger . . . Also A Word or Two upon Mr. Pope's Rape of the Lock* (London, 1714), pp. 43–44. Geoffrey Tillotson records some other responses to the poem's bawdy in TE, 2:87–93, especially p. 90 n. 1. See also n. 50, below.

32 See TE, 7:124n; *Iliad*, I.771, regarding the gods' laughter at Vulcan: yet Homer "takes care not to mention a word of his Lameness. It would have been cruel in him and Wit out of Season, to have enlarg'd with Derision upon an Imperfection which is out of one's Power to remedy."

33 "A Dissertation on the Amazons. From the History of the Amazons, written in French by the Abbé de Guyon," in *The Gentleman's Magazine* 11 (1741):203. For further information regarding this version see John Lawrence Abbott, "Dr. Johnson and the Amazons," *PQ* 44 (1965):484–95. See also item 53 of J. D. Fleeman, *Preliminary Handlist of Copies of Books Associated with Dr. Samuel Johnson*, Oxford Bibliographical Society Occasional Publication no. 17 (Oxford: Bodleian Library, 1984). This shows Johnson's reading of the entry under "Amazons" in Pierre Danet, *Complete Dictionary of Greek and Roman Antiquities* (London, 1700).

As this and other references make plain, the Amazon was not unattractive merely because she was a woman warrior. Boadicea in England and La Pucelle in France were martial heroines who received the nation's well-earned applause. In most instances the differences between the attractive female warrior and the repellent Amazon is acceptance of the conventional mediating power of God, the state, or the male to whom she is or hopes to be attached. Once this female warrior has done her job, she surrenders the arms of war for the arms of man. Spenser's Britomart, for example, so behaves towards

Artegall when she defeats the martially and sexually aggressive and unmanning Radegund in Book v, Cantos 4–7 of *The Faerie Queene*. Spenser there carefully distinguishes between Radegund as warlike and cruel Amazon, and Britomart as championesse, warrioresse, Britonesse, and conqueresse who nonetheless re-establishes Artegall's authority. For further discussion of this issue, see Susanne Woods, "Spenser and the Problem of Women's Rule," *HLQ* 48 (1985):141–58. In a note to *Iliad* XIV.216, Pope makes plain how, in his judgment, women are most likely to prevail, "by pure cunning, and the Artful Management of their Persons; For there is but one way for the weak to subdue the mighty, and that is by Pleasure" (TE, 8:170n). For a benevolent playing out of such a victory and an Amazonian transformation from hostile to amiable sexual relations, see Samuel Wesley, *Battle of the Sexes* (1723), 2nd ed. (London, 1724), pp. 11–27. In this well-resolved combat "the jarring Kinds agree, / With Reconcilement dear, and cordial Amity" (p. 27). Simon Shepherd studies the less accommodating combats in *Amazons and Warrior Women. Varieties of Feminism in Seventeenth-Century Drama* (New York: St. Martin's Press, 1981); see especially pp. 5–17. Shepherd actually deals only with the earlier seventeenth century, and thinks that "the Amazons of classical authors tend to be glorious Figures" (p. 13).

34 Biddle, *Virgil's Bucolicks Englished. Whereunto is added the Translation of the two first Satyrs of Iuvenal* (London, 1634), sig. c5^r; Dryden, CE, vol. 4, *Poems 1693–1696*, ed. A. B. Chambers *et al.* (Berkeley and Los Angeles: Univ. of California Press, 1974), p. 171, line 365. The Amazon is not in Juvenal's sixth satire.

35 Danet, *A Complete Dictionary of the Greek and Roman Antiquities*, "Amazones"; Gautruche, *Nouvelle histoire poétique* (1671; Paris, 1725), p. 141 ("elles se livroient à de certains Hommes qu'elles prenoient au hazard"); Claude Marie Guyon, *Histoire des amazones anciennes et modernes* (1698; Paris, 1740), as translated in Johnson, n. 33 above, *Gentlemen's Magazine* 11 (1741), 203; Chesterfield, letter of 14 June (old style) 1750 to Madame du Boccage, as in his *Miscellaneous Works*, ed. Matthew Maty (London, 1777), 2:242, letter 85; number 1710 in *The Letters of . . . Chesterfield*, ed. Bonamy Dobrée (London: Eyre and Spottiswoode, 1932), 4:1555–58, p. 1556 quoted, in French. As these and other references suggest, Amazons were popular topics of discourse. For some others of the scholarly sort, see Joannes Columbus, *Disputatio de imperio amazonum* (Stockholm, 1678); Pierre Petit, *De Amazonibus dissertatio* (Paris, 1685), and Andreas Sundius, *De Patria amazonum* (Uppsala, 1716). These enjoyed other editions as well. Less learned, or patient, readers were aided by earlier works cited and by other translations and summaries like those of Pierre Petit's *Traité historique sur les amazones* (Paris, 1718), and [Joseph Towers'] useful *Dialogues concerning the Ladies. To which is added an Essay on the Antient Amazons* (London, 1785). Literary performances include those by Antoine Houtar de la Motte, *Marthesie, première reine des amazones* (1699), Louis le Maingre de Bouciqualt, *Les Amazones revoltées* (Paris, 1730), and Madame Marie Anne le Page Fiquet du Boccage, *Les Amazones* (Paris, 1749).

36 [Nahum Tate, *et al.*] *The Life of Alexander the Great. Written in Latin by Quintus Curtius Rufus, and Translated into English by several Gentlemen in the University of Cambridge* (London, 1690), pp. 193–94. This version includes the traditional Amazonian display of the left breast with a draped right breast "burnt off, that they may with the greater facility, shoot Arrows or throw Darts" (p. 193). Such an image long was preserved, as in D.M., *Ancient Rome and Modern Britain Compared. A Dialogue, In Westminster Abbey, Between Horace and Mr. Pope. A Poem* (London, 1793), which may also explain Alexander's cool response to Thalestris. "Pope" here says:

Our fair to be victorious are subdued,
But flying kill, and conquer when pursued.
With Amazonian terror nods no crest,
No dart is pointed from the mangled breast:

> That breast preserved, a readier death supplies,
> And all their darts are pointed from their eyes. (p. 22)

37 See Plutarch, *Alexander*, 46; Diodorus Siculus, *Bibliotheca historicae*, VIII.17.77.1–3; Quintus Curtius Rufus, *Historiarum Alexandri magni Macedonis*, VI.5.24–36. See also Marcus Junianus Justinus, epitome of Pompeius Trogus, *Historiae Phillipicae*, XII.3.5–7, and Strabo, *Geographia*, XI.5.3–4.

38 *Love of Fame, The Universal Passion. In Six Characteristical Satires*, 2nd ed. (London, 1728), p. 111.

39 See William Blake Tyrell, *Amazons. A Study in Athenian Mythmaking* (Baltimore: The Johns Hopkins Press, 1984), pp. 56, 113, 128. For example, "in classical Athens [Amazons] existed expressly to die each time they were seen in paintings or their name was spoken" (p. 113). Tyrell's is only one among the several recent studies of Amazons. The most extensive plates of classical Amazons are in Dietrich von Bothmer, *Amazons in Greek Art*, Oxford Monographs on Classical Archaeology (Oxford: Clarendon Press, 1957), and especially *Lexicon iconographicum mythologia classicae* (Zurich and Munich: Artemis Verlag, 1941), plates, 1.ii, 440–532, and commentary by Pierre Devambe, 1.i, 586–653, 653–662, especially 639–41. I count thirty-three plates in which Greek warriors fatally pull Amazons by the hair; there are several others in which they hold Amazons by the helmet or neck. In most cases, it is difficult to determine whether the woman's right breast has been removed or deaccentuated; but there are few such candidates, perhaps for Greek aesthetic purposes. For other Amazonian encounters in the visual arts, see illustrations for the *Histoire universelle* (*c.* 1223–30), in Hugo Buchtal, *Miniature Paintings in the Latin Kingdom of Jerusalem* (Oxford: Clarendon Press, 1957), pp. 68, 81–82, 86, 91–92, and plates 107 a, b, c; 108 a, b, c; 109 a, b, c; 113 a, c; 114 a, b, c (the last especially graphic); 116 a, b, c; and 121 c, "Alexander the Great and the Queen of the Amazons." See also two chronologically distant but brutally similar images: Pietro Buonaccorsi, called Perino del Vaga (1501–47), *The Battle of the Amazons*, in *Roman Drawings of the Sixteenth Century from the Musée du Louvre Paris* (Chicago: The Art Institute of Chicago, 1979), pp. 98–99; and Max Beckmann's *Amazonenschlacht* (1911), as reproduced in *Max Beckmann Katalog der Gemälde*, ed. Erhard and Barbara Göpel (Bern: Kornfeld und Cie, 1976) 1:108–9, catalogue number 146, and 2: plate 57.

   Amazons in Roman history have recently been studied by Giampiera Arrigoni, "Amazzoni alla Romana," *Rivista Storica Italiana* 96 (1984): 871–919. T. Sturge Moore's fine *The Rout of the Amazons* (London: Duckworth, 1903) treats the Amazon with elegiac respect. It is a poem worth reclaiming.

40 The term is from *The Scriblerian* 17 (1985):134, describing recent critical attitudes in general and the approach of C. N. Manlove (n. 2 above) in particular.

41 "Transformation in *The Rape of the Lock*," *ECS* 2 (1969):216. This essay is among the most valuable discussions of the poem.

42 Geoffrey Tillotson transcribes this and other comments in TE, 2:395. The analogy with Clarissa's speech is the more telling if, as seems likely, Pope was thinking of Boileau's Canto 6, in which Piété offers a long address that re-establishes theological and clerical order. For a useful discussion of *Le Lutrin* and its moral seriousness, see J. Douglas Canfield, "The Unity of Boileau's *Le Lutrin: The Counter-Effect of the Mock-Heroic*," *PQ* 53 (1974):42–58.

43 The shared values of the narrator and Clarissa have been noted by William F. Cunningham, Jr., in "The Narrator of *The Rape of the Lock*," in *Literary Studies: Essays in Memory of Francis A. Drumm*, ed. John H. Dorenkamp (Boston: College of the Holy Cross, 1973), pp. 139–40, and Sheila Delany, "Sexual Politics in Pope's *Rape of the Lock*," in *Weapons of Criticism*, p. 188 (n. 2 above).

44 For Madame Dacier, see *L'Iliade D'Homère traduite en François, avec des remarques* (Paris, 1711), 2:241–43 for her translation, and 2:538–39 for her "Remarques," which observe

that Homer has given this extraordinary wisdom "au fils de Jupiter." For Pope, see TE, 8:263n; *Iliad*, XII.387n. George Chapman had long ago glossed this speech as *"never equalled by any (in this kind) of all that have written"* (*The Whole Works of Homer, Prince of Poets* [London, 1614], 1:165). For objections to Clarissa's speech as a positive adaptation of Sarpedon, see Robert W. Williams (n. 29 above), "Fate and . . . Narrative," pp. 36–39. He also objects that Clarissa cannot be a norm because her counsel relates only to the values of this world of men rather than of God. My discussion of "use" below may help to remove her from the index.

45 Burnet and Duckett offer a nasty, and familiar, version of the exchange between Diomedes and Glaucus:

> *Saturn's* Son in the mean Season,
> From *Glaucus* stole away his Reason,
> Who changed with *Diomede* (O Ass!)
> His Arms of Gold for his of Brass:
> And Armour worth a Hundred Cows,
> For one not worth a Hundred Sows.   (p. 29, italics and roman type reversed)

46 In rejecting Clarissa's wisdom regarding the transience of beauty, Belinda shows herself unrepresentative of the beautiful woman's psychology as exemplified in Helen. "*Should Venus leave thee, ev'ry Charm must fly,*" shows the expected result: "This was the most dreadful of all Threats, Loss of Beauty and of Reputation. *Helen* who had been Proof to the personal Appearance of the Goddess, and durst even reproach her with Bitterness just before, yields to this, and obeys all the Dictates of Love" (TE, 7:216n; *Iliad*, III.515). Clarissa, on the other hand, offers human alternatives to the loss of beauty.

47 The line is quoted from TE, 3.ii, *Epistles to Several Persons*, ed. F. W. Bateson, 2nd ed. (London: Methuen & Co.; New Haven, Conn.: Yale Univ. Press, 1961), p. 154. Bishop William Warburton commented on the sacred contexts of *use* in this line. See his edition of *The Works of Alexander Pope Esq.* (London, 1751), 3:291n. For Swift's undated sermon "On Mutual Subjection," see *Jonathan Swift. Irish Tracts 1720–1723 and Sermons*, ed. Herbert Davis and Louis Landa (Oxford: Basil Blackwell, 1963), pp. 142, 144. Earl R. Wasserman comments on such stewardship in Pope's *Epistle to Bathurst. A Critical Reading with an Edition of the Manuscripts* (Baltimore: The Johns Hopkins Press, 1960, p. 27.

48 See Samuel Wesley, *Poems on Several Occasions* (London, 1736), p. 113, "On the Rose; from Anacreon." That flower is "Dear to *Venus* and her Boy" (p. 112). See also *Midsummer Night's Dream*, I.i.69–78, where Theseus tells Hermia that those who master their blood as nuns are "Thrice blessed," though "earthlier happy is the rose distill'd / Than that which, withering on the virgin thorn, / Grows, lives, and dies in single blessedness" (lines 76–78). Arthur W. Hoffman has found several of Pope's allusions to Spenser's *Epithalamion* and, especially, *Prothalamion*. See Hoffman's "Spenser and *The Rape of the Lock*," *PQ* 49 (1970):530–46.

49 *The Spectator*, ed. Donald F. Bond (Oxford: Clarendon Press, 1965), 2:9, 11 (No. 128), and 3:80, 82. Pope's "Epistle to Miss Blount; With the Works of Voiture" (1712) also praises good humor in the woman. Somewhat later, Samuel Wesley also used a comparable image to suggest a well-balanced woman. He says in "To Kitty, a Poetical Young Lady,"

> What tho' her Wit should never fail?
> How few will long endure her?
> The Ship that Ballast wants by Sail
> Is overset the surer.   (*Poems on Several Occasions*, p. 297.)

As Mary Astell long had made plain, good humor also was a desirable male trait in the perennial mating dance. Women are more constant in love than men, she says, "For not usually fixing our Affection on so mutable a thing as the *Beauty* of a *Face*, which a

Thousand accidents may destroy, but on *Wit, Good Humour,* and other *Graces* of the *Mind,* as well as of the *Body,* our Love is more durable, and constant in proportion to the longer continuance of those Qualities in the Object" (*An Essay in Defence of the Female Sex* [London, 1696], pp. 129-30). Like eighteenth-century commentators, Astell is concerned with not violating "*Modesty* and *Decorum* at the price of our Fame and Reputation" (p. 130). Astell discusses Amazons, and a possible reason for their growth as a nation, on p. 24.

50 H. Stanhope [William Bond], *The Progress of Dulness. By an Eminent Hand. Which will serve for an Explanation of the Dunciad* (London, 1728), p. 29. For comparable observations, see John Dennis, "Remarks on Mr. Pope's *Rape of the Lock,*" *Critical Works,* 2:347; [James Ralph], *Sawney. An Heroic Poem. Occasion'd by the Dunciad. Together with a Critique of that Poem address'd to Mr. T——d, Mr. M.——r, Mr. Eu——n, &c.* (London, 1728), p. 19. The line also has two other possible contexts. Rape was associated with the Amazon myth, especially with Theseus, who raped either an unnamed Amazon, or Antiope, Hippolyte, Melanippe, or Glance. See Tyrell, *Amazons,* pp. 3-6, 91-92 (n. 39 above). Moreover, as Pope, following Eustathius, says about the *Iliad,* VIII.343n, "nothing was more common than for Heroes of old to take their Female Captives to their Beds; . . . such Captives were then given for a Reward of Valour, and as a Matter of Glory" (TE, 7:413n).

51 For another point of view regarding Berenice, see Eric Rothstein, The Routledge History of English Poetry, vol. 3, *Restoration and Eighteenth-Century Poetry 1660-1780* (Boston: Routledge & Kegan Paul, 1981), p. 26. Claudius Aelian records another wifely, civilizing, function of Berenice, who refused to allow Ptolemee to play dice when he was deciding which men should be condemned to death. See *Claudius Aelianus his Various History,* trans. Thomas Stanley (n. 12 above), XIV.43. Pope himself mentions Berenice's hair and some symbolic values of cut hair in *Iliad* XVIII.566n (TE, 8:349n) and *Iliad* XXIII.166n (TE, 8:495-96n). For a fuller English version of the Berenice story, see the translation of Jean de la Chapelle's *The Adventures of Catullus, and History of his Amours with Lesbia. Intermixt with Translations of his Choicest Poems. By Several Hands* (London, 1707), especially pp. 256-64; there are several verbal parallels with Pope's *Rape of the Lock.* The first French edition appeared in 1680-81, the fifth in 1725. For other erotic Catullan suggestions see the unsigned *Basia: Or The Charms Of Kissing. Translated from the Latin of Catullus and Secundus, And the Greek of Menage,* 2nd ed. (London, 1719). James A. S. McPeek observes that "nearly all the significant French and English epithalamies . . . conform unexceptionally to the Catullan tradition": *Catullus in Strange and Distant Britain,* Harvard Studies in Comparative Literature, vol. 15 (Cambridge, Mass.: Harvard Univ. Press, 1939), p. 236. See pp. 103-43, especially 140-43 for Pope, and pp. 144-236 for relevant texts. The "Coma Berenices" is well edited as number 66 in D. F. S. Thomson, *Catullus. A Critical Edition* (Chapel Hill: The Univ. of North Carolina Press, 1978).

8. "Such as Sir Robert Would Approve"?

1 I have considered the dangers of ignoring the first two kinds of knowledge in "Johnson's *London* and Juvenal's *Third Satire:* The Country as 'Ironic' Norm," in this volume.

2 The first quotation is from Thomas R. Edwards, *This Dark Estate: A Reading of Pope* (Berkeley: Univ. of California Press, 1963), p. 93; the second from Howard D. Weinbrot, *The Formal Strain: Studies in Augustan Imitation and Satire* (Chicago: Univ. of Chicago Press, 1969), p. 157.

3 The first set of quotations is from Thomas E. Maresca, *Pope's Horatian Poems* (Columbus: Ohio Univ. Press, 1966); the second from the most recent contribution to the debate, that by Cedric D. Reverand II, "*Ut pictura poesis,* and Pope's 'Satire II. i'," *ECS* 9 (1976):556. Reverand lists other readings of the poem that view Pope as "the victor in the argument": p. 555, n. 4.

4 The extremely complex manuscript of the poem is in the Berg Collection of the New York Public Library. Many of its readings, however, are reproduced in *The Works of Alexander Pope*, ed. John Wilson Croker, Whitewell Elwin, and William John Courthope (London, 1881), 3:289–300. It has recently been transcribed and well edited in Maynard Mack's *The Last and Greatest Art: Some Unpublished Poetical Manuscripts of Alexander Pope* (Newark, Del.: Univ. of Delaware Press, 1984).

5 For this response, see *The Tenth Satyr of Juvenal, English and Latin* (London, 1687) in *The Complete Works of Thomas Shadwell*, ed. Montague Summers (London: The Fortune Press, 1927), 5:292. Shadwell also claims that his father taught him the lute, and that he was thought a good classicist at Bury School, Suffolk, and Caius College, Cambridge. Some of his other responses were more general, and appreciably more shrill, hostile, and rude, perhaps with justification.

6 There is valuable discussion of Walpole's view of corruption in Isaac Kramnick, *Bolingbroke and his Circle: The Politics of Nostalgia in the Age of Walpole* (Cambridge, Mass.: Harvard Univ. Press, 1968), pp. 121–24.

7 On 18 January 1731 Hill makes "a gentle complaint" regarding "a paragraph in the notes of a late edition of the *Dunciad*" (2:285, and note). Pope's equivocal reply on 26 January – you attacked me first, you are not intended in the initials A. H., I did not write the note – evokes Hill's angry response of 28 January and his threat to publish "An Essay on Propriety, and Impropriety, in Design, Thought, and Expression, illustrated by Examples, in both Kinds from the Writings of Mr. Pope." Though Pope's response on 5 February urges Hill to publish his essay, he also promises to leave out the note and to specify that Hill was not meant, if he can influence the editors. On 10 February Hill accepts the offer, and promises to send Pope the manuscript of "the *Essay on Propriety*, as soon as it is finished," so that Pope can expunge what he wishes. On 15 February Pope more firmly says that "I am very desirous to leave out that *Note*, if you like so." For these exchanges, see *The Correspondence of Alexander Pope* (Oxford: Clarendon Press, 1956), 3:164–77; referred to hereafter as *Correspondence*. Several of the letters, and others of interest, are in *The Works of the Late Aaron Hill, Esq.* (London, 1753), 1:27–38. Hill finished the "Essay on Propriety" in 1739, but burnt it "in a long and melancholy illness" after it was half transcribed for the press. *Works*, 2:217, 13 January 1741, to Mallet.

8 The adversarius was not labelled "Fortescue" until Warburton's edition of 1751, though Pope clearly had his friend and attorney in mind from the outset. See Pope's letter of 18 February 1733 in *Correspondence*, 3:351. In April of 1733 he shows that he still thinks of Fortescue in terms reminiscent of the "F" of his imitation, whom he calls "my Council learned in the laws" (line 142). In this letter he says that if Fortescue is elevated to the bench, "Twickenham will be as much at the service of my lord judge, as it was of my learned council." *Correspondence*, 3:364.

9 Quotations from this and Pope's other satires are from TE, vol. 4, *Imitations of Horace*, ed. John Butt, 2nd ed., rev. (London and New Haven: Methuen and Yale Univ. Press, 1961).

10 *The Correspondence of Jonathan Swift*, ed. Harold Williams (Oxford: Clarendon Press, 1963–65), 4:131–32. Some members of the opposition, however, were more pleased with Pope's tones than concerned for his health. See the anonymous *The Wrongheads: A Poem. Inscrib'd to Mr. Pope. By a Person of Quality* (31 May; London, 1733):

> Shall knaves and fools commend the world's applause,
> And censure 'scape, because they 'scape the laws?
> No – *Pope* forbids, and fir'd with honest rage,
> Resolves to mend, as well as charm the age.
> Nor fears the cause of virtue to defend,
> Nor blushes to confess himself her friend.   (p. 3)

In general, the opposition was as delighted as the administration was appalled by Pope's severity. Ministerial writers, however, were more precise in considering Pope's specific devices in *Fortescue*.

11 This and most other dates are taken from David F. Foxon, *English Verse 1701–1750* (Cambridge: Cambridge Univ. Press, 1975).

12 As quoted in Bertrand A. Goldgar, *Walpole and the Wits: The Relation of Politics to Literature, 1722–1742* (Lincoln: Univ. of Nebraska Press, 1976), p. 129. The author of *The False Patriot: An Epistle to Mr. Pope* (March; London, 1734), also bemoans Pope's fall into "the Party-Fight" (p. 5), and misplaced devotion to Bolingbroke (pp. 4, 5, 8). Like the ministerial adversarius at the end of the *Epilogue to the Satires*, this author urges Pope to return to the innocuous *Essay on Man* (1733–34): "Recall your Muse, lur'd into Faction's Cause, / And sing, great Bard, of Heav'ns and Natures Laws" (p. 11). As late as 1781 Samuel Johnson thought Pope's use of Bolingbroke a mistake, for he was not someone "a good man would wish to have his intimacy with . . . known to posterity; he can derive little honour from the notice of . . . Bolingbroke." *Lives of the English Poets*, ed. George Birkbeck Hill (Oxford: Clarendon Press, 1905), 3:205. Johnson's objection may be based on personal as well as political animus.

13 On 28 August Lord Hervey himself completed *An Epistle from A Nobleman To a Doctor of Divinity* (William Sherwin). It was not intended for publication, but nonetheless did appear on 10 November, and takes Pope to task for several poems, including *Fortescue* (pp. 6–7). For further information regarding this *Epistle*, see Robert Halsband, *Lord Hervey Eighteenth-Century Courtier* (New York: Oxford Univ. Press, 1974), pp. 161–65. One of Hervey's objections, here as in the *Verses*, is that Pope is merely a bad imitator of Horace. That same point, together with others of a familiar and ugly sort, also appears in [?] Gerard's *An Epistle to the Egregious Mr. Pope, In which the Beauties of his Mind and Body are amply displayed* (14 February; London, 1734). Pope not only betrays and attacks all his benefactors, but

> Poor *Imitation* is thy best of Praise;
> Thy bold Adventures are but Second Hand
> Were *none* to lead, Thy Wit is at a Stand.   (p. 11)

14 This work also was printed as "A Just Imitation of the First Satire of the Second Book of Horace. In a Dialogue between Mr. Pope and the Ordinary of Newgate. With Achilles Dissected," by Alexander Burnet. The apparently pseudonymous Guthry may be Burnet, or perhaps Curll, the publisher. On 8 March 1733 Pope writes to Fortescue regarding both this and the *Sequel* below. "There has been another thing wherein Pigott is abused as my Learned Council, written by some Irish attorney; & Curll has printed a Parody on my own words which he is as proud of as his own production, saying, he will pay no more of his Authors but can write better himself." *Correspondence*, 3:354–55. My source for Guthry is *Mr. Pope's Literary Correspondence. Volume the Second* (London, 1735).

15 Another, opposition, work may not be a direct comment on *Fortescue*, but suggests the power of Sir Robert and roughly parallels Pope's point at the end of his poem. The author of *The State Juggler: Or, Sir Politick Ribband* (London, 1733) has Sir Politick sing an air called "Let Ambition fire thy mind," and shows that such ambition is everywhere in the land, and that his friends thus can "Each Fool's censorious Taunt deride, / Law and Gospel's on our Side" (Air 7) – as Pope's poem had also made clear.

16 Thomas Bentley's *Letter to Mr. Pope*, for example, is *Occasioned by Sober Advice from Horace, &c.* The anonymous *An Epistle to Alexander Pope, Esq; Occasion'd by some of his Late Writings* (4 February; London, 1735), also is a larger overview that berates several of Pope's miserable and partisan performances, and has him purport to say:

> See this old cloak, 'twas *Horace*'s of Old,
> Patch'd thus by *Bentley*, worth its Weight in Gold;

In this I domineer, repeat old Saws,
And sell 'em to the Crowd, *Apollo*'s Laws. (p. 2)

Bolingbroke also comes in for his share of blame in the degradation of politics and Pope (p. 5). The anonymous *A Sequel to Tit for Tat* (1734), and *The Satirists: A Satire* (1733–34?) also consider *Fortescue*. Many relevant works are listed and analyzed in J. V. Guerinot, *Pamphlet Attacks on Alexander Pope 1711–1744: A Descriptive Bibliography* (New York: New York Univ. Press, 1969).

17 For some of these, including cutting off ears, see Giles Jacobs, *A New Law Dictionary*, 8th ed. (London, 1762), "Libel." See also C. R. Kropf, "Libel and Satire in the Eighteenth Century," *ECS* 8 (1974–75): 153–68, and Robert Halsband, "Libels and Satires! Lawless Things Indeed!" *ECS* 8 (1975):475–77.

18 As far as we can tell from Pope's responses to Fortescue's letters, that lawyer remained concerned for his client's wellbeing, may have intervened on his behalf with Walpole, urged alteration of Pope's attack on Lady Mary, and in general knew that Pope's noble defence, however elegant as a poem, had no legal substance whatever. See *Correspondence*, 8 March 1733 (3:354), and 18 March 1733 (3:357). The ultimate utility of Pope's poem may be summed up when, on the latter date, he tells Fortescue that "[I] hope I shall have long life, because I am much threaten'd" (3:357).

9. Conventions of Classical Satire

1 TE, vol. 5, *The Dunciad*, James Sutherland, 3rd ed. (London: Methuen & Co.; Yale Univ. Press, 1963), p. 290, lines 282–84.

2 King, trans., *The Art of Love in Imitation of Ovid* (London), p. xxxix.

3 Clubbe, *Six Satires of Horace In a Style Between Free Imitation and Literal Version* (Ipswich), p. v.

4 *Letters on the Study . . . of History* (London, 1752), 1:67.

5 *Abbot Charles Batteux, A Course of the Belles Lettres; or, the Principles of Literature. Translated from the French . . . By Mr. Miller* (London), 3:144. The article on satire (by the Chevalier de Jaucourt) in the *Encyclopédie* (Neufchâtel, 1765), 14: 697–702, includes Batteux's "Parallèle des satyriques romains & françois par M. le Batteux." See Miller's translation, 3:192–95, which substitutes Dryden and Young for the French satirists.

6 For some of the better-known commentary on Trebatius, see André Dacier, *Oeuvres d'Horace en latin et en françois, avec des remarques critiques et historiques*, 3rd ed. (Paris, 1709), 7:21–22: "Il fut aussi en grande consideration auprès d'Auguste, qui ne faisoit rien sans le consulter" (p. 22). Trebatius was, of course, glossed and discussed in the other standard editions, encyclopedias, and dictionaries in Latin, French, and English.

7 For some valuable modern discussion of Horace's satire and its use of Lucilius, see Eduard Fraenkel, *Horace* (Oxford: Clarendon Press, 1957; rpt. 1966), pp. 145–53; Niall Rudd, *The Satires of Horace: A Study* (Cambridge: Cambridge Univ. Press, 1966), pp. 86–131; and Gordon Williams, *Tradition and Originality in Roman Poetry* (Oxford: Clarendon Press, 1968), pp. 443–59.

8 I have discussed anti-Augustanism and its relationship to history, politics, and literature, in "History, Horace, and Augustus Caesar: Some Implications for Eighteenth-Century Satire," in this volume and at greater length in *Augustus Caesar in "Augustan" England: The Decline of a Classical Norm* (Princeton: Princeton Univ. Press, 1978). Modern classicists often disagree with the eighteenth century's notion of the relationship between Augustus and Horace, and Horace's unthreatening tones. See, for example, Niall Rudd's "Dryden on Horace and Juvenal," in *The Satires of Horace*, pp. 258–73.

9 *The Roman History, from the Building of the City, To the Perfect Settlement of the Empire, by Augustus Caesar* (London, 1695–98), 1:428; 2:3–4.

10 *A Dissertation Upon the most celebrated Roman Poets. Written Originally in Latin,* trans. Christopher Hayes (London, 1718), pp. 47, 49. This is a small part of the evidence against Horatian satiric dominance by the early eighteenth century. Although a few modern commentators have, haltingly, recognized the Juvenalian (but not Persian) intrusions in Pope's satires and imitations of Horace, the dominant emphasis long has been on an Horatian Pope in an Horatian age. See, for example, among many possible citations from distinguished critics, Peter Dixon, *The World of Pope's Satires: An Introduction to the Epistles and Imitations of Horace* (London: Methuen & Co., 1968), p. 30 and Howard Erskine-Hill, "Augustans on Augustanism: England, 1655–1759," *Renaissance and Modern Studies* 11 (1967):74. According to the former, "The first two decades of the eighteenth century had seen Horace established as the type of the satirist," and to the latter, "Imitation [by Pope and others] . . . shows a conscious and thoughtful act of identification by the modern poet with a poet of Augustan Rome."

11 I have not discovered Wickstead's first name. His poem is *An Ode for the Year MDCCXVII. To the King* (London), pp. 2–3.

12 *The Works of Tacitus* (London, 1728–31), 1:49–50; Syme, *Tacitus* (Oxford: Clarendon Press, 1958), 1:432.

13 *A Poetical Translation of the Elegies of Tibullus; and of the Poems of Sulpicia* (London, 1759), 1:vi and 2:70n. In the same note Grainger wishes "that the Nine may always devote their Raptures to the Service of their Country, and never prostitute their Talents, in flattering Tyranny, or inflaming the Passions of guilty Greatness" (2:71n).

14 *Plain Truth, or Downright Dunstable* (London), pp. 15–16. This poem was widely circulated and read at Tom's Coffee House, Deveraux Court. See the British Library's copy, shelf mark 11630/1-22 c. 13.

15 See, for example, Bubb Dodington's *Epistle to . . . Walpole* (1725), and the *London Journal* for 8 January and 5 February 1726. Horatianism, in this context, aims to support the administration and, in the *Journal* for 5 February, win "the Smiles of the Great Man."

16 TE, vol. 6, *Minor Poems*, ed. Norman Ault and John Butt (London: Methuen & Co.; Yale Univ. Press, 1954), p. 376. The poem was published in 1738; its date of composition is unknown, though sometime near 1737 or 1738 seems reasonable. Later in this essay, quotations from Pope's imitation of Horace, *Satires* I.ii, are from vol. 4 of the Twickenham Edition, *Imitations of Horace*, ed. John Butt, 2nd ed. (London, 1953). I also call this poem *Fortescue*.

17 "The Inspector," No. 5, 11 March 1751, in *The London Daily Advertiser, and Literary Gazette*.

18 References to Rigaltius are from *D. Junii Juvenalis et A. Persii Flacci Satyrae, interpretatione ac notis Ludovicus Prateus* (London, 1694), sig. b2ᵛ: "Nempe his vocibus erectis & liberis diram servitutem fortissimi viri exsecrabantur"; and sig. b5ᵛ: "scribebat seculo Caesarum flagitiis contaminatissimo, legibus una cum elisa magistratuum voce evanidis, Romana illa quondam virtute sopore paene letali marcescente."

19 *Decimus Junius Juvenalis, and Aulus Persius Flaccus Translated* (Oxford, 1673), p. 275, n. 11.

20 Dennis, "To Matthew Prior, Esq. Upon the Roman Satirists," in *The Critical Works of John Dennis*, ed. Edward Niles Hooker (Baltimore: Johns Hopkins Univ. Press, 1943), 2:218. For Dryden, *John Dryden: Of Dramatic Poesy and Other Critical Essays*, ed. George Watson, Everyman's Library (London: Dent; New York: Dutton, 1962), 2:134–35 (Horace), 132.

21 Trapp, *Praelectiones Poeticae* (1711–1719), trans. William Boyer and William Clarke as *Lectures on Poetry* (London, 1742), p. 228; Crusius, *Lives of the Roman Poets*, 3rd ed. (London, 1753), 2:78 (highest perfection), 2:84 (liberty), 2:89. Crusius admires much about Horace and, to a lesser extent, Persius, but concludes: "JUVENAL has undoubtedly improved on both" (2:80).

22 Harte, *An Essay on Satire, Particularly the Dunciad* (London, 1730), p. 17; Brown, *An Essay on Satire; Occasion'd by the Death of Mr. Pope* (London, 1745), pp. 26, 22 (lofty epic).

23 (London), p. vii; Boscawen, *The Satires, Epistles and Art of Poetry of Horace* (London, 1797), p. x.

24 *D. Junii Juvenalis* (n. 18, above), sig. b5ᵛ.

25 See his examination of Juvenal's satires, in "Extraits de mon journal," *Miscellaneous Works*, ed. John, Lord Sheffield (London, 1796), 2:103–4 (love of liberty), 2:117–18; Johnson, *Lives of the English Poets*, ed. G. Birkbeck Hill (Oxford: Clarendon Press, 1905), 1:447.

26 "On Satire and Satirists," in *Essays Moral and Literary* (London, 1778), 2: 159.

27 *Something Like Horace: Studies in the Art and Allusion of Pope's Horatian Satires* (Nashville, Tenn.: Vanderbilt Univ. Press, 1969), p. 6.

28 In addition to Loveling and Whitehead, cited within, see the anonymous *Advice to an Aspiring Young Gentleman* (London, 1733), in imitation of the fourth satire, the pseudonymous work by Griffith Morgan D'Anvers, *Persius Scaramouch; or, A Critical and Moral Satire . . . In Imitation of the First Satire of Persius* (London, 1734), and — Dudley, *The First Satire of Persius, Translated into English Verse* (London, 1739). Loveling's poem has been discussed by Cynthia S. Dessen. See "An Eighteenth-Century Imitation of Persius, Satire I," *Texas Studies in Literature and Language* 20 (1978):433–56. For further discussion of Persius in the eighteenth century, see "Persius, the Opposition to Walpole, and Pope," in this volume. The prevailing attitude towards Persius is exemplified by Raman Selden, who believes that Lucilius and Persius "were not used directly as models by the English Augustan satirists." See *English Verse Satire 1590–1765* (London: George Allen & Unwin, 1978), p. 11

29 *The Satires of Persius, Translated into English Verse* (London, 1741–42), pp. 3–4.

30 See *Joseph Spence: Observations, Anecdotes, and Characters of Books and Men Collected from Conversation*, ed. James M. Osborn (Oxford: Clarendon Press, 1966), 1:143–44, item 321a.

31 "Sur les satiriques Latins. Première Mémoire . . . Horace," read to the Académie des Inscriptions et Belles Lettres, 11 April 1777. See the Académie's *Mémoires de Littérature* 43 (1776–79):179. Later in the Mémoire Dusaulx praises the accuracy of Batteux's description of Horace, which I have cited above: Dusaulx, p. 195n.

32 (London, 1739), p. 13. Gerard's effort is described in J. V. Guerinot, *Pamphlet Attacks on Alexander Pope 1711–1744: A Descriptive Bibliography* (New York: New York Univ. Press, 1969), pp. 245–47.

33 CE, vol. 4, *Poems 1693–1696*, ed. A. B. Chambers, William Frost, and Vinton A. Dearing (Berkeley: Univ. of California Press, 1974), pp. 273–75, lines 223–26, 235–36. The quotation from Juvenal, below, is from the same edition.

34 On 27 October, for instance, the *Gazetteer* says that opposition satirists, including a recognizable, small, hunchbacked, "late Satyrist" should be "clubb'd or rather bastinadoed" in the old Roman manner.

35 Cedric D. Reverand II has recently argued, unconvincingly, I believe, for Pope's triumph in this poem, especially so in the noble lines in defense of Virtue (105–17). See his "*Ut pictura poesis*, and Pope's 'Satire II.i,'" *ECS* 9 (1975–76):553–68. For a thorough review of Pope's literary uses of "Virtue" in his opposition poems, see Paul Gabriner, "Pope's 'Virtue' and the Events of 1738," in *Scripta Hierosolymitana* 25 (1973):96–119. I have discussed Pope's "triumph" and contemporary responses to it in "'Such as Sir Robert Would Approve'? Answers to Pope's Answer from Horace", in this volume.

36 The poem appeared as an unsigned contribution in the *Daily Gazetteer* for 16 June 1739, as "Q. HORATII FLACCI ad CURIONEM Epistola." It also appeared in Newcomb's *A Miscellaneous Collection of Original Poems* (London, 1740), pp. 52–56.

37 Thomas E. Maresca, *Pope's Horatian Poems* (Columbus: Ohio State Univ. Press, 1966), p. 67.

38 TE, vol. 1, *Pastoral Poetry and an Essay on Criticism*, ed. E. Audra and Aubrey Williams (London: Methuen & Co.; Yale Univ. Press, 1961), p. 7, from the Preface to Pope's *Works*, 1717.

10. Persius, the Opposition to Walpole, and Pope

1 The standard view has been stated by Raman Selden, who believes that Lucilius and Persius "were not used directly as models by the English Augustan satirists" (*English Verse Satire 1590–1765* [London: George Allen & Unwin, 1978], p. 11). For other views, however, see William Frost, "English Persius: The Golden Age," *ECS* 2 (1968):77–101, and especially Cynthia Dessen's study of Benjamin Loveling's *First Satire of Persius Imitated* (1740): "An Eighteenth-Century Imitation of Persius, Satire 1," *Texas Studies in Language and Literature* 20 (1978):433–56. Some of Persius' apparently political qualities, and consequent utility for the opposition to Walpole, are discussed in this useful essay as well. For more classically oriented studies, see Cynthia Dessen, *Iunctura Callidus Acri: A Study of Persius' Satires*, Illinois Studies in Language and Literature, No. 59 (Urbana: Univ. of Illinois Press, 1968), and J. C. Bramble, *Persius and the Programmatic Satire: A Study in Formal Imagery* (Cambridge: Cambridge Univ. Press, 1974).

2 These are, respectively, Barten Holyday, *Aulus Persius Flaccus His Satires Translated into English* (Oxford, 1616; reprinted with his Juvenal in 1673); John Dryden *et al.*, *The Satires of Decimus Junius Juvenalis . . . Together with the Satires of Aulus Persius Flaccus* (London, 1693); Henry Eelbeck, *A Prosaic Translation of Aulus Persius Flaccus's Six Satyrs* (London, 1719); Thomas Sheridan, *The Satyrs of Persius* (Dublin, 1728); John Senhouse, *The Satires of Aulus Persius Flaccus, Translated into English Prose* (London, 1730); John Stirling, *A. Persii Flacci, Satirae: or, The Satires of A. Persius Flaccus . . . For the Use of Schools* (London, 1736); Thomas Brewster, *The Satires of Persius* (London, 1741–42; printed individually from 1733); Edmund Burton, *The Satyrs of Persius* (London, 1752); Martin Madan, *A New and Literal Translation of Juvenal and Persius* (London, 1789); Sir William Drummond, *The Satires of Persius* (London, 1797); *The Satires of Aulus Persius Flaccus; Translated into English Verse* (London, 1806); Francis Howes, *The Satires of A. Persius Flaccus* (London, 1809); William Gifford, *The Satires of Aulus Persius Flaccus* (London, 1817, in vol. 2 of his Juvenal). This list should be supplemented with the several editions of Holyday's Persius (5th ed., 1650), Dryden's Juvenal and Persius (7th ed., 1754), and Brewster's Persius (2nd ed., 1751), which also was reprinted in *D. Junii Juvenalis et A. Persii Flacci Satirae Expurgatae: In Usum Scholarum* (London, 1784; also includes Johnson's *London* [1738] and *Vanity of Human Wishes* [1749]), and in Edward Owen's *The Satires of Juvenal . . . Also Dr. Brewster's Persius* (London, 1785). William Gifford's Persius appeared in 1821 as well.

3 For these, see Oldham, *Some New Pieces* (London, 1684), with its separate pagination and title page for *Satyrs upon the Jesuits*, 3rd ed. (London, 1685), sig. A2^r; F. A., *The Third Satyr of A. Persius, In Way of a Dialogue, or Dramatick Interlude* (London, 1685); Brown, *The Works of Mr. Thomas Brown, Serious and Comical*, 5th ed. (London, 1720), 1:56–59; the six different imitators are discussed more fully below; Thomas Neville, *Imitations of Juvenal and Persius* (London, 1769); [Edward Burnaby Greene], *The Satires of Persius Paraphrastically Imitated and Adapted to the Times* (London, 1799); *The Fourth Satire of Persius Imitated, and Much Enlarged, In Application to the Right Honourable William Pitt* (London, 1784); William Gifford, *The Baviad. A Paraphrastic Imitation of the First Satire of Persius* (London, 1791); George Daniel, *The Modern Dunciad. A Satire. With Notes Biographical and Critical* (London, 1814).

4 André Dacier's edition and translation of Horace probably was the best known such

version in the seventeenth and eighteenth centuries, and includes a "Préface sur les Satires d'Horace, Où l'on explique l'origine & le progrès de la Satire des Romains; & tous les changemens qui lui sont arrivez." Dacier quickly announced his indebtedness to "le savant Casaubon." See *Oeuvres d'Horace en Latin et en François, avec des Remarques*, 3rd ed. (Paris, 1709), 6:1 and passim. The third is the revised and preferred edition. For brief discussion of contemporary knowledge of Dacier, see Howard D. Weinbrot, *The Formal Strain: Studies in Augustan Imitation and Satire* (Chicago: Univ. of Chicago Press, 1969), pp. 60–68.

5 As translated by Peter E. Medine, in "Isaac Casaubon's *Prolegomena* to the *Satires* of Persius: An Introduction, Text, and Translation" *English Literary Renaissance* 6 (1976):288. Subsequent quotations are given in the text. Casaubon's distinction between satiric kinds already was becoming commonplace. "Description in Horace," for example, "is humbler, in Persius grander, in Juvenal often sublime" (p. 294).

6 *The Satires of . . . Persius* (n. 2 above), p. 1. Subsequent citations from Senhouse are given in the text.

7 *A General Dictionary, Historical and Critical*, tr. John Peter Bernard, Thomas Birch, John Lockman, *et al.* (London, 1734–41), 7:327. Subsequent references are cited in the text. See also the Abbé le Monnier, *Satires de Perse* (Paris, 1771), pp. xix–xxi. Le Monnier is aware of, and comments upon, Bayle in several places – pp. xvii–xviii, for example.

8 *Aulus Persius Flaccus His Satires* (n. 2 above), sig. A3^v. Subsequent citations from Holyday are given in the text.

9 *The Satires of A. Persius Flaccus* (n. 2 above), sig. [π]3^r. Subsequent citations from Stirling are given in the text.

10 *Satires de Perse, Traduites en François, avec des Remarques* (Paris, 1776), pp. xxviii (sagesse) and 116 (peine de la vie).

11 *A Prosaic Translation of Aulus Persius Flaccus's Six Satyrs* (1719; n. 1 above), p. 15n. Subsequent citations from Eelbeck are given in the text.

12 CE, vol. 4, *Poems, 1693–1696*, ed. A. B. Chambers, William Frost, Vinton A. Dearing (Berkeley and Los Angeles: Univ. of California Press, 1974), p. 255.

13 *The Satires of Persius*, 2nd ed. (London, 1739), pp. 6, 60.

14 Abbé de la Valterie, trans., *Les Satyres de Juvénal et de Perse* (Paris, 1680), 2:sig. Liii^r. The translation of Persius is dedicated to Boileau.

15 *The Satires of Persius paraphrastically imitated* (n. 3 above), pp. xxvii–xxviii.

16 *The Satires of Aulus Persius Flaccus* (n. 2 above), p. xvi. Subsequent citations from this edition are given in the text.

17 *Something like Horace: Studies in the Art and Allusion of Pope's Horatian Satires* (Nashville, Tenn: Vanderbilt Univ. Press, 1969), p. 6. Aden also observes that in this respect "Pope more nearly resembles [Persius] than he does either Horace, whom he ostensibly imitates, or Juvenal, with whom he has very little in common at all" (p. 7).

18 *The Satires of A. Persius Flaccus* (n. 2 above), p. xvii. Subsequent references are cited in the text.

19 *The Satyrs of Persius* (n. 2 above), p. 19. Subsequent citations are given in the text.

20 The translation is from the Loeb Classical Library, *Juvenal and Persius*, trans. G. G. Ramsay (London and Cambridge, Mass.: William Heinemann and Harvard Univ. Press, 1961), p. 327. Dryden's version is "All, all is admirably well for me" (*Poems, 1693–1696*, n. 12 above, p. 273). Sheridan is slightly more expansive and, perhaps unexpectedly, energetic: "Why then, let their Geese be all Swans for me – I shall not dispute it – Every thing is fine – It is all admirable." *Persius* (n. 2 above), p. 23. Quotations from Persius' Latin are from *D. Junii Juvenalis, et A. Persii Flacci Satirae*, ed. Ludovicus Prateus, 7th ed. (London, 1736).

21 For Holyday, see *Decimus Junius Juvenalis, and Aulus Persius Flaccus Translated and Illustrated* (Oxford, 1673), p. 341, "An Apostrophe of the Translator to his Authour Persius." For

F. A., see *The Third Satyr of A. Persius* (n. 3 above), p. 3.

22 Scaliger, *Poetices Libri Septem* (Lyons, 1561), p. 323. ("Persii vero stilus, morosus"); Rapin, *Reflections on Aristotle's Treatise of Poesie* [trans. Thomas Rymer] (London, 1674), p. 139; Boileau, *Oeuvres de M. Boileau Despréaux*, ed. M. de Saint-Marc (Paris, 1747), 1:116; Batteux, Abbot Charles Batteux, *A Course of the Belles Lettres: or, the Principles of Literature. Translated from the French . . . by Mr. Miller* (London, 1761), 3:155; *Encyclopédie, ou Dictionnaire raisonné* (Neufchâtel, 1765), 14:701, "Satyre." The article is by the Chevalier de Jaucourt, and includes the "Parallèle des satyriques romains & françois" by Batteux (see Miller's translation, 3:192–95, which substitutes Dryden and Young for the French satirists); Greene, *The Satires of Persius*, p. xxxiv.

23 As one important citation of Burnet's remark in his *Discourse of the Pastoral Care* (1692), pp. 162–63, see Dryden's "Discourse concerning the Original and Progress of Satire," prefatory to Juvenal and Persius of 1693, in *Poems, 1693–1696*, p. 56. Burnet singles out Persius' second satire. His judgment appears as late as 1789 in Martin Madan's *Juvenal and Persius* (n. 2 above), 1:4. Jaffray, *An Essay for Illustrating the Roman Poets for the Use of Schools* (Edinburgh, 1705), p. 11. Le Noble, *Satires de Perse traduites en vers François* (Amsterdam, 1706), sig. *5ʳ. This is one of the three ways in which Persius is preferable to Horace or Juvenal. But all are "admirables dans leurs manières & exelens dans leurs genres" (sigs. *4ᵛ–5ʳ).

24 *Observations on the Greek and Roman Classics. In a Series of Letters to a Young Nobleman* (London, 1753), pp. 261–62. In the "Inspector," No. 136, Hill refers to Persius' "one continued insulting sneer" (*The Inspector* [London, 1753], 2:254). See also Dryden's "Discourse," where Persius "rather insulted over Vice and Folly, than expos'd them, like *Juvenal* and *Horace*" (*Poems, 1693–1696*, p. 52).

25 *The Progress of Satire* (London, 1798), p. 8. This poem is reprinted in Boscawen's *Poems* (London, 1801). The association of Persius and Juvenal – with full awareness of differences as well – was familiar. See, for example, [William Combe's?] *Belphegor. The Diabo-Lady. Or, A Match in Hell* (London, 1777). The author claims that he is Juvenalian (sig. A1ᵛ); the "editor," however, adds that "we are of the opinion that he more resembles *Persius*; whose writings are both more severe and obscure" (sig. a3ʳ).

26 F. A., *The Third Satyr of A. Persius*, pp. 3, 4.

27 Robert Halsband states that this poem was "composed by Hervey during the 1720s," and was published in 1730 and 1739. I have not seen the 1730 version, and quote from that of London, 1739. The "Christian stoic point of view," according to Halsband, "is not characteristic of his thinking" (*Lord Hervey, Eighteenth-Century Courtier* [New York: Oxford Univ. Press, 1974], p. 325, n. 38).

28 Pope often was invoked by other satirists as the lonely warrier defending decency against its powerful enemies. The "patriot" author of *The Wrongheads. A Poem. Inscrib'd to Mr. Pope. By a Person of Quality* (London, 1733), for instance, asks and answers his own indignant question:

> Shall knaves and fools commend the world's applause,
> And censure 'scape, because they 'scape the laws?
> No – *Pope* forbids, and fir'd with honest rage,
> Resolves to mend, as well as charm the age;
> Nor fears the cause of virtue to defend,
> Nor blushes to confess himself her friend. (p. 3)

See also Paul Whitehead, *The State Dunces. Inscrib'd to Mr. Pope* (London, 1733), pp. 2–5, Thomas Gilbert, *A View of the Town* (London, 1735), p. 18, and Whitehead's (?) *State of Rome Under Nero and Domitian*, above. The attribution to Whitehead is questioned by David Foxon, in *English Verse, 1701–1750* (Cambridge: Cambridge Univ. Press, 1975), 2:755.

29 For further discussion of Pope and Augustus, see Howard D. Weinbrot, *Augustus Caesar*

in "Augustan" England: The Decline of a Classical Norm (Princeton: Princeton Univ. Press, 1978), pp. 137-41, 182-217.

30 All line references are from the Twickenham Edition of the Poems of Alexander Pope. To avoid excessively complex annotations, I have cited all of the allusions by means of the specific volume of the Twickenham Edition (TE), where the source of the discovery may also be found. The pastoral "Summer" line 75, alludes to Persius II.78 (TE, 1:77). Allusions to Persius' Prologue appear in the "Messiah" (1712), line 4 (*Prol.* 2-3; TE, 1:112), and the *Dunciad* of 1743, 1.304 (*Prol.* 6; TE, 5:291). Allusions to Satire I, are in the *Essays on Criticism* (1711), line 17 (Dryden's Persius, 1.110; TE, 1:241) and line 337 (1.63-66, TE 1:276), "Essay on Homer" (1.4; TE, 7:62), and the *Iliad*, IV.55 (1.4-5, 50-51; TE, 7:223, where Pope also mentions the commentary of the old scholiast on Persius). Allusions to Satire III are in the *Dunciad* of 1743, 4:151 (III.56; TE, 5:356), and the *Iliad*, XIX.209 (III.105; TE, 8:381).

31 For the remarks in letters, see *The Correspondence of Alexander Pope*, ed. George Sherburn (Oxford: Clarendon Press, 1956), 1:99 (to Cromwell); 2:231 (to Broome); 2:523 (to Sheridan); and 3:420 (to Arbuthnot). For the remarks in 1739 and 1742, see Joseph Spence, *Observations, Anecdotes, and Characters of Books and Men*, ed. James M. Osborn (Oxford: Clarendon Press, 1966), 1:228 (No. 540), and 1:150 (No. 336).

32 Both William Gifford and G. G. Ramsay use Pope's words to describe Cornutus' relationship with his pupil. See Gifford's Persius of 1817 (n. 2 above), p. xv, and Ramsay's Juvenal and Persius (n. 20), p. xxiii.

33 For examples of such practice, see the imitations of Persius and *The State of Rome Under Nero and Domitian*, discussed above. See also Maynard Mack's *The Garden and the City: Retirement and Politics in the Later Poetry of Pope, 1731-1743* (Toronto: Univ. of Toronto Press, 1969), pp. 166-67, 180 n. 4.

34 *The Satires of Persius Translated into English Verse*, 2nd ed. (London, 1751), pp. 5-6. Someone, perhaps an eighteenth-century reader, has tried to erase "By A. Pope" from the title page of the 1741 edition in the Princeton University Library.

35 *The First Satire of the Second Book of Horace Imitated* (1733), in TE, vol. 4, *Imitations of Horace*, ed. John Butt, 2nd ed. corr. (London and New Haven: Methuen and Yale Univ. Press, 1961), pp. 15 (lines 101-4), 19 (lines 145-46). Quotations from the *Epistle to Dr. Arbuthnot* (1735) and *One Thousand Seven Hundred and Thirty Eight* also are from this edition. For a comment on the association of "Richard" and George II, see Mack, *Garden and the City*, p. 140.

36 Compare Benjamin Loveling's passage from his *First Satire of Persius Imitated* of 1740:

> Well, well, I've done; my Muse correct thy Lays,
> All, all have Virtues, and let all have Praise:
> Sir *W—l—* in Senate shines for Freedom bold,
> *P—* has a strong Antipathy to Gold;
> *Horace* each Gift of Nature and of Art,
> And *R—d* Sense, and *G—ch* an honest Heart.
>   Peace, Peace, ye wicked Wits, imagine here
> A Messenger, a special Jury there;
> Let Sense and Goodness both attend on State,
> Nor charge one Vice or Folly on the Great.   (p. 17)

37 Pope himself glosses line 72 of *Arbuthnot*: "The Story is told by some [*Ovid Met.* XI.146 and Persius *Sat.* 1.121] of his Barber, but by *Chaucer* of his Queen. See Wife of Bath's Tale in *Dryden*'s Fables [lines 157-200]." The information in brackets is John Butt's. Dryden also clarifies the allusion in his own Persius, where we see that "by *Midas*, the Poet meant *Nero*" (*Poems, 1693-1696*, p. 279n). Dryden is following Casaubon, p. 664 n. 240. See also Prateus, *D. Junii Juvenalis, et A. Persii Flacci Satirae*, p. 324n, on *Auriculas asini, Mida rex habet*; Prateus adopts "Casaubonus, Lubinus & alii."

38 Pope apparently assumes such recollection of the myth in *The Dunciad* of 1743 when he has Settle happily proclaim of Cibber: "See, see, our own true Phoebus wears the bays! / Our Midas sits Lord Chancellor of Plays" (3:323–24) (TE, vol. 5, *The Dunciad*, ed. James Sutherland, 3rd ed. [London, and New Haven: Methuen and Yale Univ. Press, 1963], p. 335).

39 *The Garden and the City*, p. 130; see also p. 138, and "An Essay on Kicking" there mentioned. For the context of *Fog's Weekly Journal*, see Weinbrot, *Augustus Caesar in "Augustan" England*, pp. 111–12. The remark regarding the "audacious parallel" is written on the British Library's Burney Collection copy.

40 At one point Pope made his meaning behind line 71 – "His very Minister who spy'd them first" – even more overt. The Huntington Library owns Jonathan Richardson, Jr.'s, transcription of several of Pope's manuscript versions to his own set of Pope's 1735 *Works*. Page 61 of that *Arbuthnot* (HEH 6009) includes an illuminating annotation, in Richardson's hand: "Depressis scrobibus vitium regale *minister* / Credidit. Auson. Paulino xx[v] iii. 18." Pope probably thought the citation too bold and dropped it.

41 *Oeuvres de Boileau*. Texte de l'édition Gidel, Notes and Preface by Georges Mongrédien (Paris: Editions Garnier Frères, 1952), p. 64, line 224. Boileau is of course not attacking Louis XIV but Chapelain as king of his literary enemies. Pope may be looking at Boileau through English spectacles. Compare this section from the 1712 translation of Boileau's ninth satire, with Pope's Midas-section in *Arbuthnot*. This "Boileau" provides Midas, the choleric tone, and the ineffectual satirist, adopted at different places in *Fortescue*, *Arbuthnot* and parts of *One Thousand Seven Hundred and Thirty Eight*:

> When his pretended Right [to high poetic praise] some Fools proclaim,
> My Choler with Disdain is in a Flame,
> And if I durst not vent my raging Spleen,
> Or tell the World my Grievance with my Pen,
> Like the fam'd Barber I shou'd dig a Hole,
> And there discharge the Burthen of my Soul.
> There whisper to the Reeds that *Midas* wears
> Beneath his Royal Crown an Asses Ears.
> What hurt has my impartial Satire done?
> Its talent is not baulkt, it labours on;
> *Folio*'s on *Folio*'s still are brought to light,
> And *L—s* Garret's groan beneath the Weight. (*The Works of Mons. Boileau. Made English from the last Paris Edition By Several Hands*, 2nd ed. [London, 1736], 1:244–45)

42 *Idée de la Poësie Angloise, ou Traduction des Meilleurs Poëtes Angloises* (Paris), 3:96–97 (*Arbuthnot*), 239 (*To a Lady*).

43 *A New and Literal Translation of . . . Persius* (n. 2 above), 2:3 of the unnumbered Preface.

11. Johnson's *London* and Juvenal's Third Satire

1 For some of the relevant works, see Edward A. and Lillian D. Bloom, "Johnson's *London* and Its Juvenalian Texts," *HLQ* 34 (1970):1–23; "Johnson's *London* and the Tools of Scholarship," ibid. 34 (1971):115–39; and "Johnson's 'Mournful Narrative': The Rhetoric of *London*," in *Eighteenth-Century Studies in Honor of Donald F. Hyde*, ed. W. H. Bond (New York: The Grolier Club, 1970), pp. 107–44; Howard D. Weinbrot, *The Formal Strain: Studies in Augustan Imitation and Satire* (Chicago: Univ. of Chicago Press, 1969), pp. 165–91; Donald J. Greene, *The Politics of Samuel Johnson* (New Haven, Conn.: Yale Univ. Press, 1960), pp. 81–111; D. V. Boyd, "Vanity and Vacuity: A Reading of Johnson's Verse Satires," *ELH* 39 (1972): 387–403.

2 For a recent discussion of several pitfalls in the way of reading imitations, see William

Kupersmith, "Pope, Horace and the Critics: Some Reconsiderations," *Arion* 9 (1970):205–19.

3 Mary Lascelles, in *New Light on Dr. Johnson*, ed. Frederick W. Hilles (New Haven, Conn.: Yale Univ. Press, 1959), pp. 41–42.

4 Ibid., pp. 42–44. Lascelles apparently assumes that Johnson read the third satire for the first time, or reread it with new spectacles, while in London during 1737–38. In fact he took "Dryden's Juvenal" with him to Oxford in 1728, and had it with him in 1735 (see Allen Lyell Reade, *Johnsonian Gleanings* [London: Privately printed for the author by Percy Lund, 1928] 5:225, 115; *The Letters of Samuel Johnson*, ed. R. W. Chapman [Oxford: Clarendon Press, 1952], 1:4–6; James L. Clifford, *Young Sam Johnson* [New York: McGraw-Hill, 1955], pp. 156–57). The rest of this paper deals with the likelihood of Johnson's myopia. Moreover, Lascelles is probably mistaken in regarding Juvenal's towns as insignificant, cold, dull, and desolate. Aquinum, Baiae, Gabii, Cumae, Fabrateria, Frusino, Praeneste, Sora, Tivoli, and Volsinii were either towns of great beauty, of minor but real commercial, agricultural, or vinicultural distinction, or of religious or historical importance. This information has been gathered in William Smith's *Dictionary of Greek and Roman Geography* (London, 1854). Some of the same information would have been available to Johnson in Strabo, Stephanus' *Dictionarium historicum, geographicum, poeticum* (1561), and Louis Moréri's *Grand dictionnaire historique* (1674).

5 *New Light on Dr. Johnson*, p. 46.

6 John Hardy, "Johnson's *London*: The Country versus the City," in *Studies in the Eighteenth Century: Papers Presented at the David Nichol Smith Memorial Seminar, Canberra 1966*, ed. R. F. Brissenden (Toronto: Univ. of Toronto Press, 1968), pp. 253, 258.

7 William Kupersmith, "Declamatory Grandeur: Johnson and Juvenal," *Arion* 9 (1970): 58, n. 5. This is an otherwise valuable essay. Ian Donaldson, "The Satirists' London," *EIC* 25 (1975):106–22.

8 William S. Anderson, "Studies in Book 1 of Juvenal," in *Yale Classical Studies*, ed. Harry M. Hubbel, 15 (New Haven, Conn: Yale Univ. Press, 1957):57–63. Anderson also mentions the manuscript titles of the poem: "De urbis incommodis et de digressu Umbricii," and "Quare Umbricius urbem deserat" (p. 56, n. 29). For further useful discussion of Juvenal's satire (along the nonironic lines suggested), see Anna Lydia Motto and John R. Clark, "*Per iter tenebricosum*: The Mythos of Juvenal 3," *Transactions of the American Philological Association* 96 (1965): 265–76, and William S. Anderson, "*Lascivia* vs. *ira*: Martial and Juvenal," *California Studies in Classical Antiquity* 3 (1970):1–34.

9 See *The Formal Strain*, pp. 181–89. It is also suggested by his probable knowledge of Barten Holyday's "Argument" to his translation of the Third Satire. Since "No place for Honest men is left . . . / *Umbritius* then from *Rome* departs, / Because he wants the *Roman* Arts" (*Decimus Junius Juvenalis and Aulus Persius Flaccus* [Oxford, 1673], p. 36). Of course it is also suggested in the poem itself, especially at line 119 where, according to Holyday, "No place / Is for a *Roman* left at *Rome*" (p. 39).

10 *The Satires of Decimus Junius Juvenalis*, 3rd ed. (London, 1702), pp. 238–39. Subsequent quotations are from this edition and are cited in the text.

11 Johnson uses lines 5–8, above, as the illustrative quotation for the noun "Mark" in the *Dictionary* (1755). Basil Kennett cites much of the final paragraph as an example of Roman "Panegyricks upon the honest People of the first Ages of the Commonwealth" (*Romae Antiquae Notitia* [London, 1696], p. 63).

12 Martin Madan, *A New and Literal Translation of Juvenal and Persius* (London, 1789), 1:137–39. Samuel Derrick's extremely scarce *The Third Satire of Juvenal Translated into English Verse* (London, 1755), pp. 15–16, describes comparable "rural joys" (p. 15). Thomas Sheridan's prose translation of 1739 (reprinted 1745, 1769, 1777) also is faithful to a similar vision.

13 All Latin quotations from the third satire are from *D. Junii Juvenalis, et A. Persii Flacci Satirae*, ed. Ludovicus Prateus, 7th ed. (London, 1736). As the Blooms have shown in "Johnson's *London* and Its Juvenalian Texts" (see n. 1), this was the text (but not necessarily this reprint) which Johnson knew best, though the annotations of Schrevelius were more influential.

14 For a brief statement regarding "The Duties of a 'Client'" in Juvenal's Rome, see Jérôme Carcopino, *Daily Life in Ancient Rome*, trans. E. O. Lorimer (London: George Routledge & Sons, 1946), pp. 171–73.

15 "Introducitque Umbritium haruspicem sui temporis amicum suum, parentem ob pravitatem morum ab Urbe discedere: cui ad notanda vitia dat partes suas. Ait ergo Poeta: Quamvis non possim non commoveri, quod amicus meus Umbritius ab Urbe discedat, tamen habita discessus ratione laudo ejus consilium, quod relicta urbe Roma, statuat migrare Cumas." As quoted in *D. Junii Juvenalis . . . Satyrae*, ed. Henricus Christianus Henninius (Utrecht, 1685), p. 455.

16 *D. Junii Juvenalis et Auli Persii Flacci Satyrae*, ed. Cornelius Schrevelius (Leyden, 1671), p. 56.

17 Prateus' "Interpretatio," a prose gloss in simpler Latin, reinforces the meaning of the lines and of the commentary (see pp. 37–38 and 56–57).

18 "Ex urbe migrans quocunque te receperis, optimum putato domicilium, ubi tuam habeas domum & hortum tam exiguum, ut vix una ipsum discurrat lacerta. *Lubin*" (Schrevelius, *Junii Juvenalis . . . Satyrae*, p. 89).

19 *The Works of Mr. John Oldham, Together with His Remains* (London, 1686; new pagination and title page for *Poems and Translations. By the Author of The Satyrs upon the Jesuits* [London, 1684], p. 199).

20 Edward Burnaby Greene, *The Satires of Juvenal Paraphrastically Imitated, And Adapted to the Times* (London, 1763), pp. 33–34. On August 18, 1763 Gibbon records his initiation to the third satire, and praises it without mentioning irony. By 16 September he had read the fourteenth satire as well and was impressed with the simple country scene (described above) ("Extraits de mon journal," in *Miscellaneous Works*, ed. John, Lord Sheffield [London, 1796], 2:95–96, 113).

21 Madan, 1:138; I. and M. Casaubon (with J. C. Scaliger and H. C. Henninius), *D. J. Juvenalis Satyrae . . . accedit Auli Persi Flacci* (Leyden, 1695), p. 908, n. 231; Sir William Smith, *A Smaller Latin-English Dictionary*, rev. J. F. Lockwood (London: John Murray, 1962 [1st ed., London, 1855]). The illustrative or "iconographic" evidence also supports the conservative view of Cumae as a place for one's retreat. The illustration in Holyday's *Juvenal* (facing p. 47) shows a pleasant coast, groves, roads, and different structures, including theaters, homes, and military camps, on the way to Cumae. Holyday tells us that this "Baian prospect and delight" is from "Bertellius in his Theater of the Italian Cities" (p. 44). The illustration to Dryden's *Juvenal* is more eloquent, if less pleasant (facing p. 30; 3rd ed., 1702): the walls of Rome are in the background and Umbritius and Juvenal, at the edge of the Tiber, are in the foreground. Behind them is the once sacred grove of Numa in which, from left to right, we see a rape, the untended altar of the god overgrown with weeds, Jewish merchants plying their wares, and one of the sacred trees being chopped down. Behind Umbritius and Juvenal are the farmer's two horses being whipped forward by the servant and a cart which holds two children and a variety of personal effects, including what may be the household gods.

22 Boileau, *Satires de Perse et de Juvénal. Expliquées, traduites et commentées par Boileau, publiées d'après le manuscrit autographe, par L. Parrelle* (Paris, 1827), 1:169 (see also *Les Satires de Boileau commentées par lui-même et publiées avec des notes par Frédéric Lachèvre" Reproduction du commentaire inédit de Pierre Le Verrier avec les corrections autographes de Despréaux* [Courménil, 1906], p. 55). Bossuet, among others, seconded Boileau's interpretation. In 1684 he

commented upon the satires of Juvenal and Persius for the benefit of the Grand Dauphin of France. He glosses "vacuis" (line 2) in this way: "C'est a dire que Cumes est une ville vuide des desordres et des embarras de Rome; c'est une raison fort bone qui oblige Umbritius d'y aller habiter." And he says of the lizard (line 231): "être le maitre de quelque chose; on dit encore *unius vermiculi*" (see *Oeuvres inédites de J.-B. Bossuet. . . . Tome 1: Le Cours royal complet sur Juvénal*, ed. Auguste-Louis Ménard [Paris, 1881], pp. 81, 100). The translations by Martignac (Paris, 1683), Tarteron (Paris, 1695), and Dusaulx (Paris, 1770; 2nd ed. 1782; 3rd ed. 1789) are silent regarding irony.

23 *Oeuvres de Boileau Despréaux*, ed. M. de Saint-Marc (Amsterdam, 1772), 1:14. Italics and roman type are inverted in the text.

24 For a convenient gathering of further comments in Latin, see the Casaubon edition (n. 21 above) and its "Cento variorum." For other translations and comments in English see *Juvenal's Sixteen Satyrs*, trans. Sir Robert Stapylton (London, 1673); [Thomas Sheridan], *Satires of Juvenal . . . With . . . Notes, Relating to the Laws and Customs of the Greeks and Romans* (London, 1739); *The Satires of Decimus Junius Juvenalis*, trans. William Gifford (London, 1802), (Gifford's Juvenal was reprinted in Philadelphia in 2 vols. in 1803); *Satires of Decimus Junius Juvenalis*, trans. Rev. William Heath Marsh (London, 1804); *A New Translation with Notes, of the Third Satire of Juvenal*, trans. John Duer (New York, 1806); *The Satires of Juvenal*, trans. Francis Hodgson (London, 1807). The relevant commentary concerns the opening of the poem and the main country passage, especially lines 229 and 231. Other translators – Edward Owen in 1785, for example – say nothing, presumably because they regard the lines as clear enough without their gloss. Hodgson (pp. 32, 376–77) believes that Juvenal himself wishes to stay in Rome; but he does not attribute irony to Juvenal – simply a tolerance for the needs of his less literary friend.

25 YE, vol. 6, *Poems*, ed. E. L. McAdam, Jr., with George Milne (New Haven, Conn.: Yale Univ. Press, 1964):50. Subsequent quotations are from this text.

26 *Poems*, p. 48, n. 5.

27 A. D. Moody, "The Creative Critic: Johnson's Revisions of *London* and *The Vanity of Human Wishes*," *RES* n.s. 22 (1971):140–41.

28 *Boswell's Life of Johnson*, ed. George Birkbeck Hill, rev. L. F. Powell (Oxford: Clarendon Press, 1934–50), 1:324–25. Subsequent quotations are from this edition.

29 For some of these interpretive squabbles, see Casaubon, p. 908; Gifford, pp. 97–98; Hodgson, p. 380. Boswell's final remark is justified.

12. No "Mock Debate"

1 As quoted in Thomas Gibbons, *Rhetoric; or, A View of its Principal Tropes and Figures* (London, 1767), p. 187. Gibbons is considering the rhetorical figure erotesis, "by which we express the emotion of our minds, and infuse an ardor and energy into our discourses, by proposing questions" (p. 176).

2 For the 1738 remarks, see Samuel Johnson, "Examination of a Question Proposed in the [Gentleman's] Magazine of June, p. 310," YE, vol. 10, *Political Writings*, ed. Donald J. Greene (New Haven: Yale University Press, 1977), pp. 9–10. The essay is an attribution – but a generally accepted one. Unless otherwise specified, quotations from Johnson's works are from the Yale Edition. For the *Preceptor*, see *The Works of Samuel Johnson, LL.D* (Oxford, 1825), 5:237–38. Subsequent references from this edition will be cited in the text as *Works*. The definition is quoted from Johnson's *Dictionary of the English Language* (London, 1755), as are subsequent citations. Bacon's other remark is in *The Essays . . . of Francis Lo. Vervlam* (London, 1625), p. 196.

3 *A Philosophical Enquiry into the Origin of our Ideas of the Sublime and Beautiful*, ed. J. T. Boulton (London: Routledge & Kegan Paul, 1958), pp. 12–13. Compare Johnson's remark in the Preface to *Shakespeare* (1765): "it is natural to delight more in what we find

or make, than in what we receive" (*Johnson on Shakespeare*, ed. Arthur Sherbo [New Haven: Yale Univ. Press, 1968], p. 104). For further discussion of such reader-involvement in authorial invention, see Howard D. Weinbrot. "The Reader, the General, and the Particular: Johnson and Imlac in Chapter Ten of *Rasselas*," *ECS* 5 (1971):86–96; and Eric Rothstein, "'Ideal Presence' and the 'Non Finito' in Eighteenth-Century Aesthetics," *ECS* 9 (1976):307–32.

4 Quotations are from Samuel Johnson, YE, vol. 6, *Poems*, ed. E. L. McAdam, Jr., with George Milne (New Haven: Yale Univ. Press, 1964). I should add that the questions also appear, in varying quantity and quality, in all the other seventeenth- and eighteenth-century imitations and translations of Juvenal's tenth satire.

5 Lawrence Lipking, "Learning to Read Johnson: *The Vision of Theodore* and *The Vanity of Human Wishes*," *ELH* 43 (1976):532. There have been several useful discussions of the *Vanity* in recent years. For some of these, see Walter Jackson Bate, "Johnson and Satire Manqué," in *Eighteenth-Century Studies in Honor of Donald F. Hyde*, ed. W. H. Bond (New York: Grolier Club, 1970), pp. 145–60; Donald Greene, *Samuel Johnson* (New York: Twayne, 1970), pp. 56–63; William Kupersmith, "Declamatory Grandeur: Johnson and Juvenal," *Arion* 9 (1970):52–72; R. Selden, "Dr. Johnson and Juvenal: A Problem in Critical Method," *CL* 22 (1970):289–302; D. V. Boyd, "Vanity and Vacuity: A Reading of Johnson's Verse Satires," *ELH* 39 (1972):387–403; William Kupersmith, "'More like an Orator than a Philosopher': Rhetorical Structure in *The Vanity of Human Wishes*," *SP* 72 (1975):454–72; and John E. Sitter, "To *The Vanity of Human Wishes* through the 1740's," *SP* 74 (1977):445–64.

6 William Henry Hall observes that satire may be more effective in "the cause of religion and virtue than a sermon; since it gives pleasure, at the same time that it creates fear or indignation." To induce pleasure, "The satirist should always preserve good humour; and however keen he cuts, should cut with kindness" ("Satire," *The New Royal Encyclopaedia* [London, 1789]).

7 As quoted in Gibbon's *Rhetoric*, p. 188. For the full context, see "A Paraphrase on Part of the Book of Job," *The Works of Dr. Edward Young* (London, 1783), 4:108, where Young also observes that "*Longinus* has a chapter on interrogations" – that is section 18 in modern editions.

8 See, for example, Henry Gifford, "*The Vanity of Human Wishes*," *RES* n.s. 6 (1955): 158; and Patrick O'Flaherty, "Johnson as Satirist: A New Look at *The Vanity of Human Wishes*," *ELH* 34 (1967): 83–84, 86–87. Bruce King, however, is more accurate in his "Late Augustan, Early Modern," *SR* 76 (1968):139–42. See also Howard D. Weinbrot, *The Formal Strain: Studies in Augustan Imitation and Satire* (Chicago: Univ. of Chicago Press, 1969), pp. 199–200.

9 D. E. Eichholz offers a helpful discussion of Democritus' scorn in "The Art of Juvenal and his Tenth *Satire*," *Greece and Rome*, 2nd ser., 3 (1956):61–69. For Epicurus, see Thomas F. Mayo, *Epicurus in England, 1650–1725* (n.p.: Southwest Press, 1934). The common association of Democritus with Epicurus was made by Ludovicus Prateus in his *D. Junii Juvenalis et A. Persii Flacci Satirae*, 7th ed. (London, 1736), p. 200, note to line 34. Subsequent quotations are from this text, which Johnson knew well. Annotated editions of Juvenal and of Horace (*Epistles*, I.xii.12) offered glosses and relevant biographical information regarding Democritus. Standard reference works like Louis Moréri's *Grand Dictionnaire historique* (Lyons, 1674), Pierre Bayle's *Dictionnaire historique et critique* (Rotterdam, 1697), and Thomas Stanley's *History of Philosophy*, 2nd ed. (London, 1687) offered more abundant information. The quotation above, regarding man as diseased, is from Stanley, p. 760. Humphrey Prideaux discusses Democritus' "wholly ... atheistical scheme" in *The Old and New Testament Connected ...*, 3rd ed. (London, 1717), 1:323. I am indebted to Mrs. Joanne Murphy for some of these, and several other, contemporary references to Democritus.

10 Johnson uses this method of question and delayed answer by the reader with Swedish Charles as well (lines 191–92). The device was a familiar one, and also appears in Pope's *Epistle to Bathurst* (1733), lines 335–36, and its answer in the tale of Balaam. Randall Minshull (?) also uses questions to involve and to implicate the reader in *The Miser, A Poem: From the First Satire of the First Book of Horace* (London, 1735). Here the speaker asks the smug reader: "What – Why dost laugh? but only change the name, / The Fable [of Tantalus] proves thy self the very same" (p. 19). See also two remarks on Persius' use of questions in Edmund Burton, *The Satyrs of Persius* (London, 1752), p. 32; and Vicesimus Knox, *Essays Moral and Literary* (London, 1778), 2:151.

11 "Glance" here probably has the third meaning of the noun, "A snatch of sight; a quick view" (*Dictionary*). The illustrative quotation is favorable: "The ample mind takes a survey of several objects with one *glance. Watts's Improvement of the Mind*"; but the context of the poem and other definitions in the *Dictionary* suggest negative use here. The courtiers of Henry VIII, for example, "Mark the keen glance, and watch the sign to hate" Wolsey (line 110). The word there connotes the fourth or fifth definitions of the verb, from the noun, "To view with a quick cast of the eye; to play the eye," and "To censure by oblique hints." Bacon's illustration of the last meaning suggests the hostility of such glancing already seen in the language describing Democritus: "Some men *glance* and dart at others, by justifying themselvs by negatives; as to say, this I do not." The lines also associate Democritus with the destructive qualities of hostile Fate, who "wings with ev'ry wish th' afflictive dart" (line 15).

Moreover, Johnson had already dissociated his speaker from even the hint of superficiality. At line 2 of the *Vanity* he invites us to "Survey mankind, from China to Peru." The first word had originally been written "O'erlook" in the manuscript, and was no doubt corrected because of its denotations of "5. To pass by indulgently . . . 6. To neglect; to slight" (*Dictionary*). For further discussion of Johnson's changes from manuscript to printed version, see A. D. Moody, "The Creative Critic: Johnson's Revisions of *London* and *The Vanity of Human Wishes*," *RES* n.s. 22 (1971):137–50.

12 Rejection of such mockery would have been familiar, as Edward Young's remarks in the Preface to *Love of Fame* suggest: "Some Satyrical Wits, and Humorists, like their Father *Lucian*, laugh at every thing indiscriminately; which betrays such a poverty of wit, as cannot afford to part with any thing; and such a want of virtue, as to postpone it to a jest. Such writers encourage Vice and Folly, which they pretend to combat, by setting them on an equal foot with better things: And while they labour to bring every thing into contempt, how can they expect their own parts should escape?" (2nd ed. [London, 1728], sig. a1ᵛ.

13 Samuel Johnson, YE, vol. 14, *Sermons*, ed. Jean Hagstrum and James Gray (New Haven: Yale Univ. Press, 1978), pp. 262, 267, 268; subsequent references are cited as *Sermons*. For further discussion of Johnson's sermons and some of their major themes, see Paul K. Alkon, *Samuel Johnson and Moral Discipline* (Evanston, Ill.: Northwestern Univ. Press, 1967), pp. 51–53, 191–209; and James Gray, *Johnson's Sermons: A Study* (Oxford: Clarendon Press, 1972). The sermons and the *Vanity* are of course different works in different genres at different times; but Gray is correct in saying that in the sermons Johnson "stuck to his own beliefs and staunchly defended his own orthodoxy" (p. 185; see also p. 186). Many other remarks in the sermons are valuable as glosses to the *Vanity*; see, for example, Johnson's discussion of charity, pity, and courtesy in Sermon 11 (*Sermons*, pp. 123, 125). Furthermore, the distinction between inefficacious philosophy and friendly religion was so commonplace that even Fielding's misguided Man of the Hill could understand and use it; see *The History of Tom Jones*, ed. Martin C. Battestin and Fredson Bowers (Middletown, Conn.: Wesleyan Univ. Press, 1975), Book 8, chap. 13 (pp. 470–71 and p. 470, n. 1).

14 See the *Spectator*, ed. Donald Bond (Oxford: Clarendon Press, 1965), 2:205–6. James H.

Sledd and Gwin J. Kolb note Johnson's completed reading for the *Dictionary* in *Dr. Johnson's "Dictionary": Essays in the Biography of a Book* (Chicago: Univ. of Chicago Press, 1955), p. 107; for the time of the writing of the *Vanity*, see *Poems*, p. 90.

15 See *The Formal Strain*, p. 168 and p. 168, n. 10.

16 *Boswell's Life of Johnson*, ed. George Birkbeck Hill, rev. L. F. Powell (Oxford: Clarendon Press, 1934–50), 3:265–66. For some of Johnson's comments on questions, and Boswell as annoying questioner, see 2:472; and 3:57, 268.

17 Charles, even more than the reader, has lost control in his narcissistic attraction to himself and his deadly way of life: "War sounds the trump, he rushes to the field" (line 198). Johnson also may be playing on the other, nonmusical meaning of trump: "A winning card; a card that has particular privileges in a game" (*Dictionary*).

18 See also Johnson's Preface to the *Preceptor*: "To counteract the power of temptations, hope must be excited by the prospect of rewards, and fear by the expectation of punishment; and virtue may owe her panegyricks to morality, but must derive her authority from religion" (*Works*, 5.244).

19 Much of the rest of this sermon, on Ecclesiastes 1:14, provides a gloss on what Johnson means by the vanity of human wishes; see *Sermons*, pp. 129–30.

20 The narrator's changing but respectful, collaborative, if pedagogical, relationship with the reader is well illustrated in his use of *thee*, *thou*, and *thy* when addressing us. By 1749 *thou* had long passed out of common speech; it was indeed considered insulting "to thou" someone who was not an intimate. But there were exceptions, and some more important than those for Quakers, pets, and abstractions. *Thou*, Johnson said in his *Dictionary*, "is used only in very familiar or very solemn language. When we speak to equals or superiors we say *you*; but in solemn language, and in addresses of worship, we say *thou*." The tones of the *Vanity*'s "thou" change from the familiar, as in "Does envy seize thee?" (line 39), to the solemn, as in "Pour forth thy fervours for a healthful mind" (line 359).

21 CE, vol. 4, *Poems, 1693–1696*, ed. A. B. Chambers, William Frost, and Vinton A. Dearing (Berkeley and Los Angeles: Univ. of California Press, 1974), pp. 221, 223. Johnson refers to Juvenal's "grandeur" in *Lives of the English Poets*, ed. George Birkbeck Hill (Oxford: Clarendon Press, 1905), 1:447.

22 Immediately thereafter, as if in contradiction to the Democritean spirit, he adds: "To gain affection, and to preserve concord, it is necessary not only to mourn with those that mourn, but to rejoice with them that rejoice."

23 The passage quoted in fact embodies Johnson's own views on the relation of learning to religion, and of even the best secular moral writing, to gospel itself. "The Vision" was printed with Dodsley's *Preceptor* as one of three examples which caution the young student "against the danger of indulging his passions, of vitiating his habits, and depraving his sentiments . . . But at this he is not to rest; for if he expects to be wise and happy, he must diligently study the Scriptures of God" (Preface to the *Preceptor*, in *Works*, 5:245). This Preface, written in April 1748, also includes a reason (over and above the Juvenalian parallels) for the several historical characters in the poem, a reason based on the questioning nature of the human mind; see *Works*, 5:239, regarding "inquiries which history alone can satisfy."

24 *A Poetical Translation of the Elegies of Tibullus; and of the Poems of Sulpicia* (London, 1759), 2:159.

25 For comments on Juvenal's ambiguous use of Fortuna, see "Extraits de mon Journal," *Miscellaneous Works of Edward Gibbon, Esquire*, ed. John, Lord Sheffield (London, 1796), 2:106–7. These comments were known and used by William Gifford in his *Satires of Decimus Junius Juvenalis* (London, 1802), p. 360.

13. Pope, his Successors, and the Dissociation of Satiric Sensibility

1 Reuben Arthur Brower, *Alexander Pope: The Poetry of Allusion* (Oxford: Clarendon Press, 1959), p. 165; Maynard Mack supports this description of Pope's career. See *The Garden and the City: Retirement and Politics in the Later Poetry of Pope 1731–1743* (Toronto: Univ. of Toronto Press, 1969), p. 234. Mack's study remains the most persuasive and eloquent defense of Pope's positive Horatian and Virgilian contexts.

2 "On Laughter and Ludicrous Composition," in *Essays* (Edinburgh, 1766). p. 662.

3 TE, vol. 6, *Minor Poems*, ed. Norman Ault and John Butt (London and New Haven: Methuen and Yale Univ. Press, 1954), p. 376.

4 For Hill, see *The Correspondence of Alexander Pope*, ed. George Sherburn (Oxford: Clarendon Press, 1956), 4:112, regarding the *Epilogue to the Satires*; for Johnson, YE, vol. 7, *Johnson on Shakespeare*, ed. Arthur Sherbo (New Haven: Yale Univ. Press, 1968), p. 66 (two modes), p. 67 (mingled drama), p. 66 (distinct kinds). Comparable evidence concerning the relationship of mingled literary forms and the complexity of life may be found in Collins' "Ode to Fear" (1746), lines 44–45, and "Ode on the Popular Superstitions of the Highlands" (1748?), and Horace Walpole's Preface to the second edition (1765) of *The Castle of Otranto*.

5 Quotations are from YE, vol. 6, *Samuel Johnson: Poems*, ed. E. L. McAdam, Jr., with George Milne (New Haven: Yale Univ. Press, 1964).

6 We know, for example, that in *The Progress of Satire* (1798) William Boscawen says of Pope: "Each graceful form the Sons of Satire choose / Springs from thy various, thy accomplish'd Muse" (p. 10).

7 *Thomas Chatterton's Art: Experiments in Imagined History* (Princeton: Princeton Univ. Press, 1978), p. 260. See also pp. 182, 199–200, and 211–12 for useful comments on the continuity, or lack of it, between eighteenth-century satiric kinds and generations, and particular satirists, especially Pope, Churchill, and Chatterton. What Donald Taylor calls "Churchillean" I prefer to call "Juvenalian," in celebration of roots.

8 Quotations are from TE, vol. 4, *Imitations of Horace*, ed. John Butt, 2nd ed. (London and New Haven: Methuen and Yale Univ. Press, 1961), and vol. 3. ii, *Epistles to Several Persons*, ed. F. W. Bateson, 2nd ed. (1961).

9 *The Fribbleriad* is quoted from *The Poetical Works of David Garrick* (1785). The word "fribble" also is used in William Kenrick's anti-Garrick poem *The Town. A Satire* (1748), p. 7, and in [Nathaniel Lancaster], *The Pretty Gentleman: Or, Softness of Manners Vindicated From the false Ridicule exhibited under the Character of William Fribble, Esq.* (1747). The work is dedicated to Garrick. Garrick included a "Beau Fribble" in his *Miss in her Teens* (1747).

10 Churchill is quoted from *The Poetical Works of Charles Churchill*, ed. Douglas Grant (Oxford: Clarendon Press, 1956).

11 Thomas Lockwood emphasizes the mid- and later eighteenth-century examination of the self as a subject. "The characteristic subject of Churchill's satire," he observes, "is the satirist himself, or the satirist in relation to the world." Lockwood rightly extends this remark to Peter Pindar. See *Post-Augustan Satire: Charles Churchill and Satirical Poetry, 1750–1800* (Seattle: Univ. of Washington Press, 1979), p. 22. Donald Taylor's discussion of Chatterton's satire (note 7 above) is consistent with this paradigm of one kind of formal satire. Discussions of "Post-Augustan" and "Romantic" satire have flourished, especially for that interesting "transitional" satirist Byron. For some of these, see Jerome McGann, "The Non-Augustan Nature of Byron's Early 'Satires,'" *Revue des langues vivantes* 34 (1970):495–503; Mary Clearman, "A Blueprint for *English Bards and Scotch Reviewers: The First Satire of Juvenal*," *Keats–Shelley Journal* 19 (1970):87–89; Frederick L. Beatty, "Byron's Imitations of Juvenal and Persius," *Studies in Romanticism* 15 (1976):333–55; and Robert F. Gleckner, "From Selfish Spleen to Equanimity:

Byron's Satires," *Studies in Romanticism* 18 (1979):173–205. Gleckner offers a useful summary of the recent critical trends.

12 The poem is quoted from *The Works of Richard Owen Cambridge, Esq.* (1803), p. 60.

13 Quotations are from *The Poetical Works of the Late Christopher Anstey, Esq.* (1808).

14 Quotations in volume 1 are from John Wolcot, *The Works of Peter Pindar, Esq*ʳ (1794); quotations in volume 5 are from *The Works of Peter Pindar, Esq.* (1801). See 1:86 for "volcanic."

15 For Dryden's comments on Milton as a synthesizer of Homer and Virgil, see his lines written for the engraving of Milton in the fourth edition of *Paradise Lost* (1688); CE, vol. 3, *Poems, 1685–1692*, ed. Earl Miner and Vinton A. Dearing (Berkeley and Los Angeles: Univ. of California Press, 1969), p. 208. For discussion of Boileau as a synthesizing satirist with an Horatian bias, see chapter 3 of my *Alexander Pope and the Traditions of Formal Verse Satire* (Princeton: Princeton Univ. Press, 1982), pp. 82–104.

INDEX

A., F., 149, 243
Accius, Lucius, 35, 72
Adam, Alexander, 33
Addison, Joseph, 18, 19, 28, 117, 119, 132, 176, 206
Aden, John M., 136, 148, 220, 242
Aelian, Claudius, 228
Aeschylus, 34
Aesopus, Claudius, 35
Afranius, Latin comic poet, 35
Akenside, Mark, 24
Alcibiades, 41, 147, 148
Alexander the Great, 112, 119, 232, 233
Amazons, 3, 111–13, 115, 117, 118, 119, 231–33, 235
Anacreon, 69
Anderson, William S., 165, 246
Andrews, Robert, 26, 210
Anne, Queen of England, 21, 142
Anstey, Christopher, 196–98, 202, 253
Antony, Mark (Caius Marcus Antonius), 28, 131
Appius, Claudius, 44
Apuleius, of Madaura, 35
Arbuthnot, Dr. John, 149, 157
Aristotle, 12, 36, 101–3, 213, 228
Artegall, in Spenser's *The Faerie Queene*, 232
Astell, Mary, 234–35
Audra, E., 241
Augustus, Caius Julius Caesar Octavianus, 2, 3, 12, 13, 21–29, 31, 32, 45, 72–74, 78, 79, 126, 130, 131, 132, 135, 138, 139, 156, 161, 186, 187, 190, 207–10, 212, 214, 216, 223, 224, 238, 239
Ausonius, Decimus Magnus, 35, 215, 245

Bacon, Francis, 172, 173, 185, 248, 250
Bailey, Nathan, 69, 206
Bassus, Caesius, 146
Bathhurst, Allen, Earl, 122, 187

Batteux, Abbé Charles, 129, 130, 140, 149, 238, 240, 243
Bayle, Pierre, 84, 86, 101, 103, 145, 219, 225, 228, 242, 249
Beattie, James, 187
Beaumont, Francis, 75
Bentley, Richard, 37, 216, 227, 228
Bentley, Thomas, 45, 46, 122, 142, 237
Bethel, Slingsby, 88, 226
Bettenham, James 158
Biddle, John, 111, 232
Birch, Thomas, 17, 228, 242
Blackmore, Sir Richard, 16, 140, 155
Blackwell, Thomas, 26, 27, 39, 107, 207, 210, 216
Blount, Sir Thomas Pope, 15
Boccage, Marie Anne le Page Fiquet du, 230, 232
Boileau-Despréaux, Nicolas, 1, 2, 5, 6, 15–16, 28, 40, 42, 68, 70, 77–78, 114, 140, 155, 161–62, 168, 169–70, 202–3, 205, 211, 215, 216, 224, 231, 233, 242, 243, 245, 247–48
    Works cited: *Le Lutrin*, 5, 114, 233; *Ode sur ... Namur*, 77; Satire One, 68, 170; Satire Three, 68; Satire Eight, 70; Satire Nine, 40, 161, 245; Satire Ten, 40
Bolingbroke, Henry St. John, Viscount, 22, 44, 45–46, 48, 49, 78, 122, 125, 128, 140, 142, 157, 187, 236, 237, 238
Bond, William (H. Stanhope), 118, 140, 235, 245, 249
Boscawen, William, 38, 135, 151, 211, 216, 240, 243, 252
Boswell, James, 15, 37, 170, 171, 178, 206, 211, 215, 248, 251
Brewster, Thomas, 42, 47, 137, 139, 144, 158, 216, 241
Bridges, Thomas, 106, 229
Britomart, in Spenser's *The Faerie Queene*, 231, 232

Broome, William, 157, 244
Brossette, Claude, 170, 221
Brower, Reuben, 28, 207, 210, 226, 252
Brown, John, 17, 29, 37, 38, 135, 188, 216
Brown, Thomas, 12, 144, 205, 241
Brutus, Lucius Junus, 208
Brutus, Marcus Junius, 18, 82, 149
Buckhurst, Charles Sackville, Baron, 54, 75, 77; *see also* Dorset
Buckingham, George Villiers, 1st Duke of, 178
Buckingham, George Villiers, 2nd Duke of, 88–89
Buckingham, John Sheffield, Earl of Mulgrave and 1st Duke of Buckingham and Normanby, 54, 209, 230
Burke, Edmund, 25, 173
Burlington, Richard Boyle, Earl, 48, 116, 200, 209
Burnet, Alexander, 237
Burnet, Bishop Gilbert, 150, 221, 222, 223
Burnet, Thomas, 104, 229, 234
Burns, Robert, 189
Burton, Edmund, 144, 148, 241, 250
Butler, Samuel, 1, 54
Butt, John, 31, 204, 208, 212, 217, 220, 236, 239, 244, 252
Byron, George Gordon, Lord, 7, 252
Bysshe, Edward, 69, 221

Caesar, Caius Julius, 23, 27, 44, 72, 130, 154, 207
Calidius, Junius, 27
Cambridge, Richard Owen, 195–97, 202, 253
Care, Henry, 85
Caroline, Queen of England, 161, 190
Casaubon, Isaac, 2, 4, 5, 16, 38, 41, 42, 47, 145, 146, 147, 164, 169, 205, 216, 242, 244, 247, 248
Castiglione, Baldassare, 36, 43
Catiline (Catilina Lucius Sergius), 15, 82, 152
Cato, Marcus Porcius (of Utica), 24–25, 44, 154, 211
Catullus, Valerius, 35, 118
Chamaeleon, 34, 215
Chambers, A. B., 204, 216, 232, 240, 242, 251
Chambers, Ephraim, 69, 211
Charles I, King of England, 81, 82, 131
Charles II, King of England, 1, 21, 22, 27, 70, 80, 81–85, 89, 91–93, 101, 225

Charles XII, King of Sweden, 178, 179, 184, 250, 251
Chartres (Charteris), Francis, 137, 140, 155
Chatterton, Thomas, 190, 252
Chesterfield, Philip Dormer Stanhope, Earl, 29, 111, 211, 232
Churchill, Charles, 8, 28, 190, 192–95, 202, 252
Cibber, Colley, 19, 79, 137, 139, 140, 154, 161, 200, 208, 209, 245
Cicero, Marcus Tullius, 15, 23–26, 30, 35, 36, 129, 209, 212, 213, 217, 229
Cinna, Caius Helvius, 27
Cleland, John, 27
Cobb, Samuel, 107
Cobham, Richard Temple, Viscount, 48, 49, 137, 152, 155, 187
Cohen, Ralph, 113
Collier, Jeremy, 12, 205
Concanen, Matthew, 124
Congreve, William, 19, 128, 166
Cooke, Thomas, 44, 124
Cooper, Thomas, 150
Cornutus, Lucius Annaeus, tutor of Persius, 13, 41, 145, 146, 156, 157, 160–62
Cornwall, Charles, 104, 106, 228, 229
Cowley, Abraham, 27, 221
Creech, Thomas, 47, 222, 223
Cromwell, Oliver, 82, 94, 156, 157, 244
Crusius, Lewis, 29, 134, 223, 239
Curtius, Quintus, 112

Dacier, André, 4, 12, 13, 15, 23, 39, 102, 145, 204, 205, 208, 212, 216, 222, 238, 241, 242
Dacier, Madame Anne le Fevre, 102, 108, 115, 228, 230, 233
Damassipus, Junius, 30, 212, 213
Danet, Pierre, 111, 231, 232
Daniel, George, 144, 241
D'Anvers, Caleb, 43, 209
D'Anvers, Griffith Morgan, 153, 154, 240
D'Aubignac, François Hedelin, Abbé, 102, 103, 116, 228
Dean, John, 89
De Crequi, Maréchal, 23
De la Motte, Antoine Houtar, 101, 103, 227, 228, 232
De la Valterie, Père, 38, 147, 216, 242
De Mably, Bonnot, 25
Demetrius, trainer of mimes, 72–73

Democritus, 78, 174, 175–79, 180, 181, 183, 184, 249, 250, 251
Demosthenes, 172
Dennis, John, 12, 16, 20, 29, 102, 114, 134, 211, 212, 235, 239
De Pons, Jean-François, 102, 228
Des Maizeaux, Pierre, 42, 217, 225, 228
Desmarets de Saint Sorlin, 101, 227
Dilke, Thomas, 69
Dodington, George Bubb, Baron, 133, 187, 239
Dodsley, Robert, 172, 251
Dolce, Lodovico, 205
Domitian (Titus Flavius Domitianus), 78, 133, 156, 243
Donaldson, Ian, 165, 246
Donne, John, 6, 186, 219
Donnelly, Jerome, 80, 89, 224
Dorset, Charles Sackville, Earl, 2, 6, 16, 28, 29, 223
Drummond, Sir William, 144, 145, 241
Dryden, John, 1, 2, 4–8, 11, 14–16, 17, 19–20, 24, 27, 28, 29, 31, 32, 33, 37, 39, 40, 41, 54, 68, 73–76, 79, 80–99, 111, 120, 134, 135, 139, 140, 144, 145, 147, 155–57, 166, 167, 169, 184, 202, 204–8, 211, 213, 214, 216, 222, 224–26, 232, 238, 241–44, 247, 253
    Works cited: *Absalom and Achitophel*, 5, 7, 19, 80–89; *Aeneid*, 214; *Astraea Redux*, 21; Discourse on Satire, 1–8, 11, 14–16, 17, 19–20, 24, 29, 32, 37, 134, 135, 145, 147, 211, 241; *Fables* 244; Juvenal and Persius, 15, 16, 31, 39, 40, 41, 111, 139, 144, 157, 166, 169, 184, 206; *Mac Flecknoe*, 1, 5, 20; *The Medal*, 4; *Ovid*, 68, 207, 247
Dryden, John, Jr., 17, 166
Duckett, George, 104, 229, 234
Dudley, Mr, 154, 158, 159, 240
Dusaulx, Jean, 25, 26, 138, 208, 210, 240, 248
Dyson, A. E., 80

Echard, Laurence, 21, 23, 131, 208
Eelbeck, Henry, 39, 144, 146, 148, 149, 216, 241, 242
Ennius, Quintus, 6, 27, 72, 223
Epicurus, 175, 249
Etherege, Sir George, 68
Euripides, 34, 36

Fabricius, Caius, 25

Fannius, Roman poet, 72
Fermor, Arabella, 100, 114, 118
Fiddes, Richard, 101, 227
Fielding, Henry, 23, 208, 215
Filmer, Sir Robert, 81, 88
Fitzcotton, Henry, 105, 229
Fitzpatrick, Thomas, 190
Fletcher, John, 75
Fortescue, William, 45, 47, 48, 77, 120–22, 124, 126, 127, 138, 141, 142, 147, 158, 187, 196, 198, 217, 236, 238, 245
Fraenkel, Eduard, 73, 222, 238
Frederick, Prince of Wales, 187
Fundanius, Roman comic playwright, 71

Galen (Galenus, Claudius), 27
Garrick, David, 190–92, 195, 202, 252
Gautruche, Père, 111, 232
George I, King of England, 20, 22, 32, 132
George II, King of England, 22, 30, 32, 78, 137, 139, 142, 152, 154, 155, 156, 161, 198, 199, 208, 244
George III, King of England, 26, 198, 199, 200, 202
Gerard, Mr, 138, 237, 240
Gibbon, Edward, 23, 29, 135, 212, 227, 247, 249, 251
Gifford, William, 15, 39, 41, 144, 147, 210, 241, 244, 248, 251
Gilbert, Thomas, 43, 243
Gildon, Charles, 12, 13, 204, 205, 231
Glaucus, in the *Iliad*, 115
Godolphin, Sidney, Earl, 54
Goldsmith, Oliver, 21, 207
Gordon, Thomas, 24, 132, 208, 209
Gould, Robert, 1, 28
Grainger, James, 132, 140, 185, 239
Greene, Edward Burnaby, 18, 144, 147, 149, 169, 207, 211, 241, 243, 247
Grey, Ford, Lord (of Warke), 82
Grotius, Hugo, 90
Gueret, Gabriel, 101, 227
Guthry, Mr, 124, 125, 237
Guyon, Claude Marie, Abbé De, 111, 231, 232

Hall, Bishop Joseph, 19
Hannibal, 183, 184
Hardy, John P., 165, 220, 227, 246
Harrison, T. W., 22, 211
Harte, Walter, 17, 134, 240
Harth, Phillip, 86, 215, 225

Hawkins, Sir John, 33
Hayley, William, 200
Heinsius, Daniel, 2, 4, 14, 37, 164, 205
Henley, John "Orator," 124, 153, 154, 159
Henry VIII, King of England, 250
Heraclitus, 175
Hervey, John, Baron, 46–48, 123, 136, 151, 152, 190, 209, 217, 237, 243
Hill, Aaron, 17, 18, 20, 42, 121, 188, 236
Hill, "Sir" John, 150
Hobbes, Thomas, 92
Holyday, Barten, 6, 39, 40, 134, 135, 144, 145, 146, 149, 216, 241, 242, 246, 247
Homer, 100–4, 107–9, 118, 119, 227–31, 234, 244, 253
Hooke, Nathan, 23, 24
Hopkins, Charles, 82
Horace (Horatius Quintus Flaccus), 2–7, 11–16, 22–33, 35, 36, 37, 38, 39, 40, 41, 44–49, 53, 54, 68–79, 108, 120, 123, 127, 128–33, 134, 135, 136, 137, 138–43, 144, 145, 147, 148, 150–51, 154, 155, 156, 157, 158, 159, 161, 162, 164, 186–90, 192, 195–99, 201–3, 205, 208–9, 211, 212, 213, 215, 216, 217, 221, 222, 224, 237, 238, 239, 240, 242, 246, 249, 252, 253
  Works cited: Ars Poetica, 36, 197; Epistles, I.i, 44, 78, 161; I.xii, 249; II.ii, 45; Odes, III.v, 28; Satires, I.iv, 70, 130; I.x, 54, 70–7, 130, 223, 224; II.i, 77, 129–31, 138–43, 148, 158, 196, 201, 238; II.ii, 39; II.iii, 30, 40; II.viii, 68
Howes, Francis, 144, 145, 148, 241
Hughes, John, 117
Hurd, Richard, 36

Jaffray, Thomas, 150, 243
James II, King of England, 2, 32, 88, 93, 99, 131, 214
Jephson, Robert, 26, 207, 209, 210
Johnson, Samuel, 7, 8, 16–17, 20, 27, 28, 31, 32–33, 36–37, 43, 48, 66, 69–70, 78, 79, 96, 111, 133, 135, 164–71, 172–85, 189, 195, 202, 206, 210, 211, 213, 214, 215, 216, 220, 221, 222, 224, 227, 231, 237, 240, 245, 248, 249, 250, 251
  Works cited: Blackwell review, 27, 210; Compleat Vindication, 170; Dictionary, 17, 32–33, 69–70, 172–73, 181, 182, 213, 216, 217, 219, 221, 222, 237, 240, 250; Dodsley's Preceptor, 172, 248, 251; Drury Lane "Prologue," 188; Guyon, trans., 111, 231; Lives of the Poets, 37, 70, 96, 135, 206, 213, 216, 217, 221, 237, 240; London, 7, 17, 78, 164–71, 220, 245, 247, 248; Marmor Norfolciense, 170; Ramblers, 36, 43, 48, 217; Sermons, 176, 182, 184–85, 250, 251; Shakespeare preface, 188, 202, 249, 252; Vanity, 7, 20, 66, 78, 172–85, 195, 248, 249–50; Vision of Theodore, 185, 249
Jones, Inigo, 200
Jonson, Ben, 75, 188
Juvenal (Decimus Junius Juvenalis), 2–8, 11, 14–17, 19, 23, 24, 25–26, 28–33, 37–41, 47, 48, 49, 53, 65, 78, 111, 129–33, 132–36, 137–38, 140–43, 144–45, 148, 150–58, 160, 162, 164–71, 174–85, 186, 187–90, 192, 193, 194, 195, 196, 197–99, 200, 201–3, 205, 206, 207, 210, 211, 212, 213, 216, 221, 232, 235, 236, 238, 239, 240, 241, 242, 243, 244, 245–48, 249, 251, 252
  Works cited: Satires I, 31, 40, 133, 137, 153, 156, 193, 199, 232, 252; II, 193, 232; III, 39, 78, 137, 142, 156, 164–71, 235, 245–48; VI, 15, 111; VII, 137, 156; VIII, 156, 212; IX 193; X, 78, 174–85, 249, 251

Kersey, John, 69
King, William, 128, 238
Knox, Vicesimus, 135, 250
Kolb, Gwin, J., x, 206, 251
Kupersmith, William, 165

Laberius, Roman mime, 71
Labeo, Atticus, 16
Laelius, C., in Horace, 23, 130, 139, 140
Langton, Bennet, 170
Lascelles, Mary, 164, 165, 220, 246
Laud, Archbishop William, 178, 179, 182
Le Bossu, René, 12, 102, 103, 204, 228
Lee, Nathaniel, 24, 207, 208
Le Monnier, Abbé, 38, 145, 216, 242
Le Noble, M., 150, 243
Le Verrier, Pierre, 40, 170, 216, 247
Lewalski, Barbara, 224, 226
Livy (Titius Livius), 23, 24, 44
Lloyd, Robert, 189
Locke, John, 81, 92, 219, 224, 226
Longinus, Dionysius, 172, 215
Louis XIV, King of France, 2, 22, 161, 207, 245

Loveling, Benjamin, 136, 137, 154, 155, 240, 241, 244
Lovelock, Julian, 80
Lubin, Eilhard, 168
Lucilius, Caius, 5, 6, 11, 13, 31, 70–76, 130, 139, 140, 154, 155, 158, 186, 197, 202, 211, 222, 238, 240, 241
Lucretius, Carus T., 39, 175
Luttrell, Narcissus, 89, 225
Lyttleton, George, Baron, 24–26, 209

M., D., 232
Mack, Maynard, 161, 204, 214, 215, 220, 227, 236, 244, 252
Madan, Martin, 144, 162, 167, 169, 241, 243, 246, 247
Maecenas, Caius, 12, 13, 44, 72, 78, 131, 186, 187, 201
Malone, Edmond, 37, 211
Manilius, Caius, 27
Marius, Caius, 15
Marlborough, John Churchill, Duke, 180
Martial, Marcus Valerius, 35, 69
Marvell, Andrew, 189
Mason, William, 200
Maxwell, William, 170
M'Doe-Roach, Patrick, 124, 125
Messala, M. Valerius Corvinus, 24, 25, 72, 209
Midas, of Phrygia, 160–62, 194, 244, 245
Middleton, Conyers, 24, 209
Milton, John, 27, 37, 48, 86, 87, 93, 116, 154, 185, 189–92, 202, 203, 253
Monmouth, James Scott, Duke, 82, 83, 86, 99
Montagu, Edward Wortly, 214
Montagu, Lady Mary Wortly, 46, 47, 123, 217, 238
Montesquieu, Charles-Louis De Secondat, Baron de la Brede, 28, 209
Moody, A. D., 170, 248, 250
Moore, John L., 70, 221
Moréri, Louis, 25, 205, 219, 246, 249
Morris, Corbyn, 29
Murphy, Arthur, 25, 195, 209
Musa, Octavius, 73

Nero (Lucius Domitius Ahenobarbus), 15, 41, 42, 136, 137, 145–50, 152, 154–57, 160, 162, 190, 243, 244
Neville, Thomas, 144, 241
Newcomb, Thomas, 46, 47, 142, 217, 240
Ninnyhammer, Nickydemus, 104, 105, 229

Oates, Titus, 89, 91, 226
Oldham, John, 1, 28, 144, 169, 211, 241, 247
Oldmixon, John, 16, 228, 230
Ormond, James Butler, Duke, 85, 88, 93
Osborn, James M., 159, 209, 211, 221–23, 240, 244
Ossory, Thomas Butler, Earl, 85, 93, 226
Otway, Thomas, 74
Ovid (Publius Ovidius Naso), 24, 30, 35, 186, 207, 208, 244
Owen, Edward, 15, 18, 39–41, 48, 207, 216, 241, 248
Ozell, John, 15, 219

Paine, Tom, 202
Palladio, Andrea, 200
Parnell, Thomas, 101, 227, 230
Patrick, Samuel, 215
Patrick, Bishop Simon, 84, 90, 98
Peacham, Henry, 32
Perrault, Charles, 101, 227, 228
Persius (Aulus Persius Flaccus), 2, 4–6, 11, 14–17, 19, 38–42, 47–49, 53, 129, 131, 133, 135, 136–40, 142–43, 144–62, 186, 190, 194, 202, 203, 205, 206, 207, 211, 216, 217, 239, 240, 241, 242, 243, 244, 247, 248, 250
  Works cited: Prologue, 41, 49, 144, 147, 244; Satires I, 38, 41, 49, 136–37, 139, 144, 146–48, 149, 153–62, 202, 240, 241, 242, 244; II, 17, 38, 39, 244; III, 17, 39, 144, 149, 241; IV, 41–42, 48, 136–37, 148, 152–53, 156, 241; V, 150, 157; VI, 38, 148, 157
Peterborough, Charles Mordaunt, Earl, 140, 142
Petre, Robert, Baron, 100
Petronius, Arbiter, 69
Phaethon, in Absalom and Achitophel, 35, 82, 92
Phalereus, Demetrius, 25
Phillips, Edward, 69, 219
Pisistratus of Athens, 104
Pitt, William, 199, 201, 202
Plain Truth or Downright Dunstable, 24
Plato, 13
Plotius, Tucca, 72
Plutarch, 142, 231, 233
Pollio, Caius Asinius, 27, 71
Polwarth, Hugh Hume, Earl (Marchmont), 49
Pompey (Sextus Pompeius Magnus), 44
Pope, Alexander, 7, 18, 19, 20, 21, 24, 28–32,

34, 35, 38, 41, 43–49, 54, 77–79, 100,
103, 106–11, 112–13, 115, 116, 118, 120,
121, 123–27, 128–29, 133, 136, 138–43,
145, 147, 151, 152, 154, 155–56, 157–63,
186–92, 193, 195, 196, 197, 198, 199,
200, 201, 202, 203, 204, 206, 207–8, 209,
210, 212, 213, 214, 215, 216, 217, 220,
221, 223, 226–27, 229–35, 235–38,
239–41, 242, 243, 244, 245, 246, 250,
252, 253

Works cited: *Arbuthnot*, 45, 54, 125, 137,
147, 156, 158–63, 187, 190–92, 195, 198,
200, 244, 245; *Augustus* (Horace, *Epistles*
II.i), 30, 45, 78–79, 187–88, 208, 220;
Bathurst, 18, 54, 200, 202, 250; *Bolingbroke*
(Horace, *Epistles*, I.i,), 44, 161, 187;
Burlington, 18–19, 186, 200; *Dunciad*, 19,
31, 54, 103, 121, 220, 221, 236, 240, 244,
245; *Epilogue to the Satires*, 30–31, 49, 139,
157, 158, 159–60, 186, 188, 199, 200,
237, 244, 245; *Essay on Criticism*, 244;
Essay on Man, 142, 157, 237; *Fortescue*
(Horace, *Satires* II.i), 45, 77, 120–27,
138–43, 147, 158–59, 187, 196, 235–38,
239, 240, 244; *Iliad*, 108, 115–16, 119,
227, 229–31, 234, 235, 244; *Rape of the
Lock*, 7, 100, 106–19, 226–27, 229–31,
233–35; *Sober Advice*, 29, 45; *To a Lady*,
18; *Windsor Forest*, 21

Pordage, Samuel, 81
Porteus, Bishop Beilby, 199
Potter, Robert, 216
Prateus, Ludovicus, 168, 239, 242, 244, 247,
249
Prior, Matthew, 16, 29, 77, 155, 204, 211, 239
Probus, M. Aurelius, 145, 150
Pulteney, William, Earl (Bath), 153
Pythagoras, 213

Quin, James, 197
Quintilian, Marcus Fabius, 34–36, 69, 209,
215

Raleigh, Sir Walter, 44
Ralph, James, 124, 235
Ramsay, Andrew-Michael, 103, 228, 242, 244
Randolph, Mary Claire, 11, 12, 15, 204
Rapin, René, 102, 103, 149, 228, 243
Rigault, Nicholas, 2, 133, 135, 205, 239
Righter, Anne, 64, 218
Robinson, K. E., 80
Rochester, John Wilmot, Earl, ix, 7, 28,
53–55, 57, 59, 60, 63–67, 68, 70, 73–77,
79, 189, 218, 219, 221, 222, 223, 224
Works cited: "Allusion to Horace," 1, 7,
68–79, 218, 220, 224; *Letter from
Artemesia*, ix, 7, 53–67, 79, 218, 219–20;
"On Poet Ninny," 189; *Satyr Against
Mankind*, 69, 70, 78, 218, 221; "Timon,"
68
Ruffhead, Owen, 18, 20, 201
Rymer, Thomas, 77, 79, 102, 223, 243

St. Evremond, Charles De, 23, 26, 101, 208,
210, 223, 228
Saint-Marc, Lefévre De, 40, 170, 216, 221,
243, 248
Sardanapalus, 90
Sarpedon, in the *Iliad*, 115, 116, 119
Satyrus, 34
Scaliger, Julius Caesar, 2, 145, 149, 243, 247
Scarsdale, Nicholas Leke, Earl, 140
Schochet, Gordon, 81, 225, 226
Schrevelius, Cornelius, 38, 168, 216, 247
Scipio, Africanus, 18, 23, 130, 139, 190
Scott, John, 37
Scroop, Sir Carr, 53
Scudamore, James, 104, 106, 229
Sedley, Sir Charles, 53, 75
Sejanus, Aelius, 18
Selis, M., 146
Seneca, Lucius Annaeus, 25, 41, 209
Senhouse, John, 144, 146, 147, 149, 241,
242
Settle, Elkanah, 74, 85, 245
Seymour, Edward, 88, 207
Shadwell, Thomas, 53, 74, 79, 120, 236
Shaftesbury, Anthony Ashley Cooper, 1st
Earl of (*Absalom and Achitophel*), 81, 86,
93, 99, 207
Shaftesbury, Anthony Ashley Cooper, 3rd
Earl of, 17, 18, 36, 206, 215
Shakespeare, William, 16, 75, 188, 189, 200,
202, 248, 249
Shelley, Percy Bysshe, 26, 126, 210
Sheridan, Thomas, 17, 41, 144, 147, 156, 157,
216, 241, 244, 246, 248
Shipley, Bishop Jonathan, 37
Shrewsbury, Countess of, 89
Siculus, Diodorus, 112, 233
Sidney, Algernon, 87
Smart, Christopher, 21, 207
Smollett, Tobias, 29, 196, 207, 211, 219
Socrates, 13, 41, 44, 173

Spence, Joseph, 28, 30, 211, 212, 221, 222, 240, 244
Spenser, Edmund, 113, 231, 234
Stair, John Dalrymple, Earl, 137, 155
Stanley, Thomas, 228, 235, 249
Stapylton, Sir Robert, 248
Steele, Sir Richard, 35, 36, 215, 217
Stepney, George, 15, 212
Stirling, John, 144, 146, 150, 241, 242
Suetonius, Caius Tranquillus, 24, 208
Swift, Jonathan, 6, 28, 41, 55, 61, 66, 67, 116, 122, 128, 170, 180, 214, 227, 234, 236
Syme, Sir Ronald, 132, 208, 239

Tacitus, Cornelius, 24, 25, 132, 208, 209, 239, 268
Taylor, Donald, 190, 252
Taylor, Bishop Jeremy, 181
Terence (Terentius, Afer, P.), 23
Terrasson, Jean, 102–4, 228
Thalestris (Queen of the Amazons), 109–13, 115, 116, 118, 119, 232
Theobald, Lewis, 200, 227
Tiberius, Claudius Nero, 27, 207, 209
Tibullus, Albius, 24, 132, 239, 251
Tigellius, Hermogines, 72–74
Topsell, Edward, 59, 219
Trapp, Joseph, 134, 205, 211, 239
Trebatius, C. Testa, 77, 129, 130, 139, 148, 158, 238
Tullius, Servius, 15

Valgius, Rufus, 27, 72
Varius, Rufus L., 71, 72
Varus, Alfenus, 27
Vico, Giambattista, 103, 228
Victor, Sextus Aurelius, 24
Vieth, David, 55, 214, 218, 221, 224, 225

Virgil (Publius Virgilius Maro), 4, 5, 22–24, 26–28, 30, 71, 72, 108, 131, 133, 186, 188, 208, 210–12, 226, 228, 229, 232, 252, 253
Voltaire (François-Marie Arouet), 25, 208–10

Waller, Edmund, 27
Walpole, Sir Robert, ix, 24, 43–45, 78, 120, 121, 124, 125, 127, 133, 137, 139–42, 144, 151–57, 161, 162, 177, 190, 199, 209, 217, 235, 236–38, 240, 241
Walter, Peter, 137, 140, 155
Warburton, Bishop William, 18, 20, 37, 113, 114, 126, 207, 209, 211–13, 217, 221, 234, 236
Ward, Addison, 137, 155, 208
Warton, Joseph, 28, 210
Warton, Thomas, 19, 199
Watson, David, 12, 16, 39
Wesley, Samuel, 103, 228, 229, 232, 234
Weston, John, 112
Whitehead, Paul, 123, 133, 137, 141, 156, 217, 240, 243
Wickstead, Mr., 132, 239
William III, King of England, 2, 31, 32, 214
Wolcot, John (Peter Pindar), 7, 8, 198, 199–202, 252, 253
Wolsey, Cardinal Thomas, 18, 178, 182
Wycherley, William, 53, 74

Yart, Abbé Antoine, 162, 163, 217
Yonge, Sir William, 122
Young, Edward, 11, 16, 19, 20, 28, 35, 37, 54, 112, 155, 173, 206, 211, 238, 243, 249, 250

Zeno, 152
Zimri, see Buckingham, George Villiers